Studies

Mathematical Logic
and Foundations
Volume 12

Second-Order
Quantifier Elimination
Foundations, Computational
Aspects and Applications

Studies in Logic Series Editor
Dov Gabbay   dov.gabbay@kcl.ac.uk

Second-Order Quantifier Elimination

Foundations, Computational Aspects and Applications

Dov M. Gabbay,

Renate A. Schmidt,

and

Andrzej Szałas

ISBN 978-1-904987-56-7

College Publications
Scientific Director: Dov Gabbay
Managing Director: Jane Spurr
Department of Computer Science
King's College London, Strand, London WC2R 2LS, UK

http://www.collegepublications.co.uk

Original cover design by orchid creative   www.orchidcreative.co.uk
Printed by Lightning Source, Milton Keynes, UK

Contents

Part 1

Introduction and Background

CHAPTER 1

Introduction to Second-Order Logic

Second-order formalisms refer to logics, where quantifiers can bind formulas or, equivalently, variables ranging over semantic entities modeling formulas.

As an example consider the extension of classical first-order logic by second-order quantifiers. We simply allow ourselves to quantify not only over elements of the underlying domain, but also over relations or, equivalently, over sets or over functions. This allows one to express sentences like "John has no good relationships with anyone" or "there is a coloring of a graph using three colors only".

In the beginning of the 20th century mathematicians realized that classical second-order quantifiers are extremely complex and that second-order reasoning often leads to paradoxes. The lack of a complete and at least partially computable proof theory has even raised doubts whether second-order logic should be considered logic at all. For many decades second-order logic has not really been present in the mainstream of research. In 1950 Henkin developed a non-standard semantics for higher-order logic, which made it partially decidable. However, this did not change the attitude towards second-order formalisms much.

In the last thirty years the situation has seriously been changing. Modal correspondence theory, common-sense and non-monotonic reasoning as well as descriptive complexity theory have focused much interest on second-order formalisms. It has appeared that various aspects of specification and reasoning require, in general, second-order formulation.

1.1. Second-Order Logic in Artificial Intelligence

Second-order logic has been intensively used in modeling common-sense, non-monotonic reasoning. A prominent example of formalization of this form of reasoning is *circumscription*, introduced by McCarthy [**147**]. Circumscription is a form of minimization, where abnormal situations or behaviors are minimized in order to reach conclusions in the context of incomplete knowledge. For example, consider a formula stating that normally my bus departs at 9:00:

$$Th(B, Ab, D) \stackrel{\text{def}}{\equiv} \forall x \big[(B(x) \land \neg Ab(x)) \to D(x, 9{:}00) \big],$$

3

where B, Ab and D stand for "my bus", "abnormal" and "departs", respectively. Suppose I want to catch my bus. Typically I have no knowledge about unusual situations which prevent my bus from departing at 9:00. In order to be able to reason and act, I usually assume that nothing abnormal happened, i.e., minimize relation Ab and vary relation D. Such minimization requires second-order formalization. Circumscription of Ab with varied D is expressed by:

$$Th(B, Ab, D) \wedge$$
$$\forall X, Y \left[(Th(B, X, Y) \wedge \forall x[X(x) \to Ab(x)]) \to \right.$$
$$\left. \forall x[Ab(x) \to X(x)] \right].$$

Modeling common-sense reasoning is discussed in Chapter 16 of this book.

Also natural language understanding requires second-order formalisms. Boolos has shown that sentences such as "some critics admire only each other" can only be expressed by second-order quantification, since the linear sequence of classical quantifiers introduces unwanted relationships. Sometimes one can use Henkin *branching quantifiers* to express such sentences, but Henkin quantifiers are modeled by (non-)existence of Skolem functions, i.e., are substantially second-order. As an example consider the sentence "every professor has a favorite topic and every student has a favorite topic, but these topics are different". The first-order formula

$$\forall x \exists t \forall y \exists t' \left[favorite(x, t) \wedge favorite(y, t') \wedge t \not\approx t' \right]$$

makes t' dependent on x and y, while our intention was to make it dependent only on y. A suitable formulation with the use of Henkin quantifiers can be given by

$$\left(\begin{array}{c} \forall x \exists t \\ \forall y \exists t' \end{array} \right) \left[favorite(x, t) \wedge favorite(y, t') \wedge t \not\approx t' \right].$$

Another example of that kind is "every player can make a choice and every other player can make an independent choice in such a way that there will be no winner". It can again be formulated with the use of Henkin quantifiers as

$$\left(\begin{array}{c} \forall x \exists u \\ \forall y \exists z \end{array} \right) \left[canChose(x, u) \wedge canChose(y, z) \wedge \right.$$
$$\left. x \not\approx y \wedge \neg win(x) \wedge \neg win(y) \right].$$

Another branch of artificial intelligence, where second-order logic demonstrates its usefulness, concentrates around approximate reasoning. As we show in Chapter 18, many important forms of reasoning are modeled by weakest sufficient and strongest necessary conditions (see Lin [**140**] and Doherty, Łukaszewicz, Szałas [**59**]) which, in turn, are substantially second-order. Suppose that we want to approximate given knowledge expressed in a richer language by using a weaker language. Then the weakest sufficient condition WSC $(\alpha; Th; P)$ and strongest necessary condition SNC $(\alpha; Th; P)$ of a formula α on the set of relation symbols P

under theory Th are characterized by the following second-order formulas:

$$\text{WSC}\,(\alpha; Th; P) \equiv \forall P'[Th \rightarrow \alpha]$$
$$\text{SNC}\,(\alpha; Th; P) \equiv \exists P'[Th \wedge \alpha],$$

where P' denotes all relation symbols appearing in the richer language and not appearing in P.

1.2. Second-Order Logic in Complexity Theory

The area of descriptive complexity has, in fact, been initiated by the paper of Fagin [74], where it is shown that NPTIME is captured over finite domains by the existential fragment of second-order logic.[1] Later Stockmeyer [195] has generalized this result showing that full second-order logic over finite domains corresponds to the polynomial time hierarchy.

For a detailed description of the area see, e.g., [64, 119].

To show how existential second-order logic can express a NPTIME-complete 3-colorability of a graph,[2] consider the following formula, where R, G, B and E stand for "red", "green", "blue" and "edge", respectively:

$$\exists R \exists G \exists B \big[\forall x[R(x) \vee G(x) \vee B(x)] \wedge$$
$$\forall x \forall y[E(x,y) \rightarrow (\neg R(x) \vee \neg R(y))] \wedge$$
$$\forall x \forall y[E(x,y) \rightarrow (\neg G(x) \vee \neg G(y))] \wedge$$
$$\forall x \forall y[E(x,y) \rightarrow (\neg B(x) \vee \neg B(y))]\big].$$

The elimination of second-order quantifiers $\exists R, \exists G, \exists B$ from the above formula would indeed be an achievement, as this would mean that PTIME=NPTIME.

Let us now concentrate on more modest applications of elimination of second-order quantifiers in estimating the complexity of potentially intractable problems. The methodology can consist of the following steps:

(1) Specify a given problem in second-order logic. The complexity of checking the validity of second-order formulas in a finite model is PSPACE-complete w.r.t. the size of the model. Thus, for all problems in PSPACE such a description exists. The existential fragment of second-order logic is NPTIME-complete over finite models. Dually, the universal fragment of second-order logic is CO-NPTIME-complete over finite models.

(2) Try to eliminate second-order quantifiers. The application of known methods, if successful, might result in:

---

[1] I.e., the fragment consisting of formulas in which all second-order quantifiers are existential and appear only in prefixes of formulas.

[2] I.e., an assignment of colors to graph nodes so that no two adjacent nodes have the same color.

- a formula of first-order logic, the validity of which (over finite models) is in PTIME and LOGSPACE;
- a formula of fixpoint logic, the validity of which (over finite models) is in PTIME.

(3) If the second-order quantifier elimination is not successful, which is likely to happen for NPTIME, CO-NPTIME or PSPACE-complete problems, one can try to identify subclasses of the problem, for which elimination of second-order quantifiers is guaranteed. In such cases tractable (or quasi-polynomial) subproblems of the main problem can be identified.

One can also prove decidability of certain problems by reducing quantifiers and dealing with a decidable theory of equality.

These methodologies are discussed and applied to the analysis of the complexity of hypergraph transversal problem in Szałas [202] and Chapter 15 of this book.

1.3. Second-Order Logic in Correspondence Theory

Modal correspondence theory has led to many techniques for eliminating second-order quantifiers. Modal correspondence theory is concerned about conditions on semantic structures reflecting modal axioms. The basic idea behind the approach is that modal axioms are translated into second-order formulas. For example consider the axiom $\Box P \rightarrow P$. It states that for all P this axiom holds, i.e., it is equivalent to $\forall P [\Box P \rightarrow P]$. Under Kripke semantics this axiom is translated into

$$\forall P [\forall x [\forall y [R(x, y) \rightarrow P(y)] \rightarrow P(x)]].$$

Elimination of the second-order quantifier $\forall P$ results in the equivalent formula $\forall x [R(x, x)]$.

The area of correspondence theory was initiated by Sahlqvist [175] and subsequently by van Benthem [209, 210]. Sahlqvist has isolated a class of modal formulas for which reduction to first-order logic is guaranteed (and which guarantee completeness).

In 1992 Gabbay and Ohlbach [84] developed a resolution-based algorithm, called SCAN.[3] Despite its name indicating the focus on correspondence theory, SCAN has a more general nature and, in fact, allows us to eliminate second-order quantifiers. Later Goranko, Hustadt, Schmidt and Vakarelov [98] showed that SCAN is complete for Sahlqvist formulas (for a proof, see Chapter 11).

The work of Gabbay and Ohlbach has inspired Szałas, who provided an algorithm [199] based on a lemma of Ackermann [2]. Ackermann's lemma allows one

---

[3]SCAN is an acronym for "Synthesizing Correspondence Axioms for Normal Logics".

to eliminate second-order quantifiers from formulas of a certain shape and obtain equivalent first-order formulas. This lemma was later substantially strengthened by Nonnengart and Szałas [155], where the resulting formula is expressed in the fixpoint calculus. The motivation behind the work [155] has been modal-fixpoint correspondence theory.

An approach based on a functional translation has been investigated by Ohlbach and Schmidt in [162].

Recently Conradie, Goranko and Vakarelov have developed an algorithm focused on modal correspondence theory [43, 44]. This algorithm is presented and extended in Chapter 13 of the current book.

The issues of correspondence theory are covered in Chapters 11–13.

1.4. Second-Order Logic in Deductive Databases

Deductive databases are often based on traditional relational databases (see [1]). Due to the complexity, second-order logic is not allowed as a practical query language. However, sometimes it is useful to apply second-order formalisms as a modeling tool and then try to eliminate second-order quantifiers. Default reasoning based on circumscription can serve as an example.

Another example follows from the observation that sometimes it is difficult or impossible to provide an explicit definition of a query. Instead, one provides a set of constraints that the result is to satisfy. Then, one can look for minimal or maximal relations satisfying these constraints. This amounts to asking queries of the form $\exists X[C(X)]$, where $C(X)$ is the conjunction of constraints and X is the relation we ask about (see Doherty, Kachniarz and Szałas [52]).

Also, whenever complete knowledge is assumed, negative information about the world is represented efficiently by accepting the closed world assumption, CWA, according to which information about the world, absent in a state, is assumed to be FALSE (see, e.g., [1]). In many applications, the assumption of complete information is not realistic and the CWA cannot be used. In such cases an open world assumption, OWA, where information not known by the agent is assumed to be UNKNOWN, is often accepted, but complicates both the representational and implementational aspects associated with the use of negative information. The CWA and OWA represent two extremes. Quite often, CWA can be applied locally. In this case one deals with the local closed world assumption LCWA. It can be observed that both CWA and LCWA can be modeled as minimization policies using second-order logic (see Doherty, Łukaszewicz and Szałas [60]). This modeling formalism can, in many cases, be reduced to first-order or fixpoint queries that can be computed in PTIME.

Yet another application of second-order logic depends on the static verification of integrity constraints, as proposed by Kachniarz and Szałas in [**122**]. Assume one wants to make sure that a given database transaction $Trans$ preserves an integrity constraint expressed by a first-order formula α. We then ask whether the initial database satisfies α and whether

$$\forall \bar{X} \left[\alpha(\bar{X}) \to Trans(\alpha(\bar{X})) \right]$$

holds, where $\bar{X}$ contains all relations appearing in α. If the elimination of second-order quantifiers $\forall \bar{X}$ is successful, one ends up in a decidable equality theory (classical or fixpoint).

These problems are more deeply addressed in Chapter 17 of this book.

1.5. Second-Order Quantifier Elimination

It is a very rare case that a given theory allows for eliminating second-order quantifier from any formula. Therefore in the area of second-order quantifier elimination one is mainly interested in providing techniques that allow one to eliminate such quantifiers in the case of classes of formulas which are as large as possible.

A natural question is why do we specify a problem in second-order logic and then eliminate second-order quantifiers? Whenever such elimination is possible, we could have formulated our problem without second-order quantification. It appears that in many particular applications a principled, general specification of given aspects of reasoning substantially requires second-order formalization. Moreover, subformalisms that allow for quantifier elimination are sometimes quite tricky, not obvious and difficult to understand, contrary to a clear specification by second-order means. It is then desirable to reduce the complexity of reasoning by eliminating second-order quantifiers whenever possible.

The fist approach to second-order quantifier elimination seems to have been given in 1935 by Ackermann [**2**]. The next important and fruitful line of research was initiated by Sahlqvist [**175**] and then by van Benthem [**209, 210**]. In 1985 Lifschitz provided some techniques specialized for reducing circumscription [**138**] (for an overview of his results, see also [**139**]). In 1992 Gabbay and Ohlbach developed SCAN [**84**]. Then Szałas provided an algorithm based on Ackermann's lemma [**199**]. This algorithm has been extended by Doherty, Łukaszewicz and Szałas to the DLS algorithm, investigated in [**56**] mainly in the context of circumscription. In 1994 Simmons [**188**] provided another algorithm. Also around the same time Bachmair, Ganzinger and Waldmann [**12**] introduced hierarchical theorem proving and showed it can be used for solving second-order quantification problems.

Nonnengart and Szałas [155] have substantially strengthened Ackermann's lemma by considering fixpoint calculus, too. This approach has also been formalized as the DLS* algorithm proposed by Doherty, Łukaszewicz and Szalas in [57].[4] In [201] Szałas has adapted the fixpoint lemma of [155] to modal contexts.

The approaches based on applications of particular elimination lemmas or theorems, like the lemma of Ackermann or the theorem of [155] are called *direct approaches*.

For an overview of the results obtained before 1999, see [154].

In 2004 Conradie, Goranko and Vakarelov developed the algorithm SQEMA [43], which is specialized to computing correspondences between modal and classical logic. In [181] and Chapter 13, Schmidt introduces an adaptation and improvement, called MSQEL.

Some applications of SCAN are published, e.g., in [27, 98, 106, 178].

Various applications of second-order quantifier elimination based on direct methods have been published, e.g., in [53, 54, 57, 58, 59, 60, 61, 63, 122, 200, 202].

Several algorithms for second-order quantifier elimination have been implemented and are available online.

- SCAN, introduced in [84] and developed and implemented by Engel and Ohlbach [70, 160, 71], is available via the website
  http://www.mpi-inf.mpg.de/departments/d2/software/SCAN/.
- DLS, developed by Gustafsson [103], is available via
  http://www.ida.liu.se/labs/kplab/projects/dls/.
- DLS and DLS*, defined in [57] and based on the fixpoint approach of [155], implemented by Magnusson [144], is available via
  http://www.ida.liu.se/labs/kplab/projects/dlsstar/.
- SQEMA, defined in [43] and implemented by Georgiev [90], is available via the address
  http://www.fmi.uni-sofia.bg/fmi/logic/sqema/.

1.6. Structure of the Book

The book is divided into four parts. The first part contains this chapter and additional background material covering the basics from complexity theory, all necessary details concerning classical propositional, first-order, second-order and fixpoint logic, as well as first-order resolution theorem proving and equality reasoning. Part 2 is devoted to second-order quantifier elimination in classical logic. We

---

[4]In fact, in [57] it has been defined under the name G-DLS.

start with the SCAN algorithm and hierarchical resolution, and then consider direct methods (based on Ackermann's lemma and the fixpoint lemma of Nonnengart and Szałas). We also discuss the possibility of incorporating background theories and consider methods specialized for particular structures not defined by means of theories. Part 3 is devoted to second-order quantifier elimination in modal logics. The last part presents selected applications of the methods discussed earlier in complexity theory, databases, common-sense reasoning, approximate reasoning, conditional reasoning, and duality theory, and mentions some further applications classical logic and mathematics.

1.7. Acknowledgments

For cooperation on the topic of second-order quantifier elimination and/or comments which helped improve the contents of this book, we are indebted to our colleagues, Willem Conradie, Patrick Doherty, Valentin Goranko, Ullrich Hustadt, Jarosław Kachniarz, Witold Łukaszewicz, Andreas Nonnengart, Hans-Jürgen Ohlbach, Ewa Orłowska, Jerzy Tyszkiewicz and Dimiter Vakarelov. Many thanks go to Joakim Gustaffson, Martin Magnusson, Torsten Engel, Hans-Jürgen Ohlbach and J. J. Palacios-Perez for their involvement with the implementation and porting of DLS and SCAN. We are also grateful to Mike Nugent for his help in the final editing of the book.

We thank the following institutions which have hosted us during our research on the book as well as on papers related to the book: King's College (London, UK), Max-Planck-Institut für Informatik (Saarbrücken, Germany), University of Economics and Computer Science (Olsztyn, Poland), University of Linköping (Linköping, Sweden), University of Manchester (Manchester, UK), University of Warsaw (Warsaw, Poland), and Warsaw School of Computer Science (Warsaw, Poland).

Work on the topic of this book has been supported by several UK EPSRC grants (GR/M88761/01, GR/R92035/01, GR/T08210/01, EP/C538536/1, EP/D056152/1) and two Polish grants (MNiI 3 T11C 023 29, MNiSW N N206 399134).

CHAPTER 2

Some Basics

In this chapter first we summarize notational conventions common to the entire book. Notation needed within particular chapters only is defined within these chapters. Second, we recall some basic facts of complexity theory necessary for the current book. A comprehensive coverage of the subject can be found, e.g., in [107, 166]. The basics of logic can be found in the next chapter.

2.1. Notational Conventions

2.1.1. Set Theory. Sets are denoted using brackets $\{,\}$. Angled brackets $\langle \ldots \rangle$ are used to denote tuples. Also $\bar{Q}$ denotes a tuple of elements of type known from the context.

The symbols $\emptyset, -, \cup, \cap, \in, \subseteq, =$ stand for the empty set and the usual operations of the *complement* of a set, *union*, *intersection* of sets and relations of *membership*, *set inclusion* and *set equality*.

By $|A|$ we understand the cardinality of A and by $|A|^+$ the least cardinal strictly greater than $|A|$.

The *powerset of a set* A is denoted by $\mathcal{P}(A)$ (i.e., $\mathcal{P}(A) \overset{\text{def}}{=} \{X \mid X \subseteq A\}$).

The *Cartesian product* of sets $U_1, \ldots, U_k$ is denoted by $U_1 \times \ldots \times U_k$. By U^k we understand the Cartesian product $\underbrace{U \times \ldots \times U}_{k \text{ times}}$.

By ω we denote the set of natural numbers.

Functions are denoted by $f : A \longrightarrow B$, where f is the name of the function, A is its domain and B the set of its values.

2.1.2. Logic. The symbols $\neg, \vee, \wedge, \rightarrow, \equiv$ stand for the standard propositional connectives denoting *negation, disjunction, conjunction, implication* and *equivalence*.

We use the symbols $\forall, \exists$ to denote *universal* and *existential* quantifiers, respectively.

11

The symbol $\approx$ is used for logical equality, whereas $=$ is used to denote syntactic equality.

For $\bar{s} = \langle s_1, \ldots, s_k \rangle$ and $\bar{t} = \langle t_1, \ldots, t_k \rangle$ we write $\bar{s} \approx \bar{t}$ to denote the conjunction $\bigwedge_{i=1}^{k} s_i \approx t_i$ and $\bar{s} \not\approx \bar{t}$ to denote $\neg(\bar{s} \approx \bar{t})$.

2.1.3. General. The notation $g(n) = O(f(n))$, where $f : \omega \longrightarrow \omega$, means that there is a real number $c > 0$ such that for all $n \in \omega$, $g(n) \leq c * f(n)$. We say that $g(n)$ is *linear* in n iff $g(n) = c * n$ for some real number $c > 0$. $g(n)$ is *exponential* in n iff $g(n) = c^n$ for some real number $c > 0$.

By $\alpha_{f_1(y_1),\ldots,e_k(x_k)}^{e_1(x_1),\ldots,e_k(x_k)}$ we understand the expression obtained from α in such a way that for any $1 \leq i \leq k$, all occurrences of e_i of the form $e_i(a)$ are replaced by $f_i(y_i)$, where y_i itself is replaced by a. For example,

$$\left(P(s) \vee P(t) \right)_{(Q(a,u) \wedge Q(u,b))(u)}^{P(x)} = \left((Q(a,s) \wedge Q(s,b)) \right) \vee \left((Q(a,t) \wedge Q(t,b)) \right).$$

In a simplified form, by α_e^x we mean the expression obtained from α by replacing all occurrences of x by e. Also, $\alpha_{e_2(\bar{x},\bar{y})}^{e_1(\bar{x})} \stackrel{\text{def}}{=} \alpha_{e_2(\bar{x},\bar{y})(\bar{x})}^{e_1(\bar{x})}$.

2.2. Basics of Complexity Theory

In complexity theory, we consider *time complexity* and *space complexity* with the intuition that the time complexity refers to the time spent during the computing process and space complexity refers to the amount of memory used during the computing process. We assume the Turing machine model.

2.2.1. Basic Complexity Classes. In order to measure complexity, we need a parameter describing the input size. We shall always assume that the input size is a natural number. Let $n \in \omega$ be an input size and let $f : \omega \longrightarrow \omega$ be a function. We shall deal with the following complexity classes:

- DTime($f(n)$), NTime($f(n)$) – problems solvable by deterministic (respectively non-deterministic) algorithms in time not exceeding $f(n)$;
- DSpace($f(n)$), NSpace($f(n)$) – problems solvable by deterministic (respectively non-deterministic) algorithms in space not exceeding $f(n)$.

The most important complexity classes considered in this book are:

- PTime – problems solvable deterministically in polynomial time,
  PTime $\stackrel{\text{def}}{=} \bigcup_{k \in \omega}$ DTime(n^k);

- NPTIME – problems solvable non-deterministically in polynomial time,
  $$\text{NPTIME} \stackrel{\text{def}}{=} \bigcup_{k \in \omega} \text{NTIME}(n^k);$$
- PSPACE – problems solvable deterministically in polynomial space,
  $$\text{PSPACE} \stackrel{\text{def}}{=} \bigcup_{k \in \omega} \text{DSPACE}(n^k);$$
- LOGSPACE – problems solvable deterministically in logarithmic space,
  $$\text{LOGSPACE} \stackrel{\text{def}}{=} \text{DSPACE}(\log(n));$$
- NLOGSPACE – problems solvable non-deterministically in logarithmic
  space, $\text{NLOGSPACE} \stackrel{\text{def}}{=} \text{NSPACE}(\log(n))$.

We do not distinguish between non-deterministic and deterministic polynomial space, since due to the Savitch theorem [**176**] these classes are equal.

It is known that $\text{LOGSPACE} \subseteq \text{NLOGSPACE} \subseteq \text{PTIME} \subseteq \text{NPTIME} \subseteq \text{PSPACE}$. It is, however, still unknown whether the inclusions are proper.

Classes containing *complements* of the problems of a given class are denoted using the prefix CO- preceding the class name. For example, CO-NPTIME denotes the class of complements of problems from NPTIME.

DEFINITION 2.1. We say that a problem P' is *polynomially reducible* to a problem P iff there is a deterministic algorithm A running in polynomial time which any input d' to P' transforms into an input d to P in such a way that $d' \in P'$ iff $d \in P$.

For a given complexity class CC, we say that a problem P is CC-*complete* iff $P \in \text{CC}$ and any problem $P' \in \text{CC}$ is polynomially reducible to P. ◁

2.2.2. Polynomial Hierarchy. Stockmeyer [**195**] has introduced the polynomial hierarchy.

By an *oracle for a problem* P we mean a querying mechanism giving answers to instances of P. Each call to the oracle is regarded as a single step. If C, C' are complexity classes, then by $C[C']$ we shall denote the class of problems with complexity in class C, provided that an oracle for C' is given.

DEFINITION 2.2. The *polynomial hierarchy* consists of sets of problems Δ_k^P, Σ_k^P, Π_k^P, for $k \in \omega$, defined as follows:

$$\Delta_0^P = \Sigma_0^P = \Pi_0^P \stackrel{\text{def}}{=} \text{PTIME}$$
$$\Delta_{k+1}^P \stackrel{\text{def}}{=} \text{PTIME}[\Sigma_k^P]$$
$$\Sigma_{k+1}^P \stackrel{\text{def}}{=} \text{NPTIME}[\Sigma_k^P]$$
$$\Pi_{k+1}^P \stackrel{\text{def}}{=} \text{CO-}\Sigma_{k+1}^P.$$

The complexity class $\mathcal{PH}$ is defined to be $\mathcal{PH} \stackrel{\text{def}}{=} \bigcup_{i \in \omega} \Sigma_i^P$. ◁

It can be proved that, for all $k \in \omega$, $\Sigma_k^P, \Pi_k^P, \Delta_k^P \subseteq$ PSPACE. It is also known that NPTIME, CO-NPTIME $\subseteq \Sigma_2^P \cap \Pi_2^P$.

2.2.3. Arithmetical Hierarchy. The arithmetical hierarchy has been defined independently by Kleene and Mostowski (see, e.g., [**173**]). Let $\langle \omega, 0, 1, +, *, = \rangle$ be the standard structure of arithmetics of natural numbers. In this section we assume that formulas are evaluated in this structure.

DEFINITION 2.3. *Arithmetical hierarchy* consists of sets of formulas $\Sigma_n^0, \Pi_n^0, \Delta_n^0$, where $n \in \omega$, defined inductively by

$$\Sigma_0^0 = \Pi_0^0 = \Delta_0^0 \stackrel{\text{def}}{=} \text{ the set of formulas without quantifiers}$$
$$\Sigma_{n+1}^0 \stackrel{\text{def}}{=} \{\exists x[A(x)] \mid x \text{ is an individual variable and } A(x) \in \Pi_n^0\}$$
$$\Pi_{n+1}^0 \stackrel{\text{def}}{=} \{\forall x[A(x)] \mid x \text{ is an individual variable and } A(x) \in \Sigma_n^0\}$$
$$\Delta_{n+1}^0 \stackrel{\text{def}}{=} \Sigma_{n+1}^0 \cap \Pi_{n+1}^0.$$

Sets definable by means of formulas of Σ_0^0 are called *(totally) decidable*, definable by formulas of Σ_1^0 are called *partially decidable* and definable by formulas of Π_1^0 are called *co-partially decidable*. Sets definable by a formula of Σ_n^0 or Π_n^0, for some $n \in \omega$, are called *arithmetical*.   ◁

We have the following theorem.

THEOREM 2.4. *For all* $n \in \omega$,

$$\Delta_n^0 \subsetneqq \Sigma_n^0 \subsetneqq \Delta_{n+1}^0, \ \Delta_n^0 \subsetneqq \Pi_n^0 \subsetneqq \Delta_{n+1}^0$$
$$\Sigma_n^0 \subsetneqq \Sigma_{n+1}^0, \ \Pi_n^0 \subsetneqq \Pi_{n+1}^0,$$

i.e., the sets $\Sigma_n^0, \Pi_n^0, \Delta_n^0$ *form a strict hierarchy.*   ◁

2.2.4. Analytical Hierarchy. The analytical hierarchy, first investigated by Kleene, is a second-order analogue of the arithmetical hierarchy and is also defined over the standard structure of arithmetics of natural numbers (see, e.g., [**107**]).

DEFINITION 2.5. *Analytical hierarchy* consists of sets of formulas $\Sigma_n^1, \Pi_n^1, \Delta_n^1$, where $n \in \omega$, defined inductively by

$$\Sigma_0^1 = \Pi_0^1 = \Delta_0^1 \stackrel{\text{def}}{=} \text{ the set of all arithmetical formulas}$$
$$\Sigma_{n+1}^1 \stackrel{\text{def}}{=} \{\exists X[A(X)] \mid X \text{ is a relation symbol and } A(X) \in \Pi_n^1\}$$
$$\Pi_{n+1}^1 \stackrel{\text{def}}{=} \{\forall X[A(X)] \mid X \text{ is a relation symbol and } A(X) \in \Sigma_n^1\}$$
$$\Delta_{n+1}^1 \stackrel{\text{def}}{=} \Sigma_{n+1}^1 \cap \Pi_{n+1}^1.$$

Sets definable by a formula of Σ_n^1 or Π_n^1, for some $n \in \omega$, are called *analytical*. Sets definable by formulas of Δ_1^1 are called *hyperarithmetical*.   ◁

We have the following theorem.

THEOREM 2.6. For all $n \in \omega$,

$$\Delta_n^1 \subsetneqq \Sigma_n^1 \subsetneqq \Delta_{n+1}^1, \ \Delta_n^1 \subsetneqq \Pi_n^1 \subsetneqq \Delta_{n+1}^1$$
$$\Sigma_n^1 \subsetneqq \Sigma_{n+1}^1, \ \Pi_n^1 \subsetneqq \Pi_{n+1}^1,$$

i.e., the sets Σ_n^1, Π_n^1, Δ_n^1 form a strict hierarchy. $\triangleleft$

CHAPTER 3

Logics and Equality Theories

In this chapter we introduce a general notion of logic and specialize it to zero-order, first-order, second-order and fixpoint logics. The framework we give is not as general as it could be, but suits our purposes well. We also consider the first-order and fixpoint versions of the theory of equality.

3.1. Definition of Logic

For the purpose of this book we assume that a logic is mainly presented via its language and semantics. An alternative way to present logics is via their language and proof systems. Of course, particular proof systems play an important rôle in algorithms we describe. However, the primary rôle in methods we present is played by semantics.

DEFINITION 3.1. By a *logic* we understand a triple $\mathcal{L} \stackrel{\text{def}}{=} \langle \mathcal{F}, \mathcal{I}, \models \rangle$, where

- $\mathcal{F}$ is a non-empty set, called the *set of formulas*, called also the *language*; of logic $\mathcal{L}$ (it is often assumed that TRUE, FALSE $\in \mathcal{F}$)
- $\mathcal{I}$ is a non-empty *class of admissible interpretations*;
- $\models \subseteq \mathcal{F} \times \mathcal{I}$ is a relation, called the *satisfiability relation*, assigning truth values for formulas under interpretations. For $I \in \mathcal{I}$ and $\alpha \in \mathcal{F}$ we write $I \models \alpha$ to mean that the truth value of formula α under interpretation I is TRUE and we write $I \not\models \alpha$ when it is not the case that $I \models \alpha$.

We say that a formula $\alpha \in \mathcal{F}$ is *satisfiable* if there is $I \in \mathcal{I}$ such that $I \models \alpha$. We say that α is a *tautology* if for all $I \in \mathcal{I}$ we have $I \models \alpha$. Formula α is a *counter-tautology* if for all $I \in \mathcal{I}$ we have $I \models \neg\alpha$.   ◁

The above definition is general enough to serve our purposes. We do not make any assumptions as to the shape of formulas as well as availability of logical connectives or operators. Similarly, no assumption is made as to the class of interpretations. We specialize Definition 3.1 whenever necessary by fixing elements of logical languages and their semantics.

3.2. Zero-Order Logics

Zero-order logics are usually referred to as propositional logics since the atoms of the underlying logical languages are propositions represented by propositional variables. More complicated formulas are then formed by using propositional connectives and operators.

The intended meaning of propositional variables is that they are evaluated by assigning truth values to them. Definition 3.1 is then specialized as follows.

DEFINITION 3.2. By a *zero-order logic* we understand any logic $\langle \mathcal{F}, \mathcal{I}, \models \rangle$, as defined in Definition 3.1, where additionally

- We assume a non-empty set V_0, called the *set of propositional* or *zero-order variables*, ranging over {TRUE, FALSE};
- We assume a non-empty set $\mathcal{C}$ of *propositional connectives*; with each $C \in \mathcal{C}$ we associate the *arity* of C, which is a natural number. Connectives of arity 1 are called *unary* and of arity 2 are called *binary*;
- $\mathcal{F}$ is defined inductively to be the smallest set containing V_0 and closed under propositional connectives, i.e., if $C \in \mathcal{C}$ is a connective of arity n and $\alpha_1, \ldots, \alpha_n \in \mathcal{F}$ then $C(\alpha_1, \ldots, \alpha_n) \in \mathcal{F}$.   ◁

For binary connectives we usually use the traditional infix notation, i.e., we write $\alpha \, C \, \beta$ rather than $C(\alpha, \beta)$.

3.2.1. Classical Propositional (Zero-Order) Logic.

Classical propositional logic is used to investigate properties of complex sentences built from elementary sentences by using propositional connectives. Whether complex sentences are true or not depends solely on logical values of elementary sentences involved in them. The meaning of sentences is given by valuations of elementary sentences together with a method of calculating values of complex sentences on the basis of their components.

3.2.2. Syntax of Classical Propositional Logic.

By Definition 3.2, any propositional logic is given as the triple $\langle \mathcal{F}, \mathcal{I}, \models \rangle$. Classical propositional logic assumes that TRUE, FALSE $\in \mathcal{F}$ and that the set of *classical propositional connectives* is $\mathcal{C} \stackrel{\text{def}}{=} \{\neg, \wedge, \vee, \rightarrow, \equiv\}$. Elements of $\mathcal{C}$ stand for *negation, conjunction, disjunction, implication* and *equivalence*, respectively.

DEFINITION 3.3. The set of classical propositional formulas, $\mathcal{F}_0$, is inductively defined according to the general schema of Definition 3.2 to be the smallest set satisfying the conditions

(1) {TRUE, FALSE} $\subseteq \mathcal{F}_0$, $V_0 \subseteq \mathcal{F}_0$;
(2) $\alpha, \beta \in \mathcal{F}_0$ implies $\neg\alpha, \alpha \wedge \beta, \alpha \vee \beta, \alpha \rightarrow \beta, \alpha \equiv \beta \in \mathcal{F}_0$.

By a *propositional literal* we understand any formula of the form p or $\neg p$, where $p \in V_0$. Literals of the form p are called *positive* and of the form $\neg p$ are called *negative*. A *propositional clause* is a disjunction of literals. A clause with at most one positive literal is called a *Horn clause* (a *propositional Horn formula*). A clause with at most one negative literal is called a *propositional dual Horn clause*. By a *propositional term* we understand any conjunction of propositional literals.   ◁

3.2.3. Semantics of Classical Propositional Logic. Below we assume that truth values are ordered, FALSE $\leq$ TRUE. By $\min\{t_1, t_2\}$ and $\max\{t_1, t_2\}$ we denote respectively the minimum and maximum of truth values t_1, t_2 w.r.t. $\leq$. The set $\mathcal{I}$ of interpretations consists of *valuations of propositional variables*, i.e.,

$$\mathcal{I} \overset{\text{def}}{=} \{v \mid v \text{ is a function, } v : V_0 \longrightarrow \{\text{TRUE}, \text{FALSE}\}\}.$$

The *satisfiability relation of classical propositional logic*, $\models$, is defined by

(1) $v \models p$ iff $v(p) = \text{TRUE}$, where $p \in V_0$;
(2) $v \models \neg\alpha$ iff $v \not\models \alpha$;
(3) $v \models \alpha \wedge \beta$ iff $\min\{v(\alpha), v(\beta)\} = \text{TRUE}$;
(4) $v \models \alpha \vee \beta$ iff $\max\{v(\alpha), v(\beta)\} = \text{TRUE}$;
(5) $v \models \alpha \rightarrow \beta$ iff $v(\alpha) \leq v(\beta)$;
(6) $v \models \alpha \equiv \beta$ iff $v(\alpha) = v(\beta)$.

3.2.4. Normal Forms for Propositional Formulas.

DEFINITION 3.4. A formula is in *negation normal form* if the formula does not contain implication and equivalence and the negation sign $\neg$ appears only in literals. We denote by $\text{NNF}(\alpha)$ the negation normal form of a formula α.[1]   ◁

We have the following proposition.

PROPOSITION 3.5. Every propositional formula can equivalently be transformed into negation normal form, i.e., $\alpha \equiv \text{NNF}(\alpha)$ for any propositional formula.   ◁

PROOF. In order to transform a formula into negation normal form one has to eliminate implication and equivalence using the equivalences provided in Table 1. Then one moves negation inside using the equivalences listed in Table 2. It can easily be observed that if no such equivalence can be applied, then the input formula is already in negation normal form.   ◁

DEFINITION 3.6. A formula is in *conjunctive normal form* iff it is a conjunction of clauses.   ◁

---

[1]In fact, there might be many formulas in the negation normal form, equivalent to a given formula. The notation $\text{NNF}(\alpha)$ is then to be understood as a formula provided by a chosen algorithm. The same remark applies to other normal forms considered in this book.

TABLE 1. Equivalences for eliminating implication and equivalence.

input formula	equivalent formula
$\neg(\alpha \equiv \beta)$	$(\neg\alpha \lor \neg\beta) \land (\alpha \lor \beta)$
$\alpha \equiv \beta$	$(\neg\alpha \lor \beta) \land (\alpha \lor \neg\beta)$
$\neg(\alpha \to \beta)$	$\alpha \land \neg\beta$
$\alpha \to \beta$	$\neg\alpha \lor \beta$

TABLE 2. Equivalences for transforming a formula into negation normal form.

input formula	equivalent formula
$\neg\neg\alpha$	α
$\neg(\alpha \land \beta)$	$\neg\alpha \lor \neg\beta$
$\neg(\alpha \lor \beta)$	$\neg\alpha \land \neg\beta$

We have the following proposition.

PROPOSITION 3.7. Every propositional formula can equivalently be transformed into conjunctive normal form.

PROOF. In order to transform a formula into conjunctive normal form one can first transform it into negation normal form and then use the equivalences listed in Table 3. It can easily be observed that if no such equivalence can be applied, then the input formula is already in conjunctive normal form.   ◁

TABLE 3. Equivalences for transforming a formula into conjunctive normal form.

input formula	equivalent formula
$\alpha \lor (\beta \land \gamma)$	$(\alpha \lor \beta) \land (\alpha \lor \gamma)$
$(\alpha \land \beta) \lor \gamma$	$(\alpha \lor \gamma) \land (\beta \lor \gamma)$

It is also convenient to perform obvious simplifications, modulo associativity and commutativity of conjunction and disjunction, based on the equivalences in Table 4.

When we use the notation $\mathrm{CNF}(\alpha)$ we mean the conjunctive normal form of a formula α defined exhaustively applying the set of rewrite rules based on equivalences in Tables 1–3 and including those of Table 4, modulo associativity and commutativity of conjunction and disjunction.

PROPOSITION 3.8. For every propositional formula α, $\alpha \equiv \mathrm{CNF}(\alpha)$.   ◁

TABLE 4. Equivalences for removing obvious redundancies.

input formula	equivalent formula
$\alpha \wedge$ TRUE	α
$\alpha \wedge$ FALSE	FALSE
$\alpha \vee$ TRUE	TRUE
$\alpha \vee$ FALSE	α
$\neg$TRUE	FALSE
$\neg$FALSE	TRUE

DEFINITION 3.9. A formula is in *disjunctive normal form* iff it is a disjunction of propositional terms.   ◁

We have the following proposition.

PROPOSITION 3.10. Every propositional formula can equivalently be transformed into disjunctive normal form.

PROOF. In order to transform a formula into disjunctive normal form one can first transform it into negation normal form and then to use the equivalences listed in Table 5. It can easily be observed that if no such equivalence can be applied, then the input formula is already in disjunctive normal form.   ◁

TABLE 5. Equivalences for transforming a formula into disjunctive normal form.

input formula	equivalent formula
$\alpha \wedge (\beta \vee \gamma)$	$(\alpha \wedge \beta) \vee (\alpha \wedge \gamma)$
$(\alpha \vee \beta) \wedge \gamma$	$(\alpha \wedge \gamma) \vee (\beta \wedge \gamma)$

3.2.5. Complexity of Classical Propositional Logic. Complexity of propositional logic is provided in Theorem 3.11, proved by Cook [45].

THEOREM 3.11. The satisfiability problem for the propositional logic is NPTIME-complete. Checking whether a propositional formula is a tautology of the propositional logic is CO-NPTIME-complete.   ◁

On the other hand, there are classes of propositional formulas for which both problems mentioned in Theorem 3.11 are in PTIME. The dichotomy theorem by Schaeffer [177] clarifies the situation. In order to formulate this theorem we need some definitions.

DEFINITION 3.12. Let $S = \{C_l, \ldots, C_m\}$ be any finite set of propositional connectives. By an *S-formula* we understand any conjunction of formulas of the form $C_i(p_1, \ldots, p_k)$, where $p_1, \ldots, p_k \in V_0$ and k is the arity of C_i. The *S-satisfiability problem* is the problem of deciding whether a given *S-*formula is satisfiable.   ◁

DEFINITION 3.13. Let $S = \{C_l, \ldots, C_m\}$ be a finite set of propositional connectives, let $A(p_1, \ldots, p_n)$ be an *S-*formula and let $p_1, \ldots, p_n$ be all propositional variables in A. Then:

   (1) A is *0-valid* iff $v \models A(p_1, \ldots, p_n)$, where v assigns FALSE to all variables $p_1, \ldots, p_n$;
   (2) A is *1-valid* iff $v \models A(p_1, \ldots, p_n)$, where v assigns TRUE to all variables $p_1, \ldots, p_n$;
   (3) A is *Horn valid* iff A is equivalent to a conjunction of Horn clauses;
   (4) A is *dual Horn valid* iff A is equivalent to a conjunction of dual Horn clauses;
   (5) A is *bijunctive* iff A is equivalent to a formula in conjunctive normal form having at most two literals in each clause;
   (6) A is *affine* iff A is equivalent to a conjunction of formulas of the form $\neg[p_1 \veebar p_2 \veebar \ldots \veebar p_k]$, where $\veebar$ stands for *exclusive or*, i.e., the connective defined by

$$p_1 \veebar p_2 \veebar \ldots \veebar p_k \stackrel{\text{def}}{\equiv} \left[(p_1 \vee p_2 \vee \ldots \vee p_k) \wedge \bigwedge_{1 \leq i < j \leq k} (\neg p_i \vee \neg p_j) \right].$$

A set F of formulas is *0-valid* (*1-valid, Horn valid, dual Horn valid, bijunctive, affine*) iff every formula in F is *0-valid* (respectively *1-valid, Horn valid, dual Horn valid, bijunctive, affine*).   ◁

Schaeffer's dichotomy theorem is formulated below.

THEOREM 3.14. Let S be a finite set of propositional connectives. If S is either 0-valid or 1-valid, Horn valid, dual Horn valid, bijunctive or affine then the *S-*satisfiability problem is in PTIME. Otherwise the *S-*satisfiability problem is NPTIME-complete.   ◁

Observe that Theorem 3.14 characterizes shapes of formulas admitting second-order quantifier elimination. For other formulas such elimination would be possible only in the case when PTIME = NPTIME.

3.3. First-Order Logics

Fist-order logics usually allow one to express properties of individuals, using terms, relations between them and quantifiers. To make this possible we introduce individual variables, functions, relations and quantifiers.

The intended meaning of individual variables is that they range over individuals of the underlying domain.

DEFINITION 3.15. By a *first-order logic* we understand any logic $\langle \mathcal{F}, \mathcal{I}, \models \rangle$, which is an extension of a zero-order logic, as defined in Definition 3.2, where additionally

- We assume a non-empty set V_1, called the *set of individual variables*, a non-empty set FUN of *function symbols* and a non-empty set REL of *relation symbols*; with each $f \in$ FUN and $R \in$ REL we associate the *arity* of f (respectively R), which is a natural number. Functions of arity 0 are called *constants*. Functions and relations of arity 1 are called *unary* and of arity 2 are called *binary*.
- We define inductively the set of *terms*, TERMS, as the smallest set containing individual variables and constants and closed under applications of function symbols, i.e., if $f \in$ FUN is a function symbol of arity n and $\tau_1, \ldots, \tau_n \in$ TERMS then $f(\tau_1, \ldots, \tau_n) \in$ TERMS.
- *Atomic formulas* are expressions of the form $R(\tau_1, \ldots, \tau_n)$, where $R \in$ REL is a n-ary relation symbol and $\tau_1, \ldots, \tau_n \in$ TERMS.
- $\mathcal{F}$ is defined inductively to be the smallest set containing propositional formulas, atomic formulas and closed under propositional connectives and first-order quantifiers $\forall x$, $\exists x$, i.e., if $C \in \mathcal{C}$ is a connective of arity n, $x \in V_1$ and $\alpha_1, \ldots, \alpha_n \in \mathcal{F}$ then $C(\alpha_1, \ldots, \alpha_n), \forall x[\alpha_1], \exists x[\alpha_1] \in \mathcal{F}$. The quantifier $\forall x$ is called *universal* and $\exists x$ is called *existential*.   ◁

3.3.1. Classical First-Order Logic.

Classical first-order logic, known also as *classical predicate logic*, serves as a means to express properties of individuals and relationships between individuals (objects of a domain). It is an extension of classical propositional logic and provides syntax that allows one to talk about individuals, relations and functions. Quantifiers $\forall$ ("for all") and $\exists$ ("exists"), ranging over individuals, are also available.

Classical first-order logic is a very powerful formalism.[2] It has a great variety of applications ranging from mathematics to computer science and artificial intelligence. It is very well developed. In particular there are many well-developed automated theorem proving methods. Thus it is widely used as a "kernel" of many other formalisms.

3.3.2. Syntax of Classical First-Order Logic.

Classical first-order logic is an extension of classical propositional logic (see Chapter 3.2.1) in the sense of Definition 3.15, page 23. In particular we have

---

[2]In fact, by the Lindström theorem, it is the strongest logic satisfying some natural conditions, with a partially decidable set of tautologies – see, e.g., [**36, 65**].

- A non-empty set V_1 of individual variables, a non-empty set FUN of *function symbols* and a non-empty set REL of *relation symbols*;
- By *atomic first-order formulas* we understand expressions of the form $R(\tau_1, \ldots, \tau_n)$, where $R \in$ REL is a n-ary relation symbol and $\tau_1, \ldots, \tau_n$ belong to TERMS;
- The *set of classical first-order formulas*, denoted by $\mathcal{F}_1$, is defined inductively to be the smallest set containing propositional formulas, atomic first-order formulas and closed under propositional connectives $\neg, \wedge, \vee,$ $\rightarrow, \equiv$ and first-order quantifiers $\forall x, \exists x$.

By a *first-order signature* (*signature*, for short) we understand any tuple of the form $\langle \langle f_i \rangle_{i \in I}, \langle R_j \rangle_{j \in J} \rangle$, where I, J are any subsets of ω and for any $i \in I, j \in J$, $f_i \in$ FUN and $R_j \in$ REL.

DEFINITION 3.16. A first-order formula is called *open* if it does not contain quantifiers. A variable occurrence is *free* in a formula if it is not bound by a quantifier, otherwise it is called *bound*. A formula is called *closed* (or a *sentence*) if it does not contain free occurrences of variables. Any set of sentences is called a *first-order theory*, or *theory*, for short. A theory is understood as a (finite or infinite) conjunction of its sentences.

By a *literal* we understand any atomic formula or its negation. Literals of the form $R(\tau_1, \ldots, \tau_n)$ are called *positive* and of the form $\neg R(\tau_1, \ldots, \tau_n)$ are called *negative*. A *clause* is a disjunction of literals. A clause with at most one positive literal is called a *Horn clause* (a *Horn formula*). A clause with at most one negative literal is called a *dual Horn clause*.   ◁

3.3.3. Semantics of Classical First-Order Logic. The semantics of first-order formulas is given by a valuation of individual variables together with an interpretation of function symbols and relation symbols as functions and relations. The interpretation of function symbols and relation symbols is given by relational structures defined below.

DEFINITION 3.17. Let $\Sigma = \langle \langle f_i \rangle_{i \in I}, \langle R_j \rangle_{j \in J} \rangle$ be a signature. By a *relational structure* over Σ we understand a tuple of the form $\langle U, \langle f_i^U \rangle_{i \in I}, \langle R_j^U \rangle_{j \in J} \rangle$, where:

- U is a non-empty set, called the *domain* or *universe* of the relational structure;
- For $i \in I$, f_i^U denote *functions* corresponding to function symbols f_i;
- For $j \in J$, R_j^U denote *relations* corresponding to relation symbols R_j.

For the sake of simplicity, in the rest of the book we often abbreviate f_i^U and R_j^U by f_i and R_j, respectively.

For a given signature Σ, by $RS(\Sigma)$ we denote the class of all relational structures built over the signature Σ.   ◁

DEFINITION 3.18. Given a relational structure $M = \langle U, \langle f_i^U \rangle_{i \in I}, \langle R_j^U \rangle_{j \in J} \rangle$, by a valuation of individual variables in M we mean any mapping $v : V_1 \longrightarrow U$.

The class of *first-order interpretations*, $\mathcal{I}_1$, is defined to consist of $\langle M, v \rangle$, where $M \in RS(\Sigma)$ and v is a valuation of individual variables in M.   ◁

By v_a^x we denote the valuation obtained from v by assigning value a to variable x and leaving all other variables unchanged, i.e.,

$$v_a^x(z) = \begin{cases} a & \text{if } z = x \\ v(z) & \text{otherwise.} \end{cases}$$

Any valuation v of individual variables is extended to provide values of terms as follows, where $f \in$ FUN is a k-argument function symbol and $t_1, \ldots, t_k \in$ TERMS:

$$v(f(t_1, \ldots, t_k)) = f^U(v(t_1), \ldots, v(t_k)).$$

Then v is extended to define the *truth value of first-order formulas* as follows, where $R \in$ REL is a k-argument relation:

(1)
$$\begin{aligned} &v(R(t_1, \ldots, t_k)) = R^U(v(t_1), \ldots, v(t_k)) \\ &v(\neg \alpha) = \begin{cases} \text{TRUE} & \text{if } v(\alpha) = \text{FALSE} \\ \text{FALSE} & \text{otherwise} \end{cases} \\ &v(\alpha \wedge \beta) = \min\{v(\alpha), v(\beta)\} \\ &v(\alpha \vee \beta) = \max\{v(\alpha), v(\beta)\} \\ &v(\alpha \rightarrow \beta) = \text{TRUE iff } v(\alpha) \leq v(\beta) \\ &v(\alpha \equiv \beta) = \text{TRUE iff } v(\alpha) = v(\beta) \\ &v(\forall x[\alpha(x)]) = \min\{v_a^x(\alpha(x)) \mid a \in U\} \\ &v(\exists x[\alpha(x)]) = \max\{v_a^x(\alpha(x)) \mid a \in U\}. \end{aligned}$$

DEFINITION 3.19. The *satisfiability relation of classical first-order logic* is defined by $M, v \models \alpha$ iff $v(\alpha) = $ TRUE.

A first-order formula α is *satisfied* in $M = \langle U, \langle f_i^U \rangle_{i \in I}, \langle R_j^U \rangle_{j \in J} \rangle$ iff there is a valuation $v : V_1 \longrightarrow U$ such that $v(\alpha) = $ TRUE. Formula α is *valid in relational structure* M iff for all valuations v, $v(\alpha) = $ TRUE. In such a case we also say that M is a *model* for α. For a set of formulas $F \subseteq \mathcal{F}_1$ and formula $\alpha \in \mathcal{F}_1$, by the *consequence relation*, denoted by $F \models \alpha$, we mean that α is satisfied in any relational structure which is a model of all formulas of F.   ◁

3.3.4. Normal Forms for First-Order Formulas.

3.3.4.1. *Basic Definitions.* We define the polarity of (occurrences of) first-order subformulas as usual. Any occurrence of a proper subformula of an equivalence has *zero polarity*. For occurrences of subformulas not under a $\equiv$ symbol, an occurrence of a subformula has *positive polarity* if it is an occurrence inside the scope of an even number of (explicit or implicit) negations, and it has *negative polarity* if it is one inside the scope of an odd number of negations.

3.3.4.2. *Negation, Conjunctive and Disjunctive Normal Forms.* Negation, conjunctive and disjunctive normal forms are defined for open formulas similarly to corresponding normal forms for propositional formulas, as defined in Definitions 3.4, 3.6 and 3.9 (see pages 19–21). Namely, an open formula is in *negation normal form* iff the negation sign appears only in literals. It is in *conjunctive normal form* iff it is a conjunction of clauses and in *disjunctive normal form* iff it is a disjunction of conjunctions of literals.

Propositions 3.5, 3.7, 3.8 and 3.10 can easily be generalized to the case of open first-order formulas. In particular, the equivalences given in Table 1 (page 20) and Table 2 (page 20), together with the rules in Table 6 for moving negation inward over quantifiers provide the rules for conversion into negation normal form. Conversion into conjunctive and disjunctive normal form do not require additional rules in addition to those in Tables 3 and 4 (page 20) and Table 5 (page 21).

TABLE 6. Equivalences for moving negation inside of quantifiers.

input formula	equivalent formula
$\neg \forall x [\alpha(x)]$	$\exists x [\neg \alpha(x)]$
$\neg \exists x [\alpha(x)]$	$\forall x [\neg \alpha(x)]$

DEFINITION 3.20. We say that an open formula α is *positive w.r.t. a relation symbol* R iff all literals containing R in its equivalent in negation normal form are positive. It is *negative w.r.t. a relation symbol* R iff all literals containing R in its equivalent in negation normal form are negative.   ◁

3.3.4.3. *Prenex Normal Form.*

DEFINITION 3.21. We say that a first-order formula is in *prenex normal form* iff it is of the form $Q_1 x_1 Q_2 x_2 \ldots Q_k x_k [\alpha]$, where $Q_1, Q_2, \ldots, Q_k \in \{\forall, \exists\}$ and α is an open formula. In such a case α is also called the *quantifier-free part of* $Q_1 x_1 Q_2 x_2 \ldots Q_k x_k [\alpha]$.

We denote by $\mathrm{PNF}(\alpha)$ the negation normal form of a formula α.   ◁

We have the following proposition.

PROPOSITION 3.22. Every classical first-order formula can equivalently be transformed into prenex normal form, i.e., $\alpha \equiv \mathrm{PNF}(\alpha)$ for any first-order formula.

PROOF. In order to transform a formula into the prenex normal form one first eliminates implication and equivalence using equivalences given in Table 1 (page 20).

Then one converts the result into negation normal form. Next the equivalences given in Table 7 are applied. If no such equivalence can be applied, then the input formula is already in prenex normal form.   ◁

TABLE 7. Equivalences for transforming a formula into prenex normal form.

input formula	equivalent formula
$\forall x[\alpha(x)] \wedge \forall y[\beta(y)]$	$\forall z[\alpha(z) \wedge \beta(z)]$ where z is a new variable
$\exists x[\alpha(x)] \vee \exists y[\beta(y)]$	$\exists z[\alpha(z) \vee \beta(z)]$ where z is a new variable
$\alpha \vee Qx[\beta(x)]$	$Qz[\alpha \vee \beta(z)]$ where $Q \in \{\forall, \exists\}$ and z is a new variable
$Qx[\beta(x)] \vee \alpha$	$Qz[\beta(z) \vee \alpha]$ where $Q \in \{\forall, \exists\}$ and z is a new variable
$\alpha \wedge Qx[\beta(x)]$	$Qz[\alpha \wedge \beta(z)]$ where $Q \in \{\forall, \exists\}$ and z is a new variable
$Qx[\beta(x)] \wedge \alpha$	$Qz[\beta(z) \wedge \alpha]$ where $Q \in \{\forall, \exists\}$ and z is a new variable

DEFINITION 3.23. By a *universal formula* we mean a formula in prenex normal form, without existential quantifiers. A formula is called *semi-universal* iff it does not contain an existential quantifier in the scope of a universal quantifier. By an *existential formula* we mean a formula in prenex normal form, without universal quantifiers. A set of universal (respectively, semi-universal, existential) formulas is called a *universal* (respectively *semi-universal, existential) theory*.

We say that a formula α is *positive w.r.t. a relation symbol R* iff the quantifier-free part of its equivalent in prenex normal form is positive w.r.t. R. It is *negative w.r.t. a relation symbol R* iff the quantifier-free part of its equivalent in prenex normal form is negative w.r.t. R.

We say that a formula $\alpha(X)$ is *monotone* (respectively *down-monotone*) w.r.t. a *relation symbol X* iff for all relations R, S if $R \subseteq S$ then $v(\alpha_R^X) \rightarrow v(\alpha_S^X)$ (respectively, $v(\alpha_S^X) \rightarrow v(\alpha_R^X)$).   ◁

Monotone formulas are also sometimes called *up-monotone*.

PROPOSITION 3.24. Any classical first-order formula positive w.r.t. a relation symbol R is monotone w.r.t. R.   ◁

3.3.5. Skolemization. By *Skolemization* we understand a process of elimination of existential quantifiers, in which new function symbols reflecting the climinated quantifiers are introduced. The method was introduced by Skolem [189].

Let us denote by $\mathrm{Sk}(\alpha)$ the result of Skolemizing α; $\mathrm{Sk}(\alpha)$ is also referred to as the *Skolemization of the formula α*. Our definition is that of *inner Skolemization* [153]. We assume that α does not contain any subformulas of zero polarity.

For convenience we also assume that every variable is bound by a unique quantifier occurrence. The construction of $\text{Sk}(\alpha)$ is based on applying the following two rules exhaustively.

Let $\beta(x_1, \ldots, x_k, x)$ be any subformula of α with free variables $x_1, \ldots, x_k$.

(1) If β has positive polarity and is of the form $\exists x[\gamma(x_1, \ldots, x_k, x)]$, we introduce a new function symbol f of arity k and replace $\beta(x_1, \ldots, x_k)$ by $\gamma(x_1, \ldots, x_k, x)^x_{f(x_1, \ldots, x_k)}$.

(2) If β has negative polarity and is of the form $\forall x[\gamma(x_1, \ldots, x_k, x)]$, we introduce a new function symbol f of arity k and replace $\beta(x_1, \ldots, x_k)$ by $\gamma(x_1, \ldots, x_k, x)^x_{f(x_1, \ldots, x_k)}$.

Recall that $\beta(x_1, \ldots, x_k, x)^x_{f(x_1, \ldots, x_k)}$ is the formula β in which all occurrences of x (in the subformula γ) are replaced by $f(x_1, \ldots, x_k)$ (the notation for forming a substitution instance used here is explained in Section 2.1.3, page 12). The new symbol f is the *Skolem function* introduced for $\exists x$, respectively $\forall x$. If β does not contain any free variables, i.e., $k = 0$, then f is a nullary function and is called a *Skolem constant*.

For example:

$$\text{Sk}\left(\exists x \forall y \exists z \forall t \exists s[R(x, y, z, t, s)]\right) = \forall y \forall t[R(a, y, f_1(y), t, f_2(y, t))]$$

$$\text{Sk}\left(\forall x \exists y[\neg(P(x, y) \vee \forall z Q(z))]\right) = \forall x[\neg(P(x, f(x)) \vee Q(a))].$$

We have the following important theorem.

THEOREM 3.25. Let α be a classical-first-order formula without any subformulas of zero polarity, and let $\text{Sk}(\alpha)$ denote its Skolemization. Then:

(1) $\models \text{Sk}(\alpha) \rightarrow \alpha$;
(2) α is satisfiable iff $\text{Sk}(\alpha)$ is satisfiable.   ◁

The order in which existential quantifiers are eliminated from the given formula matters and different results are produced depending on the order in which the rules are applied. Nested Skolem function symbols can be avoided if the rules are always applied to outermost existential quantifiers first. Techniques such as mini-scoping and antiprenex transformation, which move quantifiers inward and reduce the scope of quantifiers, are often applied before Skolemization in order to minimize the arity of Skolem functions and the number of different Skolem functions.

The converse of (1) is in general not true. However adding the appropriate Skolem axioms to the given formula α we have the following logical equivalence

(2) $\models (\alpha \wedge \exists f_1 \ldots \exists f_l[S]) \equiv \exists f_1 \ldots \exists f_l[\text{Sk}(\alpha)],$

where S denotes the set of Skolem axioms for the Skolem functions f_i. The *Skolem axiom* for a function f is the implication

$$\forall x_1 \ldots \forall x_k \left[\exists x[\beta(x)] \rightarrow \beta(x)^x_{f(x_1,\ldots,x_k)} \right],$$

if f was introduced for the formula $\exists x[\beta(x)]$.

3.3.6. Complexity of Classical First-Order Logic.

THEOREM 3.26. Checking whether a classical first-order formula is a tautology is partially decidable, but not decidable, i.e., the set of classical first-order tautologies is in $\Sigma_1^0 - \Sigma_0^0$. The set of satisfiable classical first-order formulas is in Π_1^0.   ◁

The fact that the set of tautologies of the classical first-order logic is partially computable follows from the completeness result due to Gödel [**95**]. Since a formula α is satisfiable iff $\neg \alpha$ is not a tautology, the satisfiability problem is in Π_1^0. If it was in Σ_1^0 then both checking tautologies and satisfiability would be in Σ_0^0. Uncomputability, i.e., the fact that these sets are not in Σ_0^0, is due to Church [**39**].

When fixing a finite domain relational structure, one ends up in a tractable situation, as stated in the following theorem (see Vardi [**213**]).

THEOREM 3.27. Checking whether a classical first-order formula is valid in a given finite domain relational structure is in PTIME and LOGSPACE w.r.t. the size of the domain.   ◁

3.4. Second-Order Logics

Second-order logics extend first-order logics and allow one to quantify over semantic entities attached to formulas. To make it possible we introduce second-order variables representing such entities. Most commonly such entities are sets, relations or functions.

DEFINITION 3.28. By a *second-order logic* we understand any logic $\langle \mathcal{F}, \mathcal{I}, \models \rangle$, which is an extension of any first-order logic, as defined in Definition 3.15, where additionally

- We assume a non-empty set V_2, called the *set of second-order variables* representing formulas;
- $\mathcal{F}$ is defined inductively to be the smallest set containing first-order formulas, second-order variables and closed under propositional connectives, first-order and second-order quantifiers, i.e., if $C \in \mathcal{C}$ is a connective of arity n, $x \in V_1$, $X \in V_2$ and $\alpha_1, \ldots, \alpha_n \in \mathcal{F}$ then

  $$C(\alpha_1, \ldots, \alpha_n), \forall x[\alpha_1], \exists x[\alpha_1], \forall X[\alpha_1], \exists X[\alpha_1] \in \mathcal{F}.$$

  The quantifier $\forall X$ is called *universal* and $\exists X$ is called *existential*.   ◁

3.4.1. Classical Second-Order Logic. In this book *classical second-order logic* provides the basic logic for studying second-order quantifier elimination. It is an extension of classical first-order logic and provides syntax that allows one to use quantifiers "for all" and "exists", ranging over sets, relations and functions.

Observe that semantic entities attached to a first-order formula are relations consisting of such valuations of free variables that make the formula true in a given domain and interpretation of function and relation symbols. In the current book we primarily focus on quantifiers ranging over relations. This is done without loss of generality, since sets and functions can be represented by relations.

3.4.2. Syntax of Classical Second-Order Logic. *Classical second-order logic* is an extension of classical first-order logic (see Section 3.3.1) in the sense of Definition 3.28 (page 29). In particular we have

- A non-empty set V_2, called the *set of second-order variables* (or *relation variables*), ranging over relations; with any second-order variable we associate its arity which is a natural number;
- By *atomic second-order formulas* we understand expressions of the form $\Upsilon(\tau_1, \ldots, \tau_n)$, where $\Upsilon \in \text{REL} \cup V_2$ is a n-ary relation symbol or second-order variable and $\tau_1, \ldots, \tau_n \in \text{TERMS}$;
- The set of second-order formulas, denoted by $\mathcal{F}_2$, is defined inductively to be the smallest set containing first-order formulas, atomic second-order formulas and closed under propositional connectives $\neg, \wedge, \vee, \rightarrow, \equiv$, first-order quantifiers $\forall x, \exists x$ and second-order quantifiers $\forall X$ and $\exists X$.

Although functions are special relations, sometimes for convenience we also use *function variables* ranging over functions.

By the *existential fragment of second-order logic* we understand the set of second-order formulas of the form $\exists X_1 \ldots \exists X_k[\alpha]$, where $k \geq 1$ and α is a classical first-order formula. By the *universal fragment of second-order logic* we understand the set of second-order formulas of the form $\forall X_1 \ldots \forall X_k[\alpha]$, where $k \geq 1$ and α is a classical first-order formula.

3.4.3. Semantics of Classical Second-Order Logic. The semantics of second-order formulas is given by a valuation of individual variables, valuation of second-order variables together with an interpretation of function symbols and relation symbols as functions and relations. The interpretation of function symbols and relation symbols is given by relational structures, as defined in Definition 3.17, page 24.

DEFINITION 3.29. The class of *second-order interpretations*, $\mathcal{I}_2$, is given by the tuple $\langle M, v, V \rangle$, where $M \in RS(\Sigma)$ is a relational structure, v is a valuation of individual variables in M and V assigns to second-order variables in V_2 relations of a suitable arity over the domain of M. ◁

Semantics of second-order formulas is now defined by extending semantics of first-order formulas given in Section 3.3.3. To complete the definition we assume that a second-order interpretation $\langle M, v, V \rangle$ is given, where

$$M = \langle U, \langle f_i^U \rangle_{i \in I}, \langle R_j^U \rangle_{j \in J} \rangle,$$

and extend the definition of v given by the formulas in (1) on page 25 by

(3)
$$\begin{aligned}
&v(X(t_1, \ldots, t_k)) = \text{TRUE iff } \langle v(t_1), \ldots, v(t_k) \rangle \in V(X), \text{ for } X \in V_2; \\
&v(\forall X[\alpha(X)]) = \min\{v_A^X(\alpha(X)) \mid A \subseteq U^k\}, \text{ where } X \in V_2 \text{ is } k\text{-ary}; \\
&v(\exists X[\alpha(X)]) = \max\{v_A^X(\alpha(X)) \mid A \subseteq U^k\}, \text{ where } X \in V_2 \text{ is } k\text{-ary}.
\end{aligned}$$

DEFINITION 3.30. The *satisfiability relation of classical second-order logic* is defined by $M, v, V \models \alpha$ iff $v(\alpha) = \text{TRUE}$.

A second-order formula α is *satisfied* in $M = \langle U, \langle f_i^U \rangle_{i \in I}, \langle R_j^U \rangle_{j \in J} \rangle$ iff there is a valuation v such that $v(\alpha) = \text{TRUE}$. Formula α is *valid in relational structure* M iff for all valuations v, $v(\alpha) = \text{TRUE}$. In such a case we also say that M is a *model* for α. For a set of formulas $F \subseteq \mathcal{F}_1$ and formula $\alpha \in \mathcal{F}_1$, by the *consequence relation*, denoted by $F \models \alpha$, we mean that α is valid in any relational structure which is a model of all formulas of F. By $Cn(F)$ we mean the set of all semantical consequences of F, i.e., $Cn(F) \overset{\text{def}}{=} \{\alpha \in \mathcal{F}_1 \mid F \models \alpha\}$. ◁

3.4.4. Second-Order Skolemization. *Second-order Skolemization* eliminates existential first-order quantifiers as described in Section 3.3.5. It is based on the equivalence

(4)
$$\begin{aligned}
&\exists x_1 \ldots \exists x_m \forall y_1 \ldots \forall y_k \exists y [\alpha(y_1, \ldots, y_k, y)] \wedge \exists f[S] \equiv \\
&\exists f \exists x_1 \ldots \exists x_m \forall y_1 \ldots \forall y_k \left[\alpha(y_1, \ldots, y_k, y)_{f(y_1, \ldots, y_k)}^y \right],
\end{aligned}$$

where $k \geq 1$ and S is the Skolem axiom for f, i.e.,

$$\forall y_1 \ldots \forall y_k \left[\exists y [\alpha(y_1, \ldots, y_k, y)] \rightarrow \alpha(y_1, \ldots, y_k, y)_{f(y_1, \ldots, y_k)}^y \right].$$

In some methods of second-order quantifier elimination we also apply the equivalence

(5)
$$\forall \bar{x} \exists y [\alpha(\bar{x}, y, \ldots)] \equiv \exists f \forall \bar{x} \left[\alpha(\bar{x}, y, \ldots)_{f(\bar{x})}^y \right],$$

where f is a new function symbol of arity equal to the number of variables in $\bar{x}$. Note, however, that the proof of (5) requires the axiom of choice, while (4) does not.

3.4.5. Unskolemization. By *unskolemization* we understand the elimination of Skolem constants and Skolem functions (or existential second-order quantifiers binding Skolem functions) introduced in the process of Skolemization.

In order to unskolemize, one can apply equivalence (4) or (5). This is not always possible due to dependencies introduced by first-order quantifiers. One can also use *Henkin quantifiers* (called also *branching quantifiers*), introduced by Henkin in [**104**]. For the purpose of unskolemization, following [**70**] we consider Henkin quantifiers of the form

$$
(6) \qquad
\begin{pmatrix}
\forall \bar{x}_1 \exists y_1 \\
\forall \bar{x}_2 \exists y_2 \\
\cdots \\
\forall \bar{x}_n \exists y_n
\end{pmatrix}
\alpha(\bar{x}_1, \bar{x}_2, \ldots, \bar{x}_n, y_1, y_2, \ldots, y_n)
$$

as an abbreviation for

$$
\exists f_1 \exists f_2 \ldots \exists f_n \forall \bar{x}_1 \forall \bar{x}_2 \ldots \forall \bar{x}_n \Bigg\{
$$
$$
\alpha(\bar{x}_1, \bar{x}_2, \ldots, \bar{x}_n, y_1, y_2, \ldots, y_n)_{f_1(\bar{x}_1), f_2(\bar{x}_2), \ldots, f_n(\bar{x}_n)}^{y_1, \quad y_2, \quad \cdots, \quad y_n} \Bigg\}.
$$

It should be obvious that Skolem functions can always be eliminated using Henkin quantifiers of the form (6).

It is worth emphasizing that Henkin quantifiers are much more complex than classical first-order quantifiers, since they can be used for eliminating any existential second-order quantifier.

Section 5.3 discusses unskolemization in more detail.

3.4.6. Complexity of Classical Second-Order Logic. Second-order logic over arbitrary domains is extremely complex, as the following theorem shows.

THEOREM 3.31. Checking whether a classical second-order formula is a tautology as well as whether it is satisfiable exhausts the analytical hierarchy, defined in Section 2.2.4, page 14, thus is not in Σ_k^1 nor in Π_k^1, for any $k \in \omega$.   ◁

From Theorem 3.31 we have the following immediate corollary, which shows that the problem of second-order quantifier elimination is, in general, highly undecidable.

COROLLARY 3.32. Checking whether a classical second-order formula is equivalent to a classical first-order formula exhausts the analytical hierarchy, thus is not in Σ_k^1 nor in Π_k^1, for any $k \in \omega$.   ◁

Over finite domains the situation is summarized below.

THEOREM 3.33. Checking whether a classical second-order formula is valid in a given finite domain relational structure exhausts the complexity class $\mathcal{PH}$ (see Section 2.2.2, page 13). In the case of the existential fragment the problem is NPTIME-complete and in the case of the universal fragment it is CO-NPTIME-complete. ◁

The correspondence between classical second-order logic over finite models and the polynomial hierarchy has been shown by Stockmeyer [195]. The NPTIME-completeness for the existential fragment of classical second-order logic has been proved in [74] and is known as the theorem of Fagin. CO-NPTIME-completeness for the universal fragment follows easily from Fagin's theorem.

3.5. Classical Fixpoint Logic

Fixpoint logics are important in computer science applications, since many computational processes and database query languages have a natural fixpoint characterization. Also inductive definitions usually involve fixpoints. Roughly speaking, fixpoint logics extend base logics by adding operators for expressing least and greatest fixpoints of positive formulas. For a comprehensive study of fixpoint logics see, e.g., [4] or, in the case of finite models, [64, 119]. We use the term *classical* fixpoint logic to emphasize that it is an extension of classical first-order logic.

In what follows, for the sake of simplicity, we define classical fixpoint logic by introducing least and greatest monotone fixpoints of single relational variables. Many other forms of fixpoint formulas, important in applications, like simultaneous fixpoints, can be reduced to the logic we deal with (see, e.g., [4, 64]).

3.5.1. Syntax of Classical Fixpoint Logic.
Classical fixpoint logic is an extension of classical first-order logic (see Section 3.3.1) by allowing fixpoint operators to be atomic formulas.

DEFINITION 3.34. If $\alpha(X, \bar{x})$ is a formula with free individual variables $\bar{x} = \langle x_1, \ldots, x_k \rangle$ and a free second-order variable X of arity k such that $\alpha(X, \bar{x})$ is positive w.r.t. X, then by an *atomic least (greatest) fixpoint formula* we understand a formula of the form $[\text{LFP } X(\bar{x}).\alpha(X, \bar{x})](t_1, \ldots, t_k)$ (respectively, of the form $[\text{GFP } X(\bar{x}).\alpha(X, \bar{x})](t_1, \ldots, t_k)$), where $t_1, \ldots, f_k \in \text{TERMS}$. ◁

For simplicity we omit tuples of terms $(t_1, \ldots, t_k)$ and write $[\text{LFP } X(\bar{x}).\alpha(X, \bar{x})]$ and $[\text{GFP } X(\bar{x}).\alpha(X, \bar{x})]$, when $t_1, \ldots, t_k$ is just $x_1, \ldots, x_k$.

DEFINITION 3.35. By *classical fixpoint logic* we understand logic in the sense of Definition 3.1 (page 17), with language $\mathcal{L}$ defined to be an extension of the language of classical first-order logic (see Section 3.3.2, page 23), where we also allow atomic least and greatest fixpoint formulas as atomic formulas. ◁

3.5.2. Semantics of Classical Fixpoint Logic. The semantics of classical fixpoint logic extends the semantics of classical first-order logic (see Section 3.3.3, page 24) and is given in the class of first-order interpretations, $\mathcal{I}_1$.

Let $\langle M, v \rangle$ be a fist-order interpretation. In order to provide semantics for first-order formulas it suffices to extend v to cover the case of atomic fixpoint formulas. Then v provides the *truth value of classical fixpoint formulas*:

(7)
$$v([\text{LFP}\, X(x_1, \ldots, x_k).\alpha(X, x_1, \ldots, x_k)](t_1, \ldots, t_k)) = \text{TRUE iff}$$
$$v(\alpha(X, \bar{x})_{R,\, t_1, \ldots, t_k}^{X, x_1, \ldots, x_k}) = \text{TRUE},$$
$$\text{where R is the smallest (w.r.t. } \subseteq\text{) relation satisfying}$$
$$\forall x_1, \ldots, x_k \{ R(x_1, \ldots, x_k) \equiv \alpha(X, x_1, \ldots, x_k)_R^X \};$$
$$v([\text{GFP}\, X(x_1, \ldots, x_k).\alpha(X, x_1, \ldots, x_k)](t_1, \ldots, t_k)) = \text{TRUE iff}$$
$$v(\alpha(X, \bar{x})_{R,\, t_1, \ldots, t_k}^{X, x_1, \ldots, x_k}) = \text{TRUE},$$
$$\text{where R is the greatest (w.r.t. } \subseteq\text{) relation satisfying}$$
$$\forall x_1, \ldots, x_k \{ R(x_1, \ldots, x_k) \equiv \alpha(X, x_1, \ldots, x_k)_R^X \}.$$

Observe that the least and the greatest relation required in (7) exists due to the famous fixpoint theorem due to Knaster and Tarski [**126, 206**], where the required partial order is simply the inclusion $\subseteq$ defined on relations. Then any formula $\alpha(X)$ positive w.r.t. a relational variable X is monotone w.r.t. variable X.

The following proposition shows that least and greatest fixpoints are *dual* to each other.

PROPOSITION 3.36. *Let $\alpha(X)$ be a formula monotone w.r.t. relational variable X. Then $[\text{LFP}\, X(\bar{x}).\alpha(X, \bar{x})] \equiv \neg[\text{GFP}\, X(\bar{x}).\neg\alpha(X, \bar{x})_{\neg X}^X]$. We also have the dual characterization $[\text{GFP}\, X(\bar{x}).\alpha(X, \bar{x})] \equiv \neg[\text{LFP}\, X(\bar{x}).\neg\alpha(X, \bar{x})_{\neg X}^X]$.* ◁

3.5.3. Characterization of Fixpoints.

DEFINITION 3.37. *Let $\alpha(X)$ be a formula monotone w.r.t. relational variable X. Then by the lfp-sequence and the gfp-sequence for α, denoted respectively by $\alpha{\uparrow}\xi$ and $\alpha{\downarrow}\xi$, where ξ ranges over ordinal numbers, we understand sequences defined by:*

$$\alpha{\uparrow}0 \overset{\text{def}}{=} \alpha(X)_{\text{FALSE}}^X \qquad\qquad \alpha{\downarrow}0 \overset{\text{def}}{=} \alpha(X)_{\text{TRUE}}^X$$
$$\alpha{\uparrow}(\xi + 1) \overset{\text{def}}{=} \alpha(X)_{\alpha{\uparrow}\xi}^X \qquad\qquad \alpha{\downarrow}(\xi + 1) \overset{\text{def}}{=} \alpha(X)_{\alpha{\downarrow}\xi}^X$$
$$\alpha{\uparrow}\lambda \overset{\text{def}}{=} \bigvee_{\xi < \lambda} \alpha{\uparrow}\xi \qquad\qquad \alpha{\downarrow}\lambda \overset{\text{def}}{=} \bigwedge_{\xi < \lambda} \alpha{\downarrow}\xi,$$

where $\bigvee_{\xi < \lambda}$ and $\bigwedge_{\xi < \lambda}$ stand for the infinite disjunction and conjunction. ◁

We have the following theorem due to Knaster and Tarski.

THEOREM 3.38. For any formula $\alpha(X)$ monotone w.r.t. relational variable X there is an ordinal number ζ such that $\alpha{\uparrow}(\zeta + 1) = \alpha{\uparrow}\zeta$ and $\alpha{\downarrow}(\zeta + 1) = \alpha{\downarrow}\zeta$. ◁

DEFINITION 3.39. The least ordinal ζ satisfying $\alpha{\uparrow}(\zeta + 1) = \alpha{\uparrow}\zeta$, as in Theorem 3.38, is called the *closure ordinal* for α. ◁

Observe that the closure ordinal ζ for α characterizes the least and greatest fixpoint of $\alpha(X)$ in the following sense:

$$(8) \qquad \begin{aligned} [\text{LFP}\, X(\bar{x}).\alpha(X, \bar{x})] &\equiv (\alpha{\uparrow}\zeta)(\bar{x}) \\ [\text{GFP}\, X(\bar{x}).\alpha(X, \bar{x})] &\equiv (\alpha{\downarrow}\zeta)(\bar{x}). \end{aligned}$$

DEFINITION 3.40. For a given relational structure M we define the *closure ordinal for* $\alpha(X, \bar{x})$ *in* M, denoted by $cl(\alpha(X, \bar{x}), M)$, to be the least ordinal ζ for which $M \models \alpha{\uparrow}(\zeta + 1) = \alpha{\uparrow}\zeta$. ◁

We also have the following proposition, useful in applications.

PROPOSITION 3.41. Let M be a relational structure with universe U and $\alpha(X, \bar{x})$ be a first-order formula positive w.r.t. X. Then:

(1) $cl(\alpha(X, \bar{x}), M) < |U|^{+}$;
(2) If $\alpha(X, \bar{x})$ is an existential classical first-order formula, then
$cl(\alpha(X, \bar{x}), M) \leq \omega$.

PROOF. (1) easily follows from the observation that in each stage of induction either at least one element of U is added or the fixpoint is reached.

To prove (2), suppose there is an existential positive formula $\alpha(X, \bar{x})$ such that $cl(\alpha(X, \bar{x}), M) > \omega$. Assume that $\alpha(X, \bar{x})$ is in prenex normal form, i.e., it is in the form $\exists \bar{y}[\beta(X, \bar{x}, \bar{y})]$.

Since $cl(\alpha(X, \bar{x}), M) > \omega$, there is a tuple $\bar{t} \in \alpha{\uparrow}(\omega + 1) - \alpha{\uparrow}\omega$. Thus $\bar{t} \in \alpha{\uparrow}(\omega + 1)$, i.e., by Definition 3.37, $\bar{t} \in \alpha(X)^{X}_{\alpha{\uparrow}\omega}$ therefore there is $\bar{s}$ such that $M \models \beta(X, \bar{t}, \bar{s})^{X}_{\alpha{\uparrow}\omega}$. Again by Definition 3.37, $\alpha{\uparrow}\omega \equiv \bigvee_{k<\omega} \alpha{\uparrow}k$, thus there is n such that $M \models \beta(X, \bar{t}, \bar{s})^{X}_{\alpha{\uparrow}n}$, i.e., $M \models \alpha(X, \bar{t})^{X}_{\alpha{\uparrow}n}$, which contradicts the fact that $\bar{t} \notin \alpha{\uparrow}\omega$. ◁

3.5.4. Complexity of Classical Fixpoint Logic. In the case for arbitrary structures, one can prove the following theorem (see [49]).

THEOREM 3.42. The set of classical fixpoint tautologies is in $\Pi^{1}_{2} - \Pi^{1}_{1}$. The set of satisfiable fixpoint formulas is in $\Sigma^{1}_{2} - \Sigma^{1}_{1}$. ◁

We also have the following proposition, showing that the problem of second-order quantifier elimination in the context of classical fixpoint logic is highly undecidable.

PROPOSITION 3.43. Checking whether a classical second-order formula is equivalent to a classical fixpoint formula fits the analytical hierarchy, thus is not in Σ^1_k nor in Π^1_k, for any $k \in \omega$.   ◁

When fixing a finite domain relational structure, one ends up in a tractable situation. Moreover, if a relational structure is linearly ordered, then all tractable problems are definable by fixpoint formulas as stated in the following theorem (which has independently been proved by Immerman [**118**] and Vardi [**213**]).

THEOREM 3.44. Checking whether a classical fixpoint formula is valid in a given finite domain relational structure is in PTIME w.r.t. the size of the domain. Moreover, all problems definable over such structures belonging to PTIME are expressible in the fixpoint calculus, provided that the domain is linearly ordered.   ◁

3.6. Equality Theories

In *equality theories* the only allowed relation symbol is equality $\approx$. This theory is important, since in the considered methods of second-order quantifier elimination as well as applications the use of equality is the rule rather than the exception. It is well known that the classical first-order theory of equality is decidable. Also the fixpoint theory of equality is decidable. These results allow one, among others, to show decidability of certain theories in which all relation symbols other than equality can be eliminated (see also Section 15.3, page 208).

3.6.1. First-Order Theory of Equality. The proof of the decidability of the first-order theory of equality is based on the method of elimination of *first-order* quantifiers. The key step of this method is formulated in the following lemma, where by a *Boolean combination of formulas* we understand a formula obtained by applying the classical propositional connectives to these formulas.

LEMMA 3.45. Let T be a theory and let Σ be a set of formulas, called the *basic formulas*. In order to show that every formula is equivalent under T to a Boolean combination of basic formulas, it is sufficient to show the following:

(1) Every atomic formula is equivalent under T to a Boolean combination of basic formulas;
(2) If α is a Boolean combination of basic formulas, then $\exists x[\alpha]$ is equivalent to a Boolean combination of basic formulas.

PROOF. Let E be the set of all formulas which are equivalent under T to a Boolean combination of basic formulas. We show by induction that every formula α belongs to E. If α is an atomic formula, then $\alpha \in E$ by (1). Assume that our lemma holds for formulas $\alpha_1, \ldots, \alpha_k$. If α is a Boolean combination of $\alpha_1, \ldots, \alpha_k$ then it is obvious that $\alpha \in E$. If α is $\exists x[\beta]$ and $\beta \in E$ then β is equivalent to a Boolean combination of basic formulas γ. Therefore α is equivalent to $\exists x[\gamma]$. By (2) we have that $\exists x[\gamma] \in E$, so $\alpha \in E$.   ◁

Let the *set of basic formulas of the theory of equality* consist of all atomic formulas $x \approx y$ together with sentences α_n which state that "there are more than n distinct elements". Formally, α_n may be expressed by.

(9) $\forall x_1 \ldots \forall x_n \exists y[y \not\approx x_1 \wedge \ldots \wedge y \not\approx x_n].$

For technical reasons we assume that $\alpha_0 \overset{\text{def}}{\equiv}$ FALSE (or $x \not\approx x$, for some x, if the language does not contain FALSE).

The following theorem is due to Tarski (see, e.g., [**36**]).

THEOREM 3.46. Every formula α in the language of the theory of equality is equivalent to a combination of basic formulas.

PROOF. We first easily note that every atomic formula is equivalent to a Boolean combination of basic formulas. Next, let $\alpha(x_1, \ldots, x_n)$ be an arbitrary Boolean combination of basic formulas.

By Lemma 3.45, it suffices to prove that any formula $\exists x_i[\alpha(x_1, \ldots, x_n)]$ is equivalent to a Boolean combination of basic formulas. Formula α can be equivalently transformed into prenex normal form (see, e.g., Section 3.3.4.3, page 26). We end up with a formula of the form $Q_1 X_1 \ldots Q_r x_r[\beta]$, where $Q_i \in \{\forall, \exists\}$ and β is a Boolean combination of formulas of the form $x_l \approx x_m$, $x_l \not\approx x_m$. We eliminate quantifiers one by one starting with the innermost one. If the eliminated quantifier is universal, we replace it by $\neg \exists \neg$. Therefore we can consider the existential case only, i.e., we only have to deal with the case $\exists x[\gamma]$.

To eliminate $\exists x$ we transform γ into an equivalent formula in disjunctive normal form (cf. Section 3.2.4, page 21), obtaining $\gamma_1 \vee \ldots \vee \gamma_k$, where each γ_i is a conjunction of formulas of the form $x_l \approx x_m$, $x_l \not\approx x_m$. Existential quantifier can be distributed over disjunctions and we can consider each disjunct $\exists x_i[\gamma_l]$ separately. Assume that $\gamma_l = \gamma_l' \wedge \gamma_l''$, where each atomic formula in γ_l' contains x and γ_l'' does not contain occurrences of x. In such a case, $\exists x[\gamma_l] \equiv \gamma_l'' \wedge \exists x[\gamma_l']$ and we have to consider $\exists x[\gamma_l']$ only. Equalities of the form $x \approx x$ can simply be removed. Consider equalities of the form $x \approx x_j$ with $x \not\approx x_j$. Such equalities can also be removed, but all occurrences of x_j have to be replaced by x. As a result we obtain a formula of the form $\exists x[x \not\approx x_{l_1} \wedge \ldots \wedge x \not\approx x_{l_n}]$ which is obviously equivalent to a basic formula α_k, for some k.   ◁

According to Theorem 3.46 every formula of the first-order theory of equality expresses facts stating that the domain consists of n elements, where $n \in A$ with A being a finite union of intervals of the form $a \leq n \leq b$ or $a \leq n$. Therefore, a formula of the first-order theory of equality is a tautology if and only if A reduces to the interval $1 \leq n$. This shows the decidability of the considered theory.   ◁

3.6.2. Fixpoint Theory of Equality. The fixpoint theory of equality has been considered in Szałas and Tyszkiewicz [**204**], where the decidability of the theory is established. Below we present the proof given in [**204**].[3]

In this section $\mathcal{F}_1^k$ ($\mathcal{F}^k$) stand for the sets of classical first-order (respectively fixpoint) formulas, in which only at most k distinct first-order variable symbols occur.

Below by $A(\bar{x})[\bar{t}]$ we mean the application of $A(\bar{x})$ to terms (or, dependent on the context, to domain values) $\bar{t}$.

DEFINITION 3.47. Let $\mathbb{A}, \mathbb{B}$ be two structures over a common signature. We write $\mathbb{A} \equiv_k \mathbb{B}$ iff $\mathbb{A}$ and $\mathbb{B}$ cannot be distinguished by any $\mathcal{L}_1^k$ sentence, i.e., when for every sentence α of first-order logic with k variables, $\mathbb{A} \models \alpha$ iff $\mathbb{B} \models \alpha$.

For two tuples $\bar{a} \in A^k$ and $\bar{b} \in B^k$ we write $\mathbb{A}, \bar{a} \equiv_k \mathbb{B}, \bar{b}$ iff those tuples cannot be distinguished by any $\mathcal{L}_1^k$ formula in $\mathbb{A}$ and $\mathbb{B}$, i.e., when for every formula $\alpha(\bar{x}) \in \mathcal{L}_1^k$, $\mathbb{A} \models \alpha[\bar{a}]$ iff $\mathbb{B} \models \alpha[\bar{b}]$.   ◁

Another fact that we need is a characterization of the expressive power of $\mathcal{L}_1^k$ in terms of an infinitary Ehrenfeucht–Fraïssé-style pebble game. This game characterizes the expressive power of the logic we have introduced in the sense formulated in Theorem 3.49.

DEFINITION 3.48. [The Game]

> **Players, board and pebbles:** The game is played by two players, Spoiler and Duplicator, on two structures $\mathbb{A}, \mathbb{A}'$ of the same signature, with two distinguished tuples $\bar{a} \in A^k$ and $\bar{a}' \in \mathbb{A}'$. There are k pairs of pebbles: $(1, 1'), \ldots, (k, k')$. Pebbles without primes are intended to be placed on elements of A, while those with primes on elements of A'.
> **Initial position:** Initially, pebbles are located as follows: pebble i is located on a_i, and pebble i' is located on a_i', for $i = 1, \ldots, k$.
> **Moves:** In each of the moves of the game, Spoiler is allowed to choose one of the structures and one of the pebbles placed on an element of that structure and move it onto some other element of the same structure. Duplicator must place the other pebble from that pair on some element in the other structure so that the partial function from $\mathbb{A}$ to $\mathbb{A}'$ mapping $x \in \mathbb{A}$ on which pebble i is placed onto the element $x' \in \mathbb{A}'$ on which pebble i' is placed and constants in $\mathbb{A}$ onto the corresponding constants in $\mathbb{A}'$, is a partial isomorphism. Spoiler is allowed to alternate between the structures as often as he likes, when choosing elements.

---

[3]In fact, the decidability proof given in [**204**] has been proposed by J. Tyszkiewicz and is more general than the one presented here, as it establishes the result in the case of simultaneous fixpoints, too.

Who wins?: Spoiler wins if Duplicator does not have any move that preserves the isomorphism. We say that Duplicator has a winning strategy if he can play forever despite the moves of Spoiler, preventing him from winning. ◁

The following theorem can be found, e.g., in [**14, 117, 169**].

THEOREM 3.49. Let $\mathbb{A}, \mathbb{B}$ be any two structures of a common signature. Then Duplicator has a winning strategy in the game on $\mathbb{A}, \bar{a}$ and $\mathbb{B}, \bar{b}$ iff $\mathbb{A}, \bar{a} \equiv_k \mathbb{B}, \bar{b}$. ◁

Henceforth we restrict our attention to the theory and models of pure equality. For a cardinal number $\mathfrak{m}$, let the symbol $\mathbb{E}_{\mathfrak{m}}$ stand for the only model (up to isomorphism) of pure equality of cardinality $\mathfrak{m}$.

The following theorem can be proved easily using Theorem 3.49.

THEOREM 3.50. Let $k \in \omega$. Then for any cardinal numbers $\mathfrak{m}, \mathfrak{n} \geq k$ and any two tuples $\bar{a}, \bar{b}$ of length k over $\mathbb{E}_{\mathfrak{m}}$ and $\mathbb{E}_{\mathfrak{n}}$, respectively, $\mathbb{E}_{\mathfrak{m}}, \bar{a} \equiv_k \mathbb{E}_{\mathfrak{n}}, \bar{b}$ if and only if for every $i, j \leq k$ the equivalence $a_i \approx a_j \equiv b_i \approx b_j$ holds. ◁

Henceforth if the equivalence $a_i \approx a_j \equiv b_i \approx b_j$ holds for two tuples $\bar{a}, \bar{b}$ of length k, we write $\bar{a} \equiv_k \bar{b}$. Note that already in $\mathbb{E}_k$ there are tuples which are representatives of all the equivalence classes of $\equiv_k$.

DEFINITION 3.51. The *quantifier rank of a formula* α, denoted by $r(\alpha)$, is defined inductively by setting $r(\alpha) \stackrel{\text{def}}{=} 0$ when α contains no quantifiers, $r(\neg \alpha) \stackrel{\text{def}}{=} r(\alpha)$, for any binary propositional connective $\circ$, $r(\alpha \circ \beta) \stackrel{\text{def}}{=} \max\{r(\alpha), r(\beta)\}$ and $r(\exists \alpha) \stackrel{\text{def}}{=} r(\forall \alpha) \stackrel{\text{def}}{=} r(\alpha) + 1$. ◁

An important result is the following theorem, proved in [**129**, Theorem 2.7].

THEOREM 3.52. Let $0 < n \in \omega$ and let the first-order formula α in a fixpoint formula $[\text{LFP } R.\alpha]$ have at most n free variables and be of quantifier rank at most d. Then, over the signature containing equality only, α is definable by a first-order formula β with at most n variables. ◁

Next, an application of Theorem 3.50 and the previous results, yields the following consequence.

COROLLARY 3.53. Let $0 < k \in \omega$. If $\mathbb{A}$ is a model of equality of cardinality at least k, $\bar{a} \in A^k$, and $\varphi(\bar{x}) \in \mathcal{F}^k$, then $\mathbb{A} \models \varphi[\bar{a}]$ iff $\mathbb{E}_k \models \varphi[\bar{a}']$, where $\bar{a}' \equiv_k \bar{a}$. ◁

Now we turn to the problem of satisfiability of $\mathcal{F}$ formulas over the signature containing $\approx$ only. This means that still the only predicate allowed in formulas is the equality symbol.

By the results of the previous section, we have the following equivalence:

THEOREM 3.54. A formula α of $\mathcal{F}^k$ is satisfiable if and only if it is satisfiable in one of the structures $\mathbb{E}_1, \ldots, \mathbb{E}_k$. ◁

This suggests the following algorithm for testing satisfiability of fixpoint formulas over the empty signature: for a given formula $\alpha(\bar{x}) \in \mathcal{F}^k$ we test if it is satisfied by $\langle \mathbb{A}, \bar{a} \rangle$, where $\mathbb{A}$ ranges over all (pure equality) structures of cardinality at most k, and $\bar{a}$ ranges over all equality types of vectors of length $|\bar{x}|$ of elements from A.

Concerning the complexity of this procedure, the number of structures to be tested is linear in k. The number of iterations of any fixpoint in $\mathcal{F}^k$ is bounded by $O(B(k)^\ell)$, where $B(n)$ is the n-th Bell number and ℓ the maximal number of formulas whose simultaneous fixed point is used (for the definition of Bell numbers see, e.g., [102]). Indeed, $B(k)$ is the number of $\equiv_k$-equivalence classes. Thus computing the fixpoints literally, according to the definition, takes time bounded by a polynomial of $B(k)^\ell$, and computing the first-order constructs increases this by only a polynomial factor.

Therefore the algorithm we obtained is of exponential complexity.

CHAPTER 4

Resolution Theorem Proving

The clausal second-order quantifier elimination methods discussed in this book are based on inference algorithms in which the resolution principle is fundamental. Resolution is best known as a refutational calculus for clauses, which can be viewed as formulas in implicational form. This requires that formulas are first transformed into clausal form, before clausal resolution can be applied. A generalized form of resolution can be applied directly to formulas. Due to lack of space we are not going to discuss generalized resolution; it is however "in-built" into Ackermann's lemma discussed in Chapter 6.

This chapter provides the background to resolution for first-order clause logic which forms the basis for the clausal approach to second-order quantifier elimination used in SCAN and hierarchical resolution.

4.1. Clause Logic

A *literal* is either an *atom* $P(t_1, \ldots, t_n)$ or $t_1 \approx t_2$ (also called a *positive literal*) where P is an n-ary relation symbol and $t_1, \ldots, t_n$ are terms, or a *negative literal* $\neg P(t_1, \ldots, t_n)$, or $t_1 \not\approx t_2$. An atom $t_1 \approx t_2$ is also called an *equation*, while a negative literal $t_1 \not\approx t_2$ is called an *inequation*.

We regard *clauses* as multisets of literals. A *multiset* over a set $\mathcal{L}$ is a mapping C from $\mathcal{L}$ to the natural numbers. We write $L \in C$ if $C(L) > 0$ for a literal L. A *subclause* of a clause C is a submultiset of C. We use $\bot$ to denote the empty clause.

A *positive (negative)* clause contains only positive (negative) literals. The *positive (negative) part* of a clause C is the subclause of all positive (negative) literals in C. A clause which consists of only one literal is called a *unit clause*.

A *clause set* is a set of clauses.

Clauses can be viewed as implicational formulas. Just view a clause

$$C = \neg A_1 \vee \cdots \vee \neg A_m \vee B_1 \vee \cdots \vee B_k$$

as the implication

$$(A_1 \wedge \cdots \wedge A_m) \rightarrow (B_1 \vee \cdots \vee B_k).$$

A_i, B_j denote atoms and we refer to A_i as the body atoms and to B_j as the head atoms. The positive literals in C are the head atoms B_j and the negative literals in C are the negated body atoms $\neg A_i$ (where $1 \le i \le m$, $1 \le j \le k$). (Conjunction and disjunction are assumed to bind tighter than implication.)

An *expression* is a term, an atom, a literal or a clause.

A *substitution* σ is a mapping from variables to terms which is the identity mapping almost everywhere. We define the *domain* of σ to be $dom(\sigma) = \{x \mid x\sigma \neq x\}$ and the *co-domain* of σ to be $cdom(\sigma) = \{x\sigma \mid x\sigma \neq x\}$. Thus, a substitution σ is given by a finite set of pairs

$$\{x_1/t_1, \ldots, x_n/t_n\},$$

where $x_i\sigma = t_i$ for all i, $1 \le i \le n$, and $dom(\sigma) = \{x_1, \ldots, x_n\}$. Substitution σ is called a *variable renaming* if σ is an injection and its co-domain is a set of variables. The result of applying a substitution σ to a variable x is denoted by $x\sigma$. The application of σ to a functional term is defined by

$$f(t_1, \ldots, t_n)\sigma \overset{\text{def}}{=} f(t_1\sigma, \ldots, t_n\sigma).$$

Analogously, for atoms, literals, and clauses,

$$(\neg)P(t_1, \ldots, t_n)\sigma \overset{\text{def}}{=} (\neg)P(t_1\sigma, \ldots, t_n\sigma),$$

$$(L_1 \vee \ldots \vee L_n)\sigma \overset{\text{def}}{=} L_1\sigma \vee \ldots \vee L_n\sigma.$$

If X is a set of variables, then $\sigma|_X$ denotes the restriction of σ to X, that is, $\sigma|_X$ is a substitution θ such that $dom(\theta) = dom(\sigma) \cap X$ and $x\sigma = x\theta$ for every x in $dom(\theta)$. The *composition* $\sigma\theta$ of two substitutions σ and θ is defined by $x\sigma\theta = (x\sigma)\theta$ for all variables x. If $\sigma\sigma = \sigma$ then σ is said to be *idempotent*.

An expression E' is an *instance* of an expression E if there exists a substitution σ such that $E' = E\sigma$. A substitution σ is a (syntactical) *unifier* of expressions $\{E_1, \ldots, E_n\}$ iff $E_i\sigma = E_j\sigma$ for all i, j, $1 \le i, j \le n$, and $\{E_1, \ldots, E_n\}$ are said to be *unifiable*. A unifier σ is a *most general unifier* of $\{E_1, \ldots, E_n\}$ iff for every unifier θ of $\{E_1, \ldots, E_n\}$ there exists a substitution θ' such that $\theta|_{\text{var}(\{E_1, \ldots, E_n\})} = (\sigma\theta')|_{\text{var}(\{E_1, \ldots, E_n\})}$. If $\{E_1, \ldots, E_n\}$ are unifiable, then there exists a most general unifier of $\{E_1, \ldots, E_n\}$.

An expression E' is a *variant* of an expression E if there exists a variable renaming σ such that $E' = E\sigma$. We also say E and E' are *equal modulo variable renaming*. We consider clauses C and D to be identical iff they are equal modulo variable renaming.

A *variable indecomposable* clause (or *maximally split* clause) is a clause that cannot be split into non-empty subclauses which do not share variables. The finest partition of a clause into variable indecomposable subclauses is its *variable partition*. A subclause D of a clause C is a *split component* of C iff

(1) if L' is a literal in C but not in D, then L' and D are variable-disjoint and
(2) there is no proper subclause $D' \subset D$ satisfying property (1).

An expression is called *functional* if it contains a constant or a function symbol, and *non-functional*, otherwise. The set of all free variables occurring in an expression E, or in a set of expressions N, is denoted as var(E) or var(N). An expression is called *ground* if it contains no variables.

If $C \vee L_1 \vee \ldots \vee L_n$, $n \geq 2$, is a clause and there exists a most general unifier σ of $L_1, \ldots, L_n$, then $(C \vee L_1)\sigma$ is called a *factor* of $C \vee L_1 \vee \ldots \vee L_n$. If all the L_i are positive (negative) it is called a *positive (negative) factor*.

4.2. Transformation into Clausal Form

The transformation of any (propositional or first-order) formula into clausal form can be defined in numerous ways. A simple approach consists of the following steps: transformation into prenex normal form, (outer) Skolemization, transformation into conjunctive normal form and clausification. The clausal forms obtained are however not optimal, because the Skolem terms contained in it are unnecessarily large. The Skolem terms provide a means for handling the interaction between quantifiers.

Better clausal forms with smaller Skolem terms, and more suitable for the purposes of second-order quantifier elimination, can be obtained with the following method described by Nonnengart and Weidenbach [**156**].

(1) Applying obvious simplifications by removing TRUE, FALSE and other obvious syntactic first-order tautologies.
(2) Transformation into negation normal form and removal of the connectives $\rightarrow$ and $\equiv$.
(3) Transformation into antiprenex normal form.
(4) Variable standardization.
(5) Inner Skolemization.
(6) Transformation into clausal normal form.

Section 3.2.4 describes transformation into negation normal form and the replacement of implications and equivalences. Inner Skolemization is defined in Section 3.3.5.

TABLE 8. Equivalences for transforming a formula into antiprenex normal form.

input formula	equivalent formula
$Qx[\alpha(x) \vee \beta]$	$Qx[\alpha(x)] \vee \beta$, where $Q \in \{\forall, \exists\}$ and x is not free in β
$Qx[\alpha \vee \beta(x)]$	$\alpha \vee Qx[\beta(x)]$, where $Q \in \{\forall, \exists\}$ and x is not free in α
$\forall x[\alpha(x) \wedge \beta(x)]$	$\forall x[\alpha(x)] \wedge \forall x[\beta(x)]$
$\exists x[\alpha(x)] \vee \exists y[\beta(y)]$	$\exists z[\alpha(z) \vee \beta(z)]$, where x and y are free in α and β, respectively, and z is a new variable

4.2.1. Antiprenexing. Transformation into antiprenex normal form, or *antiprenexing*, is a variation of mini-scoping. It aims to minimize the arity of Skolem
functions by moving quantifiers inward and reducing the scope of quantifiers before Skolemization.

DEFINITION 4.1. A formula is in *antiprenex normal form* if the formula is in
normal form with respect to rewrite rules based on the equivalences in Table 8. ◁

That is, the quantifiers are moved inward as far as possible, but distributivity of
existential quantification over disjunction is reversed.

PROPOSITION 4.2. Every first-order formula can be equivalently transformed into
antiprenex normal form.   ◁

4.2.2. Variable Standardization. Variable standardization transforms first-
order formulas into standardized form. A first-order formula in which all variables
are renamed apart is said to be *standardized*. That is, in a standardized formula no
variable occurs both free and bound, and no two distinct occurrences of quantifiers
bind the same variable.

4.2.3. Transformation into Clausal Normal Form. We are at a stage where
the existential quantifiers have been eliminated by Skolemization. The next step
involves moving universal quantifiers outward, transforming into conjunctive normal form and clausification.

The specific rules needed in this step are defined in Table 9. Clausification omits
the quantifier prefix and turns the conjunction of clauses into a set of clauses.

Let α be a closed first-order formula. Suppose the transformation to clausal form
turns it into a set $N = \{C_1, \ldots, C_k\}$. N is called the *clausal (normal) form* of α.
The variables in the clauses are assumed to be implicitly universally quantified.

THEOREM 4.3. Let $N = \{C_1, \ldots, C_k\}$ be the clausal form of a formula α. Then:

TABLE 9. Equivalences for transforming a formula into clausal normal form.

input formula	equivalent formula
$\forall x[\alpha(x)] \wedge \beta$	$\forall x[\alpha(x) \wedge \beta]$, where x is free in β
$\alpha \wedge \forall x[\beta(x)]$	$\forall x[\alpha \wedge \beta(x)]$, where x is free in α
$\forall x[\alpha(x)] \vee \beta$	$\forall x[\alpha(x) \vee \beta]$, where x is free in β
$\alpha \vee \forall x[\beta(x)]$	$\forall x[\alpha \vee \beta(x)]$, where x is free in α
$\alpha \vee (\beta \wedge \gamma)$	$(\alpha \vee \beta) \wedge (\alpha \vee \gamma)$
$(\beta \wedge \gamma) \vee \alpha$	$(\beta \vee \alpha) \wedge (\gamma \vee \alpha)$

(1) $\models \forall \overline{x} \, [\bigwedge N] \rightarrow \alpha$.
(2) $\models \exists f_1 \ldots \exists f_l \forall \overline{x} \, [\bigwedge N] \equiv (\alpha \wedge \exists f_1 \ldots \exists f_l [S])$, where the f_i are the Skolem functions in N and S denotes the set of Skolem axioms for these (see Section 3.3.5).
(3) α is satisfiable iff N is satisfiable. ◁

4.3. Local Guiding of Reasoning

The search space for reasoning is in general huge. In resolution, the combination of an ordering $\succ$ and a selection function S provide local guidance to reasoning. They determine which inference steps are essential and which are inessential. The combination of the ordering and selection function provide a flexible device for guiding and restricting the application of the inference rules.

4.3.1. Orderings. Guiding and restricting reasoning by orderings is only going to work if the orderings are well-founded.

DEFINITION 4.4. A *(strict) ordering* on a set X, denoted $\succ$, is a transitive and irreflexive binary relation on X. A (strict) ordering $\succ$ over X is called *well-founded* (or *Noetherian* or *terminating*), if there is no infinite decreasing chain $x_0 \succ x_1 \succ x_2 \succ \ldots$ of elements $x_i \in X$. ◁

Orderings are required to be admissible.

DEFINITION 4.5. An ordering $\succ$ is *admissible*, if the following conditions hold.

(1) It is a total, well-founded ordering on the set of ground literals.
(2) For any ground atoms A and B, it satisfies:
    $B \succ \neg A$, whenever $\neg A \succ A$, and $B \succ A$.
(3) It is stable under the application of substitutions.

An ordering is said to be *liftable* if it satisfies (3). ◁

There are many ways of defining orderings which are admissible, see e.g. [11].

DEFINITION 4.6. A ground literal L is *(strictly) maximal* with respect to a ground clause C if for any literal L' in C, $L \succeq L'$ ($L \succ L'$). In general, a literal L is said to be *(strictly) maximal* with respect to a clause C if there is a substitution σ such that for any literal L' in C, $L\sigma \succeq L'\sigma$ ($L\sigma \succ L'\sigma$).   ◁

4.3.2. Selection Function.

DEFINITION 4.7. A *selection function* S assigns to each clause a possibly empty set of occurrences of negative literals. If C is a clause, then the literal occurrences in $S(C)$ are *selected*.   ◁

No additional restrictions are imposed on the selection function.

4.4. Resolution

The basic, unrefined resolution calculus is very simple and consists of two inference rules, the resolution rule and the factoring rule, and no axioms. For propositional logic the resolution rule is just the operation that infers a clause $C \vee D$ from two clauses $C \vee A$ and $D \vee \neg A$. The factoring rule is a form of simplification which eliminates multiple copies of the same literal from one clause, that is, it infers $C \vee A$ from $C \vee A \vee A$. These two rules suffice to give us a sound and complete calculus for propositional logic and sets of ground clauses. We obtain a sound and complete inference system for full first-order logic/clause logic, if we augment the rules with unification. This calculus, the *basic resolution calculus*, due to Robinson [172] is sound and complete for full first-order logic and clause logic. It is however very prolific and therefore not very efficient. Over the years numerous refinements, simplification techniques, optimization techniques, and sophisticated data structures and algorithms have been developed. Much of these advances can be accommodated and studied in a theoretical *framework of resolution* based on refinements of inferences and a general notion of redundancy [9, 10, 11, 151].

Refinements of inference rules are defined in terms of an ordering $\succ$ and a selection function S. The idea is that inferences do not need to be performed (but can) unless they are on literals maximal under the given ordering or on literals selected by the selection function S. The selection function can override the ordering. That is, if a literal is selected then it is the preferred candidate for an inference step even though there may be "larger" literals in the clause. The ordering and selection function are used to limit the number of possible inferences. It is clear that, in general, if we can reduce the number of possible inferences without losing completeness then a proof can be found more quickly as the search space for the proof is reduced. There is a very general completeness proof which requires only very

TABLE 10. The calculus R.

Deduction:
$$\frac{N}{N \cup \{C\}}$$
if C is a factor or resolvent of premises in N.

Deletion:
$$\frac{N \cup \{C\}}{N}$$
if C is redundant with respect to N.

Replacement:
$$\frac{N \cup \{C\}}{N \cup M}$$
if C is redundant with respect to $N \cup M$, and $N \cup \{C\}$ is satisfiable iff $N \cup M$ is satisfiable.

TABLE 11. The inference rules of R.

Ordered resolution:
$$\frac{C \vee A \quad \neg B \vee D}{(C \vee D)\sigma}$$
provided (i) σ is the most general unifier of A and B, (ii) no literal is selected in C, and $A\sigma$ is strictly $\succ$-maximal with respect to $C\sigma$, and (iii) $\neg B$ is either selected, or $\neg B\sigma$ is maximal with respect to $D\sigma$ and no literal is selected in D.

Ordered factoring:
$$\frac{C \vee A \vee B}{(C \vee A)\sigma}$$
provided (i) σ is the most general unifier of A and B, and (ii) no literal is selected in C and $A\sigma$ is $\succ$-maximal with respect to $C\sigma$.

weak conditions for the admissibility of orderings and selection functions. Simplification and deletion rules are based on a general notion of redundancy, which is based on considerations of the model construction at the center of the completeness proof of the framework of resolution. Standard simplification rules like elimination of duplicate literals within a clause, tautology deletion, subsumption deletion (forward and backward subsumption deletion), condensing, etc., are instances of this notion.

4.4.1. Resolution Calculus.

DEFINITION 4.8. By R we understand the resolution calculus defined by the rules of Table 10. ◁

In our presentation we distinguish three kinds of rules: Deduction, Deletion and Replacement rules.

The Deduction rules are the *ordered resolution* and *positive factoring* rules defined in Table 11. It is assumed that the premises have no variables in common.

Premises of the form $C_1 \vee A \; [\vee \; B]$ are called *positive premises*, if the inference is with A (and B), and premises of the form $\neg B \vee D$ are called *negative premises*. A *positive* (resp. *negative*) *premise* of a clause C is a positive (resp. negative) premise of the inference step which produced C.

The ordering $\succ$ can be any admissible ordering and S is any selection function of negative literals.

4.4.2. Redundancy.
4.4.2. Redundancy. The Deletion and Replacement rules are based on a general notion redundancy.

DEFINITION 4.9. Let N be a set of clauses. A ground clause C is *redundant* in N with respect to the ordering $\succ$ if there are ground instances $C_1\sigma, \ldots, C_n\sigma$ of clauses in N such that $(C_1\sigma_1 \wedge \ldots \wedge C_n\sigma_n) \rightarrow C$ is valid and for any i, $C_i\sigma_i \prec C$. A non-ground clause C is redundant in N if every ground instance of C is redundant in N. An inference step deriving D from a positive premise C_p and a negative premise C_n is redundant in N if N contains clauses $C_{n_1}, \ldots, C_{n_m}$ all strictly smaller than C_n and $C_p, C_{n_1}, \ldots, C_{n_m} \models D$. $\triangleleft$

Tautology deletion is a familiar instance of the Deletion rule. Other examples are the forward and backward subsumption deletion rules.

DEFINITION 4.10. A clause D *subsumes* a clause C iff there exists a substitution σ such that $D\sigma \subseteq C$. $\triangleleft$

REMARK 4.11. Strictly, the notion of redundancy defined here justifies strict subsumption deletion, because the following property holds: D is redundant with respect to $N \cup \{C\}$ if there is a substitution such that $C\sigma \subset D$. Justifying non-strict subsumption deletion requires a slightly more complicated definition of redundancy which is possible [11]. $\triangleleft$

Condensing is an instance of the Replacement rule.

DEFINITION 4.12. The *condensation* cond(C) of a clause C is a minimal (with respect to the number of literals) subclause D of C such that there exists a substitution σ with $L\sigma \in D$ for every $L \in C$. A clause C is *condensed* iff cond(C) is identical to C. $\triangleleft$

These and other simplification rules are explicitly defined in Table 16 of Section 5.2.5.

Testing for redundancy in its general form is an expensive operation, because general redundancy elimination is undecidable. For this reason one does not find theorem provers that implement redundancy elimination in its full generality. Only effectively computable instances of the Deletion and Replacement rules are normally implemented in theorem provers.

4.4.3. Soundness and Completeness.

DEFINITION 4.13. A *derivation* in R is a (possibly infinite) sequence of clause sets $N_0, N_1, \ldots$ such that for every $i \geq 0$, N_{i+1} is obtained from N_i by the application of a rule in the calculus. The *limit* of a derivation is given by the set

$$N_\infty = \bigcup_{j \geq 0} \bigcap_{k \geq j} N_k$$

of persisting clauses.   ◁

DEFINITION 4.14. A set N is R *saturated up to redundancy* if the conclusion of every inference in R from non-redundant premises is either contained in N or else is redundant in N.   ◁

DEFINITION 4.15. A derivation $N(= N_0), N_1, \ldots$ from N is called *fair* iff it is the case that each clause C which can be deduced from non-redundant premises in N_∞ is contained in some N_j.   ◁

Intuitively, fairness means that no non-redundant inferences are delayed indefinitely.

The next theorem states the soundness and (refutational) completeness of R.

THEOREM 4.16. Let $N(= N_0), N_1, \ldots$ be a fair R-derivation from a set N of clauses. Suppose N_∞ is the limit of the derivation. Then:

(1) N_∞ is saturated (up to redundancy).
(2) N is satisfiable iff N_∞ is satisfiable.
(3) N is unsatisfiable iff $\bigcup_{j \geq 0} N_j$ contains the empty clause.   ◁

For proofs see, e.g., [**9, 10, 11**].

It should be noted that inferences with non-maximal and unselected literals are not forbidden, and do not affect soundness and completeness, but are provably redundant.

4.5. Superposition

There are various ways how equality reasoning can be realized. Most automated theorem proving methods for first-order clause logic with equality are based on forms of the paramodulation rule (see Table 12). Paramodulation is based on replacing terms by terms deemed equal in combination with unification.

TABLE 12. Paramodulation rule.

Paramodulation: $$\frac{C \vee s \approx t \quad D[s']}{(C \vee D_t^{s'})\sigma}$$

provided σ is the most general unifier of s and s'.

Modern resolution based theorem provers are however based on the superposition calculus [**9, 10, 11, 151**]. The superposition calculus is denoted by S. It consists of the rules of the resolution calculus R in Table 10 with the Deduce rules given by those of Table 13. Equations are defined as unordered tuples, and any non-equational atom A is encoded as an equation $A \approx$ tt, where tt is defined to have the smallest precedence among the function symbols. Thus resolution can be viewed as an instance of the negative superposition rule and factoring as an instance of the equality factoring rule.

Note that the superposition rules are specializations of the paramodulation rule.

THEOREM 4.17. Let N be a set of clauses. Then, N is unsatisfiable iff the S-saturation (up to redundancy) of N contains the empty clause.   ◁

Proofs can be found in [**9, 10, 11**].

Observe that S restricted to the inference rules for non-equational clauses coincides with the calculus R defined in the previous section.

TABLE 13. The inference rules of the superposition calculus S.

Positive superposition: $\dfrac{C \vee s \approx t \quad D \vee u[s'] \approx v}{(C \vee D \vee u_t^{s'} \approx v)\sigma}$

provided (i) σ is the most general unifier of s and s', (ii) $t\sigma \not\succeq s\sigma$, (iii) $v\sigma \not\succeq u\sigma$, (iv) $(s \approx t)\sigma$ is strictly maximal with respect to $C\sigma$, and C contains no selected literal, (v) $(u \not\approx v)\sigma$ is strictly maximal with respect to $D\sigma$, and D contains no selected literal, (vi) s' is not a variable, and (vii) $(s \approx t)\sigma \not\succeq (u \approx v)\sigma$.

Negative superposition: $\dfrac{C \vee s \approx t \quad u[s'] \not\approx v \vee D}{(C \vee D \vee u_t^{s'} \not\approx v)\sigma}$

provided (i) σ is the most general unifier of s and s', (ii) $t\sigma \not\succeq s\sigma$, (iii) $v\sigma \not\succeq u\sigma$, (iv) $(s \approx t)\sigma$ is strictly maximal with respect to $C\sigma$, and C contains no selected literal, (v) $(u \not\approx v)\sigma$ is selected, or else no literal is selected in this premise and $(u \not\approx v)\sigma$ is maximal with respect to $D\sigma$, and (vi) s' is not a variable.

Reflexivity resolution: $\dfrac{u \not\approx v \vee D}{D\sigma}$

provided (i) σ is the most general unifier of u and v, (ii) $(u \not\approx v)\sigma$ is selected, or else no literal is selected in this premise and $(u \not\approx v)\sigma$ is maximal with respect to $D\sigma$.

Equality factoring: $\dfrac{C \vee u \approx v \vee s \approx t}{(C \vee v \not\approx t \vee u \approx t)\sigma}$

provided (i) σ is the most general unifier of s and u, (ii) $(s \approx t)\sigma$ is maximal with respect to $C\sigma$, and C contains no selected literal, and (iii) $(s \approx t)\sigma \not\succeq (u \approx v)\sigma$.

Part 2

Second-Order Quantifier Elimination in Classical Logic

CHAPTER 5

Clausal Quantifier Elimination

This part of the book is devoted to quantifier elimination in classical second-order logic. Of the various methods discussed in this book this chapter focuses on what we call clausal quantifier elimination methods, in contrast to the non-clausal (direct) method discussed in the next chapter. We discuss two related clausal methods: the SCAN algorithm and hierarchical resolution. They are both based on the idea of reducing (existentially quantified) second-order formulas to equivalent first-order formulas, by generating sufficiently many *logical consequences*, eventually keeping from the resulting set of formulas only those non-redundant formulas in which no second-order variables occur.

The SCAN algorithm is due to Gabbay and Ohlbach [**84**] and has been developed, extended and implemented by Ohlbach and Engel [**70, 160**]. The material of this chapter is based on these works and also the paper [**12**] by Bachmair, Ganzinger and Waldmann on resolution-based theorem proving for hierarchical first-order theories. Although developed for quite different purposes, and differing in important respects from the SCAN algorithm, it turns out that hierarchical resolution can also be used to eliminate existential second-order quantifiers.

5.1. The SCAN Algorithm

The input of SCAN is a second-order formula of the form

$$\exists P_1 \ldots \exists P_k [\beta],$$

where the P_i are relation variables and β is a first-order formula. The aim is to eliminate the quantifiers $\exists P_i$ from the formula. This means that all occurrences of the P_i symbols need to be removed. We refer to these as the *non-base symbols*. All other relation and function symbols are assumed to be the *base symbols*.

The SCAN algorithm involves three stages.

(1) Transformation of the input formula to clausal form including Skolemization.
(2) Constraint resolution.
(3) Reverse Skolemization (unskolemization).

TABLE 14. The C-resolution calculus.

Deduction:
$$\frac{N}{N \cup \{C\}}$$

where C is a C-resolvent or C-factor of premises in N.

Purification:
$$\frac{N \cup \{C \vee (\neg)P(s_1, \ldots, s_n)\}}{N}$$

if P is a non-base symbol and no non-redundant inferences with respect to the particular literal $(\neg)P(s_1, \ldots, s_n)$ in the premise $C \vee (\neg)P(s_1, \ldots, s_n)$ and the rest of the clauses in N can be performed.

In the first stage SCAN converts the input formula into clausal form. In the second stage SCAN performs a certain form of constraint resolution, called C-*resolution*. It generates all and only resolvents and factors with the second-order variables that are to be eliminated and in the process deletes clauses with which no non-redundant C-inferences are possible. If this stage terminates and clauses remain then the third stage attempts to reintroduce the first-order quantifiers eliminated during Skolemization in stage one.

If $\exists P_1 \ldots \exists P_k[\beta]$ is the given formula then clausification and Skolemization as described in Section 4.2 produces a clause set N for β. The implicit quantifier prefix of N contains the quantifiers over the non-base symbols and the newly introduced Skolem functions in N. That is, the clause set represents the formula $\exists P_1 \ldots \exists P_k \exists f_1 \ldots \exists f_l \forall \bar{x}[N]$. The latter logically implies $\exists P_1 \ldots \exists P_k[\beta]$, but not conversely.

For the next stage, where constraint resolution inferences are performed the quantifiers are not important and are therefore dropped (they become implicit). Thus N becomes the input to the C-resolution stage and we note the non-base symbols $P_1, \ldots P_k$ which we want to eliminate from N.

An on-line implementation is available of SCAN [160, 71]. The SCAN algorithm described in this chapter differs however in important details from the implementation.

5.2. Constraint Resolution

5.2.1. The C-resolution calculus.

DEFINITION 5.1. By C we denote the *constraint resolution* calculus defined by the two rules in Table 14.   ◁

TABLE 15. The inference rules of C.

C-Resolution:

$$\frac{C \vee P(s_1, \ldots, s_n) \quad D \vee \neg P(t_1, \ldots, t_n)}{C \vee D \vee s_1 \not\approx t_1 \vee \ldots \vee s_n \not\approx t_n}$$

provided P is a non-base symbol, the two premises have no variables in common, and $C \vee P(s_1, \ldots, s_n)$ and $D \vee \neg P(t_1, \ldots, t_n)$ are distinct clauses.

(Positive) C-Factoring:

$$\frac{C \vee P(s_1, \ldots, s_n) \vee P(t_1, \ldots, t_n)}{C \vee P(s_1, \ldots, s_n) \vee s_1 \not\approx t_1 \vee \ldots \vee s_n \not\approx t_n}$$

provided P is a non-base symbol.

The Deduction rule computes new clauses using the two rules, C-*resolution* and C-*factoring*, defined in Table 15. As usual we assume the clauses are normalized by variable renaming so that the premises of the C-resolution do not share any variables. The condition of the C-resolution rule, that the clauses must be distinct, prevents self-resolution.

The clause $C \vee P(s_1, \ldots, s_n)$ is called the *positive premise* and the clause $D \vee \neg P(t_1, \ldots, t_n)$ the *negative premise* of the inference step. The conclusion is called a C-*resolvent* with respect to P. The conclusion of the C-factoring rule is called a C-*factor* with respect to P.

The Purification rule deletes a clause when *all possible* non-redundant inferences on *one* literal have been performed. In this case the clause may be deleted even though inferences are possible with another non-base literal in the clause. These inferences are provably unnecessary.

The purification rule of C should not be confused with the purity deletion rule of Davis-Putnam algorithms (referred to as extended purity deletion in Engel [70]). A clause set N is "pure" in the standard sense in a relation symbol P, if P occurs only positively or only negatively in N. The purification rule deletes also such "pure" clauses and any factors on pure literals, provided these are pure with respect to a non-base symbol. Standard purity deletion with respect to base symbols does not preserve the required logical equivalence. Observe that the purification rule removes clauses that would not be deleted by the standard purity deletion rule.

Similar as in Section 4.4 a *derivation* in C is a (possibly infinite) sequence of clause sets $N_0, N_1, \ldots$ such that for every $i \geq 0$, N_{i+1} is obtained from N_i by the application of a rule in the calculus. The *limit* of a derivation is given as before by the set

$$N_\infty = \bigcup_{j \geq 0} \bigcap_{k \geq j} N_k$$

of persisting clauses.

5.2.2. Redundancy. In C it suffices to assume an inference step is *redundant* if it produces a clause already present in the derivation. However a stronger notion of redundancy may be employed. In particular, any equivalence preserving deletion and reduction rules may be applied, see Section 5.2.5 below.

We say a set N is C-*saturated up to redundancy with respect to the non-base symbols* if the conclusion of every inference in C with respect to the non-base symbols from non-redundant premises is either contained in N or else is redundant in N.

We say a set N is *closed under* C if N is C-saturated up to redundancy with respect to the non-base symbols and purification is not applicable.

5.2.3. Correctness. The formulation of the next theorem is a strengthening of the corresponding theorem in the original Gabbay-Ohlbach paper [84], where a proof sketch can be found. The theorem is also a consequence of a related theorem for H-resolution (Theorem 5.16 below).

THEOREM 5.2. Let N be a set of clauses and suppose $P_1, \ldots, P_k$ are the non-base symbols in N. Let $N(= N_0), N_1, \ldots$ be a fair C-derivation from N with limit N_∞. Then:

  (1) N_∞ is C-closed with respect to $P_1, \ldots, P_k$.
  (2) None of the non-base symbols occur in N_∞.
  (3) N_∞ is equivalent to $\exists P_1 \ldots \exists P_k [N]$.   ◁

Hence, C-resolution yields a saturated set N_∞ of clauses in which the specified second-order variables are eliminated. This set may be infinite, but if C-resolution terminates then N_∞ is finite. If no clauses remain after purification, i.e., N_∞ is empty, then N is tautologous. If C-resolution produces the empty clause, i.e., FALSE $\in N_\infty$, then N is unsatisfiable.

5.2.4. Unskolemization. If N is the clause set for a second-order formula α then we are interested in whether N_∞ can be expressed as a formula without Skolem functions. It is possible to eliminate Skolem functions by reintroducing first-order quantifiers, but this is not always possible as we see in Section 5.3.

5.2.5. Simplifications. The C-resolution calculus can be freely enhanced by any equivalence preserving simplification rules. Table 16 lists some common simplification rules. Each of the rules M/N in the table have the property that $M \models N$ iff $N \models M$ and are therefore equivalence preserving.

The first two rules are deletion rules while the other rules are replacement rules. They all reduce a clause set to a "simpler", logically equivalent set.

TABLE 16. Simplification rules.

Tautology deletion: $\dfrac{N \cup \{C\}}{N}$

if C is a tautology.

Subsumption deletion: $\dfrac{N \cup \{C, D\}}{N \cup \{C\}}$

if C subsumes D, i.e., there is a substitution σ such that $C\sigma \subseteq D$.

Subsumption resolution: $\dfrac{N \cup \{C \vee L, D \vee C\sigma \vee \overline{L}\sigma\}}{N \cup \{C \vee L, D \vee C\sigma\}}$

where $\overline{L}$ denotes the complement of the literal L.

Subsumption factoring: $\dfrac{N \cup \{C \vee L \vee L\sigma\}}{N \cup \{C \vee L\sigma\}}$

Condensation: $\dfrac{N \cup \{C\}}{N \cup \{\mathrm{cond}(C)\}}$

Constraint elimination: $\dfrac{N \cup \{C \vee s \not\approx t\}}{N \cup \{C\sigma\}}$

if σ is a most general unifier of $s \approx t$ (that is, $s\sigma \approx t\sigma$ and σ is the most general substitution with this property).

The subsumption resolution rule combines a resolution step between the two premises and the subsumption by (the simplification of) the resolvent $D \vee C\sigma$ of the premise $D \vee C\sigma \vee \overline{L}\sigma$. In the subsumption factoring rule the factor $C \vee L\sigma$ subsumes the premise, and can replace it because the factor is clearly simpler than the equivalent premise.

The condensation rule replaces a clause by its condensation (see Definition 4.12). It makes sense that the condensation rule is applied eagerly, that is, whenever a clause set N_i in a derivation contains a clause C which is not condensed, the condensation rule is applied to N_i to derive N_{i+1} in which C is replaced by $\mathrm{cond}(C)$.

In the absence of equality in the original problem the only equality rule included is the constraint elimination rule. It is similar to reflexivity resolution, or equality resolution, except that it also replaces the premise. It is not always possible to remove constraints, namely, when s and t are not unifiable, e.g., it is not possible to eliminate the constraint $a \not\approx f(x)$.

It should be observed that these rules are not restricted to non-base clauses. Because the rules preserve logical equivalence they can be applied arbitrarily. In fact, any simplification rule compatible with the general redundancy criterion of resolution theorem proving [**11, 12**] preserve logical equivalence and therefore may be used without invalidating Theorem 5.2. The theorem remains also true if we permit standard resolution and factoring inference on base literals.

5.2.6. Completeness and Termination for Propositional Non-base Symbols. C-resolution with a weak form of simplification is guaranteed to successfully eliminate quantifiers over propositional variables, i.e., nullary relation symbols.

THEOREM 5.3. Let C^{cond} denote the calculus C including either condensation or subsumption deletion. If the non-base symbols are propositional variables, then every derivation of a procedure based on C^{cond} or a refinement of C^{cond} is finitely bounded. On termination the clause set returned is logically equivalent to the input problem.

PROOF. Because the term depth of clauses remains the same during a derivation and the number of variables in variable-disjoint subclauses does not increase we can conclude that it is not possible to derive unboundedly many clauses in a C-resolution calculus enhanced with subsumption deletion or condensation. The second statement is a consequence of Theorem 5.2.   ◁

5.2.7. Examples. The first example is adapted from [**154**] and illustrates the first two steps of the SCAN algorithm.

EXAMPLE 5.4. The formula

$$\exists P \forall x \forall y \exists z [(\neg P(a) \vee Q(x)) \wedge (P(y) \vee Q(a)) \wedge P(z)]$$

is equivalent to

$$\exists P \big[\forall x [\neg P(a) \vee Q(x)] \wedge \forall x [P(x) \vee Q(a)] \wedge \exists z [P(z)] \big]$$

in which the quantifiers were moved inwards in order to minimize the dependencies in Skolem terms and the variable names normalized (y has become x). The clausal form is:

    1. $\neg P(a) \vee Q(x)$ given

    2. $P(y) \vee Q(a)$ given

    3. $P(c))$ given

where c is a new Skolem constant. P is the non-base symbol we want to eliminate. Resolving clause 1 and clause 2 (upon the first literal in each case) we derive

    4. $Q(x) \vee Q(a) \vee a \not\approx x$ 1.1, 2.1

This is equivalent to

> 5. $Q(a)$ 4, c-elim., cond.

by applying constraint elimination and condensation. Clause 4 is replaced by clause 5 and we indicate this by striking out the number of the deleted clause. Resolving 1 and 3 we obtain

> 6. $Q(x) \vee a \not\approx c$ 1.1, 3.1

Since all possible C inferences have been performed with clause 1 purification deletes it. Clauses 2 and 3 are also removed by purification since now there is no more clause in the derivation with a negative P-literal. Clauses 5 and 6 remain and are returned.   ◁

The next example proves the Leibniz equivalence principle. The use of subsumption deletion and condensation in the derivation is important.

EXAMPLE 5.5. The formula $\forall P[P(x) \equiv P(y)]$ is equivalent to $x \approx y$. Considering the negation, we want to prove the following:

$$\exists P[\neg(P(x) \equiv P(y))] \equiv x \not\approx y.$$

Because free first-order variables are interpreted existentially in refutational theorem proving, the clausal form of the left-hand side consists of the following two ground clauses, where a and b denote Skolem constants.

> 1. $P(a) \vee P(b)$ given
> 2. $\neg P(a) \vee \neg P(b)$ given

Choose clause 2 and resolve exhaustively on the first literal.

> 3. $a \not\approx a \vee P(b) \vee \neg P(b)$ 2.1, 1.1

This clause is a tautology and is therefore redundant.

> 4. $P(a) \vee a \not\approx b \vee \neg P(b)$ 2.1, 1.2
> 5. $a \not\approx a \vee a \not\approx b \vee \neg P(b) \vee \neg P(b)$ 2.1, 4.1

Condensation and constraint elimination are applicable and mean clause 5 can be replaced by the next clause.

> 6. $a \not\approx b \vee \neg P(b)$ 5, cond. & c-elim.

Clause 6 subsumes also clause 4. Now the clause 2 can be purified away because no more inferences with the persistent clauses are possible on the first literal.

~~7.~~	$a \not\approx b \vee P(b) \vee a \not\approx b$	6.2, 1.1
8.	$a \not\approx b \vee P(b)$	7, cond.
~~9.~~	$P(a) \vee b \not\approx b \vee a \not\approx b$	6.2, 1.2
10.	$P(a) \vee a \not\approx b$	9, c-elim.
~~11.~~	$a \not\approx b \vee b \not\approx b \vee a \not\approx b$	6.2, 8.2
12.	$a \not\approx b$	11, cond. & c-elim.

Clause 12 subsumes all clauses containing the inequality $a \not\approx b$. If all these clauses are deleted then the clauses 1 and 12 remain. Since no inferences are possible on clause 1 it can be purified away and clause 12 remains and the derivation process stops. By Theorem 5.2 and the obvious unskolemization this proves the equivalence we set out to establish.   ◁

The next example illustrates that the C-resolution stage does not need to terminate. Nevertheless, in this case a successful reduction to first-order logic is still possible. This demonstrates the improved scope of Theorem 5.2.

EXAMPLE 5.6. Let N consist of the following clauses.

1. $\neg P(x) \vee P(f(x))$		given
2. $\neg P(x) \vee Q(x)$		given
3. $P(a)$		given

We obtain the following infinite derivation.

4.	$x \not\approx a \vee P(f(x)) \quad \equiv P(f(a))$	1.1, 3.1
5.	$x \not\approx a \vee Q(x) \quad \equiv Q(a)$	2.1, 3.1
6.	$x \not\approx f(a) \vee P(f(x)) \quad \equiv P(f(f(a)))$	1.1, 4.1
7.	$x \not\approx f(a) \vee Q(x) \quad \equiv Q(f(a))$	2.1, 4.1
	$\vdots$ etc.	

Note that once an inference step has been performed on any non-base unit clause purification deletes it. In the limit the result is an infinite set of clauses:

$$\{Q(a), Q(f(a)), \ldots\}.$$

This proves that $\exists P[N] \equiv \{Q(f^n(a)) \mid 0 \le n\}$.   ◁

The next example illustrates that there is a difference in efficiency depending on the order in which the non-base symbols are eliminated.

EXAMPLE 5.7. In this example we want to eliminate both P and Q.

$\quad$ 1. $\neg P(x) \lor P(f(x)) \lor Q(x)$ $\qquad\qquad$ given

$\quad$ 2. $P(a)$ $\qquad\qquad$ given

$\quad$ 3. $Q(b)$ $\qquad\qquad$ given

$\quad$ 4. $\neg P(b)$ $\qquad\qquad$ given

Let us eliminate P first and start performing all possible inferences with clause 1 on the first literal.

$\quad$ 5. $a \not\approx x \lor P(f(x)) \lor Q(x)$ $\qquad\qquad$ 1.1, 2.1

Clause 1 can now be deleted because no more inferences are possible on its first literal. Resolve clauses 2 and 4, and then 5 and 4 to get:

$\quad$ 6. $a \not\approx b$ $\qquad\qquad$ 2.1, 4.1

$\quad$ 7. $f(x) \not\approx b \lor a \not\approx x \lor Q(x)$ $\qquad\qquad$ 5.2, 4.1

Purification with respect to P deletes clauses 2, 4 and 5. Purification with respect to Q also deletes clauses 3 and 7. Clause 6 is returned.

The same conclusion can be obtained in significantly fewer steps if we start by applying the C-resolution steps with respect to Q first. Since Q occurs only positively the only rule applicable to both clauses containing a Q literal is purification. This removes clauses 1 and 3 and leave 2 and 4. One further C-resolution step gives us $a \not\approx b$. $\qquad\qquad\qquad$ ◁

This shows the choice of order in which non-base symbols are eliminated is important. In the example clearly the better order of elimination is $Q > P$, i.e., it is better to eliminate Q first because this makes C-resolution steps with the more complex P-literals in clause 1. superfluous.

5.3. Unskolemization

If the C-resolution stage produces a (possibly infinite) set N_∞ then the specified second-order variables (the non-base symbols) have been eliminated. But, in general, a non-empty set N_∞ contains Skolem functions. These are implicitly quantified by existential second-order quantifiers (see (2), page 28). If N_∞ is non-empty and does not contain the empty clause, then in the third stage, SCAN attempts (where possible) to restore the quantifiers from the Skolem functions. The aim is to reduce $\exists f_1 \ldots \exists f_l \forall \bar{x}[N_\infty]$ to an equivalent formula α without the $\exists f_j$ quantifiers. This is done by unskolemization. Although $\exists f_1 \ldots \exists f_l \forall \bar{x}[N_\infty]$ can always be reduced to an equivalent formula involving second-order Henkin quantifiers, it is not always possible to reduce this formula to a first-order formula. However, in contrast to C-resolution, unskolemization is guaranteed to terminate with an equivalent first-order formula or an equivalent second-order formula. We say unskolemization is *successful* when a first-order formula is returned.

If all three stages of the SCAN algorithm terminate and unskolemization is successful, then the result is a first-order formula logically equivalent to the second-order input formula.

5.3.1. Introducing First-Order Quantifiers.
Let us now concentrate on unskolemization, the process of reversing Skolemization. Our aim is to eliminate the functions introduced during Skolemization and to restore first-order quantifiers. This means we need to replace the Skolem terms by variables which are existentially quantified by explicit quantifiers. In the process the universal quantifiers are re-introduced for variables in the clausal form which were implicitly assumed to be universal quantified. Unskolemization, like Skolemization, must preserve satisfiability and unsatisfiability.

Unskolemizing the Skolemization (not necessarily in clausal form) of a first-order formula is not difficult. It not difficult either to unskolemize the result of transformation to clausal form back into first-order logic. The process of unskolemization becomes generally difficult after inference steps have been applied to the clause set, or if some of the function symbols in clause set are not the result of Skolemization.

5.3.2. Term Flattening and Variable Abstraction.
Specific unskolemization algorithms are described in McCune [149] and Engel [70]. Due to lack of space, we do not discuss these in detail but concentrate on most important transformation steps used in both algorithms which are sufficient to perform unskolemization by hand.

The most important operations during unskolemization are variable renaming, term flattening and variable abstraction. Recall the definition of variable renaming from Section 4.1. Term flattening and variable abstraction are closely related operations and can be specified as rewrite rules; see Table 17.[1] Note that the positions mentioned in the definition of the rules need not be all the positions of occurrences of the relevant term in C.

---

[1] By a "position below a function symbol" we mean a position of a subterm of the term with f as top symbol. We view terms as being represented by trees, more specifically, a term $f(t_1, \ldots, t_n)$ is represented by the tree with f at the root and n children each being a tree representation of $t_1, \ldots, t_n$. Thus, the terminology. Similarly, formulas can be viewed as trees.

TABLE 17. Term flattening and variable abstraction.

Term flattening:
$$\frac{N \cup \{C(s)\}}{N \cup \{C(x) \vee s \not\approx x\}}$$

provided x is a fresh variable that does not occur in C and s is a non-variable term occurring at positions $p_1, \ldots, p_k$ below a function symbol. $C(x)$ denotes the clause obtained from $C(s)$ by replacing s at positions $p_1, \ldots, p_k$ by x.

Variable abstraction:
$$\frac{N \cup \{C(y)\}}{N \cup \{C(x) \vee y \not\approx x\}}$$

provided x is a fresh variable that does not occur in C and y is a variable occurring at positions $p_1, \ldots, p_k$. $C(x)$ denotes the clause obtained from $C(y)$ by replacing y at positions $p_1, \ldots, p_k$ by x.

LEMMA 5.8. The operations of term flattening and variable abstraction preserve logical equivalence.

PROOF. We prove that for any term s, $C(s) \equiv C(x) \vee s \not\approx x$. Since $C(x) \vee s \not\approx x$ can be obtained from $C(s)$ by a paramodulation step with the equality axiom $y \not\approx z \vee y \approx z$; this proves the left-to-right direction. The right-to-left direction is simulated by resolving $C(x) \vee s \not\approx x$ with $y \approx y$. ◁

Term flattening is applied to eliminate non-variable arguments from Skolem terms. The following example illustrates the use of this technique.

EXAMPLE 5.9. Clauses

$\quad$ 1. $P(a, f(a)) \vee Q(g(a, x))$
$\quad$ 2. $R(f(b)) \vee Q(h(f(b), y))$

are respectively replaced by these two clauses.

$\quad$ 1'. $P(z_1, f(z_1)) \vee Q(g(z_1, x)) \vee a \not\approx z_1$
$\quad$ 2'. $R(z_1) \vee Q(h(z_1, y)) \vee f(z_2) \not\approx z_1 \vee b \not\approx z_2$

The clause

$\quad$ 3. $P(a, f(g(x), a)) \vee Q(f(a, y), y)$

is replaced by

$\quad$ 3'. $P(a, f(z_1, z_2)) \vee Q(f(z_2, y), y) \vee g(x) \not\approx z_1 \vee a \not\approx z_2$.

Considered separately, $1'$ and $2'$ can now be easily unskolemized to the following first-order formulas

$$\exists v_a \forall z_1 \exists v_f \forall x \exists v_g [P(z_1, v_f) \vee Q(v_g) \vee v_a \not\approx z_1] \qquad \text{(for } 1')$$

$$\exists v_b \forall z_1 \exists v_f \forall y \exists v_h [R(z_1) \vee Q(v_h) \vee v_f \not\approx z_1 \vee v_b \not\approx z_2]. \qquad \text{(for } 2')$$

For clause $3'$ a first-order solution is not apparent however.   ◁

5.3.3. Sufficient Conditions for Unskolemization. When using inner Skolemization the clausal form N of an input formula has the following properties.

(U1) There is no nesting of Skolem functions.

(U2) Every occurrence of a function symbol f in N has the same argument sequence.

(U3) Let C denote any clause in N. For any distinct Skolem functions f and g (with arity n and m, respectively) occurring in C, the set of arguments of f is a subset of the set of arguments of g, assuming that $n \leq m$.

(U4) Let C denote any clause in N. The sets of non-constant functional Skolem terms occurring in variable indecomposable subclauses of C are pairwise disjoint.

We have formulated these properties so that they provide also sufficient conditions for unskolemization to work. Our intention is to use these as guidelines for preparing a clause set for successful unskolemization. Note that condition (U3) is purposely formulated so that the order of arguments in it is irrelevant. In a clause set resulting from Skolemization the terms have the form $f(x_1, \ldots, x_n)$ and $g(x_1, \ldots, x_m)$, i.e., the argument sequence of the first term is a prefix of the argument sequence of the second term. For unskolemization the less restrictive property is sufficient.

We further require that:

(U5) Logical equivalence is preserved by all transformations.

Property (U1) is the easiest property to achieve for any given clause set N. Just apply term flattening to every clause in N. Transforming a set satisfying (U1) so that it also satisfies properties (U2) and (U3) requires variable renaming. First though it is useful to rename the variables of clauses apart. This means variable renaming is used to ensure that no two clauses in the set have any variables in common. Then, again using variable renaming and possibly abstraction of variables, we attempt to unify Skolem terms with the same top symbol. More precisely, for any function symbol f we want to transform the clause set so that any term involving f has the same argument sequence. The order of the arguments is important and no repetitions are allowed in the sequence. Variable abstraction is needed for the removal of duplicate arguments. For example

$$P(f(x, x)) \quad \text{is rewritten to} \quad P(f(x, z_1)) \vee x \not\approx z_1.$$

The introduction of quantifiers is based on applying this equivalence from right-to-left.

$$\exists \bar{x} \begin{pmatrix} \forall \bar{y}_1 \exists z_1 \\ \vdots \\ \forall \bar{y}_k \exists z_k \end{pmatrix} \alpha(\bar{x}, \bar{y}_1, z_1, \ldots, \bar{y}_k, z_k)$$

$$\equiv \exists f_1 \ldots \exists f_k \exists \bar{x} \forall \bar{y}_1 \ldots \forall \bar{y}_k \left[\alpha(\bar{x}, \bar{y}_1, z_1, \ldots, \bar{y}_k, z_k)^{z_1, \ldots, z_k}_{f(\bar{y}_1), \ldots, f(\bar{y}_k)} \right].$$

The introduction of quantifiers can be done independently for blocks of clauses which do not share any function symbols. The last step in the conversion is the linearization of the quantifiers. This is not always possible, as the examples in the next section show.

The success of unskolemization may depend on the way in which the rewriting steps are done. All possible rewritings may need to be done when attempting to unskolemize a set of clauses.

5.3.4. Correctness. Suppose $\text{UnSk}(\exists f_1 \ldots \exists f_k[\alpha])$ denotes the unskolemization with respect to $f_1, \ldots, f_k$ of the formula $\exists f_1 \ldots \exists f_k[\alpha]$ obtained by using term flattening, variable abstraction and logical equivalence preserving variable renamings.

THEOREM 5.10. For any set of clauses N with Skolem functions $f_1, \ldots, f_k$, then

$$\text{UnSk}(\exists f_1 \ldots \exists f_k \forall \bar{x}[N]) \equiv \exists f_1 \ldots \exists f_k \forall \bar{x}[N].$$

PROOF. By Lemma 5.8.   ◁

5.3.5. Examples.

EXAMPLE 5.11. Recall the set of clauses derived in Example 5.4 was:

$$Q(a)$$

$$Q(x) \vee a \not\approx c.$$

Only c was a Skolem constant, because a was present in the original input problem. Restoring quantifiers we get $Q(a) \wedge \exists y \forall x[Q(x) \vee a \not\approx y]$.   ◁

EXAMPLE 5.12. This example is from Engel [**70**].

$$1. \ P(a, f(a)) \vee Q(g(a, x))$$

$$2. \ R(f(b)) \vee Q(g(b, y)).$$

Term flattening replaces the clauses by:

$1'. P(z_1, f(z_1)) \lor Q(g(z_1, x)) \lor a \not\approx z_1$

$2'. R(z_1) \lor Q(g(z_1, y)) \lor b \not\approx z_1$

Properties (U1), (U3) and (U4) are satisfied. In order for property (U2) to hold the Skolem terms $g(z_1, x)$ and $g(z_1, y)$ need to be unified. First we make sure all clauses are pairwise variable disjoint, by using an appropriate variable renaming.

$1''. P(x_1, f(x_1)) \lor Q(g(x_1, x_2)) \lor a \not\approx x_1$

$2''. R(y_1) \lor Q(g(y_1, y_2)) \lor b \not\approx y_1$

A further variable renaming, $\{y_1/x_1, y_2/x_2\}$, ensures that the argument sequences below g are unique.

$1'''. P(x_1, f(x_1)) \lor Q(g(x_1, x_2)) \lor a \not\approx x_1$

$2'''. R(x_1) \lor Q(g(x_1, x_2)) \lor b \not\approx x_1$

This clause set now satisfies all the properties above, and unskolemizes to the following.

$$\exists v_a \exists v_b \forall x_1 \exists v_f \forall x_2 \exists v_g \begin{bmatrix} (P(x_1, v_f) \lor Q(v_g) \lor v_a \not\approx x_1) \\ \land (R(x_1) \lor Q(v_g) \lor v_b \not\approx x_1) \end{bmatrix} \qquad \triangleleft$$

EXAMPLE 5.13. For the following set unskolemization appears to be impossible. The example is a small modification of the previous example in which $g(b, y)$ has been replaced by $h(f(b), y)$.

$1. P(a, f(a)) \lor Q(g(a, x))$

$2. R(f(b)) \lor Q(h(f(b), y))$

Term flattening gives:

$1'. P(z_1, f(z_1)) \lor Q(g(z_1, x)) \lor a \not\approx z_1$

$2'. R(z_1) \lor Q(h(z_1, y)) \lor f(z_2) \not\approx z_1 \lor b \not\approx z_2$

Variable renaming to ensure the clauses are variable disjoint gives:

$1''. P(x_1, f(x_1)) \lor Q(g(x_1, x_2)) \lor a \not\approx x_1$

$2''. R(y_1) \lor Q(h(y_1, y_2)) \lor f(y_3) \not\approx y_1 \lor b \not\approx y_3$

A further variable renaming, $\{y_3/x_1\}$, ensures that the argument sequences below each function symbol are unique.

$1'''. P(x_1, f(x_1)) \lor Q(g(x_1, x_2)) \lor a \not\approx x_1$

$2'''. R(y_1) \lor Q(h(y_1, y_2)) \lor f(x_1) \not\approx y_1 \lor b \not\approx x_1$

Introducing quantifiers we get:

$$\exists v_a \begin{pmatrix} \forall x_1 \exists v_f \forall x_2 \exists v_g \\ \forall y_1 \forall y_2 \exists v_h \end{pmatrix} \begin{array}{l} (P(x_1, v_f) \vee Q(v_g) \vee a \not\approx x_1) \\ \wedge (R(y_1) \vee Q(v_h) \vee v_f \not\approx y_1 \vee b \not\approx x_1) \end{array}$$

In this case it is not possible to rewrite the formula as a first-order formula.   ◁

5.4. Hierarchical Resolution

It is not difficult to see that both the C-resolution rule and the C-factoring rule can be simulated by term abstraction, ordinary resolution and factoring on abstracted, flat non-base literals followed by constraint elimination. (An expression is *flat* if it does not contain any nested occurrences of non-variable terms.) It is possible to formalize C-resolution within the setting of hierarchical theorem proving of Bachmair, Ganzinger and Waldmann [**12**]. This framework was not developed as a framework for second-order quantifier elimination but can be seen to be a by-product of it.

However, hierarchical theorem proving does not merely give us a reformulation of C-resolution but allows us to use additional refinements to control in which order non-base symbols are eliminated and define stronger simplification rules to force termination in cases where C-resolution does not terminate. The hierarchical theorem proving approach can also be used as a method for eliminating not only relation symbols but also function symbols. Being based on the superposition calculus, provision is made for powerful equality reasoning.

In this section we focus on a specialization of this calculus for second-order quantification problems. For the sake of keeping the presentation simple we assume that the language does not include equality and the non-base symbols are relation symbols. However the key principles and results carry over to the more general case without these restrictions (though not straightforwardly).

5.4.1. The H-Resolution calculus.

DEFINITION 5.14. By H we denote the resolution calculus defined by the rules of Table 18 where H-resolvents and H-factors are derived in accordance with the rules in Table 19.   ◁

The abstraction rule is crucial preparation of the clauses because the inference rules are restricted to abstracted literals. Observe that inferences on base literals are also allowed.

The ordering $\succ$ is defined in such a way that non-base literals are always larger than base literals. Such orderings exists and can be defined in various ways, for example, using a precedence under which the non-base symbols are larger than any other symbols in the language and lifting the ordering to literals and clauses

TABLE 18. The H-resolution calculus.

Deduction:
$$\frac{N}{N \cup \{C\}}$$
where C is a H-resolvent or H-factor of premises in N.

Term abstraction:
$$\frac{N \cup \{C(s)\}}{N \cup \{C(x) \vee s \not\approx x\}}$$
provided x is a fresh variable that does not occur in C and s is a non-variable term occurring in an argument position of a non-base relation symbol. $C(x)$ denotes the clause obtained from $C(s)$ by replacing s in this position and possibly other positions by x.

Reduction:
$$\frac{N \cup M}{N \cup M'}$$
if for every clause C in M is redundant with respect to $N \cup M'$.

TABLE 19. The inference rules of H.

H-Resolution:
$$\frac{C \vee P(x_1, \ldots, x_n) \quad D \vee \neg P(y_1, \ldots, y_n)}{(C \vee D)\sigma}$$
provided (i) σ is the most general unifier of $x_1 \not\approx y_1 \wedge \ldots \wedge x_n \not\approx y_n$, (ii) $P(x_1, \ldots, x_n)$ is strictly maximal with respect to C and no literal is selected in C, (iii) $\neg P(y_1, \ldots, y_n)$ is either selected and no literal is selected in D, or no literal is selected in the right premise and $\neg P(y_1, \ldots, y_n)$ is maximal with respect to D. (We assume as usual that the two premises have no variables in common.)

(Positive) H-Factoring:
$$\frac{C \vee P(x_1, \ldots, x_n) \vee P(y_1, \ldots, y_n)}{(C \vee P(x_1, \ldots, x_n))\sigma}$$
provided (i) σ is the most general unifier of $x_1 \not\approx y_1 \wedge \ldots \wedge x_n \not\approx y_n$, (ii) $P(x_1, \ldots, x_n)$ is maximal with respect to C and no literal is selected in C.

---

by a lexicographic path ordering or a recursive path ordering. We stipulate that no base literals are selected by the selection function.

The notions of derivation, limit N_∞, and fairness are defined as in Section 4.4. Saturation up to redundancy with respect to non-base symbols is defined as in Section 5.2.

5.4.2. Redundancy. Redundancy of clauses and inferences can be defined as in Section 4.4.2. With this notion of redundancy and our assumption about the ordering used, it can be shown that except for constraint elimination and subsumption deletion all the rules of Table 16 are examples of reduction rules, but see Remark 4.11 about the use of non-strict subsumption deletion.

5.4.3. Purification. The calculus H does not include a purification rule. Because of the restrictions imposed by the ordering and the selection function on the application of the inference rules, the purification rule of the C-resolution calculus is too strong. It is easy to give examples showing that applying purification as defined in Table 14 leads to incorrect results. Rather than adapting the purification rule, which is possible, we choose to assume as in **[12]** that non-base clauses are removed when saturation is achieved (in the limit). This means a procedure based on H-resolution calculus needs to remove the clauses containing non-base symbols when the derivation terminates. This variation is theoretically insignificant.

5.4.4. Soundness and Completeness. We first consider soundness and completeness of the H-resolution calculus. Notice that in this theorem saturation is not limited to the non-base symbols.

THEOREM 5.15. Let N be a set of clauses. Let $N(= N_0), N_1, \ldots$ be a fair H-derivation from N with limit N_∞. Then:

(1) N_∞ is H-saturated up to redundancy.
(2) N is satisfiable iff N_∞ is satisfiable.
(3) N is unsatisfiable iff $\bigcup_{j \geq 0} N_j$ contains the empty clause.   ◁

A proof of the above theorem is given in **[12]**.

It follows that if N is unsatisfiable then by completeness H-resolution derives the empty clause, i.e., FALSE $\in N_\infty$. This is however not generally true for C-resolution.

5.4.5. Correctness. For the correctness of H-resolution as a procedure for eliminating the non-base (relation) symbols we need the following additional notation.

If Σ denotes a set of symbols, then let $N \backslash \Sigma$ denote the set of clauses N with all clauses removed that contain a symbol in Σ.

THEOREM 5.16. Let N be a set of clauses and suppose $P_1, \ldots, P_k$ are the non-base symbols in N. Let $N(= N_0), N_1, \ldots$ be a fair H-derivation from N with limit N_∞. Then:

(1) N_∞ is H-saturated (up to redundancy) with respect to $P_1, \ldots, P_k$.
(2) $N_\infty \backslash \{P_1, \ldots, P_k\}$ is equivalent to $\exists P_1 \ldots \exists P_k[N]$.

PROOF. The proof is based on [**12**].   ◁

5.4.6. An Example.

EXAMPLE 5.17. Reconsider Example 5.5.

~~1.~~	$P(a) \vee P(b)$	given
~~2.~~	$\neg P(a) \vee \neg P(b)$	given

In order to apply H inference rules non-variable terms need to be abstracted away from non-base symbols.

$1'.$	$P(x) \vee a \not\approx x \vee P(y) \vee b \not\approx y$	1, abstr.
$2'.$	$\neg P(x) \vee a \not\approx x \vee \neg P(y) \vee b \not\approx y$	2, abstr.
~~3.~~	$a \not\approx x \vee P(y') \vee b \not\approx y'$ $\vee\, a \not\approx x \vee \neg P(y) \vee b \not\approx y$	$2'.1, 1'.1$

Constraint elimination produces the clause $3'$, which is a tautology and therefore redundant.

~~$3'.$~~	$a \not\approx a \ \vee P(b) \vee \neg P(b)$	3, c-elim.
~~4.~~	$P(x') \vee a \not\approx x' \vee b \not\approx x$ $\vee\, a \not\approx x \vee \neg P(y) \vee b \not\approx y$	$2'.1, 1'.3$
$4'.$	$P(x') \vee a \not\approx x' \vee a \not\approx b \vee \neg P(y) \vee b \not\approx y$	$2'.1, 1'.3$
~~5.~~	$a \not\approx x' \vee \neg P(y') \vee b \not\approx y'$ $\vee\, a \not\approx x' \vee a \not\approx b \vee \neg P(y) \vee b \not\approx y$	$2'.1, 4'.1$
6.	$a \not\approx b \vee \neg P(y) \vee b \not\approx y$	5, cond. & c-elim.

Clause $4'$ now becomes redundant because it is subsumed by clause 6.

~~7.~~	$a \not\approx b \vee b \not\approx y \vee a \not\approx y \vee P(y') \vee b \not\approx y'$	$6.2, 1'.1$
8.	$a \not\approx b \vee P(y') \vee b \not\approx y'$	7, cond. & c-elim.

We skip the derivation of the clauses corresponding to 9 and 10 of Example 5.5 because they are not significant.

~~11.~~	$a \not\approx b \vee b \not\approx y \vee a \not\approx b \vee b \not\approx y$	$6.2, 8.2$
12.	$a \not\approx b$	11, cond. & c-elim.

This derivation mimics almost exactly the derivation of Example 5.5 and can be seen to be essentially mimicked by the derivation in Example 5.5. There is an important difference though. The H-resolution calculus does not include a purification rule, which means that the clause $2'$ corresponding to a clause which was removed by purification after step 6, persists. In H-resolution only redundant clauses are eliminated. Because clause $2'$ and also clause $1'$ do not become redundant they persist throughout the derivation. This means that until the last clause is derived inferences are possible on the third literal of clause $2'$. In this example a good strategy is to derive $a \not\approx b$ as quickly as possible, because then these inferences and those producing clauses 9 and 10 become redundant. ◁

Section 11.1.2 gives an example that shows the usefulness of being able to select negative non-base symbols in H-resolution.

CHAPTER 6

Direct Methods

Roughly speaking, in direct methods one provides:

(1) Theorems which allow one to eliminate second-order quantifiers from formulas of a certain shape;
(2) Algorithms which allow one to transform a class formulas into the shape required by the provided theorems.

Of course, in the case of the classical second-order logic we have Corollary 3.32 (see page 32) and Proposition 3.43 (see page 36). Thus algorithms mentioned in (2) above cannot work for all formulas having classical first-order or fixpoint equivalents.

One of the strengths of direct methods is that they allow one to relatively easily characterize theories, where second-order quantifier elimination is guaranteed.

6.1. Ackermann's Lemma

Let us now quote the lemma of Ackermann, formulated in [2] (recall that notation $\beta(X)_{\alpha(\bar{x},\bar{z})}^{X(\bar{x})}$ is explained in Section 2.1.3, page 12).

LEMMA 6.1. Let X be a relation variable and $\alpha(\bar{x},\bar{z})$, $\beta(X)$ be classical first-order formulas, where the number of distinct variables in $\bar{x}$ is equal to the arity of X. Let α contain no occurrences of X.

If $\beta(X)$ is positive w.r.t. X then

$$(10) \qquad \exists X\{\forall\bar{x}[X(\bar{x}) \to \alpha(\bar{x},\bar{z})] \wedge \beta(X)\} \ \equiv \ \beta(X)_{\alpha(\bar{x},\bar{z})}^{X(\bar{x})}.$$

If $\beta(X)$ is negative w.r.t. X then

$$(11) \qquad \exists X\{\forall\bar{x}[\alpha(\bar{x},\bar{z}) \to X(\bar{x})] \wedge \beta(X)\} \ \equiv \ \beta(X)_{\alpha(\bar{x},\bar{z})}^{X(\bar{x})}.$$

PROOF. We prove equivalence (10). A proof of (11) can be carried out similarly.

Let $\langle M, v, V \rangle$ be a second-order interpretation (see Definition 3.29, page 30).

($\to$) Assume that $M, v, V \models \exists X\{\forall\bar{x}[X(\bar{x}) \to \alpha(\bar{x},\bar{z})] \wedge \beta(X)\}$. Since $\beta(X)$ is positive w.r.t. X, it is monotone w.r.t. X. Therefore, for any v' extending v to cover variables in $\bar{x}$ we have that $M, v', V \models X(\bar{x}) \to \alpha(\bar{x}, \bar{z})$, thus we also have that $M, v', V \models \beta(X)_{\alpha(\bar{x},\bar{z})}^{X(\bar{x})}$. Observe now that $\beta(X)$ is not within the scope of the quantifier $\forall \bar{x}$, thus v and v' are equal on variables in $\beta(X)$. In consequence, $M, v, V \models \beta(X)_{\alpha(\bar{x},\bar{z})}^{X(\bar{x})}$.

($\leftarrow$) Assume that $M, v, V \models \beta(X)_{\alpha(\bar{x},\bar{z})}^{X(\bar{x})}$. Define $X(\bar{x}) \stackrel{\text{def}}{\equiv} \alpha(\bar{x}, \bar{z})$. Then, obviously $M, v, V \models \forall \bar{x}[X(\bar{x}) \to \alpha(\bar{x}, \bar{z})]$ as well as $M, v, V \models \beta(X)$ holds. Thus we have exhibited X satisfying $\forall \bar{x}[X(\bar{x}) \to \alpha(\bar{x}, \bar{z})] \wedge \beta(X)$, i.e., we have that $M, v, V \models \exists X \forall \bar{x}[X(\bar{x}) \to \alpha(\bar{x}, \bar{z})] \wedge \beta(X)$.   ◁

A closer look at the proof indicates that Lemma 6.1 can be generalized by requiring that $\beta(X)$ is monotone (respectively, down-monotone) rather than positive (negative) w.r.t. X (see also Lemma 7.8, page 92). However, monotonicity of first-order formulas is not decidable.

6.2. The DLS Algorithm

The DLS algorithm has been provided by Doherty, Łukaszewicz and Szalas in [**56**] as an extension of the algorithm given by Szałas in [**199**]. Online implementations of DLS are available (see [**103, 144**]).

DLS takes a formula of the form $\exists X[\alpha(X)]$, where α is a first-order formula, as an input and returns its first-order equivalent or reports failure. The failure of the algorithm does not mean that the second-order formula at hand cannot be reduced to its first-order equivalent. As already indicated (see Corollary 3.32, page 32), the problem we are dealing with is totally undecidable. Of course, the algorithm can also be used for formulas of the form $\forall X[\alpha(X)]$, since the latter formula is equivalent to $\neg \exists X[\neg \alpha(X)]$. Thus, by repeating the algorithm one can deal with formulas containing any sequence of second-order quantifiers.

The elimination algorithm consists of four phases:

(1) Preprocessing;
(2) Preparation for Ackermann's lemma;
(3) Application of Ackermann lemma;
(4) Simplification.

These phases are described in Sections 6.2.1-6.2.4, where it is always assumed that whenever the goal specific for a current phase is reached, then the remaining steps of the phase are skipped.

To increase clarity below we present the DLS algorithm in a simplified form.

6.2.1. Preprocessing. The purpose of this phase is to transform the formula $\exists X[\alpha(X)]$ into a form that separates positive and negative occurrences of the quantified relation variable X. The form we want to obtain is

$$(12) \qquad \exists \bar{x} \exists X \left[(\alpha_1(X) \wedge \beta_1(X)) \vee \cdots \vee (\alpha_n(X) \wedge \beta_n(X)) \right],$$

where, for each $1 \leq i \leq n$, $\alpha_i(X)$ is positive w.r.t. X and $\beta_i(X)$ is negative w.r.t. X.

The steps of this phase are the following:

(1) Eliminate implication and equivalence using the equivalences provided in Table 1 (page 20);

(2) Remove redundant quantifiers, i.e., quantifiers binding variables not appearing in formulas which are in the scope of these quantifiers;

(3) Rename individual variables until all quantified variables are different and no variable occurs both bound and free;

(4) Using the equivalences provided in Tables 2 and 6 (pages 20 and 26), move the negation connective to the right until all its occurrences immediately precede atomic formulas;

(5) Move the universal quantifiers to the right and the existential quantifiers to the left, applying as long as possible the equivalences from Table 7 (page 27);

(6) distribute all top-level conjunctions over the disjunctions occurring in conjuncts, applying the equivalences from Table 5 (page 21).

If the resulting formula is not in the form (12), then report the failure of the algorithm. Otherwise replace (12) by its equivalent given by

$$(13) \qquad \exists \bar{x} \left[\exists X[\alpha_1(X) \wedge \beta_1(X)] \vee \cdots \vee \exists X[\alpha_n(X) \wedge \beta_n(X)] \right].$$

Try to find a formula equivalent to (13) by applying the next phases in the algorithm to each disjunct in (13) separately. If the first-order equivalents of each disjunct are successfully obtained then return their disjunction, preceded by the prefix $\exists \bar{x}$, as the output of the algorithm.

6.2.2. Preparation for Ackermann's Lemma. The goal of this phase is to transform a formula of the form $\exists X[\alpha(X) \wedge \beta(X)]$, where $\alpha(X)$ (respectively $\beta(X)$) is positive (respectively negative) w.r.t. X, into one of the forms (10) or (11) given in Lemma 6.1. Both forms can always be obtained and both transformations should be performed because none, one or both forms may require Skolemization. Unskolemization, which occurs in the next phase, could fail in one form, but not the other. In addition, one form may be substantially smaller than the other. The steps of this phase are based on equivalences from Table 5 (page 21) together with equivalences (14) and (15), where $\bar{x}$ consists of new variables:

(14)
$$\gamma(\bar{t}) \equiv \forall \bar{x}[\bar{x} \approx \bar{t} \rightarrow \gamma(\bar{x})]$$
$$\neg\gamma(\bar{t}) \equiv \forall \bar{x}[\gamma(\bar{x}) \rightarrow \bar{x} \not\approx \bar{t}]$$

(15) $\gamma(\bar{t}_1) \vee \cdots \vee \gamma(\bar{t}_n) \equiv \exists \bar{x}[(\bar{x} \approx \bar{t}_1 \vee \cdots \vee \bar{x} \approx \bar{t}_n) \wedge \gamma(\bar{x})]$

as well as the Skolem equivalence (5) given on page 31.

After applying the above equivalences one has to restore implication $\rightarrow$ wherever required, using the equivalences provided in Table 1 (page 20).

6.2.3. Application of Ackermann's Lemma. The goal of this phase is to eliminate the second-order quantification over X, by applying the lemma of Ackermann, and then try to unskolemize the function variables possibly introduced. This latter step employs the Skolem equivalence (4) (page 31).

In fact, any unskolemization procedure, e.g., the one described in Section 5.3 (page 63) can also be applied here.

6.2.4. Simplification. Generally, application of Ackermann's lemma often involves the use of equivalences (14) in the left to right direction. If so, the same equivalence may often be used after application of the lemma in the right to left direction, substantially shortening the resulting formula.

Some other simplifications preserving the equivalence of the resulting formula can also be done.

6.2.5. Examples. Let us illustrate applications of Ackermann's lemma and the DLS algorithm on some examples, where, for clarity, we simplify or skip some obvious steps.

EXAMPLE 6.2. Consider

(16) $\exists X \{\forall x [X(x) \rightarrow \forall y[R(x,y)]] \wedge [X(a) \vee X(b)]\}.$

Formula (16) is in the form (10) of Lemma 6.1. An application of the lemma results in $\forall y[R(a,y)] \vee \forall y[R(b,y)]$.

Similarly, formula

(17) $\exists X \{\forall x \forall y[R(x,y) \rightarrow X(x)] \wedge [\neg X(a) \vee \neg X(b)]\}$

is in the form (11) of Lemma 6.1, according to which formula (17) is equivalent to $\neg\forall y[R(a,y)] \vee \neg\forall y[R(b,y)]$.   ◁

EXAMPLE 6.3. Consider

(18) $\exists X \{\forall x \forall y[X(x,y) \rightarrow R(x,y)] \wedge [X(a,b) \vee X(b,c)]\}.$

Formula (18) is in the form (10) of Lemma 6.1. An application of the lemma results in $R(a,b) \vee R(b,c)$.   ◁

EXAMPLE 6.4. Consider

(19) $\exists X \{ \forall x \forall y [R(x,y) \rightarrow X(x)] \wedge [X(a) \vee \neg X(b)] \wedge \neg X(c) \}.$

In formula (19) positive and negative occurrences of X are not separated. We then transform (19) to

(20) $\exists X \{ \forall x \forall y [R(x,y) \rightarrow X(x)] \wedge X(a) \wedge \neg X(c) \}$
         $\vee \exists X \{ \forall x \forall y [R(x,y) \rightarrow X(x)] \wedge \neg X(b) \wedge \neg X(c) \}$

and deal with both disjuncts of (20) separately.

The calculations for the first disjunct of (20) are

$$\exists X \{ \forall x \forall y [R(x,y) \rightarrow X(x)] \wedge X(a) \wedge \neg X(c) \} \equiv$$
$$\exists X \{ \forall x \forall y [R(x,y) \rightarrow X(x)] \wedge \forall x [x \approx a \rightarrow X(x)] \wedge \neg X(c) \} \equiv$$
$$\exists X \{ \forall x [(x \approx a \vee \forall y [R(x,y)]) \rightarrow X(x)] \wedge \neg X(c) \}.$$

Now we apply Lemma 6.1(11) and obtain the following equivalent formula:

(21) $\neg [c \approx a \vee \forall y [R(c,y)]].$

The second disjunct of (20) is already in the form required in Lemma 6.1(11), thus is equivalent to

(22) $\neg \forall y [R(b,y)] \wedge \neg \forall y [R(c,y)].$

Combining results (22) and (21) we find that the formula

$$\neg [c \approx a \vee \forall y [R(c,y)]] \vee [\neg \forall y [R(b,y)] \wedge \neg \forall y [R(c,y)]].$$

is equivalent to (20), i.e., also equivalent to (19).   ◁

EXAMPLE 6.5. Consider

(23) $\exists X \{ \forall x \exists y [X(x,y)] \wedge \forall x \exists y [\neg X(x,y)] \}.$

We first apply the Skolem equivalence (4) (see page 31) and obtain the formula

$$\exists f \exists X \{ \forall x [X(x,f(x))] \wedge \forall x \exists y [\neg X(x,y)] \},$$

which, due to equivalence (14) is equivalent to

$$\exists f \exists X \{ \forall x \forall z [z \approx f(x) \rightarrow X(x,z)] \wedge \forall x \exists y [\neg X(x,y)] \}.$$

We now apply Lemma 6.1(11) and obtain

(24) $\exists f \{ \forall x \exists y [y \not\approx f(x)] \}.$

Applying the Skolem equivalence (4) we conclude that formula (24), and thus also the initial formula (23), is equivalent to $\forall x \exists z \exists y [y \not\approx z]$, i.e., to $\exists z \exists y [y \not\approx z]$.   ◁

EXAMPLE 6.6. In formula

(25) $\exists X \{ \forall x \forall y [R(x,y) \vee X(x) \vee \neg X(y)] \wedge \forall x \forall y [S(x,y) \vee X(x) \vee X(y)] \}$

positive and negative occurrences of X cannot be separated. In consequence, DLS fails to eliminate second-order quantifier $\exists X$ from (25).   ◁

6.3. On the Strength of DLS

This section is based on [**40**], where Conradie has provided conditions for the success of DLS formulated as Theorems 6.14 and 6.18 below.

DEFINITION 6.7. A first-order formula is said to be *clean* if no variable occurs both bound and free, and no two quantifier occurrences bind the same variable.

The *scope of an occurrence of a quantifier* $Q \in \{\forall, \exists\}$ is *minimal* in a first-order formula if Q may not be moved to the right by the application of equivalences given in Table 7 (page 27).

A first-order formula is *standardized* w.r.t. a relation symbol (variable) X if it is clean, in negation normal form, and the scope of all quantifiers in the scope of which X occurs, is minimal.   ◁

DEFINITION 6.8. Given a formula α in negation normal form and a relation variable X, a conjunction (disjunction) occurrence in α is:

(1) *Benign w.r.t.* X, if it is the main connective of a subformula of the form $\gamma \wedge \delta$ ($\gamma \vee \delta$) where at least one of γ and δ contains no occurrences of X;
(2) *Malignant w.r.t.* X if it is the main connective of a subformula of the form $\gamma \wedge \delta$ ($\gamma \vee \delta$) where γ and δ contains occurrences of X of opposite polarity;
(3) *Non-malignant w.r.t.* X, if it is not malignant w.r.t. X.   ◁

EXAMPLE 6.9. In the formula

$$\forall x[\neg Q(x) \vee' P(x)] \wedge^*$$
$$\exists u\left[(P(u) \wedge' Q(u)) \wedge^\circ \forall y[\neg R(u,y) \vee' \exists z[R(y,z) \wedge' Q(z)]]\right]$$

all conjunctions and disjunctions are marked whether they are benign (with '), malignant (with *) or non-malignant (with °) w.r.t. Q.   ◁

DEFINITION 6.10. A relation symbol (variable) X, is in $\exists\forall$-*scope* in a formula α, if no occurrence of X in α is in the scope of

(1) An existential quantifier which is in the scope of a universal quantifier, or
(2) A non-benign (w.r.t. X) disjunction which is in the scope of a universal quantifier, or
(3) A malignant (w.r.t. X) conjunction which is in the scope of a universal quantifier.   ◁

EXAMPLE 6.11. In the formula

$$\forall x[\neg Q(x) \vee P(x)] \wedge \exists u\left[P(u) \wedge \forall y[\neg R(u,y) \vee \exists z[R(y,z) \wedge Q(z)]]\right],$$

which is clean and in negation normal form, P is in $\exists\forall$-scope, while Q is not in $\exists\forall$-scope. ◁

DEFINITION 6.12. A relation symbol (variable) X is in *good scope* in a formula α in negation normal form provided that

(1) No conjunction or disjunction malignant w.r.t. X occurs in the scope of a universal quantifier in α, and
(2) α contains no subformula of the form $\gamma \wedge \delta$ where γ contains a positive (negative) occurrence of X out of $\exists\forall$-scope, and δ contains a negative (positive) occurrence of X out of $\exists\forall$-scope.

A relation symbol (variable) X is in *bad scope* in α when it is not in good scope in α. ◁

EXAMPLE 6.13. In the formulas

$$\forall x \exists y \left[R(x,y) \wedge \neg P(y) \wedge \forall y [\neg R(x,y) \vee P(y)] \right]$$
$$\forall z \exists y [R(z,y) \wedge P(y)] \wedge \forall z \exists y [R(z,y) \wedge \neg P(y)]$$

the relation symbol P is in bad scope. It is in good scope in the formulas

$$\exists x \exists y [R(x,y) \wedge \neg P(y)] \wedge \forall y [\neg R(x,y) \vee P(y)]$$
$$\forall z \forall y [R(z,y) \wedge P(y))] \wedge \forall z \exists y [R(z,y) \wedge \neg P(y)].$$

Note that P is in good scope in any formula that is positive (negative) w.r.t. P. ◁

The following theorem is proved in [**40**].

THEOREM 6.14. Let α be a formula, standardized w.r.t. X. Then DLS succeeds in eliminating $\exists X$ from $\exists X \alpha$ if and only if X is in good scope in α. ◁

DEFINITION 6.15. A formula α is *restricted* w.r.t. relation variables $X_1, \ldots, X_n$ if it is standardized w.r.t. $X_1, \ldots, X_n$, and, in α,

(1) No two positive occurrences of relation variables among $X_1, \ldots, X_n$ are in the scope of the same universal quantifier, and
(2) All positive occurrences of $X_1, \ldots, X_n$ are in $\exists\forall$-scope. ◁

DEFINITION 6.16. Let α be a formula restricted w.r.t. $X_1, \ldots, X_n$. The *dependency graph of α over* $X_1, \ldots, X_n$ is the graph $D_\alpha = \langle V_A, E_A \rangle$ with vertex set $V_A = \{X_1, \ldots, X_n\}$ and edges E_A such that $\langle X_i, X_j \rangle \in E_\alpha$ iff there is a subformula $\forall x \gamma$ of α such that X_i occurs negatively in γ and X_j occurs positively in γ.

The dependency digraph of α is *acyclic* if it contains no directed cycles or loops.

A formula α, restricted w.r.t. $X_1, \ldots, X_n$, is *independent* w.r.t. $X_1, \ldots, X_n$ if its dependency graph over $X_1, \ldots, X_n$ is acyclic. ◁

EXAMPLE 6.17. The formula

$$\forall x [P(x) \vee \forall z [R(x,z) \wedge Q(z)]]$$

is not restricted w.r.t. P and Q.

The formula

$$\forall x [P(x) \vee \forall z [R(x,z) \wedge \neg Q(z)]] \wedge$$
$$\forall x [\forall y [\neg R(x,y) \vee Q(y)] \vee \exists z [R(x,z) \wedge \neg P(z)]]$$

is restricted w.r.t. P and Q but not independent w.r.t. P and Q. It can be made independent by replacing the subformula $\neg Q(z)$, e.g., with $z \neq z$.   ◁

The proof of the following theorem is given in [40].

THEOREM 6.18. DLS succeeds in computing first-order equivalents for all formulas $\exists X_1 \ldots \exists X_n \alpha$ where α is independent w.r.t. $X_1, \ldots, X_n$.   ◁

6.4. The Fixpoint Approach

The fixpoint approach to second-order quantifier elimination was introduced by Nonnengart and Szałas in [155]. It is based on a theorem, quoted below as Theorem 6.19. It generalizes Ackermann's lemma by allowing formula α in equivalences (10) and (11) to contain the eliminated relational variable X. In consequence, the resulting formulas are classical fixpoint formulas.

THEOREM 6.19. Let X be a relation variable and $\alpha(X, \bar{x}, \bar{z})$, $\beta(X)$ be classical first-order formulas, where the number of distinct variables in $\bar{x}$ is equal to the arity of X and $\alpha(X, \bar{x}, \bar{z})$ is positive w.r.t. X.

If $\beta(X)$ is positive w.r.t. X then

$$(26) \qquad \exists X \{ \forall \bar{x} [X(\bar{x}) \rightarrow \alpha(X, \bar{x}, \bar{z})] \wedge \beta(X) \} \equiv \beta(X)_{[\text{GFP } X(\bar{x}).\alpha(X,\bar{x},\bar{z})]}^{X(\bar{x})}.$$

If $\beta(X)$ is negative w.r.t. X then

$$(27) \qquad \exists X \{ \forall \bar{x} [\alpha(X, \bar{x}, \bar{z}) \rightarrow X(\bar{x})] \wedge \beta(X) \} \equiv \beta(X)_{[\text{LFP } X(\bar{x}).\alpha(X,\bar{x},\bar{z})]}^{X(\bar{x})}.$$

PROOF. We prove equivalence (26). A proof of (27) can be carried out similarly.

Let $\langle M, v, V \rangle$ be a second-order interpretation (see Definition 3.29, page 30).

($\rightarrow$) Assume that $M, v, V \models \exists X \{ \forall \bar{x} [X(\bar{x}) \rightarrow \alpha(X, \bar{x}, \bar{z})] \wedge \beta(X) \}$. Thus, there is V' extending V to cover X such that

$$M, v, V' \models \forall \bar{x} [X(\bar{x}) \rightarrow \alpha(X, \bar{x}, \bar{z})] \wedge \beta(X),$$

from which we obtain $M, v, V' \models \forall \bar{x} [X(\bar{x}) \rightarrow \alpha(X, \bar{x}, \bar{z})]$. Therefore we also have that $M, v, V' \models \forall \bar{x} [X(\bar{x}) \rightarrow [\text{GFP } X(\bar{x}).\alpha(X, \bar{x}, \bar{z})]]$.

Since $\beta(X)$ is positive w.r.t. X, it is monotone w.r.t. X. Thus

$$M, v, V' \models \beta(X)^{X(\bar{x})}_{[\text{GFP}\, X(\bar{x}).\alpha(X,\bar{x},\bar{z})]}.$$

Observe now that formula $\beta(X)^{X(\bar{x})}_{[\text{GFP}\, X(\bar{x}).\alpha(\bar{x},\bar{z})]}$ does not contain free occurrences of X (all such occurrences are bound by the fixpoint operator), which implies that V and V' are equal on its variables. In consequence,

$$M, v, V \models \beta(X)^{X(\bar{x})}_{[\text{GFP}\, X(\bar{x}).\alpha(X,\bar{x},\bar{z})]}.$$

($\leftarrow$) Assume that $M, v, V \models \beta(X)^{X(\bar{x})}_{[\text{GFP}\, X(\bar{x}).\alpha(X,\bar{x},\bar{z})]}$. Define

$$X(\bar{x}) \stackrel{\text{def}}{\equiv} [\text{GFP}\, X(\bar{x}).\alpha(X, \bar{x}, \bar{z})].$$

Then, since X is a fixpoint of $\alpha(X, \bar{x}, \bar{z})$, we have that

$$M, v, V \models \forall \bar{x}[X(\bar{x}) \equiv \alpha(X, \bar{x}, \bar{z})],$$

from which $M, v, V \models \forall \bar{x}[X(\bar{x}) \rightarrow \alpha(X, \bar{x}, \bar{z})]$.

By assumption, $M, v, V \models \beta(X)$ holds. Thus we have exhibited X such that $M, v, V \models \forall \bar{x}[X(\bar{x}) \rightarrow \alpha(\bar{x}, \bar{z})] \wedge \beta(X)$, i.e., we have that

$$M, v, V \models \exists X \forall \bar{x}[X(\bar{x}) \rightarrow \alpha(\bar{x}, \bar{z})] \wedge \beta(X). \qquad \lhd$$

Some remarks are in order here.

First, observe that Theorem 6.19 generalizes Lemma 6.1 in the sense that whenever formula $\alpha(X, \bar{x}, \bar{z})$ does not, in fact, contain X, then $[\text{LFP}\, X(x).\alpha(X, \bar{x}, \bar{z})]$ and $[\text{GFP}\, X(x).\alpha(X, \bar{x}, \bar{z})]$ are equivalent to $\alpha(X, \bar{x}, \bar{z})$ (or, being more suggestive, to $\alpha(\bar{x}, \bar{z})$).

Second, a closer look at the proof indicates that Theorem 6.19 can be generalized by requiring that $\beta(X)$ is monotone (respectively, down-monotone) rather than positive (negative) w.r.t. X. Similarly, $\alpha(X, \bar{x}, \bar{z})$ could be required to be monotone rather that positive w.r.t. X, but this would additionally require us to consider fixpoints of monotone, not only positive formulas.

Observe also that the proof of Theorem 6.19 allows us to obtain the explicit definitions of the eliminated relation variables (see the corollary below). Such definitions are important in applications (see, e.g, [58]).

COROLLARY 6.20. Let $\langle M, v, V \rangle$ be a second-order interpretation. Then:

(1) The least (w.r.t. $\subseteq$) relation X such that
$$M, v, V \models \forall \bar{x}[\alpha(X, \bar{x}, \bar{z}) \rightarrow X(\bar{x})] \wedge \beta(X),$$
if it exists, is defined by $[\text{LFP}\, X(x).\alpha(X, \bar{x}, \bar{z})]$;
(2) The greatest (w.r.t. $\subseteq$) relation X such that
$$M, v, V \models \forall \bar{x}[X(\bar{x}) \rightarrow \alpha(X, \bar{x}, \bar{z})] \wedge \beta(X),$$
if it exists, is defined by $[\text{GFP}\, X(x).\alpha(X, \bar{x}, \bar{z})]$. $\qquad \lhd$

The existence of relations mentioned in Corollary 6.20 is characterized by coherence conditions as defined below.

DEFINITION 6.21. In the case when Theorem 6.19 is applicable, by a *coherence condition* for formula $\exists X\{\forall \bar{x}[X(\bar{x}) \to \alpha(\bar{x}, \bar{z})] \wedge \beta(X)\}$ we understand its equivalent $\beta(X)_{[\text{GFP}\,X(x).\alpha(\bar{x},\bar{z})]}^{X(\bar{x})}$ and for formula $\exists X\{\forall \bar{x}[\alpha(\bar{x}, \bar{z}) \to X(\bar{x})] \wedge \beta(X)\}$ its equivalent $\beta(X)_{[\text{LFP}\,X(x).\alpha(\bar{x},\bar{z})]}^{X(\bar{x})}$. ◁

By Theorem 6.19 we have the following immediate corollary.

COROLLARY 6.22. Let $\langle M, v, V \rangle$ be a second-order interpretation and let the assumptions of Theorem 6.19 be respectively satisfied. Then:

(1) The least (w.r.t. $\subseteq$) relation X such that
$$M, v, V \models \forall \bar{x}[\alpha(\bar{x}, \bar{z}) \to X(\bar{x})] \wedge \beta(X)$$
exists in $\langle M, v, V \rangle$, iff $M, v, V \models \beta(X)_{[\text{LFP}\,X(x).\alpha(\bar{x},\bar{z})]}^{X(\bar{x})}$. Thus the coherence condition for formula $\exists X\{\forall \bar{x}[X(\bar{x}) \to \alpha(\bar{x}, \bar{z})] \wedge \beta(X)\}$ is $\beta(X)_{[\text{LFP}\,X(x).\alpha(\bar{x},\bar{z})]}^{X(\bar{x})}$;

(2) The greatest (w.r.t. $\subseteq$) relation X such that
$$M, v, V \models \forall \bar{x}[X(\bar{x}) \to \alpha(\bar{x}, \bar{z})] \wedge \beta(X)$$
exists in $\langle M, v, V \rangle$ iff $M, v, V \models \beta(X)_{[\text{GFP}\,X(x).\alpha(\bar{x},\bar{z})]}^{X(\bar{x})}$. Thus the coherence condition for formula $\exists X\{\forall \bar{x}[X(\bar{x}) \to \alpha(\bar{x}, \bar{z})] \wedge \beta(X)\}$ is $\beta(X)_{[\text{GFP}\,X(x).\alpha(\bar{x},\bar{z})]}^{X(\bar{x})}$. ◁

6.5. The DLS* Algorithm

The DLS* algorithm, introduced by Doherty, Łukaszewicz and Szalas in [57], extends DLS (see Section 6.2) by allowing one to deal with a class of formulas in which positive and negative occurrences of the eliminated second-order relational variable are not separated. Namely, instead of applying Ackermann's lemma, where such separation is required (and reflected in DLS in the step described in Section 6.2.1), one applies Theorem of Nonnengart and Szałas 6.19, in which two forms of non-separated formulas are allowed.

An online implementation of DLS* is available (see [144]).

DLS* takes a formula of the form $\exists X[\alpha(X)]$, where α is a first-order formula, as an input and returns its fixpoint equivalent or reports failure. The failure of the algorithm does not mean that the second-order formula at hand cannot be reduced to its first-order equivalent. As in the case of DLS, the algorithm can also be used for formulas of the form $\forall X[\alpha(X)]$.

The elimination algorithm is similar to DLS and consists of four phases:

(1) Preprocessing and preparation for the fixpoint theorem;
(2) Application of the fixpoint theorem;
(3) Simplification.

Phases (1) and (2) are described in Sections 6.5.1 and 6.5.2, where it is always assumed that whenever the goal specific for a current phase is reached, then the remaining steps of the phase are skipped. Phase (4) is the same as in the case of DLS and has been described in Section 6.2.4.

To increase clarity, the DLS* algorithm is also presented in a simplified form.

6.5.1. Preprocessing. The purpose of this phase is to transform the formula $\exists X \alpha(X)$ into a form suitable for application of Theorem 6.19. The form we want to obtain is

$$(28) \qquad \exists \bar{x} \exists X [(\alpha_1(X) \wedge \beta_1(X)) \vee \cdots \vee (\alpha_n(X) \wedge \beta_n(X))],$$

where either

- For each $1 \leq i \leq n$, $\alpha_i(X)$ is in the form[1] $\forall \bar{x}[X(\bar{x}) \rightarrow \alpha(\bar{x}, \bar{z})]$ and $\beta_i(X))$ if positive w.r.t. X;
- Or for each $1 \leq i \leq n$, $\alpha_i(X)$ is in the form[2] $\forall \bar{x}[\alpha(\bar{x}, \bar{z}) \rightarrow X(\bar{x})]$ and $\beta_i(X))$ if negative w.r.t. X.

The steps of this phase are the same as steps (1)–(6) given in Section 6.2.1, page 77, where in addition one uses equivalences from Table 5 (page 21) together with equivalences (14) and (15) defined on page 78, as well as the Skolem equivalence (4) given on page 31.

Next one restores implication $\rightarrow$ wherever required, using the equivalences provided in Table 1 (page 20).

If the resulting formula is not in the form (28), then report the failure of the algorithm. Otherwise replace (28) by its equivalent given by

$$(29) \qquad \exists \bar{x} \big[\exists X [\alpha_1(X) \wedge \beta_1(X)] \vee \cdots \vee \exists X [\alpha_n(X) \wedge \beta_n(X)] \big].$$

Try to find a formula equivalent to (29) by applying the next phases in the algorithm to each disjunct in (29) separately. If the fixpoint equivalents of each disjunct are successfully obtained then return their disjunction, preceded by the prefix $\exists \bar{x}$, as the output of the algorithm.

---

[1]This is the form required in (26) of Theorem 6.19.
[2]This is the form required in (27) of Theorem 6.19.

6.5.2. Application of the Fixpoint Theorem. This phase depends on eliminating the second-order quantification over X, by applying Theorem 6.19, and then trying to unskolemize the function variables possibly introduced. Unskolemization employs the Skolem equivalence (4) (page 31).

6.5.3. An Example. To illustrate the DLS* consider the following example.

EXAMPLE 6.23. Consider the formula of Example 6.6, where DLS has failed,

$$(30) \qquad \exists X \{\forall x \forall y [R(x,y) \lor X(x) \lor \neg X(y)] \land \forall x \forall y [S(x,y) \lor X(x) \lor X(y)]\}.$$

Moving the quantifier $\forall x$ inside and restoring implication in formula (30) one obtains its equivalent

$$(31) \qquad \exists X \{\forall y [X(y) \rightarrow \forall x [R(x,y) \lor X(x)]] \land \forall x \forall y [S(x,y) \lor X(x) \lor X(y)]\}$$

Formula (31) is in the form (26) of Theorem 6.19, so is equivalent to

$$\forall x \forall y \{ S(x,y) \lor \\ [\text{GFP}\, X(y).\forall x [R(x,y) \lor X(x)]](x) \lor \\ [\text{GFP}\, X(y).\forall x [R(x,y) \lor X(x)]]\},$$

where the second-order quantifier $\exists X$ of (31) is eliminated.   ◁

CHAPTER 7

Direct Methods for Chosen Background Theories

In this chapter we show some case studies showing how the general methods considered previously can be adapted to particular background theories as well as higher-order contexts. Integrating methods of second-order quantifier elimination with background theories is important for applications. For example, it is well known that particular properties of accessibility relations allow one to obtain first-order correspondences for more modal axioms. Another example here is that certain relations defined on a given finite domain add expressiveness to the fixpoint calculus. Therefore, the fixpoint calculus augmented in that way can allow for more reductions.

7.1. Elementary Set Theory Ω

Elementary set theory Ω has been considered in the context of modal logics by D'Agostino, Montanari and Policriti in [**47**]. A proof system for this theory can be found in Omodeo, Orłowska and Policriti [**163**]. The current section is based on the work of Orłowska and Szałas [**164**].

7.1.1. Syntax. The language is built over the following symbols:

- A denumerable set VAR of individual variables;
- Binary function symbols $\overset{\circ}{\cup}$, $\overset{\circ}{-}$, representing union and difference;
- The binary function symbol $\mathcal{P}()$, representing the powerset;
- Binary predicates $\overset{\circ}{\in}$ and $\overset{\circ}{\subseteq}$, used in the infix notation, representing membership and inclusion;
- Propositional connectives $\neg, \vee, \wedge, \rightarrow, \equiv$;
- Quantifiers $\forall, \exists$.

The *set of terms*, TERMS, is defined as the least set satisfying the following

- VAR $\subseteq$ TERMS;
- If $t, t' \in$ TERMS, then $t \overset{\circ}{\cup} t', t \overset{\circ}{-} t', \mathcal{P}(t) \in$ TERMS.

The *set of formulas*, FORMS, is defined as the least set satisfying the conditions:

- If $t, t' \in$ TERMS, then $t \mathbin{\mathring{\in}} t', t \mathbin{\mathring{\subseteq}} t' \in$ FORMS (*atomic formulas*);
- FORMS is closed under applications of propositional connectives and quantifiers.

7.1.2. Semantics. By a *model of* elementary set theory Ω we mean any model $S = \langle U, \mathbin{\mathring{\cup}}, \mathbin{\mathring{-}}, \mathcal{P}, \mathbin{\mathring{\in}}, \mathbin{\mathring{\subseteq}} \rangle$ of the axioms

$$
(32) \quad
\begin{aligned}
& x \mathbin{\mathring{\in}} y \mathbin{\mathring{\cup}} z \equiv x \mathbin{\mathring{\in}} y \vee x \mathbin{\mathring{\in}} z \\
& x \mathbin{\mathring{\in}} y \mathbin{\mathring{-}} z \equiv x \mathbin{\mathring{\in}} y \wedge x \mathbin{\mathring{\notin}} z \\
& x \mathbin{\mathring{\subseteq}} y \equiv \forall z [z \mathbin{\mathring{\in}} x \to z \mathbin{\mathring{\in}} y] \\
& x \mathbin{\mathring{\in}} \mathcal{P}(y) \equiv x \mathbin{\mathring{\subseteq}} y.
\end{aligned}
$$

The semantics of Ω w.r.t. a model $S = \langle U, \mathbin{\mathring{\cup}}, \mathbin{\mathring{-}}, \mathcal{P}, \mathbin{\mathring{\in}}, \mathbin{\mathring{\subseteq}} \rangle$ is defined in the standard way, by extending valuations VAR $\longrightarrow U$ in order to provide values for terms and truth values for formulas.

Given a model of Ω, $S = \langle U, \mathbin{\mathring{\cup}}, \mathbin{\mathring{-}}, \mathcal{P}, \mathbin{\mathring{\in}}, \mathbin{\mathring{\subseteq}} \rangle$, a valuation $v : $ VAR $\longrightarrow U$ and a formula $\alpha \in$ FORMS, we write $S, v \models \alpha$ to mean that α is satisfied in S under valuation v and $S \models \alpha$ to mean that α is valid in S, i.e., for any valuation v, $S, v \models \alpha$.

We say that model $S \langle U, \mathbin{\mathring{\cup}}, \mathbin{\mathring{-}}, \mathcal{P}, \mathbin{\mathring{\in}}, \mathbin{\mathring{\subseteq}} \rangle$ is *partially ordered* if $\langle U, \mathbin{\mathring{\subseteq}} \rangle$ is a partial order. If $\langle U, \mathbin{\mathring{\subseteq}} \rangle$ is a complete partial order, we also say that S is a *complete partial order*. In such a case the least and the greatest element of U w.r.t. $\mathbin{\mathring{\subseteq}}$ exist and are denoted by $\bot$ and $\top$, respectively, and we often expand S by explicitly listing elements $\bot$ and $\top$.

A term $F(\bar{x}, z) \in$ TERMS is *up-monotone* (respectively, *down-monotone*) w.r.t. z in model S iff for any valuation v in S it is the case that if $v(z') \mathbin{\mathring{\subseteq}} v(z'')$ then $S, v \models F(\bar{x}, z') \mathbin{\mathring{\subseteq}} F(\bar{x}, z'')$ (respectively, $S, v \models F(\bar{x}, z'') \mathbin{\mathring{\subseteq}} F(\bar{x}, z')$).

Analogously, a formula $\alpha(\bar{x}, z) \in$ FORMS is *up-monotone* (respectively, *down-monotone*) w.r.t. z in model S iff for any valuation v in S it is the case that if $v(z') \mathbin{\mathring{\subseteq}} v(z'')$ then $S, v \models \alpha(\bar{x}, z') \to \alpha(\bar{x}, z'')$ (respectively, $S, v \models \alpha(\bar{x}, z'') \to \alpha(\bar{x}, z')$).

7.1.3. Ackermann-Like Lemma for Ω. Let us first formulate Ackermann-like lemma. This lemma, under the additional assumption that the underlying model is a complete partial order, is subsumed by Lemma 7.4, but it is frequently used in applications, so we formulate it separately.

LEMMA 7.1. [Ackermann-like Lemma] Let $S = \langle U, \mathbin{\mathring{\cup}}, \mathbin{\mathring{-}}, \mathcal{P}, \mathbin{\mathring{\in}}, \mathbin{\mathring{\subseteq}} \rangle$ be a partially ordered model of Ω and let $F(\bar{z}) \in$ TERMS be a term not containing y.

If $\alpha(\bar{x}, y) \in$ FORMS is a formula up-monotone w.r.t. y in S, then

$$
(33) \quad S \models \exists y \big[y \mathbin{\mathring{\subseteq}} F(\bar{z}) \wedge \alpha(\bar{x}, y) \big] \equiv \alpha(\bar{x}, y)^{y}_{F(\bar{z})}.
$$

If $\alpha'(y) \in$ FORMS is a formula down-monotone w.r.t. y in $\mathcal{S}$, then

(34) $\qquad \mathcal{S} \models \exists y [F(\bar{z}) \overset{\circ}{\subseteq} y \wedge \alpha'(y)] \equiv \alpha'(y)^y_{F(\bar{z})}$.

PROOF. We prove (33). The proof of (34) is similar.

($\rightarrow$) Let $\mathcal{S}$ be a model of Ω and let v be a valuation in $\mathcal{S}$ such that

$$\mathcal{S}, v \models \exists y [y \overset{\circ}{\subseteq} F(\bar{z}) \wedge \alpha(\bar{x}, y)].$$

Let v' be a valuation extending v by assigning a domain value to y such that

$$\mathcal{S}, v' \models y \overset{\circ}{\subseteq} F(\bar{z}) \text{ and } \mathcal{S}, v' \models \alpha(\bar{x}, y).$$

By up-monotonicity of α we have that also $\mathcal{S}, v' \models \alpha(\bar{x}, y) \rightarrow \alpha(\bar{x}, y)^y_{F(\bar{z})}$. Therefore $\mathcal{S}, v' \models \alpha(\bar{x}, y)^y_{F(\bar{z})}$. Observe that $\alpha(\bar{x}, y)^y_{F(\bar{z})}$ does not contain free occurrences of y. Thus we conclude that $\mathcal{S}, v \models \alpha(\bar{x}, y)^y_{F(\bar{z})}$.

($\leftarrow$) Let v be a valuation in $\mathcal{S}$ such that $\mathcal{S}, v \models \alpha(\bar{x}, y)^y_{F(\bar{z})}$. Consider a valuation v' different from v at most on y and such that $v'(y) \overset{\text{def}}{=} F(v(\bar{z}))$. Then we have $\mathcal{S}, v' \models y \overset{\circ}{\subseteq} F(\bar{z})$ and $\mathcal{S}, v' \models \alpha(\bar{x}, y)$. Therefore we also have that $\mathcal{S}, v \models \exists y [y \overset{\circ}{\subseteq} F(\bar{z}) \wedge \alpha(\bar{x}, y)]$. $\qquad \triangleleft$

EXAMPLE 7.2. This example, considered in [164], automatizes a reasoning step in searching for correspondences, as done in [163]. Here we eliminate quantifier $\forall y$ from

(35) $\qquad \forall y [u \overset{\circ}{\in} y \vee z \overset{\circ}{\nsubseteq} y]$.

The elimination starts with the observation that formula (35) is equivalent to $\neg \exists y [z \overset{\circ}{\subseteq} y \wedge u \overset{\circ}{\notin} y]$. It can be easily seen that formula $u \overset{\circ}{\notin} y$ is down-monotone w.r.t. y. Thus after applying (34) with $F(z) \overset{\text{def}}{=} z$ and $\alpha(y) \overset{\text{def}}{=} u \overset{\circ}{\notin} y$ we obtain $\neg u \overset{\circ}{\notin} z$. Thus formula (35) is equivalent to $u \overset{\circ}{\in} z$. $\qquad \triangleleft$

7.1.4. Fixpoints in Ω and the Fixpoint Lemma.

The following definition of fixpoints in Ω is, as usual, based on the Knaster and Tarski fixpoint theorem [126, 206].

DEFINITION 7.3. Let $F(\bar{x}, z)$ be a term up-monotone w.r.t. z and let us fix a model of Ω, which is a complete partial order, $\mathcal{S} = \langle U, \overset{\circ}{\cup}, \overset{\circ}{-}, \mathcal{P}, \overset{\circ}{\in}, \overset{\circ}{\subseteq}, \bot, \top \rangle$. Then the least and the greatest (w.r.t. $\overset{\circ}{\subseteq}$) fixpoints of F exist and are denoted by $[\text{LFP } z.F(\bar{x}, z)]$ and $[\text{GFP } z.F(\bar{x}, z)]$, respectively.

The least ordinal number α such that, for any up-monotone F, we have that $\mathcal{S} \models F^\alpha(\bar{x}, \bot) = F^{\alpha+1}(\bar{x}, \bot)$, is called the *closure ordinal* for $\mathcal{S}$. $\qquad \triangleleft$

LEMMA 7.4. [Fixpoint Lemma] Let $\mathcal{S} = \langle U, \overset{\circ}{\cup}, \overset{\circ}{-}, \mathcal{P}, \overset{\circ}{\in}, \overset{\circ}{\subseteq}, \bot, \top \rangle$ be a model of Ω which is a complete partial order. Let $F(\bar{x}, y) \in$ TERMS be a term up-monotone w.r.t. y in $\mathcal{S}$.

If $\alpha(\bar{z}, y) \in$ FORMS is a formula up-monotone w.r.t. y in $\mathcal{S}$, then

(36) $\qquad \mathcal{S} \models \exists y \left[y \overset{\circ}{\subseteq} F(\bar{x}, y) \wedge \alpha(\bar{z}, y) \right] \equiv \alpha(\bar{z}, y)^{y}_{[\text{GFP } y. F(\bar{x}, y)]}.$

If $\alpha'(y) \in$ FORMS is a formula down-monotone w.r.t. y in $\mathcal{S}$, then

(37) $\qquad \mathcal{S} \models \exists y \left[F(\bar{x}, y) \overset{\circ}{\subseteq} y \wedge \alpha'(y) \right] \equiv \alpha'(y)^{y}_{[\text{LFP } y. F(\bar{x}, y)]}.$

PROOF. We prove (36). The proof of (37) is similar.

($\rightarrow$) Assume $\mathcal{S}$ and v are such that $\mathcal{S}, v \models \exists y \left[y \overset{\circ}{\subseteq} F(\bar{x}, y) \wedge \alpha(\bar{z}, y) \right]$. Since $F(\bar{x}, y)$ is up-monotone w.r.t. y and $\mathcal{S}$ is a complete partial order, the greatest fixpoint of F, $[\text{GFP } y. F(\bar{x}, y)]$, exists and for any v' such that $\mathcal{S}, v' \models y \overset{\circ}{\subseteq} F(\bar{x}, y)$ we have that[1] $\mathcal{S}, v' \models y \overset{\circ}{\subseteq} [\text{GFP } y. F(\bar{x}, y)]$. By assumption, $\alpha(\bar{z}, y)$ holds, for some y. Thus, by up-monotonicity of α we conclude that $\mathcal{S}, v \models \alpha(\bar{z}, y)^{y}_{[\text{GFP } y. F(\bar{x}, y)]}$ holds.

($\leftarrow$) Assume $\mathcal{S}$ and v are such that $\mathcal{S}, v \models \alpha(\bar{z}, y)^{y}_{[\text{GFP } y. F(\bar{x}, y)]}$ holds. Then v' which differs from v at most on y and such that $v'(y) \overset{\text{def}}{=} [\text{GFP } y. F(v(\bar{x}), y)]$ satisfies $\mathcal{S}, v' \models y \overset{\circ}{\subseteq} F(\bar{x}, y)$ and $\mathcal{S}, v' \models \alpha(\bar{z}, y)$. Therefore we also have that $\mathcal{S}, v \models \exists y \left[y \overset{\circ}{\subseteq} F(\bar{x}, y) \wedge \alpha(\bar{z}, y) \right]$. ◁

The following example illustrates the method.

EXAMPLE 7.5. The following formula, considered in [**164**], has been motivated by [**163**] where it has been used to find a correspondence for the modal Löb axiom.

(38) $\qquad \forall y \left[v_0 \overset{\circ}{\notin} f \vee v_0 \overset{\circ}{\not\subseteq} (\overline{\mathcal{P}}(y) \overset{\cup}{\cup} y) \vee \bigvee_{i} [v_{i+1} \overset{\circ}{\notin} v_i \vee v_{i+1} \in y] \right].$

We eliminate $\forall y$ from (38). Formula (38) is equivalent to

$$\neg \exists y \left[v_0 \overset{\circ}{\in} f \wedge v_0 \overset{\circ}{\subseteq} (\overline{\mathcal{P}}(y) \overset{\cup}{\cup} y) \wedge \bigwedge_{i} [v_{i+1} \overset{\circ}{\in} v_i \wedge v_{i+1} \overset{\circ}{\notin} y] \right],$$

i.e., to

(39) $\qquad \neg \left\{ v_0 \overset{\circ}{\in} f \wedge \exists y \left[(v_0 \overset{\circ}{\cap} \mathcal{P}(y)) \overset{\circ}{\subseteq} y \wedge \bigwedge_{i} [v_{i+1} \overset{\circ}{\in} v_i \wedge v_{i+1} \overset{\circ}{\notin} y] \right] \right\},$

where $v_0 \overset{\circ}{\cap} \mathcal{P}(y)$ is an abbreviation for $f \overset{\circ}{-} ((f \overset{\circ}{-} v_0) \overset{\cup}{\cup} \overline{\mathcal{P}}(y))$.

Observe that $v_0 \overset{\circ}{\cap} \mathcal{P}(y)$ is up-monotone w.r.t. y and $\bigwedge_{i} [v_{i+1} \overset{\circ}{\in} v_i \wedge v_{i+1} \overset{\circ}{\notin} y]$ is down-monotone w.r.t. y. Thus we can apply the second part of Lemma 7.4 and obtain the following formula equivalent to (39),

(40) $\qquad \neg \left\{ v_0 \overset{\circ}{\in} f \wedge \bigwedge_{i} [v_{i+1} \overset{\circ}{\in} v_i \wedge v_{i+1} \overset{\circ}{\notin} [\text{LFP } y. (v_0 \overset{\circ}{\cap} \mathcal{P}(y))]] \right\}.$

---

[1]A standard transfinite induction argument applies here.

By unfolding the least fixpoint operator we easily notice that

$$[\textsc{Lfp}\, y.(v_0 \,\hat{\in}\, \mathcal{P}(y))] \equiv \bot.$$

Thus (40) reduces to $\neg\{v_0 \,\hat{\in}\, f \wedge \bigwedge_i [v_{i+1} \,\hat{\in}\, v_i \wedge v_{i+1} \,\hat{\not\in}\, \bot], \}$ i.e., to

$$\neg\{v_0 \,\hat{\in}\, f \wedge \bigwedge_i [v_{i+1} \,\hat{\in}\, v_i]\}.$$

Moving negation inside we obtain the formula $v_0 \,\hat{\not\in}\, f \vee \bigvee_i [v_{i+1} \,\hat{\not\in}\, v_i]$, equivalent to (38). $\lhd$

7.2. Quantifier Elimination in Higher-Order Contexts

In this section we show extensions to Ackermann's lemma (Lemma 6.1) and the fixpoint theorem (Theorem 6.19) to higher-order contexts, as proposed by Gabbay and Szałas [85].

Let us first introduce the notion of higher-order relations, where $\mathcal{P}^1(U) \overset{\text{def}}{=} U$ and $\mathcal{P}^{n+1}(U) \overset{\text{def}}{=} \mathcal{P}(\mathcal{P}^n(U))$.

DEFINITION 7.6. For $k \in \omega$ and $1 \leq n \in \omega$, k-argument *relations of order n* are defined to be subsets of $U_1 \times \ldots \times U_k$, where, for $1 \leq i \leq k$, $U_i = \mathcal{P}^{a_i}(U)$, for some $1 \leq a_i \leq n$. *Higher order relations over a set U* are relations of order $n \geq 2$.

Higher-order relation symbols denote higher-order relations. *Higher-order formulas* are defined by extending the definition of the classical second-order logic by assuming that higher-order relation symbols can occur wherever the classical first-order relation symbols can.

We shall say that a relation S is *compatible* with relation X iff S and X have the same arities and respective arguments are of the same order. $\lhd$

DEFINITION 7.7. By a *model* we understand a pair $\mathcal{M} \overset{\text{def}}{=} \langle \mathcal{I}, \mathcal{V} \rangle$, where $\mathcal{I}$ is the classical (first-order) relational structure and $\mathcal{V}$ is an assignment of domain elements to individual variables, relations to first-order variables and higher-order relations to compatible higher-order relation symbols. By $\alpha^{\mathcal{M}}$ we understand a higher-order relation of $\mathcal{M}$ which is the interpretation of α in $\mathcal{M}$.

Let $\mathcal{M}$ be a model. We shall say that a formula $\alpha(X)$ is *up-monotone* (respectively *down-monotone*) w.r.t. *a relation symbol X* in $\mathcal{M}$ iff for all relations R, S of $\mathcal{M}$ compatible with X, if $R \subseteq S$ then $\alpha^{\mathcal{M}}(R) \subseteq \alpha^{\mathcal{M}}(S)$ (respectively, $\alpha^{\mathcal{M}}(S) \subseteq \alpha^{\mathcal{M}}(R)$). $\lhd$

The following lemma, provided in [85] and extending Lemma 6.1 allows us to deal with relations of arbitrary order.

LEMMA 7.8. Let X be a predicate variable and $\alpha(\bar{x}, \bar{z})$, $\beta(X)$ be formulas with relations of arbitrary order, where the number of distinct variables in $\bar{x}$ is equal to the arity of X. Let α contain no occurrences of X at all.

If $\beta(X)$ is up-monotone w.r.t. X then

(41) $\exists X\{\forall \bar{x}[X(\bar{x}) \to \alpha(\bar{x}, \bar{z})] \wedge \beta(X)\} \equiv \beta(X)_{\alpha(\bar{x}, \bar{z})}^{X(\bar{x})}.$

If $\beta(X)$ is down-monotone w.r.t. X then

(42) $\exists X\{\forall \bar{x}[\alpha(\bar{x}, \bar{z}) \to X(\bar{x})] \wedge \beta(X)\} \equiv \beta(X)_{\alpha(\bar{x}, \bar{z})}^{X(\bar{x})}.$ ◁

The following theorem, provided in [85], can be proved by adapting the proof of Theorem 6.19.

THEOREM 7.9. Let X be a predicate variable and $\alpha(X, \bar{x}, \bar{z})$, $\beta(X)$ be formulas with relations of arbitrary order, where the number of distinct variables in $\bar{x}$ is equal to the arity of X. Let α be up-monotone w.r.t. X.

If $\beta(X)$ is up-monotone w.r.t. X then

(43) $\exists X\{\forall \bar{x}[X(\bar{x}) \to \alpha(X, \bar{x}, \bar{z})] \wedge \beta(X)\} \equiv \beta(X)_{[\text{GFP}\, X(\bar{x}).\alpha(X,\bar{x},\bar{z})](\bar{x})}^{X(\bar{x})}.$

If $\beta(X)$ is down-monotone w.r.t. X then

(44) $\exists X\{\forall \bar{x}[\alpha(X, \bar{x}, \bar{z}) \to X(\bar{x})] \wedge \beta(X)\} \equiv \beta(X)_{[\text{LFP}\, X(\bar{x}).\alpha(X,\bar{x},\bar{z})](\bar{x})}^{X(\bar{x})}.$

◁

REMARK 7.10. Observe that Theorem 7.9 subsumes Lemma 7.8. Namely if the formula $\alpha(X, \bar{x}, \bar{z})$ in (43) and (44) does, in fact, not contain X then

$$[\text{GFP}\, X(\bar{x}).\alpha(X, \bar{x}, \bar{z})] \equiv [\text{LFP}\, X(\bar{x}).\alpha(X, \bar{x}, \bar{z})] \equiv \alpha(X, \bar{x}, \bar{z})$$

and Theorem 7.9 reduces to Lemma 7.8. We consider Lemma 7.8 separately, as it simplifies the results.   ◁

For applications of Lemma 7.8 and Theorem 7.9, see [85] and Chapter 19.

7.3. Quantifier Elimination over Successor Structures

A theorem of Leivant [135] states that over successor structures every Σ_1^1 formula reduces to a Σ_1^1 formula of the form $\exists \bar{X} \forall \bar{x}[\alpha(\bar{x}, \bar{X})]$. In the current section we recall a simpler proof of this theorem, given by Eiter, Gottlob and Gurevich in [68], and show applications of the technique to elimination of second-order quantifiers over successor structures.

DEFINITION 7.11. By a *successor structure* we mean a finite relational structure M over signature containing at least a binary relation symbol S and one argument relation symbols F, L, such that there is a linear order $<$ on the universe of M such that S is the successor relation of $<$, $F(x)$ is satisfied by and only by the first (w.r.t. $<$) element and $L(x)$ is satisfied by and only by the last element. The expanded structure $\langle M, < \rangle$ is called an *ordered successor structure*. ◁

Observe that the properties required in Definition 7.11, except for finiteness, are defined by the following axioms:

(45) $\forall x \forall y \forall z [(x < y \wedge y < z) \to x < z]$

(46) $\forall x [\neg(x < x)]$

(47) $\forall x \forall y [x \approx y \vee x < y \vee y < x]$

(48) $\exists x [F(x)] \wedge \forall x [F(x) \to \forall y [\neg y < x]]$

(49) $\exists x [L(x)] \wedge \forall x [L(x) \to \forall y [\neg x < y]]$

(50) $\forall x \forall y [S(x, y) \to (x < y \wedge \neg \exists z [x < z \wedge z < y])]$

(51) $\forall x [\neg L(x) \to \exists y [S(x, y)]]$.

Formulas (45)–(48) state that $<$ is a linear order, (48) states that F defines the first element, (49) states that L defines the last element and formulas (50)–(51) state that S is the successor w.r.t. $<$.

Finiteness can be expressed by existence of $<, S, F, L$ satisfying formulas (45)-(50) plus second-order induction (as, e.g., expressed by formula (279) given on page 276).

The following theorem is due to Leivant [**135**].

THEOREM 7.12. Over successor structures, every Σ_1^1 formula (possibly with free predicate or individual variables) reduces to a Σ_1^1 formula of the form $\exists \bar{X} \forall \bar{x} [\alpha]$, where α is quantifier-free.

PROOF. We follow a simplified proof given in [**68**].

Without loss of generality, the given formula has the form $\exists \bar{Y} \forall \bar{x} \exists \bar{y} [\beta(\bar{x}, \bar{y})]$, where β is quantifier-free. We prove that the formula

(52) $\forall \bar{x} \exists \bar{y} [\beta(\bar{x}, \bar{y})]$

is equivalent to

(53) $\exists G \forall \bar{x} \forall \bar{y} \forall \bar{y}' [\gamma]$,

where G is a $(2n)$-argument relation symbol and γ is quantifier-free. The idea is that (53) asserts that $G(\bar{x}, \bar{y})$ holds if and only if $\beta(\bar{x}, \bar{z})$ holds for some $\bar{z} \leq \bar{y}$ and that $G(\bar{x}, \bar{y})$ holds for the last $\bar{y}$.

The order corresponding to S, F, L gives rise to the lexicographical order $<^n$ on n-tuples of elements and to quantifier-free formulas S^n, F^n, L^n describing the successor relation on n-tuples, the first n-tuple and the last n-tuple, respectively.

The desired γ is the conjunction of the following formulas:

$$(54) \qquad F(\bar{y}) \rightarrow [G(\bar{x}, \bar{y}) \equiv \beta(\bar{x}, \bar{y})]$$

$$(55) \qquad S(\bar{y}, \bar{y}') \rightarrow [G(\bar{x}, \bar{y}') \equiv (G(\bar{x}, \bar{y}) \vee \beta(\bar{x}, \bar{y}'))]$$

$$(56) \qquad L(\bar{y}) \rightarrow G(\bar{x}, \bar{y}).$$

We check that formula (52) is equivalent to (53). Suppose that for some successor structure M, we have $M \models$ (52). Let $G(\bar{x}, \bar{y}) \overset{\text{def}}{\equiv} \bar{y} \geq^n \min\{\bar{z} \mid \beta(\bar{x}, \bar{z})\}$. Then $M, G \models \forall\bar{x}\forall\bar{y}\forall\bar{y}'[\gamma]$. Hence, $M \models$ (53).

Conversely, suppose that $M \models$ (53) and G is a witness to that fact. Let $\bar{e}$ be the last tuple. By (56), $G(\bar{x}, \bar{e})$ holds for all $\bar{x}$. Let $m(\bar{x}) \overset{\text{def}}{=} \min\{\bar{z} \mid G(\bar{x}, \bar{z})\}$. If $F(m(\bar{x}))$ holds then, by (54), $M \models \beta(\bar{x}, m(\bar{x}))$. Otherwise we use (55) to establish that $M \models \beta(\bar{x}, m(\bar{x}))$. Thus $M \models$ (52).   ◁

The normal form for Σ_1^1 formulas provided in Theorem 7.12 can be helpful in transforming formulas into one of the forms required in the lemma of Ackermann (Lemma 6.1) or the fixpoint theorem (Theorem 6.19).

REMARK 7.13. In order to simplify the elimination process we can observe that in the proof of Theorem 7.12 equivalences in formulas (54) and (55) can be replaced by implications:

$$(57) \qquad F(\bar{y}) \rightarrow [G(\bar{x}, \bar{y}) \rightarrow \beta(\bar{x}, \bar{y})]$$

$$(58) \qquad S(\bar{y}, \bar{y}') \rightarrow [G(\bar{x}, \bar{y}') \rightarrow (G(\bar{x}, \bar{y}) \vee \beta(\bar{x}, \bar{y}'))].$$

Thus in calculations we can use the conjunction (57) $\wedge$ (58) $\wedge$ (56) rather than the conjunction (54) $\wedge$ (55) $\wedge$ (56).   ◁

EXAMPLE 7.14. Consider the formula

$$(59) \qquad \exists X \forall x \exists y [(S(x, y) \vee X(x)) \wedge \neg X(y)].$$

What makes the elimination of $\exists X$ problematic is the context of quantifiers $\forall x \exists y$ in which X occurs. Assuming that we work over successor structures, we are first able to replace $\exists y$ by a suitable existential second-order quantifier, using the technique used in the proof of Theorem 7.12 (simplified in Remark 7.13). As a result we obtain the following formula equivalent to (59),

$$\exists X \exists G \forall x \forall y \forall y' \big[$$
$$F(y) \rightarrow [G(x, y) \rightarrow \beta(x, y)] \wedge$$
$$S(y, y') \rightarrow [G(x, y') \rightarrow (G(x, y) \vee \beta(x, y'))] \wedge$$
$$L(y) \rightarrow G(x, y)\big],$$

where $\beta(x,y) \overset{\text{def}}{\equiv} (S(x,y) \vee X(x)) \wedge \neg X(y)$. Replacing $\beta(x,y)$ by its equivalent we obtain that (59) is equivalent to

(60)
$$\exists X \exists G \forall x \forall y \forall y' \big[$$
$$F(y) \to \big[G(x,y) \to \big((S(x,y) \vee X(x)) \wedge \neg X(y)\big)\big] \wedge$$
$$S(y,y') \to$$
$$\big[G(x,y') \to \big(G(x,y) \vee \big((S(x,y') \vee X(x)) \wedge \neg X(y')\big)\big)\big] \wedge$$
$$L(y) \to G(x,y)\big].$$

After simple calculations we obtain that formula (60) is equivalent to

(61)
$$\exists G \exists X$$
$$\forall x \forall y \big[\big[F(y) \wedge G(x,y)\big] \to \big[(S(x,y) \vee X(x))\big]\big] \wedge$$
$$\forall y \big[X(y) \to \forall x \big[\neg F(y) \vee \neg G(x,y)\big]\big] \wedge$$
$$\forall x \forall y \forall y' \big[\big(S(y,y') \wedge G(x,y')\big) \to \big(G(x,y) \vee S(x,y') \vee X(x)\big)\big] \wedge$$
$$\forall y' \big[X(y') \to \forall x \forall y \big[\neg S(y,y') \vee \neg G(x,y') \vee \neg G(x,y)\big]\big] \wedge$$
$$\forall x \forall y \big[L(y) \to G(x,y)\big],$$

i.e., to

(62)
$$\exists G \exists X$$
$$\forall z \big[X(z) \to$$
$$\big[\forall u \big[\neg F(z) \vee \neg G(u,z)\big] \wedge$$
$$\forall u \forall w \big[\neg S(w,z) \vee \neg G(u,z) \vee \neg G(u,w)\big]\big] \wedge$$
$$\forall x \forall y \big[\big[F(y) \wedge G(x,y)\big] \to \big[(S(x,y) \vee X(x))\big]\big] \wedge$$
$$\forall x \forall y \forall y' \big[\big(S(y,y') \wedge G(x,y')\big) \to \big(G(x,y) \vee S(x,y') \vee X(x)\big)\big] \wedge$$
$$\forall x \forall y \big[L(y) \to G(x,y)\big].$$

An application of Lemma 6.1 to (62) results in

(63)
$$\exists G$$
$$\forall x \forall y \big[\big[F(y) \wedge G(x,y)\big] \to \big[S(x,y) \vee \big[\forall u \big[\neg F(x) \vee \neg G(u,x)\big] \wedge$$
$$\forall u \forall w \big[\neg S(w,x) \vee \neg G(u,x) \vee \neg G(u,w)\big]\big]\big]\big] \wedge$$
$$\forall x \forall y \forall y' \big[\big(S(y,y') \wedge G(x,y')\big) \to$$
$$\big[G(x,y) \vee S(x,y') \vee \big[\forall u \big[\neg F(x) \vee \neg G(u,x)\big] \wedge$$
$$\forall u \forall w \big[\neg S(w,x) \vee \neg G(u,x) \vee \neg G(u,w)\big]\big]\big]\big] \wedge$$
$$\forall x \forall y \big[L(y) \to G(x,y)\big].$$

Formula (63) is equivalent to

(64)
$$\exists G$$
$$\forall x \forall y \forall y' \big[\big(S(y,y') \wedge G(x,y') \wedge \neg S(x,y') \wedge \big[\exists u \big[F(x) \wedge G(u,x)\big] \vee$$
$$\exists u \exists w \big[S(w,x) \wedge G(u,x) \wedge G(u,w)\big]\big]\big) \to G(x,y)\big] \wedge$$
$$\forall x \forall y \big[\big[F(y) \wedge G(x,y)\big] \to \big[S(x,y) \vee \big[\forall u \big[\neg F(x) \vee \neg G(u,x)\big] \wedge$$
$$\forall u \forall w \big[\neg S(w,x) \vee \neg G(u,x) \vee \neg G(u,w)\big]\big]\big]\big] \wedge$$
$$\forall x \forall y \big[L(y) \to G(x,y)\big],$$

i.e., to

$$\exists G$$
$$\forall x \forall y \big\{ \big[L(y) \vee \big(\exists y' \big[S(y,y') \wedge G(x,y') \wedge \neg S(x,y') \big] \wedge$$
$$\big[\exists u \big[F(x) \wedge G(u,x) \big] \vee$$

(65)

$$\exists u \exists w \big[S(w,x) \wedge G(u,x) \wedge G(u,w) \big] \big] \big) \big] \to G(x,y) \big\} \wedge$$
$$\forall x \forall y \big[\big[F(y) \wedge G(x,y) \big] \to \big[S(x,y) \vee \big[\forall u \big[\neg F(x) \vee \neg G(u,x) \big] \wedge$$
$$\forall u \forall w \big[\neg S(w,x) \vee \neg G(u,x) \vee \neg G(u,w) \big] \big] \big] \big].$$

Now Theorem 6.19 can be applied and results in

$$\forall x \forall y \big[\big[F(y) \wedge \Phi(x,y) \big] \to \big[S(x,y) \vee \big[\forall u \big[\neg F(x) \vee \neg \Phi(u,x) \big] \wedge$$
$$\forall u \forall w \big[\neg S(w,x) \vee \neg \Phi(u,x) \vee \neg \Phi(u,w) \big] \big] \big],$$

where

$$\Phi(x,y) \stackrel{\text{def}}{\equiv} [\text{LFP } G(x,y).$$
$$L(y) \vee \big(\exists y' \big[S(y,y') \wedge G(x,y') \wedge \neg S(x,y') \big] \wedge$$
$$\big[\exists u \big[F(x) \wedge G(u,x) \big] \vee$$
$$\exists u \exists w \big[S(w,x) \wedge G(u,x) \wedge G(u,w) \big] \big] \big)]$$ ◁

CHAPTER 8

Second-Order Quantifier Elimination in Description Logics

Description logics refer to a family of formalisms concentrated around concepts, roles and individuals. They are syntactic variants of decidable fragments of classical first-order logic. There is a rich literature on description logics. For good survey papers consult [6], and in particular papers [8, 22, 150] as well as the bibliographies provided there. These logics are one of the most frequently used knowledge representation formalisms and provides a logical basis to a variety of well known paradigms, including frame-based systems, semantic networks and KL-ONE. The main goal of description logics is to specify concepts and concept hierarchies and to reason mainly about properties reducing to subsumption. Knowledge representation systems are often assumed to be equipped with a more advanced reasoning machinery, usually employing non-monotonic or common-sense forms of reasoning. There have been attempts to integrate description logics with such forms of reasoning (see, e.g. Baader and Hollunder [7] or the most recent paper by Bonatti, Lutz and Wolter [21]), however they do not directly employ second-order formalisms. On the other hand, common-sense and non-monotonic reasoning can, in many cases, be directly formalized within classical second-order logic (see, e.g., [139, 140, 56, 59] as well as Chapter 16). Therefore the way to integrate description logics with common-sense reasoning we follow here, depends on extending description logics by second-order quantifiers allowing one to quantify over concepts. The version of second-order description logic we deal with has been introduced by Szałas in [203]. This chapter is mainly based on [203].

8.1. Description Logics

8.1.1. Basic Description Logics. Assume that sets of atomic concepts, C, and of atomic roles, $\mathcal{R}$, are given. More complex concepts and roles are built by the use of constructors given in Table 20, where concepts are represented by unary predicates and roles are represented by binary predicates. We further often

97

exploit the fact that description logics correspond to fragments of classical first-order logics. In particular, rather than formal semantics we show translation of the considered constructs into classical first-order logic.

TABLE 20. Constructors used in description logics.

Constructor name	Syntax	Translation (Tr)
concept name	A	A(x)
top		TRUE
bottom	$\perp$	FALSE
complement ($\mathcal{C}$)	$\neg E$	$\neg Tr(E, x)$
conjunction	$E \sqcap F$	$Tr(E, x) \wedge Tr(F, x)$
union ($\mathcal{U}$)	$E \sqcup F$	$Tr(E, x) \vee Tr(F, x)$
universal quantification	$\forall R.E$	$\forall y[R(x, y) \rightarrow Tr(E, y)]$
existential quantification ($\mathcal{E}$)	$\exists R.E$	$\exists y[R(x, y) \wedge Tr(E, y)]$

Various description languages are distinguished by the constructors that allow us to specify complex concepts and roles. The basic language $\mathcal{AL}$, has been introduced by Schmidt-Schauss and Smolka [187]. In $\mathcal{AL}$ one can use atomic concepts, top, bottom, negation applied to atomic concepts, intersection, universal quantification and existential quantification of the form $\exists R.\top$. The other languages of this family are extensions of $\mathcal{AL}$. They are denoted by indicating particular constructs that are allowed. For example $\mathcal{ALUEC}$ allows us to use union (indicated by $\mathcal{U}$), full existential quantification (indicated by $\mathcal{E}$) and unrestricted complement (indicated by $\mathcal{C}$), while in $\mathcal{ALUC}$ full existential quantification is excluded. In the rest of this chapter we deal with $\mathcal{ALUEC}$.

EXAMPLE 8.1. The expression $Person \sqcap Male$ describes the concept of a person who is a male, while the expression $Female \sqcap \exists hasChild.Person$ describes persons being mothers.   ◁

Expressions obtained by the use of constructs given in Table 20 are called the *concept expressions*. In addition, we allow *terminological axioms* of the form $E \sqsubseteq F$ (called *subsumptions*). The meaning of $E \sqsubseteq F$ is that the concept C is included (set-theoretically) in concept D. More precisely, we define translation Tr' from terminological axioms into first-order formulas

$$Tr'(E \sqsubseteq F) \overset{\text{def}}{\equiv} \forall x[Tr(E, x) \rightarrow Tr(F, x)].$$

In terminological axiom $E \sqsubseteq F$, E is called a *subsumee* of F and F is called a *subsumer* of E.

REMARK 8.2. In the literature terminological axioms are also of the form of an equivalence $E \equiv F$ (called *equality*), where E, F are concept expressions. The meaning of such an equality is that the concept E is equal (set-theoretically) to F. An equality whose left-hand side is an atomic concept is called a *definition*. In what follows we shall deal with sets of terminological axioms, where any equality $E \equiv F$ can be represented by the set of two subsumptions $\{E \sqsubseteq F, F \sqsubseteq E\}$. Therefore without loss of generality we have restricted the language to terminological axioms in the form of subsumptions only. $\lhd$

Observe that terminological axioms can lead to cycles. This is a well-known phenomenon (see, e.g. [8]) in the case of equalities. In order to deal with circular terminologies we further on restrict considerations to subsumptions of the form $E \sqsubseteq C$, where C is an atomic concept and understand subsumption of the form $C \sqsubseteq E$ as a set of subsumptions $\{\neg E \sqsubseteq D, \neg C \sqcup D \sqsubseteq D\}$, where D is a fresh atomic concept. This is justified by observing that $C \sqsubseteq E$ is logically equivalent to $\neg E \sqsubseteq \neg C$ and that the least fixpoint semantics, explained below, makes $D \equiv \neg C$. If E contains C then $\{\neg E \sqsubseteq D, \neg C \sqcup D \sqsubseteq D\}$ can be simplified to $\{\neg E \sqcup D \sqsubseteq D, \neg D \sqsubseteq C\}$ due to circularity of C appearing in this set. Similarly, we can replace any subsumption of the form $E \sqsubseteq F$ by the set $\{E \sqsubseteq D, F \sqcup D \sqsubseteq D\}$, where D is a fresh atomic concept.[1]

DEFINITION 8.3. We shall say that T is *circular w.r.t.* an atomic concept D provided that $D \Rightarrow_T^* D$, where $\Rightarrow_T^*$ is the transitive closure of relation $\Rightarrow_T$ such that $C \Rightarrow_T C'$ iff there is in T a terminological axiom of the form $E \sqsubseteq C'$ with C appearing in E. We say that T is circular if there is a concept D such that T is circular w.r.t. D. $\lhd$

Consider a set T of terminological axioms of the form $E \sqsubseteq C$, where E is a concept expression and C is an atomic concept. Let k be the number of concepts appearing in T. A standard technique allows us to consider T as a mapping $\mathcal{P}(U)^k \longrightarrow \mathcal{P}(U)^k$, where U is the underlying domain. In such a case we shall say that T is *monotone in the coordinate* i $(1 \leq i \leq k)$, provided that for any $A_i \subseteq A_i'$, $T(A_1, \ldots, A_i, \ldots A_k) \subseteq T(A_1, \ldots, A_i', \ldots A_k)$. We say that T is *monotone* provided that it is monotone in all its coordinates.

By the Knaster and Tarski fixpoint theorem, for any monotone T there is the least fixpoint of T. The semantics of concepts w.r.t. which T is circular and monotone is then given by the least fixpoint of T. More precisely, assume that

$$T(X_1, \ldots, X_k) = \langle T_1(X_1, \ldots, X_k), \ldots, T_k(X_1, \ldots, X_k) \rangle$$

is circular and monotone w.r.t. $X_1, \ldots, X_k$. Then $X_1, \ldots, X_k$ are defined by the least fixpoint of equivalence

$$\langle X_1, \ldots, X_k \rangle \equiv \langle T_1(X_1, \ldots, X_k), \ldots, T_k(X_1, \ldots, X_k) \rangle.$$

---

[1]We treat circular and non-circular cases separately, since the latter do not require a fixpoint semantics turning subsumptions into equalities.

EXAMPLE 8.4. The semantics of $firstHuman \sqcup \exists parent.human \sqsubseteq human$ is given by the least fixpoint of $\Gamma(X) \stackrel{\text{def}}{=} firstHuman \sqcup \exists parent.X$.

Assume that first humans had no parents. Unwinding the fixpoint of $\Gamma(X)$ results then in

$$
\begin{aligned}
\Gamma^1(\bot) = \ & firstHuman \sqcup \exists parent.\bot = firstHuman \\
\Gamma^2(\bot) = \ & \Gamma(firstHuman) = \\
& firstHuman \sqcup \exists parent.firstHuman \\
\Gamma^3(\bot) = \ & \Gamma(firstHuman \sqcup \exists parent.firstHuman) = \\
& firstHuman \sqcup \\
& \exists parent.[firstHuman \sqcup \exists parent.firstHuman]
\end{aligned}
$$

$\dots$

which reflects iterations through successive generations. ◁

EXAMPLE 8.5. Consider $T = \{K \sqcup X \sqsubseteq Y, Y \sqsubseteq X\}$. Then T is circular w.r.t. X and Y. Terminological axioms in T lead to a mapping

$$
T(X, Y) = \langle Y \sqsubseteq X, K \sqcup X \sqsubseteq Y \rangle.
$$

Therefore X, Y are defined by the least solution of the fixpoint equivalence

$$
\langle X, Y \rangle \equiv \langle Y \sqsubseteq X, K \sqcup X \sqsubseteq Y \rangle,
$$

which is $\langle K, K \rangle$. ◁

REMARK 8.6. The least fixpoint semantics construction is standard and used, e.g., in logic programming. One can then easily adopt some syntactic conditions as to monotonicity, like negation-freeness or stratification. For a comprehensive discussion of the area see, e.g., [1]. ◁

8.1.2. Second-Order Description Logics. The *set of formulas of second-order description logic*, also referred to as *second-order terminological formulas* $\mathcal{L}_{\text{II}}$, is defined as the least set satisfying the conditions:

- If T is a finite set consisting of terminological axioms or their negations then $T \in \mathcal{L}_{\text{II}}$;
- If T is a finite set of terminological axioms, C is an atomic concept and $S \in \mathcal{L}_{\text{II}}$ then $\exists_T C.S \in \mathcal{L}_{\text{II}}$;
- If $S \in \mathcal{L}_{\text{II}}$ then $\neg S \in \mathcal{L}_{\text{II}}$.

The meaning attached to second-order terminological formulas is given by the following clauses extending translation Tr':

$$
\begin{aligned}
Tr'(S) &\stackrel{\text{def}}{\equiv} \bigwedge_{\delta \in S} Tr'(\delta) \\
Tr'(\exists_T C.S) &\stackrel{\text{def}}{\equiv} \exists C[Tr'(T) \wedge Tr'(S)] \\
Tr'(\neg S) &\stackrel{\text{def}}{\equiv} \neg Tr'(S),
\end{aligned}
$$

where, as usual, $\bigwedge_{\beta \in \emptyset} Tr'(\beta) \overset{\text{def}}{\equiv} \text{TRUE}$ whereas $\bigvee_{\beta \in \emptyset} Tr'(\beta) \overset{\text{def}}{\equiv} \text{FALSE}$.

In the case of singleton sets we often simplify notation by writing δ rather than $\{\delta\}$. We also use universal quantifiers defined by $\forall_T C.S \overset{\text{def}}{\equiv} \neg \exists_T C.\neg S$.

REMARK 8.7. The above language could be extended to allow T in $\forall_T C.S$ and $\exists_T C.S$ to be any set of formulas of $\mathcal{L}_{\text{II}}$. The definition of semantics would not be changed. However, both to stay closer to the spirit of description logics as well as to simplify the considerations we deal with a restricted version of the logic.   ◁

EXAMPLE 8.8. Let T consist of the following terminological axioms:

(66) $Bird \sqcap \neg Ab' \sqsubseteq Flies$

(67) $Ab' \sqsubseteq Ab.$

Then $\exists_T Flies.Flies \sqsubseteq Bird$ as well as $\forall_{(67)} Ab'.\forall_{(66)} Flies.Ab \sqsubseteq Ab'$ are second-order terminological formulas.[2]   ◁

8.2. Elimination of Second-Order Quantifiers

8.2.1. Preliminaries. Recall that by α_e^x we mean the expression obtained from α by substituting all occurrences of x by e.

The *negation depth of an occurrence of a concept C in a concept expression E*, denoted by $n_C(E)$, is defined inductively:

- $n_C(E(C)) = 0$ when the considered occurrence of C in E is not in the scope of a negation;
- $n_C(\neg E(C)) = 1 + n_C(E(C))$;
- $n_C(E(C) \circ E'(C)) = \begin{cases} n_C(E(C)) & \text{when the considered occur-} \\ & \text{rence of } C \text{ is in } E(C), \\ n_C(E'(C)) & \text{otherwise,} \end{cases}$

  where $\circ \in \{\sqcup, \sqcap\}$;
- $n_C(QR.E(C)) = n_C(E(C))$, where $Q \in \{\forall, \exists\}$.

The definition of negation depth is extended to terminological axioms, sets of terminological axioms or their negations, and to second-order terminological formulas as follows:

- $n_C(E(C) \sqsubseteq E'(C)) = \begin{cases} 1 + n_C(E(C)) & \text{when the considered oc-} \\ & \text{currence of } C \text{ is in } E(C), \\ n_C(E'(C)) & \text{otherwise;} \end{cases}$

---

[2]In fact, the second of these formulas corresponds to the second-order part of circumscription of Ab with varied $Flies$ – cf. Section 8.3 as well as Chapter 16.

- $n_C(T) = n_C(\delta(C))$, where T is a set of terminological axioms or negations of terminological axioms and $\delta(C)$ is the member of T containing the considered occurrence of C;

- $n_C(\exists_T C.S) = \begin{cases} n_C(T) & \text{when the considered occurrence of } C \text{ is in } T, \\ n_C(S) & \text{otherwise;} \end{cases}$

- $n_C(\neg S) = 1 + n_C(S)$.

Observe that, due to our definition of universal quantifiers as dual to existential quantifiers, we have that

$$n_C(\forall_T C.S) = \begin{cases} 1 + n_C(T) & \text{when the considered occurrence of } C \text{ is in } T, \\ 2 + n_C(S) & \text{otherwise.} \end{cases}$$

We say that an occurrence of concept C is *positive* (respectively *negative*) in a concept expression E if $n_C(E)$ is even (respectively odd). An occurrence of C is *positive* (respectively *negative*) in a set of terminological axioms T if $n_C(T)$ is even (respectively odd). Likewise, an occurrence of concept C is *positive* (respectively *negative*) in a second-order terminological formula S if $n_C(S)$ is even (respectively odd).

A concept expression E is positive w.r.t. concept C provided that all occurrences of C in T are positive (respectively negative). A set of terminological axioms T is *positive* (respectively *negative*) w.r.t. concept C provided that all occurrences of C in T are positive (respectively negative). A second-order terminological formula S is *positive* (respectively *negative*) w.r.t. concept C provided that all occurrences of C in S are positive (respectively negative).

8.2.2. Ackermann-Like Lemma.
For simplicity we first deal with an Ackermann-like lemma. This lemma is subsumed by Theorem 8.11, but due to applications it is worth formulating separately.

LEMMA 8.9. Let E be a concept expression and T be a set of terminological axioms. Assume that the atomic concept X does not occur in E.

If T and T' are sets of terminological axioms or negations of terminological axioms negative w.r.t. concept X such that $T \cup \{E \sqsubseteq X\} \cup T'$ is not circular w.r.t. X, then

(68) $\exists_{T \cup \{E \sqsubseteq X\}} X.T'(X) \equiv T_E^X \cup T'^X_E$.

If T and T' are sets of terminological axioms or negations of terminological axioms positive w.r.t. concept X such that $T \cup \{X \sqsubseteq E\} \cup T'$ is not circular w.r.t. X, then

(69) $\exists_{T \cup \{X \sqsubseteq E\}} X.T'(X) \equiv T_E^X \cup T'^X_E$.   ◁

Elimination of second order universal quantifiers can be done by considering the negation $\neg\exists_T X[\neg S]$ rather than $\forall_T X[S]$ and applying Lemma 8.9.

Observe that many second-order terminological formulas can be transformed into equivalent formulas in one of the forms required in Lemma 8.9 by adopting transformation rules of the DLS algorithm.

EXAMPLE 8.10. As an example of the application of Lemma 8.9 consider T and the formula $\exists_T Flies.Flies \sqsubseteq Bird$ as in Example 8.8. Then the result of eliminating quantifier $\exists_T Flies$ from this formula is $\{Ab' \sqsubseteq Ab, Bird \sqcap \neg Ab' \sqsubseteq Bird\}$.

Consider now the second formula of Example 8.8,

$$\forall_{(67)} Ab'.\forall_{(66)} Flies.Ab \sqsubseteq Ab'.$$

We first negate $\forall_{(66)} Flies$, so consider $\neg\exists_{(66)} Flies.\neg(Ab \sqsubseteq Ab')$, which is equivalent to $\neg\neg(Ab \sqsubseteq Ab')$, i.e., to $Ab \sqsubseteq Ab'$. Therefore we consider

$$\forall_{(67)} Ab'.Ab \sqsubseteq Ab', \text{ i.e., } \neg\exists_{(67)} Ab'.\neg(Ab \sqsubseteq Ab').$$

An application of Lemma 8.9 results in $Ab \sqsubseteq Ab$, which is circular and its least fixpoint is $\bot$. Therefore Ab is here $\bot$, as expected, since we had no evidence forcing Ab to hold for some individuals. $\triangleleft$

8.2.3. The Fixpoint Theorem. Let us now formulate and prove a more advanced theorem influenced by the Theorem 6.19.

THEOREM 8.11. Let $E(X)$ be a concept expression positive w.r.t. X.

If T and T' are sets of terminological axioms or negations of terminological axioms negative w.r.t. concept X then

$$(70) \qquad \exists_{T\cup\{E(X)\sqsubseteq X\}} X.T' \equiv T \cup \{E(X) \sqsubseteq X\} \cup T'.$$

If T and T' are sets of terminological axioms or negations of terminological axioms positive w.r.t. concept X then

$$(71) \qquad \exists_{T\cup\{X\sqsubseteq E(X)\}} X.T' \equiv T \cup \{\neg E(X) \sqcup D \sqsubseteq D, \neg D \sqsubseteq X\} \cup T',$$

where D is a fresh atomic concept, not occurring in $\exists_{T\cup\{X\sqsubseteq E(X)\}} X.T'(X)$.

PROOF. Let us prove (70). The proof of (71) is analogous. Observe that

$$Tr'(\exists_{T\cup\{E(X)\sqsubseteq X\}} X.T'(X)) =$$
$$(72) \qquad \exists X\Big[Tr'(T) \wedge \forall x[Tr(E(X),x) \to X(x)] \wedge Tr'(T'(X))\Big].$$

According to Theorem 6.19, formula (72) is equivalent to

$$(73) \qquad Tr'(T) \wedge T'^X_{[\text{LFP } X(x).Tr(E(X),x)]},$$

where $[\text{LFP } X(x).Tr(E(X),x)]$ stands for the least fixpoint of $Tr(E(X),x)$.

Based on the fixpoint semantics of circular terminologies it can now easily be observed that formula (72) is equivalent to

$$Tr'(T \cup \{E(X) \sqsubseteq X\} \cup T')$$

being the translation of the right-hand side of (70).   ◁

REMARK 8.12. Observe that equality (71) introduces a new atomic concept name, D, into the result of eliminating a second-order quantifier. This is caused by the simplifying assumption as to accepting a restricted language for subsumptions. One could avoid introducing D by attaching the greatest fixpoint semantics to subsumptions of the form $X \sqsubseteq E$. Moreover, the new concept is fully defined by the least fixpoint semantics. Similarly, the concept X reappears at the right-hand sides of equivalences (70) and (71). Again this concept is fully defined by the least fixpoint semantics. Therefore both for D and X there is a tractable database querying machinery (see, e.g., [1]).   ◁

8.3. Applications

8.3.1. Circumscribing Concepts in Description Logics.
Second-order circumscription of predicates $\bar{P}$ w.r.t. theory $Th(\bar{P}, \bar{S})$ with $\bar{S}$ varied is formulated by the following formula (see, e.g., [139] and Chapter 16):

(74)
$$
\begin{aligned}
Th(\bar{P}, \bar{S}) \wedge & \\
\forall \bar{X} \forall \bar{Y} \Big\{ & \Big[Th(\bar{X}, \bar{Y}) \wedge \bigwedge_{i=1}^{n} \forall \bar{x} \big[X_i(\bar{x}) \to P_i(\bar{x}) \big] \Big] \to \\
& \bigwedge_{i=1}^{n} \forall \bar{x} \big[P_i(\bar{x}) \to X_i(\bar{x}) \big] \Big\}.
\end{aligned}
$$

In the case of description logics theory Th is given by a set of terminological axioms and predicates $\bar{P}, \bar{S}$ represent concepts. The second-order part of (74) can then be formulated by the following second-order terminological formula, where it is assumed that $\bar{P} = \langle P_1, \ldots, P_n \rangle$, $\bar{S} = \langle S_1, \ldots, S_m \rangle$, $X_1, \ldots, X_n, Y_1, \ldots, Y_m$ are fresh atomic concepts, and $T' \stackrel{\text{def}}{=} \{X_i \sqsubseteq P_i : 1 \leq i \leq n\}$:

(75)
$$
\forall_{Th(\bar{X},\bar{Y}) \cup T'} X_1 \ldots \forall_{Th(\bar{X},\bar{Y}) \cup T'} X_n.
$$
$$
\forall_{Th(\bar{X},\bar{Y}) \cup T'} Y_1 \ldots \forall_{Th(\bar{X},\bar{Y}) \cup T'} Y_m. \{P_i \sqsubseteq X_i : 1 \leq i \leq n\}.
$$

In fact, in our formalisms rather than T' we shall use

$$\{\neg P_i \sqsubseteq D_i, \neg X_i \sqcup D_i \sqsubseteq D_i : 1 \leq i \leq n\},$$

where, as before, D_i are fresh atomic concept names or, in the case when circularity w.r.t. X_i appears in $Th(\bar{X}, \bar{Y})$, we shall use the set

$$\{\neg P_i \sqcup D_i \sqsubseteq D_i, \neg D_i \sqsubseteq X_i : 1 \leq i \leq n\}.$$

EXAMPLE 8.13. Consider the following theory expressed in classical logic

$$\forall x[K(x) \rightarrow Ab(x)]$$
$$\forall x \forall y[(Ab(y) \wedge sim(x, y)) \rightarrow Ab(x)],$$

meaning intuitively that objects known to be abnormal are abnormal and objects similar to abnormal are abnormal, too. This theory can be expressed by the following terminological axioms:

$$K \sqsubseteq Ab$$
$$(\exists sim.Ab) \sqsubseteq Ab,$$

further denoted by $Th(Ab)$.

Assume we want to circumscribe Ab w.r.t. Th. The general formula (75), specialized to this case, is $\forall_{\{K \sqsubseteq X, (\exists sim.X) \sqsubseteq X\} \cup \{X \sqsubseteq Ab\}} X.[Ab \sqsubseteq X]$, which, due to the circularity w.r.t. X, is transformed to

$$\forall_{\{K \sqsubseteq X, (\exists sim.X) \sqsubseteq X, \neg Ab \sqcup D \sqsubseteq D, \neg D \sqsubseteq X\}} X.[Ab \sqsubseteq X],$$

and further to

(76) $$\forall_{\{K \sqcup \neg D \sqcup \exists sim.X \sqsubseteq X, \neg Ab \sqcup D \sqsubseteq D\}}[Ab \sqsubseteq X].$$

Formula (76) is equivalent to

$$\neg \exists_{\{K \sqcup \neg D \sqcup \exists sim.X \sqsubseteq X, \neg Ab \sqcup D \sqsubseteq D\}} \neg [Ab \sqsubseteq X].$$

An application of (70) of Theorem 8.11 results in

$$\neg \{K \sqcup \neg D \sqcup \exists sim.X \sqcup X \sqsubseteq X, \neg Ab \sqcup D \sqsubseteq D, \neg[Ab \sqsubseteq X]\}.$$

A closer analysis of this result, together with theory Th, shows that the minimal Ab satisfying Th is defined by $Ab \equiv K \sqcup \exists sim.Ab$, as could have easily been expected.   ◁

8.3.2. Approximating Terminological Axioms. Formulas of classical logic can be approximated using strongest necessary and weakest sufficient conditions as introduced by Lin in [**140**] and further developed by Doherty, Łukaszewicz and Szałas in [**59**]. Such conditions provide the best approximations of formulas using a restricted vocabulary and allow one to model various forms of reasoning, including abduction. A second-order characterization of these conditions has been provided in [**59**].

The following definitions are immediate adaptations of definitions of [**140, 59**] to the context of description logics (see also Section 18.2, page 246).

DEFINITION 8.14. By *a necessary condition of a terminological axiom A on the set of atomic concepts P under the set of terminological axioms T* we shall understand any second-order terminological formula S all whose atomic concepts are in P, such that in any model of T, $A \sqsubseteq S$. It is the *strongest necessary condition* if, additionally, for any necessary condition S' of A on P under T, we have that $S \sqsubseteq S'$ in any model of T.

By *a sufficient condition of a terminological axiom A on the set of atomic concepts P under the set of terminological axioms T* we shall understand any second-order terminological formula S all whose atomic concepts are in P, such that in any model of T, $S \sqsubseteq A$. It is the *weakest sufficient condition* if, additionally, for any sufficient condition S' of A on P under T, we have that $S' \sqsubseteq S$ in any model of T.   ◁

The following lemma adapts the corresponding lemma of [**59**] (see also Chapter 18) to the context of description logics.

LEMMA 8.15. For any concept expression E, any set of atomic concepts P and set of terminological axioms T:

  (1) The strongest necessary condition of E on P under T is defined by

  $$\exists_T Q_1. \ldots . \exists_T Q_r.E;$$

  (2) The weakest sufficient condition of E on P under T is defined by

  $$\forall_T Q_1. \ldots . \forall_T Q_r.E,$$

where $Q_1, \ldots, Q_r$ are all atomic concepts appearing in T and A but not in P.   ◁

The above characterization is substantially second-order but again, in many cases second-order quantifiers can be eliminated. The results of elimination might have new atomic concepts, but the new concepts, if any, are fully defined due to the fixpoint semantics.

EXAMPLE 8.16. Let $T = \{\exists hasChild.Person \sqsubseteq Parent\}$. Then, according to Lemma 8.15, the strongest necessary condition of $Parent \sqcap Female \sqsubseteq Mother$ on $\{Person, Female, Mother\}$ under T is

$$\exists_{\exists hasChild.Person \sqsubseteq Parent} Parent.Parent \sqcap Female \sqsubseteq Mother$$

which, according to Lemma 8.9, is equivalent to

$$\exists hasChild.Person \sqcap Female \sqsubseteq Mother.$$ ◁

CHAPTER 9

Definability and Second-Order Quantifier Elimination

There is a strong link between definability and second-order quantifier elimination. In the current chapter we apply known definability results to eliminating second-order quantifiers. Assume that in a given theory or a class of models relation R is definable by a formula α. Then, in the simplest case when $\exists R[\beta(R)]$ entails $R(\bar{x}) \equiv \alpha(\bar{x})$, where α does not contain occurrences of R, formula $\exists R[\beta(R)]$ is equivalent to $\beta_{\alpha(\bar{x})}^{R(\bar{x})}$. In more complex cases the results are not that immediate and, to our knowledge, have not been proved elsewhere.

Another topic considered in this chapter is the semantic characterization of first-order and fixpoint definability. We recall known results that might be helpful in detecting whether a given relation is or is not definable by a first-order or fixpoint formula.

In this chapter whenever a logic is not mentioned explicitly, it is assumed that it is the classical first-order logic.

9.1. Definability and Second-Order Quantifier Elimination

Let us start with the relation of implicit and explicit definability to second-order quantifier elimination.

DEFINITION 9.1. We say that the set of formulas $S(P)$ *defines* P *implicitly* iff $S(P) \cup S(P)_{P'}^{P} \models \forall \bar{x}[P(\bar{x}) \equiv P'(\bar{x})]$, where P' is a relation symbol not appearing in $S(P)$. We say that $S(P)$ *defines* P *explicitly* iff there exists a formula $\alpha(\bar{x})$ not containing occurrences of P such that $S(P) \models \forall \bar{x}[P(\bar{x}) \equiv \alpha(\bar{x})]$. ◁

We have the following lemma.

LEMMA 9.2. If $S(P)$ explicitly defines P then $\exists P \left[\bigwedge_{\gamma \in S(P)} \gamma \right]$ is equivalent to a first-order formula or, if $S(P)$ is infinite, to an infinite conjunction of first-order formulas.

PROOF. If $S(P)$ explicitly defines P then there exists a formula $\alpha(\bar{x})$ not containing occurrences of P such that $S(P) \models \forall \bar{x}[P(\bar{x}) \equiv \alpha(\bar{x})]$. It is then obvious that $\exists P \left[\bigwedge_{\gamma \in S(P)} \gamma \right]$ is equivalent to $\left[\bigwedge_{\gamma \in S(P)} \gamma \right]_{\alpha(\bar{x})}^{P(\bar{x})}$, which is a (finite or infinite) conjunction of first-order formulas.   ◁

DEFINITION 9.3. We say that the set of formulas $S(P)$ *defines P explicitly up to disjunction* iff there are formulas $\alpha_1(\bar{x}), \ldots, \alpha_n(\bar{x})$ not containing occurrences of P such that $S(P) \models \bigvee_{1 \le i \le n} \forall \bar{x}[P(\bar{x}) \equiv \alpha_i(\bar{x})]$.   ◁

LEMMA 9.4. If $S(P)$ explicitly defines P up to disjunction then $\exists P \left[\bigwedge_{\gamma \in S(P)} \gamma \right]$ is equivalent to a first-order formula or, if $S(P)$ is infinite, to an infinite conjunction of first-order formulas.

PROOF. If $S(P)$ explicitly defines P up to disjunction then there is a finite number of formulas $\alpha_1(\bar{x}), \ldots, \alpha_n(\bar{x})$ not containing occurrences of P such that

$$S(P) \models \bigvee_{1 \le i \le n} \forall \bar{x}[P(\bar{x}) \equiv \alpha_i(\bar{x})].$$

We shall prove that

$$(77) \qquad \exists P \left[\bigwedge_{\gamma \in S(P)} \gamma \right] \equiv \bigvee_{1 \le i \le n} \left\{ \forall \bar{x} \left[\bigwedge_{\gamma \in S(P)} \gamma \right]_{\alpha_i(\bar{x})}^{P(\bar{x})} \right\}.$$

($\rightarrow$) Assume that $M, v \models \exists P \left[\bigwedge_{\gamma \in S(P)} \gamma \right]$. By assumption,

$$S(P) \models \bigvee_{1 \le i \le n} \forall \bar{x}[P(\bar{x}) \equiv \alpha_i(\bar{x})],$$

therefore we have that $M, v \models \exists P \left[\bigwedge_{\gamma \in S(P)} \gamma \wedge \bigvee_{1 \le i \le n} \forall \bar{x}[P(\bar{x}) \equiv \alpha_i(\bar{x})] \right]$, i.e.,

$$M, v \models \bigvee_{1 \le i \le n} \exists P \bigwedge_{\gamma \in S(P)} [\gamma \wedge \forall \bar{x}[P(\bar{x}) \equiv \alpha_i(\bar{x})]].$$

Now the claim follows, as in Lemma 9.2.

($\leftarrow$) Assume that $M, v \models \displaystyle\bigvee_{1 \le i \le n} \left\{ \forall \bar{x} \left[\bigwedge_{\gamma \in S(P)} \gamma \right]_{\alpha_i(\bar{x})}^{P(\bar{x})} \right\}$. Then there is $1 \le i \le n$

such that $M, v \models \forall \bar{x} \left[\displaystyle\bigwedge_{\gamma \in S(P)} \gamma \right]_{\alpha_i(\bar{x})}^{P(\bar{x})}$. Thus there is P (defined by α_i) such that

$M, v \models \left[\displaystyle\bigwedge_{\gamma \in S(P)} \gamma \right]$, i.e., $M, v \models \exists P \left[\displaystyle\bigwedge_{\gamma \in S(P)} \gamma \right]$.

This proves (77) and our lemma. ◁

DEFINITION 9.5. We say that the set of formulas $S(P)$ *defines P explicitly up to parameters and disjunction* iff there are formulas $\alpha_1(\bar{x}, \bar{y}), \ldots, \alpha_n(\bar{x}, \bar{y})$ not containing occurrences of P such that $S(P) \models \displaystyle\bigvee_{1 \le i \le n} \exists \bar{y} \forall \bar{x} [P(\bar{x}) \equiv \alpha_i(\bar{x}, \bar{y})]$. ◁

The following lemma can be proved by an immediate extension of the proof of Lemma 9.4.

LEMMA 9.6. If $S(P)$ explicitly defines P up to parameters and disjunction then $\exists P \left[\displaystyle\bigwedge_{\gamma \in S(P)} \gamma \right]$ is equivalent to a first-order formula or, if $S(P)$ is infinite, to an infinite conjunction of first-order formulas. ◁

9.2. Beth Definability

The following theorem is due to Beth [**18**].

THEOREM 9.7. A set of formulas $S(P)$ defines P implicitly iff it defines P explicitly. ◁

By combining Theorem 9.7 and Lemma 9.2 we have the following corollary.

COROLLARY 9.8. If $S(P)$ implicitly defines P then $\exists P \left[\displaystyle\bigwedge_{\gamma \in S(P)} \gamma \right]$ is equivalent to a first-order formula or, if $S(P)$ is infinite, to an infinite conjunction of first-order formulas. ◁

EXAMPLE 9.9. Consider the following set $S(P)$ of formulas, where a is a constant:

(78)
$$\forall y [R(a, y) \equiv y \not\approx a] \land$$
$$P(a) \land \forall x \forall y [(P(x) \land R(x, y)) \to \neg P(y)]$$
$$\forall x \forall y [R(x, y) \lor P(x) \lor P(y)].$$

One can easily verify that P is implicitly definable and its explicit definition is $\forall x[P(x) \equiv x \approx a]$. Therefore, by Lemma 9.2, we have that $\exists P\left[\bigwedge_{\gamma \in S(P)} \gamma\right]$ is equivalent to the conjunction

$$\forall y[R(a, y) \equiv y \not\approx a] \wedge$$
$$a \approx a \wedge \forall x \forall y[(x \approx a \wedge R(x, y)) \rightarrow y \not\approx a] \wedge$$
$$\forall x \forall y[R(x, y) \vee x \approx a \vee y \approx a].$$

Observe that the last formula of (78) is added to the previous ones simply to make direct methods based on Lemma 6.1 and Theorem 6.19 inapplicable to eliminate $\exists P$ from $\exists P[S(P)]$.   ◁

9.3. Svenonius Theorem

The following theorem, extending Beth's theorem, is due to Svenonius [**198**]. For the proof see also [**36**].

THEOREM 9.10. Let Σ be a signature not containing P and $\alpha(P)$ be a formula over $\Sigma \cup \{P\}$. Then the following are equivalent:

(1) For every relational structure M over Σ, if any two models $\langle M, X_1 \rangle$, $\langle M, X_2 \rangle$ of $\alpha(P)$, where X_1, X_2 interpret P, are isomorphic,[1] then $X_1 = X_2$;
(2) $\alpha(P)$ defines P explicitly up to disjunction.   ◁

By combining Theorem 9.10 and Lemma 9.4 we have the following corollary.

COROLLARY 9.11. If $\alpha(P)$ satisfies assumptions and item (1) of Theorem 9.10 then $\exists P[\alpha(P)]$ is equivalent to a first-order formula.   ◁

9.4. Kueker Definability

In [**134**] Kueker has generalized theorems of Beth and Svenonius. For the proof see also [**36**].

THEOREM 9.12. Let Σ be a signature not containing P and $\alpha(P)$ be a formula over $\Sigma \cup \{P\}$ and let $n \geq 1$ be a natural number. Then the following are equivalent:

(1) For every relational structure M over Σ there are at most n sets X interpreting P such that $\langle M, X \rangle \models \alpha(P)$;
(2) There are formulas $\beta(\bar{y})$ and $\gamma_i(\bar{x}, \bar{y})$ $(1 \leq i \leq n)$ over Σ such that
    (i) $\alpha(P) \models \exists \bar{y}[\beta(\bar{y})]$ and

---

[1]i.e., there is a mapping $f : M \longrightarrow M$ which is one-to-one and onto and such that for any tuple $\bar{a}$ of elements of M, $\bar{a} \in X_1$ iff $f(\bar{a}) \in X_2$.

(ii) $\alpha(P) \models \forall \bar{y} \left[\beta(\bar{y}) \rightarrow \bigvee_{1 \leq i \leq n} \forall \bar{x}[P(\bar{x}) \equiv \gamma_i(\bar{x}, \bar{y})] \right].$ ◁

The following corollary relates Theorem 9.12 to second-order quantifier elimination.

COROLLARY 9.13. If $\alpha(P)$ satisfies the assumptions and item (1) of Theorem 9.12 then $\exists P[\alpha(P)]$ is equivalent to a first-order formula.

PROOF. Under our assumptions we have that item (2) of Theorem 9.12 holds. Observe that (i) and (ii) of (2) imply that $\alpha(P) \models \exists \bar{y} \left[\bigvee_{1 \leq i \leq n} \forall \bar{x}[P(\bar{x}) \equiv \gamma_i(\bar{x}, \bar{y})] \right]$,

thus also $\alpha(P) \models \bigvee_{1 \leq i \leq n} \exists \bar{y} \forall \bar{x}[P(\bar{x}) \equiv \gamma_i(\bar{x}, \bar{y})]$, i.e., $\alpha(P)$ defines P up to parameters and disjunction. Now the conclusion of our corollary follows immediately from Lemma 9.6. ◁

9.5. Chang–Makkai Definability Theorem

Recall that $|A|^+$ denotes the least cardinal strictly greater than $|A|$.

The following theorem is due to Chang [35] and Makkai [145]. For the proof see also [36].

THEOREM 9.14. Let Σ be a signature not containing P, $\alpha(P)$ be a formula over $\Sigma \cup \{P\}$ and P be of arity k. Then the following conditions are equivalent:

(1) For every infinite relational structure M over Σ,

$$|\{X \mid X \subseteq A^k \text{ and } M, X \models \alpha(P)\}| < |A|^+,$$

where U is the universe of M and X is an interpretation of P;
(2) For every infinite relational structure M over Σ,

$$|\{X \mid X \subseteq A^k \text{ and } M, X \models \alpha(P)\}| < 2^{|A|},$$

where U and X are as above;
(3) $\alpha(P)$ defines P up to parameters and disjunction. ◁

By combining Theorem 9.14 and Lemma 9.6 we have the following corollary.

COROLLARY 9.15. If $\alpha(P)$ satisfies the assumptions and item (1) or item (2) of Theorem 9.14 then $\exists P[\alpha(P)]$ is equivalent to a first-order formula. ◁

9.6. Characterization of First-Order Definability

Let us first define model theoretic tools needed to characterize first-order definability. For a more comprehensive study of these tools see, e.g., [36, 210].

DEFINITION 9.16. Let I be a non-empty set. By a *filter D over I* we understand a set of subsets of I such that

(1) $I \in D$;
(2) If $X, Y \in D$ then $X \cap Y \in D$;
(3) If $X \in D$ and $X \subseteq Z \subseteq I$, then $Z \in D$.

A filter is *proper* iff it is not the set of all subsets of I. A filter is called an *ultrafilter* iff it is a maximal (w.r.t. $\subseteq$) proper filter.   ◁

DEFINITION 9.17. Let I be a non-empty set, D be a proper filter over I, for each $i \in I$, A_i be a non-empty set and let C be the set of all functions f with domain I such that for each $i \in I$, $f(i) \in A$. for $f, g \in C$ we say that f and g are D *equivalent*, denoted by $f =_D g$, iff $\{i \in I \mid f(i) = g(i)\} \in D$.   ◁

PROPOSITION 9.18. The relation $=_D$ of Definition 9.17 is an equivalence relation over C.   ◁

DEFINITION 9.19. [Definition 9.17 continued] Let $f_D \stackrel{\text{def}}{=} \{g \in C \mid g =_D f\}$ be the equivalence class of f w.r.t. $=_D$. The *reduced product of A_i modulo D*, denoted by $\prod_D A_i$, is the set of all equivalence classes of D,

$$\prod_D A_i \stackrel{\text{def}}{=} \{f_D \mid f \in C\}.$$

We call I the *index set* for $\prod_D A_i$. When D is an ultrafilter over I, the reduced product $\prod_D A_i$ is called an *ultraproduct*.   ◁

DEFINITION 9.20. Let I be a non-empty set, D be a proper filter over I, Σ be a signature and for each $i \in I$ let M_i be a relational structure over Σ. The *reduced product* $\prod_D M_i$ is defined as follows:

- The universe of $\prod_D M_i$ is $\prod_D A_i$, where for each $i \in I$, A_i is the domain of M_i;
- Let P be an n-argument relation symbol and P_i its interpretation in M_i; the interpretation of P in $\prod_D M_i$ is the relation S such that

$$S(f_D^1, \ldots, f_D^n) \text{ holds iff } \{i \in I \mid P_i(f^1(i), \ldots, f^n(i))\} \in D;$$

- Let f be an n-argument function symbol and f_i its interpretation in M_i; the interpretation of f in $\prod_D M_i$ is the function h such that

$$h(f_D^1, \ldots, f_D^n) \stackrel{\text{def}}{=} g_D \text{ where } g(i) \stackrel{\text{def}}{=} f_i(f^1(i), \ldots, f^n(i)).$$

When D is an ultrafilter over I, the reduced product $\prod_D A_i$ is called an *ultraproduct*.   ◁

DEFINITION 9.21. Relational structures M and M' over the same signature Σ are *elementarily equivalent*, denoted by $M \equiv M'$, provided that for any classical first-order formula α over Σ, $M \models \alpha$ iff $M' \models \alpha$.   ◁

DEFINITION 9.22. A class K of relational structures is said to be an *elementary class* iff there exists a classical first-order theory T such that K is exactly the class of all models of T. If such a T is finite then K is called a *basic elementary class*.

A class K is said to be *closed under elementary equivalence* iff $M \in K$ and $M \equiv M'$ implies $M' \in K$. It is *closed under ultraproducts* iff every ultraproduct $\prod_D M_i$ of a family of structures $M_i \in K$ belongs to K.   ◁

The following theorem is due to Frayne, Morel and Scott [**79**], and Kochen [**127**] (see also [**36**]).

THEOREM 9.23. Let K be an arbitrary class of relational structures. Then

(1) K is an elementary class iff K is closed under ultraproducts and elementary equivalence;
(2) K is a basic elementary class iff both K and its complement are closed under ultraproducts and elementary equivalence.   ◁

Theorem 9.23, especially item (2), provides a non-effective criterion for checking whether a second-order quantifier can be eliminated, as indicated by the following corollary.

COROLLARY 9.24. Let K be an arbitrary class of relational structures characterized by a second-order classical formula α. Then there is a first-order formula equivalent to α iff both K and its complement are closed under ultraproducts and elementary equivalence.   ◁

We also have the following interesting lemma (see, [**36**]).

LEMMA 9.25. Σ_1^1 formulas are preserved under ultraproducts.   ◁

EXAMPLE 9.26. Consider the class of all models isomorphic to $\langle \omega, S \rangle$, where S is a successor relation (i.e., $S(x, y)$ holds if y is the successor of x). Since ultraproducts may be uncountable, this class is not preserved under ultraproducts. Therefore it is not finitely axiomatizable. On the other hand, consider the following axioms

(79)
$$\forall x \exists y [S(x, y)]$$
$$\forall z \forall y \forall z [(S(x, y) \wedge S(x, z)) \rightarrow y \approx z]$$
$$\forall x [\neg S(x, 0)]$$
$$\forall X [X(0) \wedge \forall x \forall y [(X(x) \wedge S(x, y)) \rightarrow X(y)]] \rightarrow \forall z [X(z)].$$

It can be shown that the conjunction of formulas (79) characterizes $\langle \omega, S \rangle$ up to isomorphism. Therefore, by Corollary 9.24, there is no classical first-order formula equivalent to the conjunction of of formulas (79). Therefore both SCAN and DLS fail here. However, as shown in Section 21.3.4 (page 276), Theorem 6.19 allows one to eliminate $\forall X$ from (79), obtaining its fixpoint equivalent.   ◁

Observe that the above example also provides a Π_1^1 formula which is not preserved under ultraproducts. Therefore an analogue of Lemma 9.25 does not hold for Π_1^1 formulas.

EXAMPLE 9.27. Consider the class of *torsion free Abelian groups*, i.e., the class of structures over the signature containing only a binary function symbol $\circ$ and a constant symbol 0, characterized by the following set of axioms:

(80) $\forall x \forall y \forall z [x \circ (y \circ z) \approx (x \circ y) \circ z]$ *(associativity)*

(81) $\forall x [x \circ 0 \approx x \wedge 0 \circ x \approx 0]$ *(identity)*

(82) $\forall x \exists y [x \circ y \approx 0 \wedge y \circ x \approx 0]$ *(existence of inverse)*

(83) $\forall x \forall y [x \circ y \approx y \circ x]$ *(commutativity)*

(84) $\forall x [x \not\approx 0 \rightarrow nx \not\approx 0]$ (for each $1 \leq n \in \omega$), where $nx \stackrel{\text{def}}{=} \underbrace{x \circ \ldots \circ x}_{n \text{ times}}$.

Observe that (84) represents infinitely many formulas, one for each natural number $n \geq 1$.

The class of *torsion Abelian groups*, being the Abelian groups satisfying (80)–(83) and not satisfying (84), is not closed under elementary equivalence (see, e.g., [**36**]). Therefore, by Theorem 9.23, it is not a basic elementary class. On the other hand, the following second-order formula

(85) $\forall z [z \not\approx 0 \rightarrow \exists X \forall x [X(x) \rightarrow (x \not\approx 0 \wedge X(z \circ x))] \wedge X(z)]$

is equivalent to (84), thus its negation is equivalent to the negation of (84). Hence, second-order quantifiers cannot be eliminated from (85) when the result is to be a first order formula. However, by applying Theorem 6.19, formula

$$\forall z [z \not\approx 0 \rightarrow [\text{GFP } X(x).x \not\approx 0 \wedge X(z \circ x)](z)]$$

is a fixpoint equivalent of (85).   ◁

In order to apply Theorem 6.19, the formula under second-order quantifier is to be in a particular form. Therefore we now focus on criteria when such formulas can be presented in a suitable form. We shall focus on the form required in (27), i.e.,

$$(86) \qquad \forall \bar{x}[\alpha(\bar{x}, \bar{z}) \to X(\bar{x})] \wedge \beta(X),$$

where $\alpha(\bar{x}, \bar{z}) \to X(\bar{x})$ is positive w.r.t. X and $\beta(X)$ is negative w.r.t. X.

Checking whether a formula is negative can, in fact be replaced by checking whether it is down-monotone. We shall then consider the form required in the first conjunct of (86).

First of all, one can use well-known criteria of Horn definability (see, e.g., [**36, 211**]). Here, however, we shall present criteria for the form of definability provided by van Benthem in [**211**], since this form, in fact, reflects what we really need.

DEFINITION 9.28. By a *PIA formula w.r.t.* P we understand a classical first-order formula of the form $\forall \bar{x}[\alpha(P, \bar{Q}, \bar{x}) \to P(\bar{x})]$, where $\alpha(P, \bar{Q}, \bar{x}) \to P(\bar{x})$ is positive w.r.t. P.[2] ◁

DEFINITION 9.29. A first-order formula $\alpha(P, \bar{Q})$ has the *intersection property w.r.t.* P iff in any relational structure M, whenever $M, P_i \models \alpha(P, \bar{Q})$ for all predicates in a family $\{P_i \mid i \in I\}$, $\alpha(P, \bar{Q})$ also holds for their intersection, i.e., we have that $M, \bigcap_{i \in I} P_i \models \alpha(P, \bar{Q})$. ◁

The following theorem is proved by van Benthem in [**211**].

THEOREM 9.30. The following are equivalent for all first-order formulas $\alpha(P, \bar{Q})$:

(1) $\alpha(P, \bar{Q})$ has the intersection property w.r.t. P;
(2) There is a PIA formula equivalent to $\alpha(P, \bar{Q})$. ◁

EXAMPLE 9.31. The formula $a \not\approx b \wedge \forall x[P(x, a) \vee P(x, b) \vee P(x, c)]$ does not have the intersection property. For example consider P_1, P_2 such that

$$P_1(x, y) \stackrel{\text{def}}{\equiv} y \approx a \text{ and } P_2(x, y) \stackrel{\text{def}}{\equiv} y \approx b.$$

Consider a structure where $a \not\approx b$. Then both P_1 and P_2 satisfy

$$\forall x[P(x, a) \vee P(x, b) \vee P(x, c)],$$

but their intersection, which is FALSE, does not. Therefore the formula

$$a \not\approx b \wedge a \not\approx c \wedge b \not\approx c \wedge$$
$$\forall x[P(x, a) \vee P(x, b) \vee P(x, c)] \wedge$$
$$\forall x \forall y \forall z[E(x, y) \to \neg(P(x, z) \wedge P(y, z))],$$

---

[2]The acronym PIA, introduced in [**211**], stands for "Positive antecedent Implies Atom".

expressing that the graph with edges defined by E is 3-colorable. It appears that this formula is not PIA and therefore cannot be equivalently transformed into a form required in Theorem 6.19.

Observe that we consider all relational structures here. It might still appear that in a restricted class of structures, e.g., all finite structures, the considered conjunction is equivalent to a PIA formula.   ◁

Part 3

Second-Order Quantifier Elimination in Modal Logics

Part 3

Second-Order Quantifier
Elimination in Modal Logics

CHAPTER 10

Modal Logics

Classical logic is *extensional* in the sense that one can always replace a term by an equal term and a subformula by an equivalent subformula. On the other hand, in many applications one deals with *intensional operators*, which violate extensionality. Intensional operators are called *modal operators* or *modalities*. Logics allowing such notions are called *modal logics* and sometimes *intensional logics*. Modal logics have intensively been studied (see, e.g., [**20, 38, 97, 110, 111, 136, 209**]).

In the syntactically simplest case one deals with a single unary modality $\Box$, the box operator, and its dual $\Diamond$, the diamond operator. The $\Box$ and $\Diamond$ operators have many possible readings, dependent on a particular application. Table 21 summarizes the most frequent readings of modalities.

TABLE 21. Possible readings of modalities.

readings of $\Box\alpha$	readings of $\Diamond\alpha$
α is necessary	α is possible
α is obligatory	α is allowed
always α	sometimes α
α is known	α is held possible
α is believed	α is held possible
every program state satisfies α	there is a program state satisfying α
α is provably the case	α is consistent

The different possible readings of the modalities are reflected in different types of modal logics. Table 22 summarizes the types of logics corresponding to the mentioned readings of modalities.

10.1. Mono-Modal Logics

Mono-modal (modal) logics have a single $\Box$ operator and a single $\Diamond$ operator. This is syntactically the simplest situation. Nevertheless mono-modal logics are powerful. As shown by Kracht and Wolter [**132**], multi-modal logics can be simulated by mono-modal logics.

TABLE 22. Common types of modal logics.

possible reading of modalities	type of modal logic
necessary, possible	alethic logics
obligatory, allowed	deontic logics
always, sometimes	temporal logics
known, held possible	epistemic logics
believed, held possible	doxastic logics
every (some) state of a program satisfies	logics of programs
provable, consistent	provability logics

10.1.1. Syntax. The language of propositional mono-modal logic is that of propositional logic enhanced with one unary modal operator $\Box$, the *box operator*. Let V be an enumerable set of propositional variables $p, q, r, \ldots$.

DEFINITION 10.1. A *mono-modal* (*modal*, for short) *formula* is either a propositional atom, i.e., a propositional variable or FALSE, or a formula of the form $\neg\alpha$, $\alpha \wedge \beta$ and $\Box\alpha$, where α and β denote modal formulas. TRUE, $\vee$, $\rightarrow$, and $\equiv$ are defined as usual. By definition, the modal diamond operator $\Diamond$ is the dual of the box operator, i.e., $\Diamond\alpha \overset{\text{def}}{=} \neg\Box\neg\alpha$, for any modal formula α. ◁

10.1.2. Kripke Semantics. The standard semantics of propositional modal logics is known as the *possible world semantics*, or *Kripke semantics*, after publication of Kripke's paper [**133**]. The Kripke semantics is defined in terms of relational structures called *frames* (or *Kripke structures*).

DEFINITION 10.2. A *(relational) frame* of a modal logic is a pair $F = \langle W, R \rangle$ consisting of a non-empty set of worlds W and a binary relation R over W. R is called the *accessibility relation*. ◁

DEFINITION 10.3. A *(relational) model* is a pair $M = \langle F, v \rangle$ consisting of a frame F and a *valuation* function v, where v assigns subsets of W to atomic propositional variables. The model M is said to be *based on the frame F*. Truth in any model $M = \langle W, R, v \rangle$ and any world $x \in W$ is defined inductively by:

$$M, x \models \text{TRUE}$$
$$M, x \models p \text{ iff } x \in v(p)$$
$$M, x \models \neg\alpha \text{ iff } M, x \not\models \alpha$$
$$M, x \models \alpha \wedge \beta \text{ iff both } M, x \models \alpha \text{ and } M, x \models \beta$$
$$M, x \models \Box\alpha \text{ iff } R(x, y) \text{ implies } M, y \models \alpha, \text{ for any } y \in W$$
$$M, x \models \Diamond\alpha \text{ iff } R(x, y) \text{ and } M, y \models \alpha, \text{ for some } y \in W.$$

If $M, x \models \alpha$ holds then we say α is *(locally) true at x* in M and that M *(locally) satisfies* α. A modal formula α is *(locally) satisfiable* iff there exists a model M and a world x in M such that $M, x \models \alpha$. A modal formula α is *valid in a model M*, written $M \models \alpha$, iff it is satisfiable in all worlds of M. We also say α is *globally satisfiable* in M. α is *globally satisfiable* over a frame F iff there is a valuation v such that $F, v \models \alpha$. A modal formula α is *valid in a frame F* iff it is valid in all models based on F. We then write $F \models \alpha$. We write $F, w \models \alpha$, if w is a world of the frame F and α is true in w of any model based on F, i.e., for any valuation function α is true in w.   ◁

When given a modal formula α, the problem of determining whether there exists a model M and a world x in M such that α is true at x in M is also called the *local satisfiability problem*. By contrast, the *global satisfiability problem* is the problem of determining whether there exists a model M such that for every world x in M, the given α is true at x in M.

10.1.3. An Overview of Propositional Mono-Modal Logics.

DEFINITION 10.4. We say that $\Box$ is a *normal modal operator* if it satisfies the following conditions:

$$\models \Box(\alpha \rightarrow \beta) \rightarrow (\Box\alpha \rightarrow \Box\beta)$$
$$\models \alpha \text{ implies } \models \Box\alpha.$$

By a *normal modal logic* we understand any mono-modal logic with a normal $\Box$ modality. The least normal modal logic (in the sense of the size of the set of tautologies) is denoted by **K**.   ◁

These conditions of normal modal logics are reflected in the Hilbert-like proof system defined next.

DEFINITION 10.5. A proof system for **K** is defined by extending the propositional calculus with the axiom

$$\vdash \Box(\alpha \rightarrow \beta) \rightarrow (\Box\alpha \rightarrow \Box\beta),$$

called the axiom **K**, together with the *generalization rule* (or *necessitation rule*):

$$\text{if } \vdash \alpha \text{ then } \vdash \Box\alpha.$$ ◁

The logic **K** is the weakest modal logic in the class of normal modal logic. Other normal modal logics are defined by additional axioms expressing the desired properties of modalities. Below we essentially follow the classification introduced by Lemmon [136]. The classification is based on axioms quoted in Table 23, where **D** comes from *deontic*, **T** is a traditional name of the axiom (after Feys), **4** is characteristic for logic **S4** of Lewis, **E** comes from *Euclidean* (this axiom is often

TABLE 23. Some well-known modal axioms.

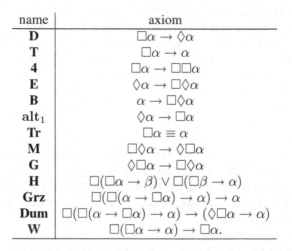

name	axiom
D	$\Box\alpha \rightarrow \Diamond\alpha$
T	$\Box\alpha \rightarrow \alpha$
4	$\Box\alpha \rightarrow \Box\Box\alpha$
E	$\Diamond\alpha \rightarrow \Box\Diamond\alpha$
B	$\alpha \rightarrow \Box\Diamond\alpha$
alt$_1$	$\Diamond\alpha \rightarrow \Box\alpha$
Tr	$\Box\alpha \equiv \alpha$
M	$\Box\Diamond\alpha \rightarrow \Diamond\Box\alpha$
G	$\Diamond\Box\alpha \rightarrow \Box\Diamond\alpha$
H	$\Box(\Box\alpha \rightarrow \beta) \vee \Box(\Box\beta \rightarrow \alpha)$
Grz	$\Box(\Box(\alpha \rightarrow \Box\alpha) \rightarrow \alpha) \rightarrow \alpha$
Dum	$\Box(\Box(\alpha \rightarrow \Box\alpha) \rightarrow \alpha) \rightarrow (\Diamond\Box\alpha \rightarrow \alpha)$
W	$\Box(\Box\alpha \rightarrow \alpha) \rightarrow \Box\alpha.$

denoted by **5**), **B** comes from Brouwer (because of its similarity with **KTB** and intuitionistic logic), **Tr** abbreviates *trivial*, **M** comes from McKinsey, **G** from Geach, **H** from Hintikka, **Grz** from Grzegorczyk, **Dum** from Dummett, and **W** from *reverse well founded* (it is also known as the Löb axiom.). These axioms are used to define many well-known modal logics.

In general, modal logics are extensions of the logic **K** with additional axioms such as those listed in Table 23. Let Δ denote a finite set of modal axioms. By KΔ we denote the smallest modal logic which contains the axioms in Δ. The notational convention $\mathbf{KX_0} \dots \mathbf{X_m}$ means the least normal logic in which formulas $\mathbf{X_0}, \dots, \mathbf{X_m}$ are accepted as axioms. Some frequently used and applied logics are listed in Table 24. The table also summarizes alternative names often used for modal logics. Sometimes modal logics coincide, for example: **KT = KDT**, **K4B = K5B**, **S5 = KT4B = KD4B = KTE**.

A modal formula α is a *theorem* of **K** or its extension iff α can be derived from the axioms by using the rules of the logic.

DEFINITION 10.6. A modal logic **KΔ** is said to be *sound* (respectively *complete*) *with respect to a class of frames* iff for any modal formula α, any frame in the class validates α if (respectively iff) α is a theorem in **KΔ**. A modal logic is said to be *complete* iff it is complete with respect to some class of frames.   ◁

The following theorem has been proved by Kripke [**133**].

THEOREM 10.7. The basic modal logic **K** is (sound and) complete with respect to the class of all frames $\langle W, R \rangle$.   ◁

TABLE 24. Some well-known modal logics.

logic	other names
KT	**T**, logic of Gödel/Feys/von Wright
KT4	**S4**
KT4B	**KT4E, S5**
K4E	**K45**
KD	deontic **T**
KD4	deontic **S4**
KD4B	deontic **S5**
KTB	logic of Brouwer
KT4M	**S4.1**
KT4G	**S4.2**
KT4H	**S4.3**
KT4Dum	**D**, logic of Prior
KT4Grz	**KGrz**, logic of Grzegorczyk
K4W	**KW**, logic of Löb
KTr	**KT4BM**, trivial logic

Soundness and completeness results for extensions of **K** are given in Section 10.4, below.

10.2. Multi-Modal Logics

10.2.1. Syntax. The language of propositional multi-modal logic extends the language of propositional monomodal logic by accepting more than one unary modal operator $\Box_1, \ldots, \Box_k$ ($k \geq 2$). Let V be an enumerable set of propositional variables $p, p_1, p_2, \ldots$.

DEFINITION 10.8. A *multi-modal* (*modal*, for short) *formula* is either a propositional atom, i.e., a propositional variable or FALSE, or a formula of the form $\neg\alpha$, $\alpha \wedge \beta$ and, for $1 \leq i \leq k$, $\Box_i\alpha$, where α and β denote modal formulas. TRUE, $\vee$, $\rightarrow$, and $\equiv$ are defined as usual. By definition, the modal diamond operator $\Diamond$ is the dual of the box operator, i.e., $\Diamond_i\alpha \stackrel{\text{def}}{=} \neg\Box_i\neg\alpha$ for any modal formula α.   ◁

10.2.2. Kripke Semantics. The semantics is a straightforward extension of that for mono-modal logics.

DEFINITION 10.9. A *frame* of a modal logic is a tuple $F = \langle W, R_1, R_2, \ldots, R_k \rangle$ of a non-empty set of worlds W and binary relations $R_1, R_2, \ldots, R_k$ over W. $R_1, R_2, \ldots, R_k$ are called the *accessibility relations*.   ◁

DEFINITION 10.10. A (*relational*) *model* is a pair $M = \langle F, v \rangle$ of a frame F and a *valuation* function v, where v assigns subsets of W to atomic propositional variables. The model M is therefore said to be *based on the frame F*. *Truth* in any model $M = \langle W, R, v \rangle$ and any world $x \in W$ is defined inductively by:

$$M, x \models \text{TRUE}$$

$$M, x \models p \text{ iff } x \in v(p)$$

$$M, x \models \neg\alpha \text{ iff } M, x \not\models \alpha$$

$$M, x \models \alpha \wedge \beta \text{ iff both } M, x \models \alpha \text{ and } M, x \models \beta$$

$$M, x \models \Box_i\alpha \text{ iff } R_i(x, y) \text{ implies } M, y \models \alpha, \text{ for any } y \in W$$

$$M, x \models \Diamond_i\alpha \text{ iff } R_i(x, y) \text{ and } M, y \models \alpha, \text{ for some } y \in W.$$

In multi-modal logics the notions of satisfiability and validity are defined as in mono-modal logics (see Definition 10.3).   ◁

10.2.3. Notation. We use the notation ϵ to denote the empty sequence and σ any (possibly empty) sequence of natural numbers. By definition let $\Box^\epsilon\alpha \overset{\text{def}}{=} \alpha$ and $\Box^{k.\sigma}\alpha \overset{\text{def}}{=} \Box_k\Box^\sigma\alpha$. Define $\Diamond^\epsilon$ and $\Diamond^\sigma$ similarly.

10.3. Translating Modal Logics into Second-Order Logic

The standard *second-order translation* of modal formulas into second-order logic is given by

$$(87) \qquad \Pi(\alpha) = \forall P_1 \ldots \forall P_m \forall x [\text{ST}(\alpha, x)],$$

where $\text{ST}(\alpha, x)$ is the (local) standard translation of a modal formula α with a free variable x, and $P_1, \ldots, P_m$ are all the unary predicates occurring in $\text{ST}(\alpha, x)$. The *standard translation* mapping ST itself is inductively defined as follows:

$$\text{ST}(\text{TRUE}, x) = \text{TRUE}$$

$$\text{ST}(p_i, x) = P_i(x)$$

$$\text{ST}(\neg\alpha, x) = \neg\,\text{ST}(\alpha, x)$$

$$\text{ST}(\alpha \wedge \beta, x) = \text{ST}(\alpha, x) \wedge \text{ST}(\beta, x)$$

$$\text{ST}(\Box_j\alpha, x) = \forall y [R_j(x, y) \rightarrow \text{ST}(\alpha, y)]$$

$$\text{ST}(\Diamond_j\alpha, x) = \exists y [R_j(x, y) \wedge \text{ST}(\alpha, y)],$$

where P_i is a unary relation symbol uniquely associated with the propositional variable p_i and R_j is a binary relation symbol representing the accessibility relation associated with $\Box_j$ and $\Diamond_j$, x is a first-order variable and y, whenever required, is a fresh variable.

An important property of the standard translation is that it preserves the truth of a modal formula at any state w of a Kripke model M. It also preserves validity of modal axioms in any frame.

THEOREM 10.11. Let α be any modal formula.

(1) For any Kripke model M and world w in it,

$$M, w \models \alpha \text{ iff } M \models ST(\alpha, x)_w^x,$$

where M is regarded as a first-order structure for the language of the standard translation.

(2) For every Kripke frame F and world w in it,

$$F, w \models \alpha \text{ iff } F \models \forall P_1 \ldots \forall P_m [ST(\alpha, x)_w^x], \text{ and}$$
$$F \models \alpha \text{ iff } F \models \forall P_1 \ldots \forall P_m \forall x [ST(\alpha, x)],$$

where F is regarded as a first-order structure for the language of the standard translation, and the P_i are the unary predicate symbols associated with the propositional variables occurring in α. ◁

Thus, validity (respectively satisfiability) of a modal formula can be expressed by a universal (respectively existential) monadic first formula. It is not difficult to prove the following.

COROLLARY 10.12. Any modal formula α is valid in $\mathbf{K}_{(m)}$ iff $\forall x[ST(\alpha, x)]$ is valid in first-order logic, and α is satisfiable in $\mathbf{K}_{(m)}$ iff $\exists x[ST(\alpha, x)]$ is satisfiable in first-order logic. ◁

$\forall x[ST(\alpha, x)]$ and $\exists x[ST(\alpha, x)]$ are referred to as the *standard first-order translation* of the modal formula α.

10.3.1. Notation. For any terms s and t, let $R^\epsilon(s, t)$ denote $s \approx t$, and let $R^{k \cdot \sigma}(s, t)$ denote $\exists x[R_k(s, x) \wedge R^\sigma(x, t)]$. The following is true.

$$ST(\Box^\sigma \alpha, s) = \forall y[R^\sigma(s, y) \rightarrow ST(\alpha, y)]$$
$$ST(\Diamond^\sigma \alpha, s) = \exists y[R^\sigma(s, y) \wedge ST(\alpha, y)].$$

10.4. Correspondence Theory

Normal modal logics can be studied systematically by considering the classes of frames they define. In general, these are subclasses of the class of all frames which define the basic modal logic $\mathbf{K}$. The most commonly used and studied modal logics are characterized by frames that satisfy first-order correspondence properties. Table 25 lists the first-order correspondence properties satisfied by classes of frames for extensions $\mathbf{K}\Delta$ for a selection of common axioms. We say, for example, that seriality is the *first-order (frame) correspondence property* of the axiom $\mathbf{D}$, reflexivity is the first-order correspondence property of the axiom $\mathbf{T}$, etc.

TABLE 25. Frame correspondence properties.

Axiom	Correspondence property	Name
D.	$\forall x \exists y [R(x,y)]$	seriality
T	$\forall x [R(x,x)]$	reflexivity
4	$\forall x \forall y \forall z [(R(x,y) \land R(y,z)) \to R(x,z)]$	transitivity
E	$\forall x \forall y \forall z [(R(x,y) \land R(x,z)) \to R(y,z)]$	Euclidicity
B	$\forall x \forall y [R(x,y) \to R(y,x)]$	symmetry
alt$_1$	$\forall x \forall y \forall z [(R(x,y) \land R(x,z)) \to y \approx z]$	functionality
Tr	$\forall x \forall y [R(x,y) \equiv (x \approx y)]$	triviality
G	$\forall x \forall y \forall z [(R(x,y) \land R(x,z))$	directedness
	$\to \exists u [R(y,u) \land R(z,u)]]$	
H	$\forall x \forall y \forall z [(R(x,y) \land R(x,z)) \to (R(y,z) \lor R(z,y))]$	

A class of frames comprising all frames satisfying a set of first-order conditions is said to be an *elementary* class. However not every modal axiom has an equivalent *first-order* frame property and therefore not every modal logic is elementary. For example, the logic **KM** is not determined by any elementary class of frames.

We are interested here in the question whether first-order correspondence properties can be derived from modal axioms. This questions has been considered by various authors (e.g. [**20, 84, 100, 154, 155, 199, 200, 209, 210**]). In general, the translations of modal axioms are second-order formulas of the form (87) above (page 124). The goal is to obtain from these second-order formulas equivalent formulas in first-order logic or fixpoint logic.

We have the following theorem of Chagrov and Chagrova [**33**], stating that finding correspondences is, in general, non-trivial.

THEOREM 10.13. It is undecidable whether a given modal formula (axiom) has a first-order correspondence property.   ◁

Nevertheless, there are classes of formulas for which first-order frame correspondence properties can be effectively computed (with second-order quantifier elimination methods).

   10.4.1. Sahlqvist Formulas. The class of Sahlqvist formulas is a syntactically defined class of modal formulas which are equivalent to first-order frame correspondence properties. Formulas in this class satisfy the well-known Sahlqvist theorem [**175**] stating that all Sahlqvist formulas define first-order conditions on frames and these properties can be effectively computed. Moreover, all Sahlqvist formulas axiomatize completely the classes of frames satisfying the corresponding first-order properties.

In the definition of Sahlqvist formulas we make use of the following notions.

DEFINITION 10.14. An occurrence of a propositional variable in a modal formula α is *positive (negative)* iff it occurs in the scope of an even (odd) number of negations. A modal formula α is *positive (negative) in a variable* p iff all occurrences of p in α are positive (negative). A modal formula α is *positive (negative)* iff all occurrences of propositional variables in α are positive (negative). ◁

DEFINITION 10.15. A *boxed atom* is a formula of the form $\Box_{k_1} \ldots \Box_{k_n} p$, where $\Box_{k_1}, \ldots, \Box_{k_n}$ is a (possibly empty) string of (possibly different) boxes and p is a propositional variable. ◁

DEFINITION 10.16. A *Sahlqvist antecedent* is a modal formula constructed from the propositional constants FALSE and TRUE, boxed atoms and negative formulas by applying $\vee$, $\wedge$, and diamonds.

A *definite Sahlqvist antecedent* is a Sahlqvist antecedent obtained without applying $\vee$ (i.e., constructed from the propositional constants FALSE and TRUE, boxed atoms and negative formulas by applying only $\wedge$ and diamonds).

A *(definite) Sahlqvist implication* is a modal formula $\alpha \to \beta$ where α is a (definite) Sahlqvist antecedent and β is a positive formula.

A *(definite) Sahlqvist formula* is a modal formula constructed from (definite) Sahlqvist implications by freely applying boxes and conjunctions, and by applying disjunctions to formulas without common propositional variables.

A *basic Sahlqvist formula* is a definite Sahlqvist formula obtained from definite Sahlqvist implications without applying conjunctions. ◁

EXAMPLE 10.17. The following are examples of Sahlqvist formulas.

the axioms **D**, **T**, **4**, **E**, **B**, **alt**$_1$, **G** (see Table 23)

$$\Diamond(\neg\Box(p \vee q) \wedge \Diamond\Box\Box q) \to \Box\Diamond(p \wedge q).$$

The following are not Sahlqvist formulas, but can be converted into Sahlqvist formulas defining the same semantic conditions by taking their contrapositions and reversing the signs of p and q.

$$\Box\Diamond p \to \Box p$$
$$\Box(p \vee q) \to \Box p.$$

The following formulas are not Sahlqvist formulas:

M $\quad \Box\Diamond p \to \Diamond\Box p$

W $\quad \Box(\Box p \to p) \to \Box p.$

They cannot be converted into Sahlqvist formulas defining the same semantic conditions, because both are known not to be first-order definable. ◁

We have the following lemma (for a proof see [**99**]).

LEMMA 10.18. Every Sahlqvist formula is semantically equivalent to a conjunction of basic Sahlqvist formulas.   ◁

THEOREM 10.19. (Sahlqvist [**175**]) Suppose α is an arbitrary Sahlqvist formula.

(1) There is a first-order formula $\beta_\alpha(x)$ in the language of first-order logic with equality and binary relational symbols, such that for every Kripke frame F and every world w in F,

$$F, w \models \alpha \quad \text{iff} \quad F \models \beta_\alpha(x)_w^x.$$

(2) Every Sahlqvist formula is canonical.   ◁

(1) of the theorem says that every Sahlqvist formula α is locally first-order definable, (2) implies that given a set of Sahlqvist axioms Δ, the logic $\mathbf{K}_{(m)}\Delta$ is complete with respect to the class of frames defined by the correspondence properties. Such a logic is called a *Sahlqvist logic*.

Sahlqvist's theorem therefore gives a sufficient condition for semantic specification in first-order logic and syntactic specification by a Hilbert axiomatization of Sahlqvist logics. Though very important, in this book we do not discuss the completeness aspect of the theorem further. Our interest is the application of second-order quantifier elimination methods which can be used for solving the first-order correspondence problem. The rest of this part of the book is devoted to this problem.

10.4.2. Applications. Modal logics are a priori second-order logics but many modal logics such as Sahlqvist logics can be characterized by first-order means. First-order definability is useful if we are interested in proof methods and automating reasoning of modal logics. It is easier to develop proof methods and theorem provers for modal logics that can be semantically encoded in first-order logic than for non-first-order definable modal logics. Currently particularly popular for automated reasoning are tableaux approaches and translation to first-order logic in combination with first-order resolution theorem provers [**75, 101, 109, 161, 184, 185**]. The benefit of a general theorem like Sahlqvist's theorem is obvious for approaches based on translation to first-order logic. It means that automated reasoning can be realized by translating modal problems into first-order logic using the standard translation mapping.

THEOREM 10.20. Let $\text{Corr}(\Delta)$ denote the set of first-order frame properties of the formulas in Δ. Let L be a first-order definable propositional multi-modal logic $\mathbf{K}_{(m)}\Delta$ which is complete with respect to the class of frames satisfying $\text{Corr}(\Delta)$. Then, for any formula α,

(1) α is locally satisfiable in L iff $\mathrm{Corr}(\Delta) \wedge \exists x[\mathrm{ST}(\alpha, x)]$ is satisfiable in first-order logic, and

(2) α is globally satisfiable in L iff $\mathrm{Corr}(\Delta) \wedge \forall x[\mathrm{ST}(\alpha, x)]$ is satisfiable in first-order logic. $\lhd$

For instance, α is locally satisfiable in **K4** iff

$$\forall x \forall y \forall z[(R(x,y) \wedge R(y,z)) \rightarrow R(x,z)] \wedge \exists x[\mathrm{ST}(\alpha, x)]$$

is satisfiable in first-order logic.

First-order definability is also useful for developing for example tableau calculi or natural deduction calculi. The common first-order relational correspondence properties can be easily captured as so-called structural inference rules for labeled semantic tableau of first-order definable logics, see for example [13, 32]. [16, 214] investigate how first-order relational correspondence properties can be systematically used in the definition of labeled natural deduction calculi for modal logics.

10.5. Extended Modal Logics and Quantified Modal Logic

10.5.1. Modal Tense Logic. *Modal tense logic* is defined like multi-modal logic with the difference that the language includes a converse modality $\Box_i^{\smile}$ for every modality $\Box_i$, and its dual $\Diamond_i^{\smile}$. Thus we can view modal tense logic as an extension of multi-modal logic with converse modalities. The alternative semantic view is to regard modal tense logic as a multi-modal logic (not as an extension of it) in which the modalities are interpreted over relations and converse relations.

Let V be an enumerable set of propositional variables $p, p_1, p_2, \ldots$.

DEFINITION 10.21. A *modal tense formula* is a propositional variable, FALSE, or a formula of the form $\neg\alpha$, $\alpha \wedge \beta$ and, for $1 \le i \le k$, $\Box_i \alpha$ and $\Box_i^{\smile} \alpha$, where α and β denote modal tense formulas. TRUE, $\vee$, $\rightarrow$, $\equiv$, $\Diamond_i$ are defined as usual. The converse diamond operator $\Diamond_i^{\smile}$ is specified by $\Diamond_i^{\smile} \alpha \stackrel{\mathrm{def}}{=} \neg\Box_i^{\smile}\neg\alpha$, where α denotes an arbitrary modal tense formula. $\lhd$

The semantics of modal tense logic is given by a Kripke model $M = \langle W, \langle R_i \rangle_i, v \rangle$ and the satisfiability relation defined as before, except that the interpretation of converse modalities is defined by the condition

$$M, x \models \Box_i^{\smile} \alpha \text{ iff } R_i(y, x) \text{ implies } M, y \models \alpha, \text{ for all } y \in W.$$

The notions of satisfiability and validity are defined as before.

The standard translation of modal tense formulas is an extension of the mapping ST from Section 10.3. The defining condition for converse modalities is:

$$\mathrm{ST}(\Box_i^{\smile} \alpha, x) = \forall y[R_i(y, x) \to \mathrm{ST}(\alpha, y)].$$

It is not difficult to prove

$$M, w \models \alpha \text{ iff } M \models \mathrm{ST}(\alpha, x)_w^x,$$

and:

THEOREM 10.22. Let α be a modal tense formula. α is valid (satisfiable) in modal tense logic iff $\forall x \, \mathrm{ST}(\alpha, x)$ is valid in first-order logic $\exists x[\mathrm{ST}(\alpha, x)]$ is satisfiable in first-order logic). ◁

10.5.2. First-Order Modal Logics. *First-order modal logics* have been extensively studied in the literature; for a survey see, e.g., [88].

In first-order modal logics we allow the elements of the classical first-order language, including first-order quantifiers.

DEFINITION 10.23. Let **S** be a propositional normal modal logic. Then the system **Q1S** is obtained from **S** by adding the principles of the first-order logic and rules

(88) $\quad t \approx t' \vdash \Box t \approx t'$

(89) $\quad t \not\approx t' \vdash \Box t \not\approx t'$

(90) $\quad t \approx t$

(91) $\quad t \approx t' \vdash p(t) \to p(t'), \quad$ where $p(t)$ and $p(t')$ are atoms

(92) $\quad \forall \bar{y}[\Box \alpha(\bar{y})] \to \Box \forall \bar{y}[\alpha(\bar{y})].$

Formula (92) is called the *Barcan formula*. ◁

It is worth noting that by assuming rules (88) and (89) we accept the *rigid terms semantics*, where the interpretation of terms is the same in all worlds of Kripke frames.

It is important to note, that **Q1K** (thus also any quantified normal modal logic) entails the converse of the Barcan formula (see, e.g., [88]):

(93) $\quad \Box \forall \bar{y}[\alpha(\bar{y})] \to \forall \bar{y}[\Box \alpha(\bar{y})].$

The standard translation can now be extended by adding the clauses

$$\begin{aligned}
&\mathrm{ST}(p(\bar{y}), x) = P(x, \bar{y}) \\
(94) \quad &\mathrm{ST}(\forall z[\alpha], x) = \forall z[\mathrm{ST}(\alpha, x)] \\
&\mathrm{ST}(\exists z[\alpha], x) = \exists z[\mathrm{ST}(\alpha, x)],
\end{aligned}$$

to the clauses given in Section 10.3 defining ST. P is a new relation symbol, which differs from the relation symbol p in the first coordinate, reflecting the dependence of p on worlds.

10.5.3. Second-Order Modal Logics.
In second-order modal logics formulas may involve quantifiers binding relation variables. Examples or second-order modal formulas are $\forall p[\Box p \to p]$ and $\forall p \exists q \Box \forall z[p(z) \lor q(z)]$.

In modal logic there are various ways of defining the semantics of second-order quantification [29, 77, 78, 123]. We use the standard definition in which the semantics of quantified relations is defined in terms of quantification over p-equivalent models.

Let p be a relation symbol (nullary or not) and let M and M' be two models of our modal logic. We say M and M' are p-*equivalent* if M and M' differ only in the valuation of p. More generally, M and M' are $(p_1, \ldots, p_m)$-*equivalent* if M and M' differ only in the valuation of the relation symbols $p_1, \ldots, p_m$ $(m > 0)$.

Now the semantics of second-order modal formulas is defined as before, but truth of formulas involving quantified relations is defined by

$$M, x \models \forall p[\alpha] \text{ iff for any model } M' \text{ } p\text{-equivalent to } M, \text{ } M', x \models \alpha$$
$$M, x \models \exists p[\alpha] \text{ iff for some model } M' \text{ } p\text{-equivalent to } M, \text{ } M', x \models \alpha.$$

Second-order quantifiers essentially involve quantification over valuations. For, consider the propositional case, and suppose $M = \langle F, v \rangle$. Then $M, x \models \forall p[\alpha]$ iff for any valuation v' which is identical to v but differs only in the assignment to p, α is true at x in the model $\langle F, v' \rangle$. This means second-order quantification is interpreted as quantification ranging over the set of all sets of possible worlds. In alternative semantics second-order quantifiers range over a designated set of subsets of the set of possible worlds.

The standard translation ST is an extension of the previous definitions with

$$\text{ST}(\forall p[\alpha], x) = \forall P[\text{ST}(\alpha, x)]$$
$$\text{ST}(\exists p[\alpha], x) = \exists P[\text{ST}(\alpha, x)],$$

where P is a new relation symbol, as in (94).

EXAMPLE 10.24. Let R be the accessibility relation of the underlying Kripke frame. The standard translation, in the world x, of the formula

$$\forall p \exists q \Box \forall z[p(z) \lor q(z)]$$

is given by

$$\text{ST}(\forall p \exists q \Box \forall z[p(z) \lor q(z)], x) =$$
$$\forall P \exists Q \left[\forall y[R(x, y) \to \forall z[P(y, z) \lor Q(y, z)]] \right]. \qquad \triangleleft$$

CHAPTER 11

Clausal Quantifier Elimination in Modal Logics

In this chapter we explore the application of the approach of SCAN in modal logic. In particular, we focus on using clausal quantifier elimination methods for automating modal correspondence theory. We consider the problem of reducing modal axioms to first-order frame correspondence properties.

11.1. Computing Correspondences

The main motivation of Gabbay and Ohlbach for developing the SCAN algorithm was the automation of correspondence theory in modal logic [**84**]. In particular, the aim was to develop algorithms and programs which can be used to inter-translate corresponding properties of modal logics and their underlying Kripke structures. Here we focus on the problem of automatically reducing a modal axiom to its corresponding frame property. This problem can be tackled with the second-order quantifier elimination methods described in this book. The idea is to consider a modal axiom as a universally quantified second-order modal formula $\forall \bar{p}[\alpha]$ and

(1) Translate it into a second-order formula using the second-order translation $\forall \bar{P} \forall x [\mathrm{ST}(\alpha, x)]$, where $\mathrm{ST}(\alpha, x)$ denotes the standard translation (see Section 10.3);
(2) Then use a method of quantifier elimination method to eliminate the second-order quantifiers over the relation symbols.

In this chapter we focus on clausal methods, while in the next chapters we discuss direct methods.

11.1.1. Using the Standard Translation. First, we consider examples of first-order definable modal axioms.

EXAMPLE 11.1. Consider

$$\mathbf{4} \quad \forall p[\Box p \to \Box \Box p]$$
$$\mathbf{G} \quad \forall p[\Diamond \Box p \to \Box \Diamond p]$$

These axioms translate to second-order sentences:

$$\forall P \forall x [\text{ST}(\mathbf{4}, x)]$$

$$= \forall P \forall x \left[\forall y [R(x, y) \rightarrow P(y)] \right.$$
$$\left. \rightarrow \forall y [R(x, y) \rightarrow \forall z [R(y, z) \rightarrow P(z)]] \right]$$

$$\forall P \forall x [\text{ST}(\mathbf{G}, x)]$$

$$= \forall P \forall x \left[\exists y_1 [R(x, y_1) \wedge \forall z_1 [R(y_1, z_1) \rightarrow P(z_1)]] \right.$$
$$\left. \rightarrow \forall y_2 [R(x, y_2) \rightarrow \exists z_2 [R(y_2, z_2) \wedge P(z_2)]] \right].$$

The negations are:

$$\exists P \exists x [\neg \text{ST}(\mathbf{4}, x)]$$

$$= \exists P \exists x \left[\forall y [R(x, y) \rightarrow P(y)] \right.$$
$$\left. \wedge \exists y [R(x, y) \wedge \exists z [R(y, z) \wedge \neg P(z)]] \right]$$

$$\exists P \exists x [\neg \text{ST}(\mathbf{G}, x)]$$

$$= \exists P \exists x \left[\exists y_1 [R(x, y_1) \wedge \forall z_1 [R(y_1, z_1) \rightarrow P(z_1)]] \right.$$
$$\left. \wedge \exists y_2 [R(x, y_2) \wedge \forall z_2 [\neg R(y_2, z_2) \vee \neg P(z_2)]] \right].$$

Let us now consider the axioms in turn. The clausal form of the negation of the translation of axiom **4** is:

1. $\neg R(a, y) \vee P(y)$
2. $R(a, b)$
3. $R(b, c)$
4. $\neg P(c)$

Now apply C-resolution followed by constraint elimination:

5. $\neg R(a, y) \vee c \not\approx y$	1.2, 4.1
6. $\neg R(a, c)$	5, c-elim.

Clauses 1 and 4 are deleted by purification leaving clauses 2, 3 and 6. Unskolemization produces

$$\exists v_a \exists v_b \exists v_c [R(v_a, v_b) \wedge R(v_b, v_c) \wedge \neg R(v_a, v_c)],$$

which is the negation of transitivity, i.e., the result we expected according to Table 25.

The derivation for **G** is as follows.

1. $R(a, b)$
2. $\neg R(b, z_1) \vee P(z_1)$
3. $R(a, c)$
4. $\neg R(c, z_2) \vee \neg P(z_2)$
5. $\neg R(b, z_1) \vee z_1 \not\approx z_2 \vee \neg R(c, z_2)$ 2.2, 4.2
6. $\neg R(b, z_1) \vee \neg R(c, z_1)$ 5, c-elim.

Unskolemizing $\{1, 3, 6\}$ yields

$$\exists v_a \exists v_b \exists v_c \forall z_1 [R(v_a, v_b) \wedge R(v_a, v_c) \wedge (\neg R(v_b, z_1) \vee \neg R(v_c, z_1))].$$

Negating this, we obtain a formula equivalent to the correspondence property of **G** (cf. Table 25).

$$\forall v_a \forall v_b \forall v_c \exists z_1 [(R(v_a, v_b) \wedge R(v_a, v_c)) \rightarrow (R(v_b, z_1) \wedge R(v_c, z_1))]. \quad \triangleleft$$

Axioms **4** and **G** are examples of Sahlqvist axioms for which the SCAN algorithm and H-resolution is guaranteed to succeed, see Section 11.2.

Not every modal axiom has an equivalent first-order frame property. The axiom we consider next is not first-order definable with respect to the standard relational semantics.

EXAMPLE 11.2. Consider McKinsey's axiom

M $\forall p [\Box \Diamond p \rightarrow \Diamond \Box p].$

It's negation is

$\neg$**M** $\exists p [\Box \Diamond p \wedge \Box \Diamond \neg p].$

The clausal form of the translation of $\neg$**M** and C-resolution derivation is:

1. $\neg R(a, x) \vee R(x, f(x))$
2. $\neg R(a, x) \vee P(f(x))$
3. $\neg R(a, x) \vee R(x, g(x))$
4. $\neg R(a, x) \vee \neg P(g(x))$
5. $\neg R(a, x) \vee f(x) \not\approx g(y) \vee \neg R(a, y)$ 2.2, 4.2

The result of stage (2), namely C-resolution, is the set of clauses $\{1, 3, 5\}$. In the next step we attempt unskolemization. First we rename the variables of clauses apart:

$$1'.\ \neg R(a, x_1) \lor R(x_1, f(x_1))$$
$$3'.\ \neg R(a, y_1) \lor R(y_1, g(y_1))$$
$$5'.\ \neg R(a, z_1) \lor f(z_1) \not\approx g(z_2) \lor \neg R(a, z_2)$$

We can unify $f(x_1)$ with $f(z_1)$ and $g(y_1)$ with $g(z_2)$ to get:

$$1''.\ \neg R(a, x_1) \lor R(x_1, f(x_1))$$
$$3''.\ \neg R(a, y_1) \lor R(y_1, g(y_1))$$
$$5''.\ \neg R(a, x_1) \lor f(x_1) \not\approx g(y_1) \lor \neg R(a, y_1)$$

but it is not possible to rewrite the clause $5''$ so that the sets of arguments of the f-term and the g-term are related by a subset relationship and preserving logical equivalence or satisfiability-equivalence. (It is possible to unify the argument sets of the two terms, but $5''$ is not logically equivalent to $\neg R(a, x_1) \lor f(x_1) \not\approx g(x_1) \lor \neg R(a, x_1)$.) Thus unskolemization returns only a formula involving a Henkin quantifier, which is still second-order, because of the presence of $\exists v_f$ and $\exists v_g$.

$$\exists v_a \begin{pmatrix} \forall x \exists v_f \\ \forall y \exists v_g \end{pmatrix} \begin{bmatrix} (\neg R(a, x) \lor R(x, v_f)) \land (\neg R(a, y) \lor R(y, v_g)) \\ \land (\neg R(a, x) \lor v_f \not\approx v_g \lor \neg R(a, y)) \end{bmatrix}. \quad \lhd$$

EXAMPLE 11.3. The disjunction of the axioms **D** and **M** reduces to seriality of the accessibility relation. That is:

$$\forall p[(\Box p \to \Diamond p) \lor (\Box \Diamond p \to \Diamond \Box p)] \equiv \forall x \exists y [R(x, y)].$$

In order to prove this we negate the modal formula and try to derive the negation of seriality,

$$\exists p[\Box p \land \Box \neg p \land \Box \Diamond p \land \Box \Diamond \neg p].$$

Translating the formula and clausifying we obtain these clauses:

$$1.\ \neg R(a, x) \lor P(x)$$
$$2.\ \neg R(a, x) \lor \neg P(x)$$
$$3.\ \neg R(a, x) \lor R(x, f(x))$$
$$4.\ \neg R(a, x) \lor P(f(x))$$
$$5.\ \neg R(a, x) \lor R(x, g(x))$$
$$6.\ \neg R(a, x) \lor \neg P(g(x))$$

Then we derive:

$$7. \; \neg R(a, x) \lor \neg R(a, x) \qquad\qquad 1.2, 2.2$$
$$8. \; \neg R(a, x) \qquad\qquad 7, \text{cond.}$$

Now, all further inferences become redundant because clause 8 subsumes all the other clauses. The result returned after unskolemization and negation is therefore $\forall x \exists y R(x, y)$. ◁

The previous example involves McKinsey's axiom for which currently all direct second-order quantifier elimination algorithms fail, see Example 13.12 in Chapter 13. Direct methods based on Ackermann's lemma need to transform the input formula (be it in modal form for MSQEL and SQEMA, or in first-order form for DLS) into a form so that Ackermann's lemma can be applied in one macro inference step. This is not possible here. SCAN does not fail outright but outputs a formula which involves quantifiers over functions and is therefore second-order. This formula may still be useful though.

11.1.2. The Utility of Refinements in the H-Resolution Calculus. The ordering refinement and the selection function in the H-resolution calculus provide mechanisms for controlling the inferences performed. They can be used to specify in which order the inferences have to be performed and can therefore also be used to limit the inference steps being performed. Having such techniques is extremely useful. The next example illustrates how, when chosen appropriately, the refinements can prevent all inferences for the considered problem (it is of course not always possible to prevent all inferences).

EXAMPLE 11.4. Consider the formula (provided by Szałas, cf. [42]):

$$(95) \qquad \forall p[\Box(p \lor \Box \neg p) \to \Diamond(p \land \Diamond \neg p)].$$

Formula (95) is equivalent to FALSE. The clausal form of its negation is:

$$1. \; \neg R(a, x) \lor P(x) \lor \neg R(x, y) \lor \neg P(y) \qquad\qquad \text{given}$$
$$2. \; \neg R(a, x) \lor \neg P(x) \lor \neg R(x, y) \lor P(y) \qquad\qquad \text{given}$$

In this example we opt to use a selection function which selects the negative literals in both clauses. No inferences and no reduction steps are possible. This means the set is saturated up to redundancy with respect to P. By Theorem 5.16, $N = \{1, 2\}$ is equivalent to the empty sct, i.e., TRUE. Negating we get FALSE as an equivalent for (95), as expected.

It would appear that without selecting literals increasingly longer non-redundant clauses are generated and the derivation does not terminate. The example therefore clearly illustrates the usefulness of a selection function. ◁

11.2. Completeness for Sahlqvist Formulas

Although the quantifier elimination methods are not complete for arbitrary modal logic formulas they are complete for the class of Sahlqvist formulas [**43, 98**]. By completeness here we mean that the algorithm terminates and returns first-order correspondence properties for a given modal formula. In this section we show that SCAN (based on C-resolution) is complete for Sahlqvist's class. This was first proved by Goranko, Hustadt, Schmidt and Vakarelov [**98**].

Let SCAN* be the extension of the SCAN algorithm with the pre-processing and post-processing necessary for computing first-order correspondences for modal logic formulas. The pre-processing involves translating the given modal formula to the second-order formula $\Pi(\varphi)$ and negating the result. The post-processing involves negating the result output of SCAN, if it terminates.

In the following, we show that SCAN* is complete for Sahlqvist formulas. We need to prove that for any second-order formula α' obtained by pre-processing from a Sahlqvist formula α, SCAN can compute a first-order equivalent for α'. To this end, we have to show two properties:

(1) The computation of C-resolvents and C-factors terminates when applied to the set $\text{Cls}(\alpha')$ of clauses associated with α', i.e., SCAN can generate only finitely many new clauses in the process;

(2) The resulting first-order formula, which in general may contain Skolem functions, can be successfully unskolemized.

We first consider the case when α is a definite Sahlqvist implication.

THEOREM 11.5. Given any definite Sahlqvist implication α, SCAN* effectively computes a first-order formula $\text{Corr}(\alpha)$ which is logically equivalent to α.

PROOF. Let $\alpha = Ant \to Pos$. In the pre-processing stage, SCAN* computes $\Pi(\alpha)$ and negates the result. Since $\Pi(\alpha) = \forall P_1 \ldots \forall P_m \forall x [\text{ST}(\alpha, x)]$, the negation $\neg\Pi(\alpha)$ is equivalent to

$$\exists P_1 \ldots \exists P_m \exists x [\text{ST}(\neg\alpha, x)] = \exists P_1 \ldots \exists P_m \exists x [\text{ST}(Ant \land \neg Pos, x)].$$

So, the initial clause set N we obtain after clausification and Skolemization is given by $\text{Cls}(\text{ST}(Ant \land \neg Pos, a))$ where a is a Skolem constant. The definite Sahlqvist antecedent Ant is constructed from propositional constants, boxed atoms and negative formulas by applying only $\land$ and diamonds. In addition $\neg Pos$ is also a negative formula, since Pos is a positive formula. Thus, $Ant \land \neg Pos$ is itself a definite Sahlqvist antecedent. Note that

$$\text{ST}(\beta \land \gamma, a_i) = \text{ST}(\beta, a_i) \land \text{ST}(\gamma, a_i)$$
$$\text{ST}(\Diamond_{k_i}\beta, a_i) = \exists y [R_{k_i}(a_i, y) \land \text{ST}(\beta, y)].$$

Skolemization replaces the existentially quantified variable y by a new constant a_{i+1} which replaces any occurrence of y in $R_{k_i}(a_i, y) \wedge \mathrm{ST}(\beta, y)$. Consequently,

$$\mathrm{Cls}(\mathrm{ST}(\beta \wedge \gamma, a_i)) = \mathrm{Cls}(\mathrm{ST}(\beta, a_i)) \cup \mathrm{Cls}(\mathrm{ST}(\gamma, a_i))$$

$$\mathrm{Cls}(\mathrm{ST}(\Diamond_{k_i}\beta, a_i)) = \{R_{k_i}(a_i, a_{i+1})\} \cup \mathrm{Cls}(\mathrm{ST}(\beta, a_{i+1})).$$

It follows by a straightforward inductive argument that we can divide the clause set $N = \mathrm{Cls}(\mathrm{ST}(Ant \wedge \neg Pos, a))$ into a set N_n of clauses which stems from negative formulas occurring in $Ant \wedge \neg Pos$ and a set N_p of clauses which stems from the translation of the propositional constants TRUE and FALSE, and boxed atoms.

The translation of boxed atoms with respect to a constant a_i is given by

$$\mathrm{ST}(\Box_{k_1} \ldots \Box_{k_n} p_j, a_i) =$$

$$\forall x_1 \Big[R_{k_1}(a_i, x_1) \rightarrow \forall x_2 \big[R_{k_2}(x_1, x_2) \rightarrow \cdots$$

$$\cdots \forall x_n [R_{k_n}(x_{n-1}, x_n) \rightarrow P_j(x_n)] \ldots \big] \Big],$$

where $n \geq 0$. Clausification transforms $\mathrm{ST}(\Box_{k_1} \ldots \Box_{k_n} p_j, a_i)$ into a single clause of the form

$$\neg R_{k_1}(a_i, x_1) \vee \bigvee_{l=1}^{n-1} \neg R_{k_l}(x_l, x_{l+1}) \vee P_j(x_n),$$

for $n \geq 0$. In the case of $n = 0$, the clause we obtain consists of a single positive ground literal $P_j(a_i)$. Besides clauses of this form, N_p can only contain the empty clause, which is the result of translation of the propositional constant FALSE, while the translation of TRUE is eliminated during clausification.

Thus, every clause in N_p contains at most one relation symbol P_j. Moreover, all clauses in N_p only contain positive occurrences of unary relation symbols P_j. In contrast, by definition, all occurrences of propositional variables p_j in the negative formulas in $Ant \wedge \neg Pos$ are negative. So, the corresponding occurrences of unary relation symbols P_j in N_n are all negative as well.

We have to establish the following.

The derivation always terminates for the formulas (clauses). We define a function μ_1 that assigns to each clause C a triple $\mu_1(C) = \langle n_C^P, n_C^R, d_C \rangle$ of natural numbers such that n_C^P is the number of P_i-literals in C, n_C^R is the number of all remaining literals in C, and d_C is the depth of C. We call $\mu_1(C)$ the *complexity* of clause C. It is straightforward to show that for a given triple $c = \langle n^P, n^R, d \rangle$ of natural numbers the preimage of c under μ_1 contains only finitely many clauses (up to renaming of variables). We also define an ordering $\succ$ on $\mathbb{N} \times \mathbb{N} \times \mathbb{N}$ by the lexicographic combination of the ordering $>$ on the natural numbers with itself. Obviously, the ordering $\succ$ is well-founded.

We have already established that no clause in N contains a positive P_i-literal as well as a negative P_j-literal and the clauses in N_p have the property that each clause which contains a positive P_i-literal contains exactly one such literal. It follows that in any C-resolution derivation from N no inference steps by C-factoring are possible. Furthermore, any C-resolvent D obtained by C-resolution with positive premise C_p and negative premise C_n does not contain a positive P_i-literal, and D contains fewer P_i-literals than C_n. Thus, $\mu_1(C_n) \succ \mu_1(D)$. Since no other inference steps are allowed in the C-resolution calculus, we have established that the conclusion of any inference step in a derivation from N is of strictly smaller complexity than one of its premises. The application of a deletion rule only replaces a clause C of complexity $\mu_1(C)$ by a clause D with smaller complexity $\mu_1(D)$. It follows that any derivation from N terminates.

The restoration of the quantifiers does not fail. To ensure that the restoration of quantifiers does not fail once the derivation from N has terminated, we can show by induction that for any clause C in a derivation from N,

(1) C contains only inequations of the form

$$b \not\approx z, \quad b \not\approx c, \quad b \not\approx f(z), \quad y \not\approx z, \quad y \not\approx c, \quad \text{or} \quad y \not\approx f(z);$$

(2) There are no two inequations in C of the form $y \not\approx f(z)$ and $y \not\approx g(z)$ with $f \neq g$, and

(3) If C contains negative P_i-literals then these are of the form $\neg P_i(z)$, $\neg P_i(c)$ or $\neg P_i(f(z))$, where c is a Skolem constant and f is a unary Skolem function.

An alternative formulation of property (2) is that for any two inequations $x_1 \not\approx f(y)$ and $x_2 \not\approx g(z)$ in C with $f \neq g$ we have $x_1 \neq x_2$.

Inspection of the unskolemization procedure (see Section 5.3) shows that properties (1) and (2) are sufficient to ensure that unskolemization is successful, and property (3) enables us to show that the other two properties are preserved in inference steps. ◁

The theorem can be extended to the case of basic Sahlqvist formulas, obtained from definite Sahlqvist implications by applying boxes and disjunctions to formulas not sharing relation variables.

In contrast to definite Sahlqvist antecedents, Sahlqvist antecedents can include disjunction as a connective. This makes the proof of completeness of SCAN with respect to Sahlqvist implications much more involved. The cornerstone of the proof is the notion of a *chain*.

Let $(t_1, \ldots, t_n)$ be an ordered sequence of pairwise distinct terms. A *chain* C over $(t_1, \ldots, t_n)$ is a clause containing only literals of the form $(\neg)R_{k_i}(s, t)$ and $(\neg)P_j(u)$ such that the following three conditions are satisfied:

(1) For every i, $1 \leq i \leq n-1$, either $\neg r_{k_i}(t_i, t_{i+1})$ or $r_{k_i}(t_i, t_{i+1})$ is in c;

(2) For every $(\neg)r_{k_i}(u, v) \in c$, $u = t_j$ and $v = t_{j+1}$ for some j, $1 \leq j \leq n - 1$;

(3) For every $(\neg)p_j(u) \in c$, $u = t_j$ for some j, $1 \leq j \leq n$.

LEMMA 11.6. Let C be a chain over $(t_1, \ldots, t_n)$. Then there does not exist an ordered sequence $(s_1, \ldots, s_m)$ of pairwise distinct terms which is distinct from $(t_1, \ldots, t_n)$ such that C is also a chain over $(s_1, \ldots, s_m)$.   ◁

The *length* of a chain C over $(t_1, \ldots, t_n)$ is n. Note that by Lemma 11.6 the chain C uniquely determines $(t_1, \ldots, t_n)$. So, the length of a chain is a well-defined notion.

The link between the clauses we obtain from translating Sahlqvist formulas or modal formulas, in general, and chains is not as straightforward as one may hope. For example, consider the Sahlqvist antecedent $\neg p_1 \vee \Box p_2 \vee \Box p_3$. The clausal form of its translation consists of the single clause

$$\neg P_1(a) \vee \neg R(a, x) \vee P_2(x) \vee \neg R(a, y) \vee P_3(y).$$

It is straightforward to check that we cannot arrange the terms a, x, and y in an ordered sequence S such that the whole clause would be a chain over S. Instead the clause consists of at least two chains: $\neg P_1(a) \vee \neg R(a, x) \vee P_2(x)$ over (a, x) and $\neg R(a, y) \vee \neg P_3(y)$ over (a, y), or alternatively, $\neg R(a, x) \vee P_2(x)$ over (a, x) and $\neg P_1(a) \vee \neg R(a, y) \vee \neg P_3(y)$ over (a, y). However, we could also divide the clause into three or more chains, for example, $\neg P_1(a)$ over (a), $P_2(x)$ over (x), $P_3(y)$ over (y), $\neg R(a, x)$ over (a, x) and $\neg R(a, y)$ over (a, y).

In the following we only consider *maximal chains*. A chain C over $(t_1, \ldots, t_n)$ is *maximal* with respect to a clause D iff C is a variable indecomposable subclause of D and there is no chain C' over $(s_1, \ldots, s_m)$, $m > n$, such that C' is a subclause of D and for every i, $1 \leq i \leq n$, $t_i \in \{s_1, \ldots, s_m\}$.

Under this definition our example clause can only be partitioned into three maximal chains, $\neg P_1(a)$ over (a), $\neg R(a, x) \vee P_2(x)$ over (a, x), and $\neg R(a, y) \vee P_3(y)$ over (a, y). We can see the obvious link between the modal subformula of $\neg p_1 \vee \Box p_2 \vee \Box p_3$ and these three maximals. So, it makes sense to say that the first chain *is associated with* the negative formula $\neg p_1$, the second *is associated with* the boxed atom $\Box p_2$, and the third with the boxed atom $\Box p_3$. In general, more than one maximal chain can be associated with a single negative formula, while exactly one maximal chain is associated with a boxed atom. We call a maximal chain which is associated with a boxed atom a *positive chain*, while all the chains associated with a negative formula are called *negative chains*.

It turns out that in the case of boxed atoms, the clauses we obtain have another important property: The clauses consist of a single maximal chain which is *rooted*. A chain C over $(t_1, \ldots, t_n)$ is *rooted* iff t_1 is a ground term.

LEMMA 11.7. Let α be a Sahlqvist implication. Then any clause C in $\mathrm{Cls}(\neg \Pi(\alpha))$ can be partitioned into a collection $\mathcal{D}$ of maximal chains. For any two maximal chains D and D' in $\mathcal{D}$, either D and D' are identical or they share at most one variable. In addition, if a maximal chain D in $\mathcal{D}$ is associated with a boxed atom in α, then D is rooted and shares no variables with other maximal chains in $\mathcal{D}$. ◁

THEOREM 11.8. Given any Sahlqvist implication α, SCAN* effectively computes a first-order formula $\mathrm{Corr}(\alpha)$ which is logically equivalent to α.

PROOF. Let $\alpha = Ant \to Pos$. We know that

$$\mathrm{Cls}(\neg \Pi(\alpha)) = \mathrm{Cls}(\mathrm{ST}(Ant, a)) \cup \mathrm{Cls}(\mathrm{ST}(\neg Pos, a)),$$

where a is a Skolem constant. We also know that all clauses in $N_0 = \mathrm{Cls}(\neg \Pi(\alpha))$ satisfy the conditions stated in Lemma 11.7. In particular, any clause C in $\mathrm{Cls}(\neg \Pi(\alpha))$ can be partitioned into a collection $\mathcal{D}$ of maximal chains.

In the following a literal with a unary relation symbol among $P_1, \ldots, P_k$, is referred to as a **P**-literal, and a literal with a binary relation symbol (not including equality) is an **R**-literal.

We know that a chain associated with a boxed atom contains exactly one positive **P**-literal $P_i(t_i)$, where t_i is either a Skolem constant or a variable, and in the following we denote such a chain by $C^+[P_i(t_i)]$ or $C_j^+[P_i(t_i)]$. Chains associated with a negative formula may contain one or more negative **P**-literals $\neg P_1(t_1), \ldots, \neg P_n(t_n)$, where each t_i is either a Skolem constant, a variable, or a Skolem term of the form $f(x)$. We denote these chains by

$$C^-[\neg P_1(t_1), \ldots, \neg P_n(t_n)] \text{ or } C_j^-[\neg P_1(t_1), \ldots, \neg P_n(t_n)].$$

Let $C^+[\text{TRUE}]$ denote the clause we obtain by removing the **P**-literal $P_i(t_i)$ from the chain $C^+[P_i(t_i)]$. Analogously, let $C^-[\text{TRUE}, \ldots, \neg P_n(t_n)]$ denote the clause obtained by removing $\neg P_1(t_i)$ from the chain $C^-[\neg P_1(t_1), \ldots, \neg P_n(t_n)]$.

Unlike in the case of definite Sahlqvist implications, since a clause in N_0 can contain more than one positive **P**-literal, inference steps by C-factoring are possible. Such an inference step would derive a clause $D_1 \vee C_1^+[P(t_1)] \vee C_2^+[\text{TRUE}] \vee t_1 \not\approx t_2$ from a clause $D_1 \vee C_1^+[P(t_1)] \vee C_2^+[P(t_2)]$. Since t_1 and t_2 are either variables or constants, the constraint $t_1 \not\approx t_2$ can take the forms

$$b \not\approx z, \quad b \not\approx c, \quad y \not\approx z, \quad \text{or} \quad y \not\approx c.$$

In all cases, except where b and c are distinct constants, a most general unifier σ of t_1 and t_2 exists, and constraint elimination replaces

$$D_1 \vee C_1^+[P(t_1)] \vee C_2^+[\text{TRUE}] \vee t_1 \not\approx t_2$$

by

$$(D_1 \vee C_1^+[P(t_1)] \vee C_2^+[\text{TRUE}])\sigma.$$

Note that this clause is identical to $D_1 \vee (C_1^+[P(t_1)] \vee C_2^+[\text{TRUE}])\sigma$, that is, the subclause D_1 is not affected by the inference step nor does it influence the result of the inference step. A problem occurs in the following situation: The clause $P(a) \vee \neg R(a,x) \vee P(x)$ is a chain over (a,x) and a C-factoring step is possible which derives $P(a) \vee \neg R(a,x) \vee a \not\approx x$. This C-factor is simplified by constraint elimination to $P(a) \vee \neg R(a,a)$. However, an **R**-literal like $\neg R(a,a)$ with two identical arguments is not allowed in a chain. We could modify the definition of a chain to allow for these literals, but it is simpler to consider a clause like $P(a) \vee \neg R(a,a)$ as shorthand for $P(a) \vee \neg R(a,x) \vee a \not\approx x$.

It is important to note that the condition that a maximal chain associated with a boxed atom does not share any variables with other chains may no longer be true for C-factors. For example, consider the clause

$$\neg R(a,x) \vee P(x) \vee \neg R(a,u) \vee \neg R(u,v) \vee P(v),$$

obtained from $\neg\Pi(\Box p \vee \Box\Box p \to \text{TRUE})$, which can be partitioned into two maximal chains, $\neg R(a,x) \vee P(x)$ over (a,x) and $\neg R(a,u) \vee \neg R(u,v) \vee P(v)$ over (a,u,v). This clause has the C-factor

$$\neg R(a,x) \vee P(x) \vee \neg R(a,u) \vee \neg R(u,v) \vee v \not\approx x.$$

Constraint elimination replaces this C-factor by

$$\neg R(a,x) \vee P(x) \vee \neg R(a,u) \vee \neg R(u,x)$$

which can be partitioned into two maximal chains $\neg R(a,x) \vee P(x)$ over (a,x) and $\neg R(a,u) \vee \neg R(u,x)$ over (a,u,x) that share the variable x. Let us call such clauses *factored positive chains*.

Note that the length of chains in a C-factor is the length of chains in the premise clause. Also, the depth of terms in a C-factor is the same as in the premise clause. Let there be c_p positive chains in the clauses of N_0. Then we can potentially derive $2^{c_p} - 1$ factored positive chains.

A C-resolvent can only be derived from a clause $D_1 \vee C^+[P_i(t_i)]$ and a clause $D_2 \vee C^-[\neg P_1'(t_1'), \ldots, \neg P_n'(t_n')]$ where one of the P_j', $1 \leq j \leq n$, is identical to P_i. Without loss of generality, we assume that $P_i = P_1'$. Then the resolvent is

$$D_1 \vee C^+[\text{TRUE}] \vee D_2 \vee C^-[\text{TRUE}, \neg P_2'(t_2'), \ldots, \neg P_n'(t_n')] \vee t_i \not\approx t_1'.$$

The term t_i is either a Skolem constant b or a variable y, while the term t_1' can either be a Skolem constant c, a variable z or a Skolem term $f(z)$. Thus, $t_i \not\approx t_1'$ has one of the following forms:

$$b \not\approx z, \quad b \not\approx c, \quad b \not\approx f(z), \quad y \not\approx z, \quad y \not\approx c, \quad \text{or} \quad y \not\approx f(z).$$

If t_i and t_1' are unifiable by a most general unifier σ, then constraint elimination replaces the C-resolvent by

$$(D_1 \vee C^+[\text{TRUE}] \vee D_2 \vee C^-[\text{TRUE}, \neg P_2'(t_2'), \ldots, \neg P_n'(t_n')])\sigma,$$

which is identical to

$$D_1 \vee D_2 \vee C^+[\text{TRUE}] \vee (C^-[\text{TRUE}, \neg P_2'(t_2'), \ldots, \neg P_n'(t_n')])\sigma.$$

If t_i is a variable, then the t_i and t_1' must be unifiable, since t_i cannot occur in t_1'. Furthermore, if t_i and t_1' are unifiable, then the most general unifier is either the identity substitution or a substitution replacing t_i by t_1'. However, if t_i and t_1' are not unifiable, then the constraint $t_i \not\approx t_1'$ cannot be eliminated. In this case t_i must be a Skolem constant b and t_1' is either a Skolem constant c distinct from b or a Skolem term $f(z)$. Again, no terms deeper than terms in N_0 occur.

We focus on the union of negative chains that occur within a single clause and share variables. We call these *joined negative chains*. Joined negative chains are variable indecomposable subclauses of the clauses in which they occur and they are variable-disjoint from the rest of the clause. A C-resolution inference step involves one such joined negative chain and one factored positive chain, and the result is again a joined negative chain. Let c_n be the number of joined negative chains in N_0 and let there be at most n_Q occurrences of **P**-literals in any joined negative chain. Then at most $c_n \times n_Q \times 2^{c_p}$ joined negative chains can be derived by one or more C-resolution inference steps.

Each clause in a derivation $N_0, N_1, \ldots$ is a collection of factored positive chains and joined negative chains without duplicates modulo variable renaming. Any clause containing duplicates modulo variable renaming would immediately be replaced by its condensation. Given there are $2^{c_p} - 1$ factored positive chains and $c_n \times n_Q \times 2^{c_p}$ joined negative chains, we can derive at most $2^{c_n \times n_Q \times 2^{c_p} + 2^{c_p} - 1}$ distinct clauses. This ensures the termination of the derivation.

As to reverse Skolemization, again the P_i-literals in N have one of the forms

$$P_i(b), \quad P_i(y), \quad \neg P_i(z), \quad \neg P_i(c) \quad \text{or} \quad \neg P_i(f(z)),$$

where b denotes any Skolem constant, f denotes any Skolem function, and y and z arbitrary variables. The possible forms of inequality literals in all C-resolvents and C-factors are then

$$b \not\approx z, \quad b \not\approx c, \quad b \not\approx f(z), \quad y \not\approx z, \quad y \not\approx c, \quad \text{or} \quad y \not\approx f(z),$$

i.e., the form of inequality literals is $s \not\approx t$, where s and t are variable-disjoint, s is either a variable or a constant, and t is either a variable, a constant or a Skolem term of the form $f(x)$. What is again crucial is that no derived clause contains two inequations $y \not\approx s$ and $y \not\approx t$, where s and t are compound terms. This cannot happen. Consequently, restoration of the quantifiers can always be successfully accomplished during reverse Skolemization.   ◁

Finally, the general case of a Sahlqvist formula α obtained from Sahlqvist implications by freely applying boxes and conjunctions, as well as disjunctions to formulas sharing no common propositional variables can be dealt with by induction of the number of applications of such disjunctions. The basis of the induction (with no such applications) has been established by Theorem 11.8.

We can now state the completeness of SCAN for the Sahlqvist class.

THEOREM 11.9. Given any Sahlqvist formula α, SCAN* effectively computes a first-order formula $\mathrm{Corr}(\alpha)$ which is logically equivalent to α.   ◁

It is not difficult to see that the same results hold for an algorithm based on H-resolution rather than C-resolution.

11.3. Computing Functional Correspondence Properties

An alternative semantics to the relational Kripke semantics is the *functional semantics* of modal logic [**105, 157, 158, 159, 162, 178**]. In the functional semantics accessibility between worlds is defined by sets of functions rather than relations. First-order translations corresponding to the functional semantics have been introduced and studied by a variety of authors, including [**5, 75, 152, 158, 179**].

11.3.1. Functional Semantics.

DEFINITION 11.10. A *functional frame* is a quadruple

$$F = \langle W, \langle de_i \rangle_i, \langle AF_i \rangle_i, [\cdot, \cdot] \rangle,$$

with W a non-empty set of worlds, $\langle de_i \rangle_i$ a family of subsets of W, $\langle AF_i \rangle_i$ a family of sets of total functions from W to W, and $[\cdot, \cdot] : W \times \bigcup_i AF_i \longrightarrow W$ the functional application operation. Each AF_i is called a set of *accessibility functions*.

DEFINITION 11.11. A *functional model* is a pair $\langle F, v \rangle$ of a functional frame and a valuation mapping of propositional variables to subsets of W. *Truth* in any functional model M and any world $x \in W$ is inductively defined as follows.

$$M, x \models \text{TRUE}$$

$$M, x \models p \text{ iff } x \in v(p)$$

$$M, x \models \neg\alpha \text{ iff } M, x \not\models \alpha$$

$$M, x \models \alpha \wedge \beta \text{ iff both } M, x \models \alpha \text{ and } M, x \models \beta$$

$$M, x \models \Box_i\alpha \text{ iff } x \notin de_i \text{ implies for any } u \in AF_i, M, [xu] \models \alpha$$

$$M, x \models \Diamond_i\alpha \text{ iff } x \notin de_i \text{ and for some } u \in AF_i \text{ and } M, [xu] \models \alpha.$$

The intuition of the functional semantics is that accessibility is specified in terms of quantification over transitions, rather than quantification over successor worlds. Intuitively, $\Box_i\alpha$ is true in a world x means that if x is not a dead-end world then for any transition u, the formula α is true in the world $[xu]$. Thus $[xu]$ represents the world reached from the world x via the transition u. Similarly, $\Diamond_i\alpha$ is true in a world x means that x is not a dead-end world and there is a transition u to a world $[xu]$ in which α is true.

Any modal logic complete with respect to the relational semantics is also complete with respect to the functional semantics as shown by Schmidt [178]. More specifically, a functional model can be defined from a relational model $M = \langle W, \langle R_i \rangle_i, v \rangle$ by letting

$$W^\perp \stackrel{\text{def}}{=} W \cup \{\perp\}, \text{ and } de_i \stackrel{\text{def}}{=} \{x \mid \neg\exists y \, R_i(x, y)\}.$$

Further, let AF_R be the set of functions g defined by $g(x) = \sigma(x)$, if $x \notin de_i$ and σ is a choice function selecting an element from the R_i-image of x, and $g(x) = \perp$, otherwise. The g are well-defined (total) functions from $W^\perp$ to $W^\perp$ and the structure

$$M^f = \langle W^\perp, \langle de_i \rangle_i, \langle AF_i \rangle_i, [\cdot, \cdot], v \rangle$$

is a well-defined functional model.

THEOREM 11.12. Let φ be a modal formula and let $M = \langle W, \langle R_i \rangle_i, v \rangle$ be a relational model. For any $x \in W$,

$$M, x \models \varphi \text{ iff } M^f, x \models \varphi. \qquad \triangleleft$$

11.3.2. Functional Correspondence Theory. As is the case for the relational correspondence properties, the correspondence properties of axioms with respect to the functional semantics can be derived using second-order quantifier elimination methods. Table 26 lists modal axioms for which the given properties were derived automatically using SCAN.

TABLE 26. Functional correspondence properties.

D $\quad\Box p \to \Diamond p$
$\quad\quad \forall x[\neg de(x)]$

T $\quad\Box p \to p$
$\quad\quad \forall x \exists u\big[\neg de(x) \wedge x \approx [xu]\big]$

B $\quad p \to \Box\Diamond p$
$\quad\quad \forall x \forall u \exists v\big[(\neg de(x) \to \neg de[xu]) \wedge (\neg de(x) \to x \approx [xuv])\big]$

4 $\quad\Box p \to \Box\Box p$
$\quad\quad \forall x \forall u \forall v \exists u'\big[(\neg de(x) \wedge \neg de[xu]) \to [xuv] \approx [xu']\big]$

4^2 $\quad\Box^2 p \to \Box^3 p$
$\quad\quad \forall x \forall u_1 \forall u_2 \forall u_3 \exists v_1 \exists v_2\big[(\neg de(x) \wedge \neg de[xu_1] \wedge \neg de[xu_1 u_2]) \to$
$\quad\quad\quad\quad\quad\quad\quad\quad (\neg de[xv_1] \wedge [xu_1 u_2 u_3] \approx [xv_1 v_2])\big]$

E $\quad\Diamond p \to \Box\Diamond p$
$\quad\quad \forall x \forall u \forall v \exists u'\big[(\neg de(x) \to \neg de[xv]) \wedge (\neg de(x) \to [xu] \approx [xvu'])\big]$

G $\quad\Diamond\Box p \to \Box\Diamond p$
$\quad\quad \forall x \forall u \forall v \exists u' \exists u''\big[\neg de(x) \to$
$\quad\quad\quad\quad\quad\quad\quad\quad (\neg de[xu] \wedge \neg de[xv] \wedge [xuu'] \approx [xvu''])\big]$

H $\quad\Box(\Box p \to q) \vee \Box(\Box q \to p)$
$\quad\quad \forall x\ \forall u \forall u' \exists v \exists v'\big[(de(x) \vee \neg de[xu] \vee [xu] \approx [xu'v']) \wedge$
$\quad\quad\quad\quad\quad\quad (de(x) \vee \neg de[xu'] \vee [xu'] \approx [xuv]) \wedge$
$\quad\quad\quad\quad\quad\quad (de(x) \vee [xu] \approx [xu'v'] \vee [xu'] \approx [xuv]) \wedge$
$\quad\quad\quad\quad\quad\quad (de(x) \vee \neg de[xu] \vee \neg de[xu'])\big]$

alt$_1$ $\quad\Diamond p \to \Box p$
$\quad\quad \forall x \forall u \forall v\big[de(x) \vee [xu] \approx [xv]\big]$

w.d. $\quad\Box\Box p \to \Box p$
$\quad\quad \forall x \forall u \exists v \exists u'\big[\neg de(x) \to (\neg de[xv] \wedge [xu] \approx [xvu'])\big]$

Mk $\quad(\Box p \wedge q) \to \Diamond(\Box\Box p \wedge \Diamond q)$
$\quad\quad \forall x \exists u\big[\neg de(x) \wedge \neg de[xu] \wedge (\exists v\ [xuv] \approx x) \wedge$
$\quad\quad\quad\quad (\forall u'\ de[xuu'] \vee (\forall v' \exists v''' \ [xuu'v'] \approx [xv''']))\big]$

THEOREM 11.13. **[178]** The pairs (α, β) of modal axioms and first-order formulas in Table 26 are such that for every functional frame F and any world W of F

$$F, w \models \alpha \text{ iff } F \models \beta(x)^x_w. \quad\quad\quad\quad\quad \triangleleft$$

For some axioms (such as **D**, **T** and **4**) these properties may be simplified by a form of globalization, as is established by Ohlbach and Schmidt **[162, 179]**.

An important advantage of the translations based on the functional semantics is that a wider class of modal logics can be embedded into first-order logic than can be done with the standard translation method, cf. [**162, 178**]. It is beyond the scope of the book to give more details. These can be found in, e.g., [**159, 161, 162, 178**].

CHAPTER 12

Direct Methods in Modal Logics

In this chapter we concentrate on direct methods for modal logics. We first provide Theorem 12.2 proved by Szałas in [201]. Then we also formulate Theorem 12.7, not published elsewhere, which allows one to deal with multi-modal logics. Even if mono-modal logics we deal with can simulate multi-modal logics (see [132]), a separate theorem is useful, and allows one to avoid all complications arising from the simulation.

The rest of the chapter is devoted to direct methods based on semantical translation, as proposed in [155, 199].

12.1. The Mono-Modal Case

In this section we assume that the considered modal logics are **Q1K** (in the first-order case) and **K** (in the propositional case).

12.1.1. The Elimination Theorem. Below, for $i \in \omega$, by ∇^i we denote any sequence of modalities $\Box$, $\Diamond$ of length i. For example, ∇^2 can be $\Box\Diamond$, $\Diamond\Box$, $\Box\Box$ or $\Diamond\Diamond$. Writing $\beta(\nabla^i\gamma)$ we mean that γ appears in β only in subformulas of the form $\nabla^i\gamma$ which themselves are not within the scope of any other modalities.

In order to prove Theorem 12.2 we need the following proposition.

PROPOSITION 12.1. For any normal modal logic and any $i \in \omega$,

$$\models \Box^i(\alpha \to \beta) \to [\nabla^i\alpha \to \nabla^i\beta].$$

PROOF. We proceed by induction on i.

The case when $i = 0$ is obvious. Assume that the theorem holds for a given $i \in \omega$, i.e., $\models \Box^i(\alpha \to \beta) \to [\nabla^i\alpha \to \nabla^i\beta]$. By assumption, the considered logics are normal, so we have that $\models \Box[\Box^i(\alpha \to \beta) \to [\nabla^i\alpha \to \nabla^i\beta]]$, and, in consequence,

(96) $\qquad \models \Box^{i+1}(\alpha \to \beta) \to \Box[\nabla^i\alpha \to \nabla^i\beta].$

Therefore we also have that $\models [\Box^{i+1}(\alpha \to \beta) \to [\Box\nabla^i\alpha \to \Box\nabla^i\beta]]$, i.e., when ∇^{i+1} begins with $\Box$, $\models [\Box^{i+1}(\alpha \to \beta) \to [\nabla^{i+1}\alpha \to \nabla^{i+1}\beta]]$.

What remains to show is the case when ∇^{i+1} begins with $\Diamond$. However, in **K** we have that $\models \Box(\gamma \rightarrow \delta) \rightarrow (\Diamond\gamma \rightarrow \Diamond\delta)$. Thus from (96) we also have that $\models \Box^{i+1}(\alpha \rightarrow \beta) \rightarrow \Box[\nabla^i\alpha \rightarrow \nabla^i\beta] \rightarrow [\Diamond\nabla^i\alpha \rightarrow \Diamond\nabla^i\beta]$, i.e., also when ∇^{i+1} begins with $\Diamond$, we have that $\models \Box^{i+1}(\alpha \rightarrow \beta) \rightarrow [\nabla^{i+1}\alpha \rightarrow \nabla^{i+1}\beta]$.   ◁

THEOREM 12.2. Consider any normal modal logic validating the Barcan formula.[1] Let i be any natural number. Assume that $\alpha(X)$ is a classical first-order formula positive w.r.t. X.

If $\beta(\nabla^i X)$ is a modal first-order formula positive w.r.t. $\nabla^i X$ then

$$(97) \quad \exists X\{\forall\bar{x}[\Box^i(X(\bar{x}) \rightarrow \alpha(X(\bar{t})))] \wedge \beta(\nabla^i X(\bar{s}))\} \equiv \beta^{X(\bar{x})}_{[\text{GFP}\, X(\bar{x}).\alpha(X(\bar{t}))]}.$$

If $\beta(\nabla^i \neg X)$ is a modal first-order formula positive w.r.t. $\nabla^i \neg X$ then

$$(98) \quad \exists X\{\forall\bar{x}[\Box^i(\alpha(X(\bar{t})) \rightarrow X(\bar{x}))] \wedge \beta(\nabla^i \neg X(\bar{s}))\} \equiv \beta^{X(\bar{x})}_{[\text{LFP}\, X(\bar{x}).\alpha(X(\bar{t}))]}.$$

If α does not contain X, then the right-hand sides of equivalences (97) and (98) reduce to $\beta^{X(\bar{x})}_{\alpha(\bar{x})}$.

PROOF. We prove (97). The proof of (98) is similar.

Assume first that $\forall\bar{x}[\Box^i(X(\bar{x}) \rightarrow \alpha(X(\bar{t})))] \wedge \beta(\nabla^i X(\bar{s}))$ holds. By the Barcan formula we have that $\Box^i\forall\bar{x}(X(\bar{x}) \rightarrow \alpha(X(\bar{t}))$ holds, i.e., also

$$\Box^i\forall\bar{x}[X(\bar{x}) \rightarrow [\text{GFP}\, X(\bar{x}).\alpha(X(\bar{t}))]].$$

We now apply the converse Barcan formula (see (93), page 130), obtaining

$$\forall\bar{x}\Box^i[X(\bar{x}) \rightarrow [\text{GFP}\, X(\bar{x}).\alpha(X(\bar{t}))]].$$

Applying Proposition 12.1 we now conclude that

$$\forall\bar{x}[\nabla^i X(\bar{x}) \rightarrow \nabla^i[\text{GFP}\, X(\bar{x}).\alpha(X(\bar{t}))]].$$

By assumption, β is positive w.r.t. $\nabla^i X$, thus also monotone w.r.t. $\nabla^i X$. We then conclude that $\beta^{X(\bar{x})}_{[\text{GFP}\, X(\bar{x}).\alpha(X(\bar{t}))]}$ holds.

Let us now prove the converse implication. Assume that $\beta^{X(\bar{x})}_{[\text{GFP}\, X(\bar{x}).\alpha(X(\bar{t}))]}$ holds. We shall define X satisfying $\forall\bar{x}[\Box^i(X(\bar{x}) \rightarrow \alpha(X(\bar{t}))) \wedge \beta(\nabla^i X(\bar{s}))]$ and thus show that it indeed exists. Set $X(\bar{x})$ to be a relation such that

$$\Box^i\forall\bar{x}[X(\bar{x}) \equiv [\text{GFP}\, X(\bar{x}).\alpha(X(\bar{t}))]].$$

By the converse Barcan formula we also have that

$$\forall\bar{x}\Box^i[X(\bar{x}) \rightarrow [\text{GFP}\, X(\bar{x}).\alpha(X(\bar{t}))]].$$

Formula $\beta(\nabla^i X(\bar{s}))$ is then obviously satisfied.

---

[1]Recall that the Barcan formula is defined as (92) on page 130.

Consider $\forall \bar{x}[\Box^i(X(\bar{x}) \to \alpha(X(\bar{t})))]$. This formula is also satisfied, as X is defined to be a fixpoint of $\alpha(X)$ exactly in the modal context $\Box^i$.   ◁

Observe that Theorem 12.2 subsumes Theorem 6.19. To see this, it suffices to fix $i = 0$ and consider β's without modalities.

The following fact follows directly from Theorem 12.2.

COROLLARY 12.3. Let i be any natural number. Assume that $\alpha(X)$ is a classical propositional formula positive w.r.t. X.

If $\beta(\nabla^i X)$ is a modal propositional formula positive w.r.t. $\nabla^i X$ then

(99) $\exists X\{\Box^i[X \to \alpha(X)] \wedge \beta(\nabla^i X)\} \equiv \beta^X_{[\text{GFP } X.\alpha(X)]}.$

If $\beta(\nabla^i \neg X)$ is a modal propositional formula positive w.r.t. $\nabla^i \neg X$ then

(100) $\exists X\{\Box^i[\alpha(X) \to X] \wedge \beta(\nabla^i \neg X)\} \equiv \beta^X_{[\text{LFP } X.\alpha(X)]}.$

If α does not contain X, then the right-hand sides of equivalences (99) and (100) reduce to β^X_α.   ◁

12.1.2. Examples. For the sake of simplicity we shall deal with propositional modal logics only.

EXAMPLE 12.4. Second-order quantifier elimination can be used to prove modal tautologies. The idea here depends on a simple observation that a formula $\alpha(\bar{P})$ is a tautology iff formula $\forall \bar{P}\alpha(\bar{P})$ is a tautology, too. Now elimination of second-order quantifiers results in a formula that does not contain variables of $\bar{P}$, thus is substantially simplified.

Let us start with the second-order formulation of axiom **D**, i.e., $\forall P[\Box P \to \Diamond P]$. It is equivalent to $\neg \exists P[\Box P \wedge \Box \neg P]$, i.e., to $\neg \exists P[\Box(\text{TRUE} \to P) \wedge \Box \neg P]$. An application of Corollary 12.3 results in an equivalent formula $\neg \Box \neg \text{TRUE}$, thus **D** is equivalent to $\Diamond \text{TRUE}$.

Consider now another propositional modal formula:

(101) $[\Box(P \to Q) \wedge \Box \neg Q] \to \Diamond \neg P.$

In order to prove it, we quantify universally over P and Q,

(102) $\forall Q \forall P[[\Box(P \to Q) \wedge \Box \neg Q] \to \Diamond \neg P].$

Formula (102) is equivalent to $\neg \exists Q \exists P[\Box(P \to Q) \wedge \Box \neg Q \wedge \Box P]$. After application of Corollary 12.3, eliminating $\exists P$, we then obtain its equivalent $\neg \exists Q[\Box \neg Q \wedge \Box Q]$, i.e., $\neg \exists Q[\Box(Q \to \text{FALSE}) \wedge \Box Q]$, thus the application of Corollary 12.3 to eliminate $\exists Q$ results in $\neg \Box \text{FALSE}$, i.e., formula (102) is equivalent to $\Diamond \text{TRUE}$. Thus formula (101) is valid iff formula $\Diamond \text{TRUE}$ is valid. Now the reasoning is substantially simplified. The formula $\Diamond \text{TRUE}$ is not a theorem of **K**, but one can easily note that it is a theorem, e.g., of any extension of **KD**.

Consider now another formula,

(103) $(\Diamond P \wedge \Diamond Q) \rightarrow \Diamond(P \wedge Q)$.

The same property can be expressed equivalently without using variable Q, thus in a simpler form. To see this note that formula (103) is equivalent to

(104) $\forall Q[(\Diamond P \wedge \Diamond Q) \rightarrow \Diamond(P \wedge Q)]$.

Formula (104) is equivalent to $\neg \exists Q[(\Diamond P \wedge \Diamond Q) \wedge \Box(\neg P \vee \neg Q)]$, i.e., to

(105) $\neg \exists Q[\Box(Q \rightarrow \neg P) \wedge (\Diamond P \wedge \Diamond Q)]$.

An application of Corollary 12.3 to (105) results in $\neg[\Diamond P \wedge \Diamond \neg P]$, thus formula (103) is equivalent to $\Diamond P \rightarrow \Box P$.   ◁

EXAMPLE 12.5. In order to check whether a query α follows from a database D, one has to check whether $\bigwedge D \rightarrow \alpha(P)$ is valid. This is equivalent to checking the validity of $\forall \bar{P}[\bigwedge D \rightarrow \alpha(\bar{P})]$, where $\bar{P}$ consists of all Boolean variables appearing in α and $\bigwedge D$ denotes the conjunction of all formulas in D. According to the reduction to absurdity paradigm, usually applied in the context of deductive databases, one negates the implication and tries to show a contradiction. Negated implication is of the form $\exists \bar{P}[\bigwedge D \wedge \neg \alpha(\bar{P})]$ and one can apply second-order quantifier elimination.

Consider an exemplary deontic database, where $\Box \alpha$ stands for "α is obligatory" and $\Diamond \alpha$ stands for "α is allowed". Assume the database contains, among others, the following simple rules, where S stands for a "serious violation of a rule", F stands for a "failure" and W stands for a "warning":

(106) $\Box(S \rightarrow F)$
         $\Box(F \rightarrow W)$.

Assume that the database contains also fact $\Diamond S$ and no other rules or facts involve W or F. If other rules or facts in the database involve W or F, the second-order quantification in (107) and (108) would have to bind those rules and facts, too. Our query is $\Diamond W$. We are then interested to check whether the conjunction of rules (106) and fact $\Diamond S$ implies the query, i.e., whether

(107) $\forall W[(\Box(S \rightarrow F) \wedge \Box(F \rightarrow W) \wedge \Diamond S) \rightarrow \Diamond W]$.

In order to apply formula (100) of Corollary 12.3 we consider

$\neg \exists W[\Box(S \rightarrow F) \wedge \Box(F \rightarrow W) \wedge \Diamond S \wedge \Box \neg W]$.

After applying formula (100) of Corollary 12.3 we obtain:

$\neg[\Box(S \rightarrow F) \wedge \Diamond S \wedge \Box \neg F]$,

which, taking into account the contents of the database, reduces to $\neg \Box \neg F$. Thus (107) is equivalent to $\Diamond F$. We still do not know whether $\Diamond F$ holds, thus ask whether it follows from the database. The suitable query is formulated as

(108) $\forall F\big[(\Box(S \to F) \land \Box(F \to W) \land \Diamond S) \to \Diamond F\big].$

After similar calculations as before we obtain that the query is equivalent to

$$\neg\Box(S \to W) \lor \Diamond S,$$

which is TRUE, as $\Diamond S$ is a fact contained in the database. Thus also the answer to the initial query is TRUE, as might have been expected.   ◁

EXAMPLE 12.6. Assume we are given the following theory, where $\Box$ stands for "usually", $\Diamond$ stands for "sometimes", B stands for "being accompanied by a partner", C for "going to a cinema", T for "going to a theater" and P for "going to a pub". Assume that the situation is described by the following theory Th:

(109) $\Box(B \to (T \lor C)) \land \Box(\neg B \to P) \land \Box(P \to (\neg T \land \neg C)).$

Suppose one wants to describe the concept $\Box\neg P$ in terms of B only, perhaps occurring within the scope of modal operators. As explained in Section 18.2, page 246, the appropriate approximations of theory (109) w.r.t. $\Box\neg P$ are given by

(110) $\exists P \exists T \exists C[Th \land \Box\neg P]$

and

(111) $\forall P \forall T \forall C[Th \to \Box\neg P].$

Consider first (110). In order to eliminate quantifier $\exists C$ we transform equivalence (110) into the following equivalent form:

$$\exists P \exists T \exists C\big[\Box[(B \land \neg T) \to C] \land \Box(\neg B \to P)$$
$$\land \Box[P \to (\neg T \land \neg C)] \land \Box\neg P\big].$$

The application of formula (100) of Corollary 12.3 to eliminate $\exists C$ results in:

$$\exists P \exists T \Box(\neg B \to P) \land \Box(P \to (\neg T \land \neg(B \land \neg T))) \land \Box\neg P,$$

which is equivalent to

$$\exists P \exists T \Box(\neg B \to P) \land \Box(P \to (\neg T \land \neg B)) \land \Box\neg P,$$

i.e., by simple calculations, to

$$\exists P \exists T \Box(\neg B \to P) \land \Box(T \to \neg P) \land \Box(P \to \neg B) \land \Box\neg P,$$

We now apply Corollary 12.3 to eliminate $\exists T$ and obtain

$$\exists P \Box(\neg B \to P) \land \Box(P \to \neg B) \land \Box\neg P,$$

equivalent to $\exists P \Box(\neg B \to P) \land \Box\neg P$. Now the application of formula (100) of Corollary 12.3 results in $\Box B$.

The elimination of second-order quantifiers from formula (111) is quite similar and we obtain $\neg\Diamond\neg B$. Thus the equivalent of (111) is also $\Box B$. It can be observed (see Section 18.2) that (111) is the weakest abduction for $\Box\neg P$ under theory Th. Thus, given the theory Th, the weakest condition that guarantees to usually not go to a pub is to be usually accompanied by partner. $\lhd$

12.2. The Multi-Modal Case

In this section we provide a generalization of Theorem 12.2 to the case of multi-modal logics.

12.2.1. The Elimination Theorem. Let $i \in \omega$ and $S = \Box_{j_1}\Box_{j_2}\ldots\Box_{j_i}$ be a sequence of modal operators. We say that a sequence of modal operators $O_{j_1}O_{j_2}\ldots O_{j_i}$ is *compatible* with S if, for each $1 \le k \le i$, O_{j_k} is either $\Box_{j_k}$ or $\Diamond_{j_k}$. For example, $\Diamond_1\Box_2$ is compatible with $\Box_1\Box_2$, while $\Diamond_2\Box_2$ is not.

Writing $\beta(\bar{\nabla}\gamma)$ we mean that γ appears in β only in subformulas of the form $\bar{\nabla}\gamma$ which themselves are not within the scope of any other modalities.

THEOREM 12.7. Let $\alpha(X)$ be a classical first-order formula positive w.r.t. X, i be any natural number and sequence $\bar{\nabla} = O_{j_1}O_{j_2}\ldots O_{j_i}$ of modal operators be compatible with $\bar{\Box} = \Box_{j_1}\Box_{j_2}\ldots\Box_{j_i}$.

If $\beta(\bar{\nabla}X)$ is a modal first-order formula positive w.r.t. $\bar{\nabla}X$ then

$$(112) \qquad \exists X \big\{ \forall \bar{x}\,[\bar{\Box}(X(\bar{x}) \to \alpha(X(\bar{t})))] \wedge \beta(\bar{\nabla}X(\bar{s})) \big\} \equiv \beta^{X(\bar{x})}_{[\text{GFP}\,X(\bar{x}).\alpha(X(\bar{t}))]}.$$

If $\beta(\bar{\nabla}\neg X)$ is a modal first-order formula positive w.r.t. $\bar{\nabla}\neg X$ then

$$(113) \qquad \exists X \big\{ \forall \bar{x}\,[\bar{\Box}(\alpha(X(\bar{t})) \to X(\bar{x}))] \wedge \beta(\bar{\nabla}\neg X(\bar{s})) \big\} \equiv \beta^{X(\bar{x})}_{[\text{LFP}\,X(\bar{x}).\alpha(X(\bar{t}))]}.$$

If α does not contain X, then the right-hand side of equivalences (112) and (113) reduce to $\beta^{X(\bar{x})}_{\alpha(\bar{x})}$.

PROOF. Analogous to the proof of Theorem 12.2. $\lhd$

It is clear that Theorem 12.7 subsumes Theorem 12.2. The following fact follows directly from Theorem 12.7.

COROLLARY 12.8. Assume that $\alpha(X)$ is a classical propositional formula positive w.r.t. X and let $\bar{\nabla}$ be a sequence of modalities compatible with $\bar{\Box}$.

If $\beta(\bar{\nabla}X)$ is a modal propositional formula positive w.r.t. $\bar{\nabla}X$ then

$$(114) \qquad \exists X \big\{ \bar{\Box}[X \to \alpha(X)] \wedge \beta(\bar{\nabla}X) \big\} \equiv \beta^X_{[\text{GFP}\,X.\alpha(X)]}.$$

If $\beta(\bar{\nabla}\neg X)$ is a modal propositional formula positive w.r.t. $\bar{\nabla}\neg X$ then

$$(115) \qquad \exists X \big\{ \bar{\Box}[\alpha(X) \to X] \wedge \beta(\bar{\nabla}\neg X) \big\} \equiv \beta^X_{[\text{LFP}\,X.\alpha(X)]}.$$

If α does not contain X, then the right-hand sides of equivalences (114) and (115) reduce to β_α^X. ◁

12.3. Computing Correspondences

In order to compute correspondences one can also translate modal axioms using the standard translation and eliminate second-order quantifiers using Lemma 6.1 or Theorem 6.19. This section, based on the work of Szałas [199] in the case of first-order correspondences and on Nonnengart and Szałas [155] in the case of fixpoint correspondences, illustrates this technique.

12.3.1. Examples of Computing First-Order Correspondences.

EXAMPLE 12.9. Consider first the modal schema

(116) $\Box P \to P$

The second-order translation, $\Pi((116), x)$ results in

$$\forall X \forall x [\forall y (R(x, y) \to X(y)) \to X(x)],$$

equivalent to $\neg \exists x \exists X [\forall y (R(x, y) \to X(y)) \land \neg X(x)]$. Now an application of Lemma 6.1(11) results in $\neg \exists x [\neg R(x, x)]$, equivalent to $\forall x R(x, x)$, the reflexivity of R.

Consider

(117) $\Box P \to \Box \Box P.$

The second-order translation, $\Pi((117), x)$, results in

$$\forall X \forall x [\forall y [R(x, y) \to X(y)] \to \forall z [R(x, z) \to \forall u (R(z, u) \to X(u))]].$$

It is equivalent to

$$\neg \exists x \exists X [\forall y [R(x, y) \to X(y)] \land \exists z [R(x, z) \land \exists u (R(z, u) \land \neg X(u))]].$$

An application of Lemma 6.1(11) results in

$$\neg \exists x \exists z [R(x, z) \land \exists u (R(z, u) \land \neg R(x, u))],$$

which is equivalent to $\forall x \forall z \forall u [(R(x, z) \land R(z, u)) \to R(x, u)]$, i.e., to the transitivity of R. ◁

EXAMPLE 12.10. Consider the axiom

(118) $\Box (P \lor Q) \to (\Box P \lor \Box Q).$

The second-order translation, $\Pi((118), x)$, results in

$$\forall X \forall Y \forall x [\forall y [R(x, y) \to (X(y) \lor Y(y))] \to \\ \forall z [R(x, z) \to X(z)] \lor \forall v [R(x, v) \to Y(v)]],$$

equivalent to

$$\neg \exists x \exists X \exists Y \big[\forall y[(R(x,y) \wedge \neg X(y)) \to Y(y))] \wedge$$
$$\exists z[R(x,z) \wedge \neg X(z)] \wedge \exists v[R(x,v) \wedge \neg Y(v)]\big].$$

The elimination of $\exists Y$ by an application of Lemma 6.1(11) results in

(119) $\neg \exists x \exists X \big[\exists z[R(x,z) \wedge \neg X(z)] \wedge \exists v[R(x,v) \wedge \neg (R(x,v) \wedge \neg X(v))]\big].$

Formula (119) is equivalent to

$$\neg \exists x \exists X \big[\exists z[R(x,z) \wedge \neg X(z)] \wedge \exists v[R(x,v) \wedge (\neg R(x,v) \vee X(v))]\big].$$

DLS transforms this formula into its equivalent

$$\neg \exists x \exists z \exists X \big[\forall u[X(u) \to u \not\approx z] \wedge$$
$$R(x,z) \wedge \exists v[R(x,v) \wedge (\neg R(x,v) \vee X(v))]\big].$$

The elimination of $\exists X$ by an application of Lemma 6.1(10) results in

$$\neg \exists x \exists z \big[R(x,z) \wedge \exists v[R(x,v) \wedge (\neg R(x,v) \vee v \not\approx z)]\big],$$

which is equivalent to $\forall x \forall z \forall v\big[(R(x,z) \wedge R(x,v)) \to (z \approx v \wedge R(x,z))\big]$, i.e., to
$\forall x \forall z \forall v[(R(x,z) \wedge R(x,v)) \to z \approx v]$.   ◁

12.3.2. Completeness for Sahlqvist Formulas. Conradie in [40] provided the following theorem.

THEOREM 12.11. DLS succeeds in computing the first-order frame correspondent of all Sahlqvist formulas.   ◁

In fact, the theorem given in [40] is even stronger, as DLS succeeds on all inductive formulas (for a definition of inductive formulas see Section 13.3.2, page 178).

12.3.3. Examples of Computing Fixpoint Correspondences. Fixpoint correspondences can be computed using Theorem 6.19 of Nonnengart and Szałas.

EXAMPLE 12.12. Consider the Löb axiom

(120) $\Box(\Box P \to P) \to \Box P$

The second-order translation, $\Pi((120), x)$, results in

$$\forall X \forall x \big[\forall y[R(x,y) \to [\forall z(R(y,z) \to X(z)) \to X(y)]] \to$$
$$\forall u[R(x,u) \to X(u)],$$

which is equivalent to[2]

(121) $\neg \exists x \exists X \forall y \big[[R(x,y) \wedge \forall z[R(y,z) \to X(z)]] \to X(y) \wedge$
$\exists y[R(x,y) \wedge \neg X(y)].$

---

[2]For the sake of simplicity we rename u by y.

An application of Theorem 6.19(27) to (121) gives

$$\neg\exists x\exists y\big[R(x,y)\wedge\neg[\textsc{Lfp}\,X(y).R(x,y)\wedge\forall z(R(y,z)\rightarrow X(z))]\big],$$

which is equivalent to

(122) $\quad\forall x\forall y\big[R(x,y)\rightarrow[\textsc{Lfp}\,X(y).R(x,y)\wedge\forall z(R(y,z)\rightarrow X(z))]\big].$

To further analyze this axiom, let

$$\Gamma(X(y))\stackrel{\mathrm{def}}{\equiv}\big[R(x,y)\wedge\forall z[R(y,z)\rightarrow X(z)]\big].$$

Now

$$\Gamma^0(\textsc{False})\equiv\textsc{False}$$
$$\Gamma^1(\textsc{False})\equiv R(x,y)\wedge\forall z\neg R(y,z)$$
$$\Gamma^2(\textsc{False})\equiv\Gamma(\Gamma(\textsc{False}))\equiv\Gamma(R(x,y)\wedge\forall z\neg R(y,z))\equiv$$
$$R(x,y)\wedge\forall z[R(y,z)\rightarrow(R(x,z)\wedge\forall z_1\neg R(z,z_1))]$$
$$\Gamma^3(\textsc{False})\equiv\Gamma(\Gamma^2(\textsc{False}))\equiv$$
$$\Gamma(R(x,y)\wedge\forall z[R(y,z)\rightarrow(R(x,z)\wedge\forall z_1\neg R(z,z_1))])\equiv$$
$$R(x,y)\wedge\forall z\big[R(y,z)\rightarrow[R(x,z)\wedge$$
$$\forall z_2(R(z,z_2)\rightarrow(R(x,z_2)\wedge\forall z_1\neg R(z_2,z_1)))]\big]$$

$\cdots$

Thus the Löb axiom (120) expresses that the relation R is transitive and reverse well-founded. Transitivity of R can be seen by unfolding the fixpoint twice and the reverse well-foundedness of R then follows from the fact that

$$\forall x\forall y\big[R(x,y)\rightarrow[\textsc{Lfp}\,X(y).R(x,y)\wedge\forall z(R(y,z)\rightarrow X(z))]\big]$$

implies

$$\forall x\forall y\big[R(x,y)\rightarrow[\textsc{Lfp}\,X(y).\forall z(R(x,z)\rightarrow X(z))]\big]$$

under the transitivity assumption.   ◁

Next we consider a modal schema which is not validated by any frame, i.e., its second-order translation is equivalent to FALSE. It is interesting that SCAN is not able prove this fact. Similarly, the application of Lemma 6.1 is not possible here.

EXAMPLE 12.13. Consider the axiom schema

(123) $\quad\square(\square P\rightarrow P)\rightarrow P.$

The second-order translation, $\Pi((123),x)$, results in

$$\forall X\forall x\Big[\forall y\big[R(x,y)\rightarrow[\forall z(R(y,z)\rightarrow X(z))\rightarrow X(y)]\big]\rightarrow X(x)\Big],$$

which is equivalent to

$$\neg\exists x\exists X\Big[\forall y\big[[R(x,y)\wedge\forall z(R(y,z)\rightarrow X(z))]\rightarrow X(y)\big]\wedge\neg X(x)\Big].$$

An application of Theorem 6.19(27) results in

$$\neg\exists y\neg[\text{LFP }X(y).R(x,y)\wedge\forall z(R(y,z)\rightarrow X(z))]^y_x,$$

equivalent to

(124) $\forall y[\text{LFP }X(y).R(x,y)\wedge\forall z(R(y,z)\rightarrow X(z))]^y_x.$

Let $\Gamma(X(y))\overset{\text{def}}{\equiv}R(x,y)\wedge\forall z(R(y,z)\rightarrow X(z))$. Now

$$\Gamma^0(\text{FALSE})\ \equiv\ \text{FALSE}$$
$$\Gamma^1(\text{FALSE})\ \equiv\ R(x,y)\wedge\forall z\neg R(y,z).$$

Thus $\Gamma^2(\text{FALSE})^y_x\equiv R(x,x)\wedge\forall z\neg R(x,z)\ \equiv\ \text{FALSE}$. Therefore FALSE is a fixpoint and it is the least fixpoint, hence the schema (123) is equivalent to FALSE, i.e., no frame validates this schema.   ◁

EXAMPLE 12.14. Consider the following axiom schema:

(125) $\square(P\rightarrow\Diamond P)\ \rightarrow\ (\Diamond P\rightarrow\square\Diamond P)$

which is sometimes called the *modified Löb Axiom* (see van Benthem [210]).[3] The second-order translation, $\Pi((125),x)$, results in

$$\forall X\forall x\big[\forall y[R(x,y)\rightarrow(X(y)\rightarrow\exists z(R(y,z)\wedge X(z)))]\rightarrow$$
$$\exists u[R(x,u)\wedge X(u)]\rightarrow\forall v[R(x,v)\rightarrow\exists w(R(v,w)\wedge X(w))]\big],$$

which is equivalent to

$$\neg\exists x\exists X\big[\forall y[R(x,y)\rightarrow(X(y)\rightarrow\exists z(R(y,z)\wedge X(z)))]\wedge$$
$$\exists u[R(x,u)\wedge X(u)]\wedge\exists v[R(x,v)\wedge\forall w(\neg R(v,w)\vee\neg X(w))]\big]$$

and further to

$$\neg\exists x\exists v\exists X\big[\forall y[X(y)\rightarrow(R(x,y)\rightarrow\exists z(R(y,z)\wedge X(z)))]\wedge$$
$$\exists u[R(x,u)\wedge X(u)]\wedge R(x,v)\wedge\forall y[X(y)\rightarrow\neg R(v,y)]\big],$$

i.e., to

(126) $\neg\exists x\exists v\exists X\big[\forall y[X(y)\rightarrow[\neg R(v,y)\wedge$
$(R(x,y)\rightarrow\exists z(R(y,z)\wedge X(z)))]\wedge$
$\exists u[R(x,u)\wedge X(u)]\wedge R(x,v)\big].$

An application of Theorem 6.19(26) to (126) results in

(127) $\neg\exists x\exists v\exists u\big[R(x,u)\wedge R(x,v)\wedge$
$[\text{GFP }X(y).R(x,y)\rightarrow\exists z(R(y,z)\wedge X(z))]^y_u\big].$

---

[3]Under a temporal interpretation this schema is often examined in its equivalent form $(\Diamond P\wedge\Diamond\square\neg P)\rightarrow\Diamond(P\wedge\square\neg P)$, i.e., "if P has not yet stopped being true but does so eventually then there is a final moment of P's truth".

Moving negation inside and applying Proposition 3.36 (page 34) we obtain the following formula equivalent to (127),

$$\forall x \forall v \forall u \big[[R(x,u) \wedge R(x,v)] \rightarrow$$
$$[\textsc{Lfp}\, X(y).R(x,y) \wedge \forall z (R(y,z) \rightarrow X(z))]_u^y \big].$$

A strong relation of (125) to the Löb axiom can now be observed. ◁

EXAMPLE 12.15. Consider the temporal logic formula, known as Segerberg's axiom,

(128) $\Box(P \rightarrow \bigcirc P) \rightarrow (P \rightarrow \Box P),$

where $\Box$ should be interpreted as *always* or *henceforth* and $\bigcirc$ as *at the next moment of time*.

The second-order translation, $\Pi((128), x)$, results in

$$\forall X \forall x \big[\forall y [R_\Box(x,y) \rightarrow (X(y) \rightarrow \forall z (R_\bigcirc(y,z) \rightarrow X(z)))] \rightarrow$$
$$[X(x) \rightarrow \forall u (R_\Box(x,u) \rightarrow X(u))] \big],$$

which is equivalent to

$$\neg \exists x \exists X \big[\forall y [R_\Box(x,y) \rightarrow (X(y) \rightarrow \forall z (R_\bigcirc(y,z) \rightarrow X(z)))] \wedge$$
$$X(x) \wedge \exists u (R_\Box(x,u) \wedge \neg X(u)) \big],$$

i.e., to

$$\neg \exists x \exists u \exists X \big[\forall y [X(y) \rightarrow (R_\Box(x,y) \rightarrow \forall z (R_\bigcirc(y,z) \rightarrow X(z)))] \wedge$$
$$X(x) \wedge R_\Box(x,u) \wedge \forall y [X(y) \rightarrow y \not\approx u] \big],$$

and finally to

(129)
$$\neg \exists x \exists u \exists X \big[\forall y [X(y) \rightarrow$$
$$[y \not\approx u \wedge (R_\Box(x,y) \rightarrow \forall z (R_\bigcirc(y,z) \rightarrow X(z)))]] \wedge$$
$$X(x) \wedge R_\Box(x,u) \big].$$

An application of Theorem 6.19(26) to formula (129) results in

(130)
$$\neg \exists x \exists u \big[R_\Box(x,u) \wedge$$
$$[\textsc{Gfp}\, X(y).y \not\approx u \wedge (R_\Box(x,y) \rightarrow \forall z (R_\bigcirc(y,z) \rightarrow X(z)))]_x^y \big].$$

Moving negation inside and applying Proposition 3.36 (page 34) we obtain

$$\forall x \forall u \big[R_\Box(x,u) \rightarrow$$
$$[\textsc{Lfp}\, X(y).y \approx u \rightarrow (R_\Box(x,y) \wedge \exists z (R_\bigcirc(y,z) \wedge X(z)))]_x^y \big],$$

which simplifies to

(131) $\forall x \forall u \big[R_\Box(x,u) \rightarrow [\textsc{Lfp}\, X(y).y \approx u \rightarrow \exists z (R_\bigcirc(y,z) \wedge X(z))]_x^y \big],$

i.e., this formula states that $R_\Box$ is included in the reflexive and transitive closure of $R_\bigcirc$, a property which is not expressible by means of classical logic but expressible by means of fixpoint logic. ◁

CHAPTER 13

Lazy Quantifier Elimination in Modal Logics

This chapter focuses on a lazy version of the direct approach to modal logic. Conradie, Goranko and Vakarelov [**41, 42, 43, 44**] have developed an algorithm, called SQEMA, for reducing second-order modal formulas into a modal hybrid language and first-order logic. The name SQEMA is short for second-order quantifier elimination for modal formulas using Ackermann's lemma. They have shown completeness and canonicity results for this algorithm. In particular, they have shown completeness with respect to Sahlqvist formulas and substantially extended it to the class of monadic inductive formulas (due to Goranko and Vakarelov [**100**]). They also show that any formula on which SQEMA succeeds is canonical. Together with the completeness results this provides a strengthening of Sahlqvist's correspondence theorem [**175**].

In this chapter we follow Schmidt [**181**] and modify and extend the SQEMA algorithm in a number of ways. In the original presentation SQEMA transforms formulas into (a disjunction of formulas in) negation normal form. Because negation normal form has a number of drawbacks, we use a different normal form. We transform formulas into a form using a limited number of logical operators. As a result our calculus has fewer rules. More importantly, the method now succeeds quicker because more cases of obvious redundancies can be detected and eliminated with little effort. In the negation normal form these redundancies are often obscured and therefore harder to detect. Another difference is that our rules are restricted by an ordering on the non-base symbols. The ordering determines in which order the rules are applied to the clauses in a derivation. The ordering can therefore be used to control how a derivation is constructed and can be used to reduce the size of the search space. A similarity to ordered resolution becomes apparent now. Furthermore, our definition separates the calculus of the inference rules from the actual realization as an algorithm or implementation. This allows the results to be sharpened and improved without being dependent on issues having to do with implementation. We call our procedure MSQEL, which is short for modal second-order quantifier elimination.

13.1. Lazy Second-Order Quantifier Elimination

The modal second-order quantifier elimination procedure MSQEL, like SQEMA, is basically a modal version of the DLS algorithm. Rather than translating the modal input formula directly into first-order logic and then passing it to a quantifier elimination algorithm, MSQEL performs the translation to first-order logic in a lazy fashion. The transformation rules are defined on a hybridized modal language which allows the use of nominals and converse modalities in restricted forms. The rules are rewrite rules which exploit (i) logical equivalences and redundancy, (ii) a limited form of Skolemization and (iii) the modal version of Ackermann's lemma proved by Conradie, Goranko and Vakarelov [43].

If the procedure succeeds it produces a formula in the hybridized modal language with all the non-base symbols eliminated. This is then finally turned into a first-order logic formula by unskolemization and the standard translation of the hybridized modal language.

What is notable and important is that MSQEL and SQEMA are defined in a manner that the procedures are guaranteed to terminate (as is DLS). Moreover, unskolemization is decidable and therefore always successful and always produces a first-order formula. However, there are modal formulas which cannot be transformed by MSQEL or SQEMA. When such formulas are derived the procedures abort and report failure.

13.1.1. Modal Hybrid Logic.

The language of *modal hybrid logic* is an extension of the language of multi-modal logic with nominals and converse modalities $\Box_1^{\smile}, \ldots, \Box_k^{\smile}$, for $k \geq 2$. Let V be an enumerable set of propositional variables $p, p_1, p_2, \ldots$ and let A be an enumerable set of nominals $a, a_1, a_2, \ldots$.

DEFINITION 13.1. A *modal hybrid formula* is either a propositional atom, i.e., a propositional variable TRUE or a nominal, or a formula of the form $\neg\alpha$, $\alpha \wedge \beta$ and, for $1 \leq i \leq k$, $\Box_i\alpha$ and $\Box_i^{\smile}\alpha$, where α and β denote modal hybrid formulas. FALSE, $\vee$, $\rightarrow$, $\equiv$, $\Diamond_i$ are defined as usual. The converse diamond operator $\Diamond_i^{\smile}$ is specified by $\Diamond_i^{\smile}\alpha \overset{\text{def}}{=} \neg\Box_i^{\smile}\neg\alpha$, where α denotes an arbitrary modal hybrid formula. ◁

Thus, modal hybrid logic is an extension of modal tense logic, namely with nominals.

The semantics of modal hybrid logic is an extension of the Kripke semantics of multi-modal logic. In particular, the semantics of modal hybrid logic is given by a model $M = \langle W, \langle R_i \rangle_i, v \rangle$ and the satisfiability relation defined as before, except that the interpretation of nominals and the converse modalities are defined by these conditions:

$$M, x \models a \text{ iff } v(a) = \{x\}$$

$$M, x \models \Box_i^{\smile} \alpha \text{ iff } R_i(y, x) \text{ implies } M, y \models \alpha, \text{ for all } y \in W.$$

The notions of satisfiability and validity are defined as before.

The standard translation of modal hybrid formulas is an extension of the mapping ST from Section 10.3 with the conditions:

$$\text{ST}(a, x) = x \approx a$$

$$\text{ST}(\Box_i^{\smile} \alpha, x) = \forall y[R_i(y, x) \rightarrow \text{ST}(\alpha, y)].$$

It is assumed here that the language of first-order logic includes constants uniquely associated to nominals. We do not distinguish nominals and the corresponding constants notationally. Thus ST is now a mapping from modal hybrid formulas to first-order formulas possibly containing constants.

13.1.2. Modal Hybrid Clauses.

DEFINITION 13.2. A *modal hybrid clause* C is a disjunction of modal hybrid formulas which is globally satisfiable (i.e., true in every world of a model). ◁

This means that any modal hybrid clause C represents $[u]C$, where $[u]$ denotes the universal modality. The semantics of the universal modality is specified by:

$$M, x \models [u]\beta \text{ iff } M, y \models \beta, \text{ for any } y \in W.$$

Accordingly, the standard translation is defined by

$$\text{ST}([u]\beta, x) = \forall y[\text{ST}(\beta, y)].$$

The standard translation of a modal hybrid clause C and a set N of modal hybrid clauses is thus given by:

$$\text{ST}(C, x) = \forall y[\text{ST}(C, y)],$$

$$\text{ST}(N, x) = \bigwedge \{\forall y[\text{ST}(C, y)] \mid C \in N\}.$$

In order to simplify the definition of the rules of the calculus we use the following notation:

- $\sharp$ denotes a box operator $\Box_i$ or $\Box_i^{\smile}$, for some i.
- $\sharp^j$ denotes a sequence of j box operators.
- $\sharp^{\smile}$ denotes $\Box_i^{\smile}$, if $\sharp = \Box_i$, and it denotes $\Box_i$, if $\sharp = \Box_i^{\smile}$, for some i. I.e., $\sharp^{\smile}$ is the *converse operator* of $\sharp$.
- $\sharp^{j,\smile}$ denotes the sequence of the converse operators of the operators in $\sharp^j$, in reverse order.

Recall that for any terms s and t, $R^\epsilon(s,t)$ denotes $s \approx t$, and $R^{k \cdot \sigma}(s,t)$ denotes $\exists x[R_k(s,x) \wedge R^\sigma(x,t)]$, where ϵ denotes the empty sequence and σ a (possibly empty) sequence of natural numbers.

Observe that the following hold:

$$\mathrm{ST}(\Box^\sigma \alpha, x) = \forall y[R^\sigma(x,y) \to \mathrm{ST}(\alpha, y)]$$

$$\mathrm{ST}(\neg a \vee \alpha, x) \equiv \mathrm{ST}(\alpha, a)$$

$$\mathrm{ST}(\neg a \vee \neg \Box_i \neg b, x) \equiv R_i(a,b)$$

$$\mathrm{ST}(\neg a \vee \neg \Box_i^{\smallsmile} \neg b, x) \equiv R_i(b,a)$$

$$\mathrm{ST}(\neg a \vee \neg \Box^\sigma \neg b, x) \equiv R^\sigma(a,b).$$

13.1.3. Modal Ackermann Lemma. Recall, two Kripke models M and M' are p-equivalent iff they are identical except that they may differ in the valuation of p, where p is (here) a propositional symbol.

THEOREM 13.3. Let α and β be modal hybrid formulas and suppose the propositional symbol p does not occur in α. Let M be an arbitrary modal hybrid model.

If p occurs only positively in β then

> (there is a model M' which is p-equivalent to M
> and $M' \models (p \to \alpha) \wedge \beta(p)$) iff $M \models \beta_\alpha^p$.

If p occurs only negatively in β then

> (there is a model M' which is p-equivalent to M
> and $M' \models (\alpha \to p) \wedge \beta(p)$) iff $M \models \beta_\alpha^p$.   ◁

13.1.4. Modal Ackermann Calculus. For any formula α, let $\sim\alpha$ denote β if $\alpha = \neg\beta$, and $\neg\alpha$ otherwise. That is, $\sim$ can be interpreted as negation but it removes a negation sign if α is a negated formula.

DEFINITION 13.4. Let $>$ denote an ordering of the non-base symbols and let $\succ$ be a reduction ordering (i.e., a well-founded, rewrite relation) on modal hybrid clauses which is compatible with $>$. Let MA be the calculus comprising the rules in Table 27, except for the sign switching rule. The calculus with the sign switching rule is denoted by MA^{sw}. We call MA the *modal Ackermann calculus*.   ◁

The ordering $>$ specifies in which sequence the non-base symbols are eliminated. The elimination process starts eliminating the largest symbol first. We say a propositional symbol p is *strictly maximal* with respect to a formula α if for any propositional symbol q in α, $p > q$.

Note that we assume that $\vee$ is commutative and associative. The rules operate on sets of modal hybrid clauses. For any rule of the form N/M, where N and M

TABLE 27. The calculus MA^{sw}.

Modal Ackermann:
$$\frac{\{\alpha_1 \vee p, \ldots, \alpha_n \vee p\} \cup N(p)}{(N^p_{\sim\alpha_1\vee\ldots\vee\sim\alpha_n})^{\neg\neg\alpha_1}_{\alpha_1}}$$

provided (i) p is a non-base symbol, (ii) p is strictly maximal with respect to each α_i, and (iii) N is negative with respect to p. We refer to the clauses $\alpha_1 \vee p, \ldots, \alpha_n \vee p$ as the *positive premises* of the rule.

Surfacing:
$$\frac{N \cup \{\alpha \vee \sharp^j \beta(p)\}}{N \cup \{\sharp^{j,\smile}\alpha \vee \beta(p)\}}$$

provided (i) p is the largest non-base symbol which occurs in $\alpha \vee \sharp^j\beta$, (ii) p does not occur in α, and (iii) $\sharp^j\beta$ is positive with respect to p. It is assumed that $j > 0$.

Skolemization:
$$\frac{N \cup \{\neg a \vee \neg\sharp^j\beta(p)\}}{N \cup \{\neg a \vee \neg\sharp^j\neg b, \neg b \vee \sim\beta(p)\}}$$

provided (i) p is the largest non-base symbol which occurs in $\neg a \vee \neg\sharp^j\beta$, (ii) $\neg\sharp^j\beta$ is positive with respect to p and (iii) b is a new nominal. It is assumed that $j > 0$.

Logical rewriting:
$$\frac{N \cup \{\alpha\}}{N \cup \{\beta\}}$$

provided (i) α and β are logically equivalent with respect to the base logic, and (ii) α is effectively reducible to β such that $\alpha \succ \beta$.

Clausifying:
$$\frac{N \cup \{\neg(\alpha \vee \beta)\}}{N \cup \{\sim\alpha, \sim\beta\}}$$

Modal purifying:
$$\frac{N(p)}{N^p_{\text{TRUE}}} \qquad \frac{N(p)}{(N^p_{\neg\text{TRUE}})^{\neg\neg\text{TRUE}}_{\text{TRUE}}}$$

provided p is a non-base symbol, N is positive with respect to p, for the left rule, and N is negative with respect to p, for the right rule.

Sign switching:
$$\frac{N(p)}{(N^p_{\neg p})^{\neg\neg p}_p}$$

provided (i) N is closed with respect to the other rules, (ii) p is the maximal non-base symbol in N, and (iii) sign switching with respect to p has not been performed before.

---

are sets of modal hybrid clauses, their meaning is characterized by the following property:

$$\bigwedge N \text{ is globally satisfiable iff } \bigwedge M \text{ is globally satisfiable.}$$

The modal Ackermann rule is the deduction rule of the MA calculus. Recall that N^γ_α means that all occurrences of γ in the set N are replaced by the formula α.

Observe that condition (ii) implies that p does not occur in $\alpha_1, \ldots, \alpha_n$ and no non-base symbol occurring in any of the α_i is larger than p. We note that the modal Ackermann rule can be viewed as a kind of (non-clausal) ordered hyperresolution rule combined with purification.

By repeated use of the surfacing rule, positive occurrences of maximal non-base symbols are moved upward in the formula tree, so that this formula can be used as left premise of the modal Ackermann rule. In order for clauses to be usable as positive premises of the modal Ackermann rule they must appear as (positive) literals in clauses. More specifically, the aim is to move positive occurrences of maximal non-base symbols occurring anywhere below a non-empty sequence of box operators "closer to the surface". This is done by moving the converse of the box operators of the boxed literal $\sharp^j \beta$ to the subclause α which does not contain this literal. Note that if α is empty then this is interpreted as $\neg\mathrm{TRUE}$ and $\sharp^j \beta$ is replaced by $\sharp^{j,\smile}\neg\mathrm{TRUE} \vee \beta$.

The Skolemization rule expands an existential formula in a clause of the form $\neg a \vee \neg\sharp^j \alpha$. Since a denotes a nominal this formula is interpreted as $M, v(a) \models \neg\sharp^j \alpha$ and is therefore an existential formula. Skolemizing the implicit quantifiers in $\neg\sharp^j \alpha$ requires only the introduction of constants and not Skolem terms with dependencies on universally quantified variables. No other form of Skolemization is performed in the calculus. That is, Skolemization is limited to top-level diamond formulas.

Because of this, and in particular, because Skolemization is limited only to the introduction of constants (nominals) and no equality constraints are used in Ackermann rule of the calculus, the surfacing rules are necessary. The Skolemization rule can be viewed as a surfacing rule for diamond literals, but it is not as general as the surfacing rule for box formulas. In particular, there is no provision in the calculus for surfacing non-base symbols occurring in β of any clause $\alpha \vee \neg\sharp^j \beta$, where α is arbitrary. It is possible to formulate a general surfacing rule for this case but this would require full Skolemization and the use of equality constraints.

Simplification is possible with the logical rewriting rule. The rule involves finding logically equivalent formulas which is in general a computationally hard problem. If the base logic is undecidable then just the testing of logical equivalence is undecidable. Even when the base logic is decidable then testing logical equivalence has at least the complexity of deduction in the base logic. For the basic multi-modal logic the complexity in PSPACE-complete, and for modal hybrid logic the complexity is EXPTIME-complete. Therefore, in practice one would not implement the rule without an effective procedure for testing and finding logical equivalents. This is the reason for including condition (ii). For correctness, the condition is not important, but it gives the rule the needed determinateness which is crucial for

TABLE 28. Equivalences for simplification.

input formula	equivalent formula
$\alpha \equiv \beta$	$\neg(\neg(\sim\alpha \vee \beta) \vee \neg(\sim\beta \vee \alpha))$
$\neg(\alpha \equiv \beta)$	$\neg(\sim\alpha \vee \beta) \vee \neg(\sim\beta \vee \alpha)$
$\alpha \rightarrow \beta$	$\sim\alpha \vee \beta$
$\neg(\alpha \rightarrow \beta)$	$\sim\alpha \vee \sim\beta$
$\alpha \wedge \beta$	$\neg(\sim\alpha \vee \sim\beta)$
$\neg(\alpha \wedge \beta)$	$\sim\alpha \vee \sim\beta$
FALSE	$\neg$TRUE
$\neg$FALSE	TRUE
$\Diamond_i \alpha$	$\neg\Box_i \sim\alpha$
$\Diamond_i^{\smile} \alpha$	$\neg\Box_i^{\smile} \sim\alpha$
$\neg\Diamond_i \alpha$	$\Box_i \sim\alpha$
$\neg\Diamond_i^{\smile} \alpha$	$\Box_i^{\smile} \sim\alpha$
$\alpha \vee \alpha$	α
$\alpha \vee \neg\alpha$	TRUE
$\alpha \vee$ TRUE	TRUE
$\alpha \vee \neg$TRUE	α
$\Box_i$ TRUE	TRUE
$\Box_i^{\smile}$ TRUE	TRUE
$\neg(\alpha \vee \beta) \vee \gamma$	$\neg(\neg(\sim\alpha \vee \gamma) \vee \neg(\sim\beta \vee \gamma))$
$\Box_i \neg(\alpha \vee \beta)$	$\neg(\neg\Box_i \sim\alpha \vee \neg\Box_i \sim\beta)$
$\Box_i^{\smile} \neg(\alpha \vee \beta)$	$\neg(\neg\Box_i^{\smile} \sim\alpha \vee \neg\Box_i^{\smile} \sim\beta)$
$\alpha \vee \Box_i \neg\Box_i^{\smile} \alpha$	TRUE
$\alpha \vee \Box_i^{\smile} \neg\Box_i \alpha$	TRUE
$\neg a \vee \neg\Box_i \neg\Box_i^{\smile} \neg a \vee \beta$	$\neg a \vee \beta$
$\neg a \vee \neg\Box_i^{\smile} \neg\Box_i \neg a \vee \beta$	$\neg a \vee \beta$
$\neg\neg\alpha$	α

termination and efficiency.[1] The rule has the advantage that it provides flexibility for using suitable and tractable instances of the rule. We apply the rule only when β is smaller than α with respect to the ordering $\succ$. Intuitively, β is then "simpler" than α with respect to the ordering.

Table 28 lists examples of logical equivalences that when used as rewrite rules from left-to-right replace formulas by equivalent smaller formulas which can be implemented efficiently. Their purpose is twofold. On the one hand they are used

---

[1]Nevertheless, the rule is still very powerful. Yet, using a notion of redundancy in the spirit of Section 4.4.2, the rule can be strengthened even further. Another possibility is to base simplification on second-order equivalence.

to transform the set into a set of general clauses and hence help prepare them for the application of the modal Ackermann rule. On the other hand they are used to simplify the formulas. The ten rules in the first block eliminate the operators $\equiv$, $\rightarrow$, $\wedge$, FALSE and $\Diamond_i$ (assuming that these are defined operators in the language). The next block of rules perform obvious propositional and modal simplifications. The rules in the third block of rules distribute disjunction and box operators over conjunctive formulas. Logical equivalence preserving simplifications based on interrelationships between the modalities and their converse modalities are exploited in the rules of the fourth block. The last rewrite rule eliminates occurrences of double negations.

Any transformation based on these logical rewrite rules clearly preserves logical equivalence in modal hybrid logic. Ignoring the distributivity of disjunction over conjunction the transformation can be implemented with constant overhead. The distributivity rule of disjunction over conjunction can lead to an exponential blow-up. In the remainder of this section we assume that the logical rewriting rule is based on a terminating rewrite system such as the rules of Table 28.

The clausifying rule replaces any top-level conjunction by the set of conjuncts appearing in the conjunctions.

The purifying rule eliminates a non-base symbol that occurs only positively or only negatively by substitution with TRUE or $\neg$TRUE. There are some similarities with the purification rule of the C-resolution calculus of SCAN. Both can be seen to eliminate clauses by the replacement of non-base literals by TRUE or $\neg$TRUE. However, the conditions under which the rules are applied are different.

The sign switching rule is only applied when the procedure has failed to eliminate the maximal non-base symbol in the set. The strategy implicit in the definition is to postpone the application of the rule as much as possible. This is however not essential for correctness or termination of the calculus.

13.1.5. Correctness and Termination of MA and MA^{sw}. For the next theorem we need the notion of Skolem formulas for the nominals introduced during an MA$^{(sw)}$-derivation. Suppose b is the nominal introduced by the Skolemization rule reducing $\neg a \;\vee\; \neg\sharp^j \alpha$ to $\neg a \;\vee\; \neg\sharp^j \neg b$ and $\neg b \vee \neg \alpha$. Then the formula $(\neg a \;\vee\; \neg\sharp^j \alpha) \rightarrow ((\neg a \;\vee\; \neg\sharp^j \neg b) \wedge (\neg b \vee \neg \alpha))$ is the *modal Skolem formula* for the nominal b.

Let N be the set of input formulas. We say a derivation in MA$^{(sw)}$ is *successful* if none of the non-base symbols occur in the result N_∞ of the derivation, and a derivation has *failed*, otherwise.

THEOREM 13.5. Let N be a set of modal hybrid clauses and suppose $p_1 > \ldots >$ p_m are the non-base symbols in N. Let $N (= N_0), N_1, \ldots$ be a $\mathsf{MA}^{(sw)}$-derivation from N with result N_∞. Then:

(1) No rules are applicable to N_∞ with respect to $p_1 > \ldots > p_m$.
(2) There is an $n \geq 0$ such that $N_n = N_\infty$, i.e., any $\mathsf{MA}^{(sw)}$-derivation with respect to $p_1 > \ldots > p_m$ terminates.
(3) If the derivation is successful, then for any $(p_1, \ldots, p_m)$-equivalent models M and M'

$$M \models \bigwedge N \wedge \bigwedge S(a_1, \ldots, a_l) \text{ iff } M' \models \bigwedge N_\infty(a_1, \ldots, a_l),$$

where $a_1 \ldots a_l$ are the nominals introduced during the derivation and $S(a_1, \ldots, a_l)$ is the set of Skolem formulas for $a_1, \ldots, a_l$.

PROOF. (1) is clear from the definition of N_∞.

(2) It is possible to define a measure $>_c$ over the derivation so that $N_i >_c N_j$ for every $1 \leq i < j$, and $>_c$ is compatible with $>$ and $\succ$. The property follows.

(3) By the modal version of Ackermann's lemma the Ackermann rule preserves equivalence in the sense of Ackermann's lemma. With the exception of the sign switching rule and the Skolemization rule every other rule in Table 27 is based on logical equivalences. For the sign switching rule we note that when applied to $N(p)$ with conclusion N', even though it is not the case that $M \models N$ iff $M \models N'$ (because $N(p) \not\equiv N'$), the following holds: $M \models N$ iff $M' \models N'$, for p-equivalent models M and M' (because $\exists p[N(p)] \equiv \exists p[N']$). Conjoining the set of Skolem formulas $S(a_1, \ldots, a_l)$ ensures logical equivalence is preserved by Skolemization.   ◁

13.1.6. Improving Successful Termination. For any given set N of formulas every $\mathsf{MA}^{(sw)}$-derivation stops after finitely many steps. This means that termination is guaranteed. But it is not guaranteed that there is a sequence of transformations that succeeds for the particular ordering of non-base symbols. As a consequence it may be necessary to attempt all possible orderings of the non-base symbols. Even when all possible orderings are tried, success cannot be guaranteed because there is no rule for bringing non-base symbols occurring below sequences of modal operators to the surface where a diamond operator occurs below a box operator. The underlying reason for the absence for such a surfacing rule is weakness in the language of modal hybrid logic. If we think of the first-order translation of diamonds below boxes then these involve unary Skolem functions which are not available in the language. Even if this can be remedied, then it is still not possible to ensure success, because some formulas such as McKinsey's axiom are just not first-order definable.

A technique which helps to improve the success rate of the elimination of the non-base symbols, is to first transform the input problem into a disjunction of smaller formulas which are then processed in separate invocations within $MA^{(sw)}$. Such transformation to disjunctive form is justified because existential quantification distributes over disjunction. It is part of the pre-processing performed in the basic algorithm of MSQEL which is described in the next section.

13.1.7. The MSQEL Procedure. Suppose that α is a given modal hybrid formula and the aim is to eliminate the set $\Sigma = \{p_1, \ldots, p_m\}$ of non-base propositional symbols from α. Analogous to SQEMA [**41, 42, 43**] and DLS [**56**], MSQEL performs the following steps.

Pre-process input: The input formula is negated so that we get $\neg\alpha$. While performing simplifications (e.g., based on the rules of Table 28), transform this into a disjunction $\bigvee_i \alpha_i$ of formulas where each α_i has the form
$$\beta \wedge \bigwedge_k \sharp\gamma_k \wedge \bigwedge_l \neg\sharp\delta_l,$$ where β is a conjunction of non-modal literals, and both γ_k and δ_l are disjunctions of the same form. However, if one of the disjuncts α_i is a negated nominal $\neg a$, then pick one of these, say $\neg a$, delete it but add it to the other disjuncts. E.g., $\neg a \vee \neg b \vee \alpha_1 \vee \alpha_2$ becomes $(\neg a \vee \neg b) \vee (\neg a \vee \alpha_1) \vee (\neg a \vee \alpha_2)$.

Reduce disjuncts: Consider each disjunct α_i in turn, select an ordering of the non-base symbols in Σ and apply the rules of the calculus MA^{sw} to the set $\{\neg a \vee \alpha_i\}$ with respect to this ordering. If this succeeds and returns a set N_i of modal hybrid clauses which are free of the non-base symbols then we say that MSQEL has *successfully reduced* α_i to N_i. If this step fails then construct a derivation with respect to a different ordering of the non-base symbols.

Translate to first-order logic: The last step is performed only when every disjunct α_i has been successfully reduced to a set N_i of modal hybrid formulas. Each set is first transformed into a set M_i of first-order formulas in the obvious way using the standard translation ST. It remains to apply unskolemization to eliminate the nominals appearing in M_i, which are now interpreted as constants. Hence, the procedure terminates successfully and, after negation, returns the formula $\neg \bigvee_i \mathrm{UnSk}(M_i)$.

The pre-processing step can be performed effectively for any modal hybrid formula. The worst-case complexity of this step is in general bounded by an exponential function in the size of the formula. Observe however that for the preservation of logical equivalence of the entire procedure, this transformation is not essential. Nevertheless the transformation is useful because it means that smaller formulas are considered in the reduction step, which increases the chances of the procedure being successful. Yet, this transformation is essential for the completeness results discussed in Section 13.3.

The reduction step involves repeated attempts of solving a disjunct with the rules of MA^{sw} by using different orderings of the non-base symbols. Unless success is reported for a particular ordering another round is necessary using a different ordering (see Example 13.10). Thus in the worst case all possible orderings may need to be attempted.

13.1.8. Correctness and Termination of MSQEL. We are now able to state the correctness and termination of the MSQEL procedure.

THEOREM 13.6. Let α be any modal hybrid formula and let $\Sigma = \{p_1, \ldots, p_m\}$ be the set of non-base symbols.

(1) Any implementation of MSQEL terminates.
(2) If a MSQEL procedure terminates successfully and returns the formula β then
    (a) β is a first-order formula, and
    (b) β corresponds to $\forall p_1 \ldots \forall p_m \alpha$ (in particular, $F, w \models \alpha$ iff $F \models \beta(x)_w^x$ if all propositional variables in α belong to Σ).

PROOF. A consequence of Theorem 13.5, and because the other transformations in the pre-processing step and the translation to first-order logic preserve logical equivalence.   ◁

13.2. Computing Correspondences

In this section we apply the procedure to a number of modal formulas. We start by considering first-order definable modal formulas.

EXAMPLE 13.7. Let us see if we can derive the seriality property for the modal axiom **D**. Its negation is:

$$\neg\mathbf{D} = \exists p[\Box p \wedge \Box\neg p].$$

We start with $\neg a \vee (\Box p \wedge \Box\neg p)$ and the goal is to eliminate p. Rewriting with respect to distributivity of disjunction over conjunction and clausifying gives us:

$$\cancel{1}. \ \neg a \vee \Box p$$
$$\cancel{2}. \ \neg a \vee \Box\neg p$$

p occurs only positively in clause 1 but is shielded by a box operator. Applying the surfacing rule to 1 we obtain

$$\cancel{3}. \ \Box^{\smallsmile}\neg a \vee p \qquad\qquad 1, \text{surf.}$$

and delete clause 1. The positive occurrence of p is now unshielded and we can apply the Ackermann rule. This replaces clauses 2 and 3 by 4.

$$4.\ \neg a\ \lor\ \Box\Box^{\smile}\neg a \qquad\qquad\qquad \text{3 into 2, Acker.}$$

Since p is now eliminated we translate clause 4 into first-order logic:

$$\forall x[\mathrm{ST}(\neg a\ \lor\ \Box\Box^{\smile}\neg a, x)] \equiv \mathrm{ST}(\Box\Box^{\smile}\neg a, a)$$
$$= \forall x\big[R(a, x) \to \forall y[R(y, x) \to y \not\approx a]\big]$$
$$\equiv \forall x\big[R(a, x) \to \forall y[\neg R(a, x)]\big] \equiv \forall x[\neg R(a, x)].$$

Unskolemization returns $\exists y \forall x[\neg R(y, x)]$. Finally negating gives the expected result: $\forall y \exists x[R(y, x)]$.   ◁

EXAMPLE 13.8. The first-order correspondence property of the axiom

$$\mathbf{alt}_1^{\kappa_1,\kappa_2} = \forall p[\Diamond^{\kappa_1}\Diamond p \to \Box^{\kappa_2}\Box p],$$

where $\kappa_1 \geq 0$ and $\kappa_2 \geq 0$, is

$$\forall x \forall y \forall z[(R^{\kappa_1+1}(x, y) \land R^{\kappa_2+1}(x, z)) \to y \approx z].$$

The negation of $\mathbf{alt}_1^{\kappa_1,\kappa_2}$ reduces to

$$\text{1. } \neg a\ \lor\ \neg\Box^{\kappa_1}\Box\neg p$$
$$\text{2. } \neg a\ \lor\ \neg\Box^{\kappa_2}\Box p$$

The Skolemization rule replaces clause 1 by these two clauses where b is a new nominal.

$$\text{3. } \neg a\ \lor\ \neg\Box^{\kappa_1}\Box\neg b \qquad\qquad \text{1, Skolem.}$$
$$\text{4. } \neg b \lor p \qquad\qquad\qquad\qquad\quad \text{1, Skolem.}$$

Now we apply the Ackermann rule to 2 and 4.

$$\text{5. } \neg a\ \lor\ \neg\Box^{\kappa_2}\Box b \qquad\qquad\quad \text{4 into 2, Acker.}$$

Clauses 3 and 5 remain and are now translated into first-order logic. Since

$$\mathrm{ST}(\neg\Box^{\kappa_1}\Box\neg b, a) = R^{\kappa_1+1}(a, b)$$
$$\mathrm{ST}(\neg\Box^{\kappa_2}\Box b, a) = \exists x[R^{\kappa_2+1}(a, x) \land x \not\approx b]$$

we have that

$$\mathrm{UnSk}(\{3, 5\}) = \exists x \exists y \exists z[R^{\kappa_1+1}(x, y) \land R^{\kappa_2+1}(x, z) \land y \not\approx z].$$

The last operation is to negate the formula which gives the result we want.   ◁

EXAMPLE 13.9. In this example we apply the Ackermann rule to multiple positive premises. The first-order correspondence property of

$$\forall p\big[(\Box p \wedge \Diamond p) \to \Box\Box p\big]$$

is

$$\forall x \forall y \forall z \forall u \big[(R(x,y) \wedge R(y,z) \wedge R(x,u)) \to (R(x,z) \vee z \approx u)\big].$$

The MA-derivation is:

1. ¬a ∨ □p
2. ¬a ∨ ¬□¬p
3. ¬a ∨ ¬□□p
4. □˘¬a ∨ p   1, surf.
5. ¬a ∨ ¬□¬b   2, Skolem.
6. ¬b ∨ p   2, Skolem.
7. ¬a ∨ ¬□□(¬□˘¬a ∨ b)   4 and 6 into 3, Acker.

We leave it to the reader to translate $\{5, 7\}$ into first-order logic.   ◁

EXAMPLE 13.10. This example is an illustration of the general sensitivity to the order in which variables are eliminated. The modal formula

$$\forall p \forall q \big[\Box(\Box p \equiv q) \to \Diamond\Box\neg p\big]$$

is equivalent to $\forall x \exists y \forall z [R(x,y) \wedge \neg R(y,z)]$; in words, every world has a successor that is a dead-end. Negating the modal formula gives:

1. ¬a ∨ □(□p ≡ q)
2. ¬a ∨ ¬◇□¬p

Suppose the ordering of the variables is $p > q$, i.e., we attempt to eliminate p first.

3. ¬a ∨ □¬□¬p   2, log. rewr.
4. □˘¬a ∨ (□p ≡ q)   1, surf.
5. □˘¬a ∨ ¬□p ∨ q   4, log. rewr., cl.
6. □˘¬a ∨ □p ∨ ¬q   4, log. rewr., cl.
7. □˘(□˘¬a ∨ ¬q) ∨ p   4, surf.
8. □˘¬a ∨ ¬□¬p   3, surf.

At this point the procedure aborts with failure, because it is not possible to isolate the positive occurrence of the maximal variable in clause 8. MSQEL now tries to reduce the problem using a different ordering, i.e., $q > p$.

$\cancel{3'}.\ \Box^{\smile}\neg a \lor (\Box p \equiv q)$ 1, surf.

$\cancel{4'}.\ \Box^{\smile}\neg a \lor \neg\Box p \lor q$ $3'$, log. rewr., cl.

$\cancel{5'}.\ \Box^{\smile}\neg a \lor \Box p \lor \neg q$ $3'$, log. rewr., cl.

$\cancel{6'}.\ \Box^{\smile}\neg a \lor \Box p \lor \Box^{\smile}\neg a \lor \neg\Box p$ $4'$ into $5'$, Acker.

$7'.\ \text{TRUE}$ $6'$, log. rewr.

$8'.\ \neg a \lor \neg\Diamond\Box\neg\text{TRUE}$ $\{2\}$, purify

The procedure returns the first-order translation of the negation of

$$\neg a \lor \neg\Diamond\Box\neg\text{TRUE}$$

which is the property we expect to obtain.

The reason that MSQEL succeeds in the second attempt is that it allows the formula to be significantly reduced by recognizing a tautology involving the symbol p (in the step from $7'$ to $8'$). In the first attempt the procedure gets itself into a hopeless situation because this tautology is not spotted.   ◁

Although it has been claimed that the DLS and SCAN algorithms fail on examples similar to the previous example, it is not difficult to solve the problem successfully with both. The solution for DLS is to base the algorithm not on negation normal forms but on a standardization similar to the one used in our modal Ackermann calculus. For SCAN all that is needed are standard methods from automated reasoning.

EXAMPLE 13.11. For McKinsey's axiom $\mathbf{M} = \forall p[\Box\Diamond p \to \Diamond\Box p]$ the problem reduces to:

$\cancel{1}.\ \neg a \lor \Box\Diamond p$

$2.\ \neg a \lor \Box\Diamond\neg p$

We then derive:

$3.\ \Box^{\smile}\neg a \lor \Diamond p$

and delete clause 1. But now no further progress can be made, because there is no rule for bringing p to the surface in clause 3. The procedure terminates unsuccessfully.   ◁

Recall that for McKinsey's axiom SCAN is able to eliminate the non-base symbols and returns a second-order formula with Henkin quantifiers, see Example 11.2.

EXAMPLE 13.12. In this example we reconsider the reduction of the disjunction of McKinsey's axiom and the axiom **D**.

$$\forall p[(\Box p \rightarrow \Diamond p) \vee (\Box \Diamond p \rightarrow \Diamond \Box p)] \equiv \forall x \exists y[R(x, y)].$$

The input to the procedure is:

$\cancel{1}.\ \neg a\ \vee\ (\Box p \wedge \Box \neg p \wedge \Box \Diamond p \wedge \Box \Diamond \neg p)$

Clausifying produces:

$\cancel{2}.\ \neg a\ \vee\ \Box p$		1, cl.
$3.\ \neg a\ \vee\ \Box \neg p$		1, cl.
$4.\ \neg a\ \vee\ \Box \Diamond p$		1, cl.
$5.\ \neg a\ \vee\ \Box \Diamond \neg p$		1, cl.

We can solve clause 2 for p and replace it by:

$6.\ \Box^{\smile} \neg a \vee p$ \hfill 2, surf.

We can replace clause 4 by:

$7.\ \Box^{\smile} \neg a \vee \Diamond p$ \hfill 4, surf.

As in the previous example, no further progress is possible, because there is no rule in the calculus for bringing p to the surface in clause 7. Consequently, the Ackermann rule is not applicable. Sign switching does not help and leads to a similar deadlock situation. The procedure fails. $\quad\triangleleft$

By contrast, in Example 11.3 we saw that C-resolution successfully computes a first-order formula. Why is this? In this particular case the clauses corresponding to the translation of clauses 6 and 3 are resolvable and the resolvent is equivalent to $\neg a \vee \Box \text{FALSE}$. Interestingly, this can be derived through logical rewriting by applying the distributivity laws in the opposite direction as defined in Table 28:

$$(\neg a \vee \Box p) \wedge (\neg a \vee \Box \neg p)$$
$$\equiv \neg a \vee (\Box p \wedge \Box \neg p) \equiv \neg a \vee \Box(p \wedge \neg p) \equiv \neg a \vee \Box \neg \text{TRUE}.$$

Now $\neg a \vee \Box \neg \text{TRUE}$ subsumes clauses 5 and 7. Thus, we have computed the expected result without applying the Ackermann rule, but this required the use of some of the logical rewriting rules in the calculus in the reverse direction and subsumption deletion. This shows there is room for improvement in the definition of MSQEL. See also the next example.

EXAMPLE 13.13. Reconsider Example 11.4:

$$\forall p[\Box(p \vee \Box \neg p) \rightarrow \Diamond(p \wedge \Diamond \neg p)] \equiv \text{FALSE}.$$

This example is interesting because MSQEL without modification fails on it (so does SQEMA), but H-resolution succeeds.

$$\text{1. } \neg a \ \vee \ \Box(p \vee \Box\neg p)$$

$$\text{2. } \neg a \ \vee \ \neg\Diamond(p \wedge \Diamond\neg p)$$

3. $\Box^{\smallsmile}\neg a \vee p \vee \Box\neg p$	1, surf.
4. $\neg a \ \vee \ \Box(\neg p \vee \Box p)$	2, log. rewr.
5. $\Box^{\smallsmile}\neg a \vee \neg p \vee \Box p$	4, surf.

Now no more MA-rules are applicable.   ◁

13.3. Completeness for Extended Sahlqvist Formulas

In the following we prove that procedures based on the modal Ackermann calculus MA succeed for the Sahlqvist class and the class of inductive formulas defined over the language of modal tense logic.

13.3.1. Sahlqvist Formulas of Modal Tense Logic.
We extend the definition of Sahlqvist formulas to modal tense logic by allowing converse modalities to be used wherever the ordinary, forward looking modalities are used in Definitions 10.14–10.16.

THEOREM 13.14. Let α be any definite Sahlqvist implication over modal tense logic. Then:

(1) For any ordering of the propositional variables in α (i.e., the non-base symbols) any derivation based on MA (without sign switching) effectively reduces $\neg a \ \vee \ \neg\alpha$, where a denotes a nominal, to a modal hybrid formula β free of non-base symbols which corresponds to α.

(2) Any MSQEL derivation without sign switching effectively computes a first-order formula which corresponds to α.

PROOF. (1) Let $\alpha = Ant \rightarrow Pos$, where Ant denotes a definite Sahlqvist antecedent and Pos denotes a positive formula. Then $\neg\alpha = Ant \wedge \neg Pos$ is a definite Sahlqvist antecedent. Recall, from Definition 10.16, this means that $\neg\alpha$ is a formula formed from propositional constants FALSE and TRUE, boxed atoms and negative formulas by applying only $\wedge$ and diamonds (or $\neg\Box_i$), with the difference that we also allow converse modalities. Boxed atoms have the form $\sharp^j p$. Now, use the clausifying rule and the logical rewriting rules to obtain a set containing clauses of the form $(j > 0)$:

empty clause: $\neg\text{TRUE}$,

boxed atom clause: $\neg a \ \vee\ \sharp^j p$,

existential clause: $\neg a \ \vee\ \neg\sharp^j \beta,$ where β is a definite antecedent,

negative clause: $\neg a \ \vee\ \gamma,$ where γ is a negative formula.

If the empty clause is derived then no further computations are necessary. Hence, suppose $\neg\text{TRUE}$ was not derived. Now transform the boxed atom clauses and existential clauses using the surfacing rule, the Skolemization rule, the logical rewriting rule and the clausifying rule. This produces clauses of the form above and also clauses of the form:

surfaced clause: $\sharp^{j,\smile}\neg a \vee p,$

relational clause: $\neg a \ \vee\ \neg\sharp\neg b.$

(For input formulas from modal logic or modal tense logic the nominals a and b are in general different but this is not crucial.) Repeat the application of these rules until all positive variables have surfaced (then no more boxed atom clauses occur in the set). It is evident that no matter what the ordering of the propositional variables is, they can be eliminated in the particular order using either the Ackermann rule or the modal purifying rule. Notice that the sign switching rule is not needed for a definite Sahlqvist implication.

(2) By (1) and Theorem 13.6. $\lhd$

THEOREM 13.15. Given any Sahlqvist formula over modal tense logic, any derivation of MSQEL (with or without sign switching) successfully computes an equivalent first-order correspondent.

PROOF. This is a consequence of the previous theorem, because the pre-processing step (see page 170) transforms any Sahlqvist formula into a disjunction of definite Sahlqvist implications. $\lhd$

The theorem states that MSQEL succeeds on all Sahlqvist formulas with forward looking and backward looking modalities, regardless of the ordering chosen on the propositional variables. It follows immediately that MSQEL succeeds also on classical Sahlqvist formulas. Again, the ordering of the propositional symbols is immaterial to the success of the method. (For efficiency reasons the ordering does matter however.) Notice that the order of applying the rules does not matter either.

REMARK 13.16. We observe that the transformation to the specific disjunctive form in the pre-processing step of the procedure is crucial for the previous theorem. For the completeness theorem of SCAN with respect to the Sahlqvist class this pre-processing is not necessary. Theorem 11.9 is therefore a stronger result in this sense, except that the theorem above has been generalized to modal tense logic.

The generalization of the results for SCAN in Section 11.2 to modal tense logic poses no technical problems.   ◁

From the proofs of the theorems in this section it is apparent that successful MA-derivations are possible for a larger classes of formulas. The next section defines a larger class for which MSQEL succeeds always.

13.3.2. Monadic Inductive Formulas. In modal correspondence theory an important problem that has received considerable attention in the literature is the characterization of classes of modal formulas which correspond to first-order properties and are canonical, and hence, can be used to provide complete axiomatizations of modal logics (cf. the survey [**43**]). In their investigation of the problem, Goranko and Vakarelov [**100**] have defined a large syntactic class of formulas, the class of *inductive formulas*, which satisfies this property. The class of inductive formulas extends the class of Sahlqvist formulas and subsumes the class of the polyadic Sahlqvist formulas introduced and studied earlier by de Rijke and Venema [**51**].

In this section we are interested in the subclass of inductive formulas of classical modal logic and modal tense logic and therefore focus only on the class of *monadic inductive formulas*. Our presentation follows Conradie et al. [**42, 43**] with the difference that we allow converse modalities. Monadic inductive formulas can be seen to be natural extensions of Sahlqvist formulas for which methods based on the substitution method, methods based on Ackermann's lemma as well as quantifier elimination based on resolution, succeed.

DEFINITION 13.17. Extend the language of modal tense logic with a special symbol $*$. By definition, the following are *box forms of* $*$:

$$*, \quad \sharp\alpha, \quad A \to \alpha,$$

provided α is a box form for $*$ and A is a positive formula. We use the notation $B(*)$ for a box form of $*$.   ◁

Observe that every box form of $*$ is equivalent to a formula of the form

$$\sharp^{j_1}(A_1 \to \sharp^{j_2}(A_2 \to \ldots \sharp^{j_n}(A_n \to *)\ldots))$$

for some $j_i \geq 0$ $(1 \leq i \leq n)$ and positive formulas $A_1, \ldots, A_n$.

DEFINITION 13.18. Let p be a propositional variable. A *box formula for* p is the formula $B(*/p)$, i.e., a box form for $*$, where $*$ is replaced by p. This particular occurrence of p is called the *head* of $B(*/p)$. Every other occurrence of a variable in $B(*/p)$ (which might include occurrences of p) is called an *inessential occurrence* in $B(*/p)$. A *box formula* is a formula which is a box formula for some propositional variable. ◁

DEFINITION 13.19. A *dependency relation* $\succ_d$ over the propositional variables of a set N of box formulas, is defined by:

> $p \succ_d q$ iff there is a box formula α in N, p occurs as an inessential variable in α and q occurs as a head in α.

Let $\succ_d^+$ denote the transitive closure of $\succ_d$. If there is no variable p such that $p \succ_d^+ p$ then $\succ_d$ is called an *acyclic dependency relation*. ◁

DEFINITION 13.20. A *monadic regular formula* is any modal tense formula built from FALSE, TRUE, negated box formulas and positive formulas by applying $\land$, $\lor$ and box modalities ($\Box_i$ and $\Box_i^{\smile}$).

A monadic regular formula α is called a *monadic inductive formula* if the dependency relationship over the set of box formulas occurring in α is acyclic. ◁

Thus, monadic regular formulas are monadic inductive formulas in which the dependency relation can be cyclic.

EXAMPLE 13.21. The following formulas are (equivalent to) monadic inductive formulas:

> all negated Sahlqvist antecedents
>
> all Sahlqvist formulas
>
> $(p \land \Box(\Diamond p \to \Box q)) \to \Diamond \Box \Box q$
>
> $\Box \Diamond (p \lor q) \lor \neg \Box(\Box p \lor \neg \Box q)$
>
> $(\Box_3(q \to p) \land \Box_4 p) \to \Box_1 \Box_2 (p \to q)$.

The following are some non-examples:

> **M** $\quad \Diamond(\Diamond p \to \Box p)$
>
> **W** $\quad \Box(\Box p \to p) \to \Box p$
>
> $\quad\quad \Box(p \lor \Box \neg p) \to \Diamond(p \land \Diamond \neg p)$. ◁

THEOREM 13.22. Let α be any monadic inductive formula over modal tense logic. Then:

(1) For any ordering of the propositional variables in α, any derivation based on MA (without sign switching) effectively reduces $\neg a \lor \neg \alpha$, where a denotes a nominal, to a modal hybrid formula β free of non-base symbols which is an equivalent correspondent to α.

(2) Any MSQEL derivation effectively computes a first-order formula which equivalently corresponds to α.

PROOF. (Sketch) $\neg\alpha$ is formed from FALSE, TRUE, box formulas and negative formulas using $\land$, $\lor$ and diamond modalities ($\Diamond_i$ and $\overset{\smile}{\Diamond_i}$). In the pre-processing phase $\neg\alpha$ is transformed into a disjunction of formulas

$$\alpha_n = \beta \land \bigwedge_k \sharp^{i_k}\gamma_k \land \bigwedge_l \neg\sharp^{j_l}\delta_l,$$

where β is a conjunction of non-modal literals, γ_k is a box formula, and δ_l is a disjunction of negated box formulas and/or positive formulas (where $i_k > 0$ and $j_l > 0$ for each k and l). The rules of MA are now applied to $\neg a \lor \alpha_n$, for each disjunct α_n. W.l.o.g. assume that the clausifying rule is applied repeatedly to $\neg a \lor \alpha_n$. It is not difficult to see that the set we get contains only clauses of the following form ($i > 0$, $j \geq 0$):

surfaced clause:	$\beta \lor p$
negative clause:	β
box formula clause:	$\beta \lor \sharp^i\gamma$
relational clause:	$\neg b \lor \neg\sharp^i\neg c$
existential clause:	$\neg b \lor \neg\sharp^j\delta$

where b, c denote nominals, β a negative formula, γ a box formula, and δ either a negated box formula or a disjunction of negated box formulas and positive formulas. (Note that when δ is a positive formula then $\neg b \lor \neg\sharp^j\delta$ is a negative clause.) By considering every type of rule in the calculus we can prove that the clauses derived by every application of a rule applied to clauses of the above form consists of clauses of this form only. In other words, this class of clauses is closed under the application of the rules of MA. Now observe that the acyclicity condition in the definition of monadic inductive formulas implies that no propositional symbol occurs both positively and negatively in a surfaced clause or a box formula clause, and no surfaced clause of box formula clauses contain more than one positive occurrence of a propositional variable. Inspection of the rules reveals that these properties are preserved by the inference rules. Finally we can convince ourselves that regardless of how the propositional variables are ordered, it is always possible to move maximal occurrences of positive propositional variables to the surface. The earlier observation that no clauses contain positive and negative occurrences of a particular propositional variable means that the elimination of any propositional variable is always possible either with the Ackermann rule or the purifying rule. It is now possible to show that for any problem and any ordering of the propositional variables all derivations terminate successfully in a finitely bounded number of steps. Both (1) and (2) now follow from earlier results.   ◁

13.4. SQEMA

The results in the previous sections are natural generalizations of results proved in Conradie et al. [**42, 43**] for modal logic formulas (rather than modal hybrid formulas or modal tense formulas) and SQEMA (rather than MSQEL), see also [**41, 44**].

13.4.1. The SQEMA Procedure.

SQEMA takes a modal logic formula as input. It applies essentially the same basic algorithm on this input as MSQEL but it is based on a different set of rules. The rules used by Conradie, Goranko and Vakarelov in [**42, 43**] operate on formulas in implicational form and formulas are transformed into negation normal form. As mentioned previously transformation into negation normal form has the drawback that obvious redundancies become harder to detect and to eliminate. For example, $\Box p \vee \Diamond \neg p$ is not picked up by the rules as defined in [**42, 43**], but can be easily reduced to $\neg$TRUE using the rules of MA (Table 27).

In the remainder of the section we assume that SQEMA is the restriction of MSQEL to input problems from modal logic, rather than modal tense logic. Strictly, SQEMA as defined here is therefore not the same as the algorithm defined in [**42, 43**], but the two versions are close enough so that the results hold also for our version of SQEMA.

13.4.2. Completeness.

Conradie et al. [**43**] prove that

- SQEMA succeeds on all Sahlqvist formulas.
- SQEMA succeeds on all monadic inductive formulas.

Their proof for monadic inductive formulas uses a certain strategy and a certain ordering compatible with the dependency relation, and thus exhibits the existence of a successful SQEMA derivation. The theorems and proofs of Sections 13.3.1 and 13.3.2 imply that the ordering of the propositional variables is immaterial and so is the order in which rules are applied. Consequently, the following slightly stronger results can be stated.

COROLLARY 13.23. Let α be any definite Sahlqvist implication. Then:

(1) For any ordering of the propositional variables in α, the non-base symbols, any derivation based on MA (without sign switching) effectively reduces $\neg a \vee \neg \alpha$, where a denotes a nominal, to a modal hybrid formula β free of non-base symbols which equivalently corresponds to α.

(2) Any SQEMA derivation without sign switching effectively computes a first-order formula which equivalently corresponds to α.   ◁

COROLLARY 13.24. Any SQEMA derivation (with or without sign switching) successfully computes an equivalent first-order correspondent, for any Sahlqvist formula.   ◁

COROLLARY 13.25. Let α be any monadic inductive formula. Then:

(1) For any ordering of the propositional variables in α, any derivation based on MA (without sign switching) effectively reduces $\neg a \lor \neg\alpha$, where a denotes a nominal, to a modal hybrid formula β free of non-base symbols which equivalently corresponds to α.

(2) Any SQEMA derivation effectively computes an equivalent first-order correspondent for α.   ◁

13.4.3. Canonicity. An important contribution of Conradie et al. [43] is the following canonicity result.

THEOREM 13.26. If SQEMA succeeds on a modal formula α then

(1) α is (d-persistent and hence) canonical, and
(2) the first-order formula returned by SQEMA is equivalent to α.   ◁

Together with the results of the previous section this implies Sahlqvist's theorem and a strengthening to monadic inductive formulas.

COROLLARY 13.27.

(1) All Sahlqvist formulas are elementary and canonical.
(2) All monadic inductive formulas are elementary and canonical.   ◁

These results were first proved in [43]. An even stronger Sahlqvist-type theorem in proved by Goranko and Vakarelov [100] for polyadic inductive formulas. See also Conradie [41] for investigations in hybrid logic.

CHAPTER 14

Back-Translation

This chapter is concerned with the problem of translating first-order formulas back into modal logic. One can translate, for instance, a modal formula into a classical second-order formula, apply second-order quantifier elimination and then, if the elimination is successful, translate the obtained first-order formula back into a modal formula, thus obtaining a modal formula that is (second-order) equivalent to the original modal formula.

Back-translation of first-order properties to modal formulas involves introducing second-order quantifiers. This second-order quantifier introduction does not necessarily just undo the elimination of the second-order quantifiers. Rather, it can be used to compute an equivalent modal formula which is more suitable, for example, it is simpler, because it contains fewer propositional variables. We discuss effective means for doing such back-translations and show how it can be used to provide a method of inter-reducing equivalent modal axioms. We also show how back-translation can be used to improve the capabilities of modal logic and description logic calculi/provers to handle problems apparently out of scope, but which can be translated to an equivalent form that can be handled.

14.1. Back-Translation for Modal Logics

14.1.1. Kracht Formulas. In [130] Kracht provided a characterization of a class of classical first-order formulas which can be translated back into Sahlqvist formulas. He also described an effective method for this back-translation.

Our definition of *Kracht formulas*, also called *first-order Sahlqvist formulas* [130], is a variation of definitions found in [20, 130, 131]. Kracht formulas are first-order formulas. Let the *(first-order) frame language* be a function-free first-order language, in which the primitive building blocks are binary relation symbols, the equality symbol $\approx$, the logical constants TRUE, FALSE, the standard connectives $\neg$, $\wedge$, $\vee$, etc. and the quantifiers $\forall$ and $\exists$.

DEFINITION 14.1. By (universal, respectively existential) *restricted quantifiers*, we mean the guarded quantifiers in these formulas, where y is a free variable of α:

$$\forall y[R_k(x,y) \to \alpha(y)] \quad \text{and} \quad \exists y[R_k(x,y) \wedge \alpha(y)].$$

By definition, a formula is *rooted in a term s* if it is a restrictedly quantified formula of the form $\forall y[R_k(s,y) \to \alpha(y)]$ or $\exists y[R_k(s,y) \wedge \alpha(y)]$. We say s is the *root* of these formulas. ◁

Note that α may contain more free variables than just y.

Recall from Section 4.2.2, in a standardized first-order formula all variables are renamed apart. A first-order formula is *mini-scoped* if the scope of all quantifiers is minimized.

DEFINITION 14.2. A first-order frame formula is called a *rooted Kracht formula* if it is a standardized, mini-scoped, rooted formula $\alpha(a)$ without any free variables which is built from FALSE, TRUE, $\wedge$, $\vee$, restricted quantifiers and formulas of the form $\neg R^\sigma(s,t)$, where σ is a possibly empty sequence of natural numbers,

- s is the innermost quantified variable in the scope of which $\neg R^\sigma(s,t)$ occurs, and
- t is a, or it is an existentially quantified variable which does not occur in the scope of a universal quantifier,

or vice versa, with the role of s and t exchanged.

A formula α is called a *Kracht formula* iff α is a conjunction of rooted Kracht formulas with no constants in common. ◁

Let α be a rooted Kracht formula. We define an ordering $<$ on the variables occurring in α as follows: $x < y$, for any restricted quantifier formula $\exists y[R(x,y) \wedge \beta(y)]$ or $\forall y[R(x,y) \to \beta(y)]$ in α. We use $<$ to also denote the corresponding ordering on the Skolem terms in the Skolemized form of α. We say y is the *tightest bound* variable in β. Similarly, we say the corresponding Skolem term is the tightest bound term in the Skolemized form of β.

EXAMPLE 14.3. Table 27 gives examples of (rooted) Kracht formulas. They are equivalent to the negation of relational properties in Table 25. ◁

The following theorem is due to Kracht (see, e.g., Theorem 5.6.1 in [131]).

THEOREM 14.4.

(1) Any Sahlqvist formula corresponds to a negated, rooted Kracht formula.
(2) Conversely, any Kracht formula corresponds to a conjunction of negated Sahlqvist formulas. ◁

TABLE 29. Examples of Kracht formulas.

$\neg \mathbf{D}$	$\forall y[R(a, y) \rightarrow \text{FALSE}]$
$\neg \mathbf{T}$	$\forall y[R(a, y) \rightarrow y \not\approx a]$
$\neg \mathbf{4}$	$\exists y\big[R(a, y) \wedge \exists z[R(y, z) \wedge \neg R(a, z)]\big]$
$\neg \mathbf{B}$	$\exists y[R(a, y) \wedge \neg R(y, a)]$
$\neg \mathbf{5}$	$\exists y\big[R(a, y) \wedge \exists z[R(a, z) \wedge \neg R(y, z)]\big]$
$\neg \mathbf{alt}_1$	$\exists y\big[R(a, y) \wedge \exists z[R(a, z) \wedge y \not\approx z]\big]$
$\neg \mathbf{G}$	$\exists y\big[R(a, y) \wedge \exists z[R(a, z) \wedge \forall u[R(y, u) \rightarrow \neg R(z, u)]]\big]$
$\neg \mathbf{H}$	$\exists y\big[R(a, y) \wedge \exists z[R(a, z) \wedge (R(y, z) \vee \neg R(z, y))]\big]$

Kracht defines a sequent-style calculus for deriving modal formulas and the corresponding Kracht formulas. This uses a bottom-up approach.

In the rest of this chapter we follow Schmidt [182] and describe a related but different method for converting first-order formulas into modal formulas. In contrast to Kracht's approach, our method proceeds in a top-down, goal-oriented fashion. Our procedure is called MSQIN, which is short for modal second-order quantifier introduction. The MSQIN procedure transforms a Kracht formula into a conjunction of rooted modal formulas.

The existence of both methods allows us to state the following.

THEOREM 14.5. There is an effective procedure for transforming a rooted Kracht formula β into a formula equivalent to a negated Sahlqvist formula. More generally, there is an effective procedure for transforming a Kracht formula β into a set of formulas $\{\alpha_1, \ldots, \alpha_n\}$, each equivalent to a negated Sahlqvist formula such that

$$\langle F, v \rangle \models \beta(a_1, \ldots, a_n)$$

iff there is a valuation mapping $B : V \longrightarrow \mathcal{P}(W)$ such that

$$\langle F, B \rangle, v(a_1) \models \alpha_1 \text{ and } \ldots \text{ and } \langle F, B \rangle, v(a_n) \models \alpha_n. \qquad \triangleleft$$

14.2. Modal Second-Order Quantifier Introduction

14.2.1. The MSQIN Procedure. The aim of the MSQIN procedure is to convert a set of first-order formulas into formulas expressible as modal logic formulas, with existentially quantified propositional variables [182].

The MSQIN procedure performs the following steps on a set N of Kracht formulas. In Section 14.3 MSQIN is applied to a larger class of formulas.

TABLE 30. The second-order quantifier introduction rules of MSQIN.

Right SQI:
$$\frac{\alpha(u)[\neg R^\sigma(s,t)]}{\alpha(u)_{\forall y[R^\sigma(s,y)\to Q_t(y)]}^{\neg R^\sigma(s,t)} \wedge \neg Q_t(t)}$$
provided (i) s is the tightest bound term in $\neg R^\sigma(s,t)$, (ii) u, t are constants, (iii) $\alpha(u)$ is rooted in u and u is the largest constant such that $\neg R^\sigma(s,t)$ occurs in $\alpha(u)$, (iv) Q_t is a unique unary relation symbol associated with t and y is a fresh variable.

Left SQI:
$$\frac{\alpha(u)[\neg R^\sigma(s,t)]}{\alpha(u)_{Q_{s,\sigma}(t)}^{\neg R^\sigma(s,t)} \wedge \forall y[R^\sigma(s,y) \to \neg Q_{s,\sigma}(y)]}$$
provided (i) t is the tightest bound term in $\neg R^\sigma(s,t)$, (ii) u, s are constants, (iii) $\alpha(u)$ is rooted in u and u is the largest constant such that $\neg R^\sigma(s,t)$ occurs in $\alpha(u)$, (iv) $Q_{s,\sigma}$ is a unary relation symbol uniquely associated with $\neg R^\sigma(s, \_)$ and y is a fresh variable.

Quantifier distribution: Distribution of existentially restricted quantifiers of the form $\exists x[R^\tau(s,x) \wedge \ldots]$ over disjunction, and universally restricted quantifiers of the form $\forall x[R^\tau(s,x) \to \ldots]$ over conjunction.

Skolemize/eliminate outer existential quantifiers: Existential quantifiers not occurring in the scope of any universal quantifiers are eliminated by Skolemization.

Introduce second-order quantifiers: The rules of Table 30 are applied exhaustively as rewrite rules. That is, the rule

Rewriting:
$$\frac{N(\alpha)}{N^\alpha_\beta}$$

is used, where α/β is a rule of Table 30. (In the table **SQI** is short for second-order quantifier introduction.)

Translate to modal logic: Define a function from unary relation symbols to propositional symbols that associates any relation symbol uniquely with a propositional symbol. We use the convention that any relation symbol Q (uppercase) is mapped to the symbol q (lowercase). Convert the obtained set of first-order formulas into labeled modal formulas using the rules in Table 31, and unskolemization where necessary. (The **LI** rule is the rule for transforming literals.)

Note that in the MSQIN procedure conjunction and disjunction are assumed to be associative and commutative. We also note that the $\Box$I and $\Diamond$I rules include the rules

$$\frac{\forall x[s \approx x \to x{:}\alpha]}{s{:}\alpha} \qquad\qquad \frac{\exists x[s \approx x \wedge x{:}\alpha]}{s{:}\alpha}$$

TABLE 31. The modal introduction rules of MSQIN.

$$
\textbf{LI:} \quad \frac{(\neg)P(s)}{s{:}(\neg)p}
$$

$$
\textbf{VI:} \quad \frac{s{:}\alpha \vee s{:}\beta}{s{:}\alpha \vee \beta}
\qquad\qquad
\textbf{\textwedge I:} \quad \frac{s{:}\alpha \wedge s{:}\beta}{s{:}\alpha \wedge \beta}
$$

provided α and β are modal formulas.

$$
\Box\textbf{I:} \quad \frac{\forall x[R^{\sigma}(s,x) \to x{:}\alpha]}{s{:}\Box^{\sigma}\alpha}
\qquad
\Diamond\textbf{I:} \quad \frac{\exists x[R^{\sigma}(s,x) \wedge x{:}\alpha]}{s{:}\Diamond^{\sigma}\alpha}
$$

provided α is a modal formula.

(where σ is the empty sequence), which are of course not really (box and diamond) introduction rules, but are constraint elimination rules.

REMARK 14.6. MSQIN is defined as a procedure involving a sequence of transformation steps. As part of these steps the rules are applied in a certain order. In particular, the definition stipulates that the modal introduction rules are applied only after no more second-order introduction rules are applicable. This is not essential however. It is possible to interleave the application of the rules in Tables 30 and 31 and the results remain the same.   ◁

REMARK 14.7. We observe that the underlying principles of MSQIN are instances of more general principles that can be used to define practical procedures for turning first-order formulas into existentially quantified second-order formulas, or modal tense formulas, modal hybrid formulas, polyadic modal formulas, etc.   ◁

14.2.2. Correctness of MSQIN.

LEMMA 14.8. Both the **SQI** rules preserve logical equivalence, i.e., if N' is obtained from N by one application of one of the rules to N in a derivation from a set of of Kracht formulas, then

$$
\exists \bar{P}[N] \equiv \exists \bar{P}\exists Q[N'],
$$

where the symbols in $\bar{P}$ are the unary relation symbols occurring in N and Q is the newly introduced relation symbol.

PROOF. An application of a **SQI** rule is reversed by the application of Ackermann's rule. Since Ackermann's rule preserves logical equivalence (Theorem 6.1), the result is immediate.   ◁

The modal introduction rules in Table 31 are correct, and it is not difficult to see that the limited form of Skolemization and unskolemization preserves equivalence as well.

14.2.3. Completeness for Kracht Formulas. The **SQI** rules replace literals of the form $\neg R^\tau(s,t)$ and, introduce in both cases, formulas of the form $\forall y[R^\sigma(s,y) \rightarrow (\neg)Q(y)]$ and $(\neg)Q(t)$. It so happens that these are expressible as modal logic formulas. This is crucial. From a modal perspective what the right **SQI** rule produces is:

$$\alpha(u)_{s:\square^\tau q}^{\neg R^\tau(s,t)} \wedge t{:}\neg q \quad (u, t \text{ are constants and } u \leq t).$$

The left **SQI** rule produces:

$$\alpha(u)_{t:q}^{\neg R^\tau(s,t)} \wedge s{:}\square^\tau\neg q \quad (u, s \text{ are constants and } u \leq s).$$

Because $\alpha(u)$ is a formula rooted in u this means that s and t do not occur outside of α, which implies that $u \leq t$, respectively $u \leq s$, for the two cases. More specifically, we notice that u is the largest constant such that $\alpha(u)$ is rooted in u and $u \leq t$, respectively $u \leq s$. In the first case s is the tightest bound variable and $\neg R^\tau(s,t)$ is a conjunct (or disjunct) in a formula β which is a positive combination of

- Formulas expressible as a labeled modal formula $s{:}\beta$ (because a **SQI** rule has already been applied), or
- Formulas of the form $\neg R^{\tau'}(s,t')$ or $\neg R^{\tau'}(t',s)$ where t' is a constant.

By *positive combination* of a set $\{\gamma_1, \gamma_2, \ldots\}$ of formulas we mean a formula built from the formulas γ_i in the set, using conjunction and disjunction.

We can show that the MSQIN procedure eventually reduces the formula β to a formula β' rooted in s, and β' is expressible as a labeled modal formula $s{:}\beta''$. By the definition of Kracht formulas, there are two cases. (i) Either β occurs immediately below a restricted quantifier, or (ii) $\beta = \alpha = \neg R^\tau(a,a)$ and $a = s = t$, where a is a minimal constant. In the case (ii) using second-order introduction, β is reducible to a modal formula. In the case (i) suppose the quantifier is a universal quantifier $\forall x[R_k(v,x) \rightarrow \ldots]$ then s is the variable x and further reduction to $v{:}\square_k\beta'$ is possible. Similarly if it was an existentially restricted quantifier. If s was a constant and s does not coincide with t then by the definition of Kracht formulas this constant was the result of Skolemization, in particular, Skolemization of an existential restricted quantifier. After restoring the existential quantifier for s using unskolemization it is possible to express $s{:}\beta''$ as part of a modal formula, analogous to the previous case.

The Skolemization performed as part of the procedure is not strictly necessary but allows for easier comparison with the second-order quantifier elimination methods discussed in this book.

THEOREM 14.9. MSQIN *is an effective procedure for transforming a rooted Kracht formula* $\beta(a)$ *into an equivalent modal formula* $a{:}\alpha$. *More generally,* MSQIN *is an*

TABLE 32. Special cases of second-order quantifier introduction rules of MSQIN.

Simple right SQI:
$$\frac{\alpha(t)[\neg R^\tau(s,t)]}{\alpha(t)_{\forall y[R^\tau(s,y)\to Q_t(y)]}^{\neg R^\tau(s,t)} \wedge \neg Q_t(t)}$$

provided (i) s is the tightest bound term in $\neg R^\tau(s,t)$, (ii) t is a constant, (iii) $\alpha(t)$ is rooted in t, (iv) Q_t is a unique unary relation symbol associated with t and y is a fresh variable.

Simple left SQI:
$$\frac{\alpha(s)[\neg R^\tau(s,t)]}{\alpha(s)_{Q_{s,\tau}(t)}^{\neg R^\tau(s,t)} \wedge \forall y[R^\tau(s,y) \to \neg Q_{s,\tau}(y)]}$$

provided (i) t is the tightest bound term in $\neg R^\tau(s,t)$, (ii) s is a constant, (iii) $\alpha(s)$ is rooted in s, (iv) $Q_{s,\tau}$ is a unary relation symbol uniquely associated with $\neg R^\tau(s, \_)$ and y is a fresh variable.

---

effective procedure for transforming a Kracht formula β into a set of modal formulas $\{a_1{:}\alpha_1, \ldots, a_n{:}\alpha_n\}$ such that

$$\langle F, v \rangle \models \beta(a_1, \ldots, a_n)$$

iff there is a valuation mapping $B : V \longrightarrow \mathcal{P}(W)$ such that

$$\langle F, B \rangle, v(a_1) \models \alpha_1 \text{ and } \ldots \text{ and } \langle F, B \rangle, v(a_n) \models \alpha_n. \qquad \triangleleft$$

We can show that when the input of the MSQIN procedure is a set of (rooted) Kracht formulas then the output of MSQIN is a set of Sahlqvist formulas. Hence we have:

THEOREM 14.10. The MSQIN procedure satisfies Theorem 14.5. $\qquad \triangleleft$

14.2.4. Simple Second-Order Quantifier Introduction. Before we apply the MSQIN procedure to a few examples we note special cases of the right and left **SQI** rules. These are given in Table 32. They are easier to apply because the side conditions are less involved. For many of the common frame correspondence properties the simple **SQI** rules are sufficient.

14.2.5. Examples. In order to demonstrate how the MSQIN procedure works, let us apply it to some of the Kracht formulas from Example 14.3.

EXAMPLE 14.11. $\neg$**D** is equivalent to

$$\forall x[R(a, x) \to \text{FALSE}].$$

The application of the $\Box$**I** rule gives

$$a{:}\Box\text{FALSE}.$$

This proves that seriality corresponds to the modal formula $\Diamond\text{TRUE}$. The more commonly used modal axiom for seriality is the formula $\mathbf{D} = \forall p[\Box p \to \Diamond p]$. This can be derived with MSQIN if we note that the formula $\forall x[R(a,x) \to \text{FALSE}]$ is equivalent to

$$\forall x[R(a,x) \to \neg R(a,x)].$$

This is a Kracht formula. The derivation of MSQIN is:

1. $\forall x[R(a,x) \to \neg R(a,x)]\}$	given
2. $\forall x[R(a,x) \to P(x)]$ $\wedge\ \forall y[R(a,y) \to \neg P(y)]$	1, simple left **SQI**
3. $a{:}\Box p \wedge \Box\neg p$	2, m. intro.

"m. intro" indicates that one of more modal introduction rules were used. The introduced symbol p is implicitly assumed to be existentially quantified. Introducing a quantifier for a and negating the result gives us a formula equivalent to the axiom $\mathbf{D}$.   ◁

EXAMPLE 14.12. Let us start with the formula

1. $\exists x\big[R(a,x) \wedge \exists y[R(a,y) \wedge x \not\approx y]\big]$	given

and see if we can derive $\neg\mathbf{alt}_1 = \neg\forall p[\Diamond p \to \Box p]$. Skolemization gives:

2. $R(a,b) \wedge R(a,c) \wedge b \not\approx c$	1, Skolem.

The ordering among the Skolem constants is $a < b < c$. We use the left **SQI** rule on the entire formula (with root a) and replace $b \not\approx c$:

3. $R(a,b) \wedge R(a,c) \wedge P(c)$ $\wedge\ \forall y[b \approx y \to \neg P(y)]$	2, left **SQI**

Now derive:

4. $R(a,b) \wedge R(a,c) \wedge c{:}p$ $\wedge\ \forall y[b \approx y \to y{:}\neg p]$	3, **LI**
5. $R(a,b) \wedge R(a,c) \wedge c{:}p \wedge b{:}\neg p$	4, $\Box\mathbf{I}$
6. $a{:}\Diamond p \wedge \Diamond\neg p$	5, m. intro.

using the introduction rules.   ◁

EXAMPLE 14.13. Assume the input is:

1. $\forall x\big[R(a,x) \to \exists y[R(x,y) \wedge \neg R^2(a,y)]\big]$	given

The ordering of the terms is: $a < x < y$. Simple left **SQI** on the entire formula, replacing $\neg R^2(a, y)$, gives us

2. $\forall x\big[R(a, x) \to \exists y[R(x, y) \wedge P(y)]\big]$ 2, simple left **SQI**
$\wedge\ \forall y[R^2(a, y) \to \neg P(y)]$

This is already expressible in modal logic as:

3. $a{:}\Box\Diamond p \wedge \Box\Box\neg p$ 2, m. intro.

With the second-order quantifier elimination methods discussed in this book we can verify that $\exists p[\Box\Diamond p \wedge \Box\Box\neg p]$ is reducible to a formula equivalent to

$$\exists x \forall y\big[R(x, y) \to \exists z[R(y, z) \wedge \neg R^2(x, z)]\big].$$ ◁

EXAMPLE 14.14. This example is a variation of an example from [20].

1. $\exists x\big[R(a, x) \wedge \exists y[R(a, y)$ given
$\wedge\ (\neg R(x, y) \vee (\neg R(y, x) \wedge y \not\approx x))]\big]$

2. $R(a, b) \wedge R(a, c)$ 1, Skolem.
$\wedge\ (\neg R(b, c) \vee (\neg R(c, b) \wedge c \not\approx b))$

The ordering of the terms is: $a < b < c$.

3. $R(a, b) \wedge R(a, c)$ 2, left **SQI**
$\wedge\ (P(c) \vee (\neg R(c, b) \wedge c \not\approx b))$
$\wedge\ \forall x[R(b, x) \to \neg P(x)]$

4. $R(a, b) \wedge R(a, c)$ 3, right **SQI**
$\wedge\ (P(c) \vee (\forall y[R(c, y) \to Q(y)] \wedge c \not\approx b))$
$\wedge\ \forall x[R(b, x) \to \neg P(x)]$
$\wedge\ \neg Q(b)$

5. $R(a, b) \wedge R(a, c)$ 4, right **SQI**
$\wedge\ (P(c) \vee (\forall y[R(c, y) \to Q(y)] \wedge Q(c)))$
$\wedge\ \forall x[R(b, x) \to \neg P(x)]$
$\wedge\ \neg Q(b)$

Observe here the symbol Q was re-used.

6. $R(a, b) \wedge R(a, c)$ 5, m. intro.
$\wedge\ (c{:}p \vee (c{:}\Box q \wedge c{:}q))$
$\wedge\ b{:}\Box p \wedge b{:}\neg q$

7. $R(a, b) \wedge R(a, c)$ 6, m. intro.
$\wedge\ c{:}(p \vee (\Box q \wedge q))$
$\wedge\ b{:}(\Box p \wedge \neg q)$

8. $a : \Diamond(\Box p \wedge \neg q) \wedge \Diamond(p \vee (\Box q \wedge q))$ 7, m. intro.

For the formula

$$\exists x \left[R(a,x) \land \exists y [R(a,y) \right.$$
$$\left. \land \, (\neg R(x,y) \lor (\neg R(y,x) \land x \not\approx y))] \right],$$

which differs from the formula above only in that the arguments in the equality literal are reversed, the result is different but equivalent.   ◁

14.3. Partial Elimination of Modal Second-Order Quantification

In conjunction with second-order quantifier elimination, back-translation can be exploited to provide a method for reducing modal axioms to equivalent (if possible different) modal axioms. For example the axiom $\mathbf{D} = \forall p[\Box p \rightarrow \Diamond p]$ is equivalent to $\Diamond$TRUE. How can this be proven? Example 14.11 suggests how (for a proof using direct methods, see Example 12.4, page 151). First apply second-order quantifier elimination to $\neg\mathbf{D}$ and then apply the MSQIN procedure to the first-order formula obtained. This produces $\neg\Diamond$TRUE. Since second-order quantifier elimination and MSQIN preserve equivalence, this shows that $\forall p[\Box p \rightarrow \Diamond p]$ is equivalent to $\Diamond$TRUE. This is a modal formula with fewer (universally quantified) propositional variables. In this instance all propositional variables have in fact been eliminated. In general, it may however not be possible or desirable to eliminate all propositional variables.

14.3.1. Rewriting Second-Order Modal Formulas. We are interested in the existence of a general method for rewriting one second-order modal formula into another equivalent second-order modal formula. Consider the method performing this sequence of steps.

Let α be a given modal axiom α and let the non-base symbols be all the propositional variables in α, which are universally quantified.

- Apply a second-order quantifier elimination method to $\neg\alpha$. If this is successful then let β be the first-order formula obtained.
- Convert β into a set N of Kracht formulas.
- Apply the MSQIN procedure to β and return a set N of second-order modal formulas.
- Turn N into a conjunction and negate it.

It follows from properties of the second-order quantifier elimination and introduction steps that, if all steps are successful, α is equivalent to the modal formula computed.

EXAMPLE 14.15. We use the method to prove that

$$\forall p \forall q [\Box(p \lor q) \rightarrow (\Box p \lor \Box q)] \; \equiv \; \forall p[\Diamond p \rightarrow \Box p].$$

We start with the (negation of the) left-hand side and use SCAN for the second-order quantifier elimination step.

~~1.~~ $\neg R(a,x) \vee P(x) \vee Q(x)$

2. $R(a,b)$

~~3.~~ $\neg P(b)$

4. $R(a,c)$

~~5.~~ $\neg Q(c)$

Let us eliminate the Q symbol first, i.e., we assume the ordering among the non-base symbols is: $Q > P$. We get:

~~6.~~ $\neg R(a,x) \vee P(x) \vee c \not\approx x$ $\qquad\qquad$ 1.3, 5.1

~~7.~~ $\neg R(a,c) \vee P(c)$ $\qquad\qquad\qquad$ 6, c-elim.

Subsumption resolution (see Table 16 in Section 5.2.5) with 4. and 7. replaces 7. by:

~~8.~~ $P(c)$ $\qquad\qquad\qquad\qquad\qquad$ 4, 7, subs. resol.

Resolve on P to eliminate it:

9. $b \not\approx c$ $\qquad\qquad\qquad\qquad\qquad$ 3, 8, c-resol.

SCAN returns the formula

$$\exists x \exists y \exists z [R(x,y) \wedge R(x,z) \wedge y \not\approx z],$$

which can be rewritten as a rooted Kracht formula, namely:

$$\exists y \big[R(a,y) \wedge \exists z [R(a,z) \wedge y \not\approx z] \big].$$

Now refer to Example 14.12 for a derivation with MSQIN of the negation of $\forall p [\Diamond p \rightarrow \Box p]$. $\qquad\qquad\qquad\qquad\qquad\qquad\qquad\qquad\qquad$ ◁

The method eliminates all second-order quantification and then re-introduces some second-order quantifiers again. This seems to involve a bit of a detour. We might thus ask whether it is possible to avoid some of the steps in the computation. The answer is yes. Below we describe a refinement which eliminates only a subset of the second-order quantifiers. For this we now extend the definition of Kracht formulas.

14.3.2. Extended Kracht Formulas. We extend the definition of the frame language to allow unary relation symbols as well. Formally, let the *extended (first-order) frame language* be a function-free first-order language, in which the primitive building blocks are unary or binary relation symbols, the equality symbol $\approx$, the logical constants TRUE, FALSE, the standard connectives, including $\neg$, $\wedge$, $\vee$, and the quantifiers $\forall$ and $\exists$.

The definitions of restricted quantifiers, rooted formulas, etc. remain unchanged. The definitions of Kracht formulas need to be adapted slightly.

DEFINITION 14.16. An extended first-order frame formula is called an *extended rooted Kracht formula* if it is a standardized, mini-scoped, rooted formula $\alpha(a)$ without any free variables which is built from FALSE, TRUE, $\wedge$, $\vee$, restricted quantifiers and formulas of the form $(\neg)P(s)$, $\neg R^\sigma(s,t)$, $\neg R^\sigma(t,s)$, where σ is a possibly empty sequence of natural numbers,

- s is the innermost quantified variable in the scope of which $(\neg)P(s)$, $\neg R^\sigma(s,t)$, $\neg R^\sigma(t,s)$ occurs, and
- t is a, or it is an existentially quantified variable which does not occur in the scope of a universal quantifier.

A formula α is called an *extended Kracht formula* iff α is a conjunction of extended rooted Kracht formulas with no constants in common.   ◁

The definition is only a slight modification of the definition of Kracht formulas. Basically, extended Kracht formulas are Kracht formulas which allow unary literals to occur without destroying the "modal patterns".

The MSQIN procedure can be used without any modification and all the results carry over to MSQIN on extended Kracht formulas.

THEOREM 14.17. MSQIN is an effective procedure for transforming an extended Kracht formula β into a set of modal formulas $\{a_1{:}\alpha_1, \ldots, a_n{:}\alpha_n\}$ such that

$$\langle F, v \rangle \models \beta(a_1, \ldots, a_n)$$

iff there is a valuation mapping $B : V \longrightarrow \mathcal{P}(W)$ such that

$$\langle F, B \rangle, v(a_1) \models \alpha_1 \text{ and } \ldots \text{ and } \langle F, B \rangle, v(a_n) \models \alpha_n.$$ ◁

Hence, the applicability of the MSQIN procedure goes beyond the class of Kracht formulas. In particular, the theorem shows that MSQIN is complete also for extended Kracht formulas.

14.3.3. Refinement of the Method. A more refined method for rewriting second-order modal formulas to equivalent second-order modal formulas is this.

Suppose α denotes any modal axiom and X is a set of non-base symbols.

- Apply a second-order quantifier elimination method to $\neg\alpha$, attempting to eliminate all symbols in X. If this step is successful, let β be the first-order formula computed.
- Convert β into a set N of extended Kracht formulas.
- Apply the MSQIN procedure to N and return a set N' of modal formulas.
- Turn N' into a conjunction and negate the formula.

The obtained formula is a modal axiom equivalent to α, whenever all steps are successful.

EXAMPLE 14.18. We use the refined method to reduce

$$\forall p \forall q [\Box(p \vee q) \rightarrow (\Box p \vee \Box q)]$$

to $\forall p[\Box p \rightarrow \Diamond p]$ without eliminating all the second-order variables first. In particular, assume q is the only non-base symbol. Eliminating the corresponding symbol Q with SCAN (but not the symbol P) gives the derivation 1.–8. from Example 14.15. SCAN returns the formula

$$\exists x \exists y \exists z [R(x,y) \wedge P(y) \wedge R(x,z) \wedge \neg P(z)]$$

which can be formulated as an extended rooted Kracht formula:

$$\exists y [R(a,y) \wedge P(y)] \wedge \exists z [R(a,z) \wedge \neg P(z)].$$

Without needing to apply any of the **SQI** rules the MSQIN procedure converts this into the modal formula $a : \Diamond p \wedge \Diamond \neg p$.   ◁

14.4. Improving the Utility of Modal Logic Deduction Systems

With the help of second-order quantifier introduction methods the utility and efficiency of modal logic deduction calculi and implemented reasoners can be improved.

Using special-purpose modal logic deduction systems one can usually only reason about modal logic formulas. For example it is not possible to handle a purely relational formula such as

$$\exists x [R(a,x) \wedge \exists y [R(a,y) \wedge x \not\approx y]].$$

As we have already seen in the previous section (in Example 14.12), MSQIN can turn this formula into an equivalent modal formula, namely $\exists p[\Diamond p \wedge \Diamond \neg p]$. This formula can now be given as input to a reasoner for modal satisfiability (e.g., a modal tableau prover). The existential second-order quantifier can be dropped because implicitly all propositional variables in the input to a satisfiability reasoner can be regarded as implicitly existentially quantified.

Thus the MSQIN procedure can be used for extending the applicability and utility of special-purpose modal logic deduction calculi and reasoners.

14.4.1. A Method. A general method for converting first-order formulas into modal formulas comprises the following sequence of steps.

Suppose α denotes a first-order formula.

- Convert α into a set N of extended Kracht formulas.
- Apply the MSQIN procedure to N and return the resulting set N' of modal formulas.

The first step is crucial, but may not always be successful. If the method terminates normally and returns a result, then α and N' are equivalent in the following sense.

Suppose α is transformed to the set $N = \{a_1{:}\alpha_1', \ldots, a_n{:}\alpha_n'\}$. Suppose MSQIN produces the set $N' = \{a_1{:}\beta_1, \ldots, a_n{:}\beta_n, b_1{:}\gamma_1, \ldots, b_m{:}\gamma_m\}$ of labeled modal formulas. It is assumed that the constants $b_1, \ldots, b_m$ do not occur in N:

$$\langle F, v \rangle \models \alpha_1'(a_1) \wedge \ldots \wedge \alpha_n'(a_n)$$

iff there is a valuation mapping $B : V \longrightarrow \mathcal{P}(W)$ and an extension v' of v such that

$$\langle F, B \rangle, v'(a_1) \models \beta_1 \text{ and } \ldots \text{ and } \langle F, B \rangle, v'(a_n) \models \beta_n \text{ and}$$
$$\langle F, B \rangle, v'(b_1) \models \gamma_1, \text{ and } \ldots \text{ and } \langle F, B \rangle, v'(b_m) \models \gamma_m.$$

What does this mean in practice? Let us consider how the property can be exploited by semantic tableau provers. For semantic modal tableau provers the input is a set of labeled modal formulas. The goal is to test the (un)satisfiability of the set by either constructing a closed tableau derivation or find a fully expanded, open branch.

Suppose we are interested in satisfiability in a modal logic L, and T is a sound and complete tableau calculus for L. Let Γ be a set of labeled modal formulas. Suppose α is a first-order formula which is equivalent to a set N of extended Kracht formula for which MSQIN produces a set N'. Further assume that the only signature symbols common to Γ and α are propositional variables and "root constants" $a_1, \ldots, a_n$. Then

$$\bigwedge \Gamma \text{ is locally satisfiable in an } L\text{-model for which } \alpha \text{ holds}$$

iff

$$T \text{ constructs an open tableau for } \Gamma \cup N'.$$

For global satisfiability similar reductions are possible.

This shows that modal logic provers can be applied even to problems apparently not in modal logic form, but which are expressible as a set of modal logic formulas.

14.4.2. Application to Description Logics. The method applies also to description logics. As for modal logics, the method can be used for utilizing special-purpose description logic provers for specifying, querying and reasoning about statements not obviously expressible in the language of the prover. This idea has been used, e.g., by Zolin [**219**].

Most description logics support reasoning with concept assertion statements, but do not always support reasoning with role assertion statements. A prover that does not support role assertions, or inequalities, evidently cannot handle the following input directly.

$$R(a,b) \wedge R(a,c) \wedge b \not\approx c.$$

However, with the MSQIN procedure this is reducible to a concept assertion:

$$a : \exists R.A \sqcap \exists R.\neg A,$$

and this can now be given to the prover. The equivalence of the two follows from Example 14.12 and the well-known correspondence between modal logics and description logics; $\exists R.A \sqcap \exists R.\neg A$ is the description logic formulation for $\Diamond p \wedge \Diamond \neg p$.

14.5. Other Applications

Another application of the methods described in this chapter is the strengthening of simplification in quantifier elimination methods based on second-order equivalence, rather than first-order equivalence.

In conclusion we note that the utility of second-order quantifier introduction methods is not limited to modal logics and description logics. All methods and results of this section transfer easily to description logics, but can also be extended to other logics. Second-order introduction techniques are increasingly becoming standard in logic and automated theorem proving where they are successfully being used for different reasons, cf. Section 21.2.

Part 4

Applications

CHAPTER 15

Applications in Complexity Theory

In this chapter we concentrate on the applications of second-order quantifier elimination techniques in estimating the complexity of potentially intractable problems. Problems which are in PSPACE can be specified by means of second-order logic. Elimination of second-order quantifiers can drastically decrease the complexity of the resulting algorithms.

Even if the quantifier elimination is not successful, one can sometimes obtain quasi-polynomial algorithms on the basis of analysis of the structure of formulas and interaction of first-order quantifiers.

This chapter is based on the paper [**202**] by Szałas.

15.1. The General Technique

As discussed in the introduction (Chapter 1), estimating the complexity of potentially intractable problems can consist of the following steps:

(1) Specify a given problem in second-order logic. The complexity of checking validity of second-order formulas in a finite model is PSPACE-complete w.r.t. the size of the model. Thus, for all problems in PSPACE such a description exists;

(2) Try to eliminate second-order quantifiers. An application of the considered methods, if successful, might result in:
- a formula of the first-order logic (in the case of SCAN or DLS), the validity of which (over finite models) is in PTIME and LOGSPACE;
- a formula of the fixpoint logic in the case of DLS* applying the fixpoint theorem (Theorem 6.19), validity of which (over finite models) is in PTIME;

(3) If the second-order quantifier elimination is not successful, which is likely to happen for NPTIME, CO-NPTIME or PSPACE-complete problems, one can try to identify subclasses of the problem, for which elimination of second-order quantifiers is guaranteed. In such cases tractable

(or quasi-polynomial) subproblems of the main problem can be identified.

This methodology is applied to the hypergraph transversal problem in the following sections. Here let us start with a simpler example.

EXAMPLE 15.1. This example concerns a game frequently considered in the literature (see, e.g., [1]), where it is solved using a three-valued semantics for database
queries. The solution considered below is based on the one given in [52].

The game is between two players. The possible moves of the games are held in
a finite binary relation *moves*, where $moves(x, y)$ indicates that when in a state x,
one can chose to move to state y. A player loses if he or she is in a state from
which there are no moves. The goal considered in [1, 52] is to compute the set of
winning states (i.e., the set of states such that there exists a winning strategy for
a player in this state). These are obtained as the extension of a unary predicate *win*.
Our additional goal is to estimate the complexity of this computation.

Let $M(x, y)$ and $W(x)$ denote the predicates *moves* and *win*, respectively.

In order to show that, we will ask whether there is a relation W, satisfying the
following conditions:

$$(132) \qquad \forall x \Big[\exists y \big[M(x, y) \wedge \forall z [\neg M(y, z)] \big] \to W(x) \Big]$$

meaning that from x there is a move to y from which the opposing player has no
move; and

$$(133) \qquad \forall x \Big[\exists y \big[M(x, y) \wedge \forall z [M(y, z) \to W(z)] \big] \to W(x) \Big],$$

meaning that from x there is a move to y from which all choices of the opposing
player lead to a state where the player that moved from x to y has a winning
strategy.

The goal is to find the minimal W satisfying both (132) and (133), i.e., the following second-order formula:

$$(134) \qquad \exists W \Big\{ \forall x \Big[\exists y \big[M(x, y) \wedge \forall z [\neg M(y, z)] \big] \to W(x) \Big] \wedge \\ \forall x \Big[\exists y \big[M(x, y) \wedge \forall z [M(y, z) \to W(z)] \big] \to W(x) \Big] \Big\}.$$

Computing W specified by formula (134) is in NPTIME. However, according to
Corollary 6.20, the definition of minimal W satisfying (134) is

$$W(x) \equiv [\text{LFP } W(x). \exists y [M(x, y) \wedge \forall z [M(y, z) \to W(z)]]].$$

This is a fixpoint formula, thus our problem is, in fact, in PTIME.   ◁

15.2. The Hypergraph Transversal Problem

15.2.1. Introduction and Preliminaries. Hypergraph theory [17] has many applications in computer science and artificial intelligence (see, e.g., [23, 66, 67, 96, 125]). In particular, the transversal hypergraph problem has attracted a great deal of attention. Many important problems of databases, knowledge representation, Boolean circuits, duality theory, diagnosis, machine learning, data mining, explanation finding, etc. can be reduced to this problem (see, e.g., Eiter and Gottlob [67]). However, its precise complexity remains open. The best known algorithm, provided by Fredman and Khachiyan in [80], runs in quasi-polynomial time w.r.t. the size of the input hypergraphs. More precisely, if n is the size of the input hypergraphs, then the algorithm of [80] requires $n^{o(\log n)}$ steps. Eiter, Gottlob and Makino's paper [69] provides a result that relates the transversal hypergraph problem to a limited non-determinism by showing that the complement of the problem can be solved in polynomial time with $O(\chi(n)*\log n)$ guessed bits, where $\chi(n)^{\chi(n)} = n$. As observed in [80], $\chi(n) \approx \log n/\log \log n = o(\log n)$.

Let us first define notions related to the transversal hypergraph problem. We provide definitions slightly adapted for further logical characterization. However, the definitions are equivalent to those considered in the literature.

DEFINITION 15.2. By a *hypergraph* we mean a triple $H = \langle V, E, M \rangle$, where

- V and E are finite disjoint sets of *elements* and *hyperedges*, respectively;
- $M \subseteq E \times V$ is an *edge membership relation*.

A *transversal* of H is any set $T \subseteq V$ such that for any hyperedge $e \in E$ there is $v \in V$ such that $(T(v) \wedge M(e, v))$ holds. A transversal is *minimal* iff it is minimal w.r.t. set inclusion. ◁

In the sequel we sometimes identify hyperedges with sets of their members, i.e., any hyperedge $e \in E$ of hypergraph $H = \langle V, E, M \rangle$ is identified with the set $\{v \in V \mid M(e, v) \text{ holds}\}$.

DEFINITION 15.3. By the *transversal hypergraph*, also called a *dual hypergraph* of a hypergraph H, we mean hypergraph H^d whose hyperedges are all minimal transversals of H. By the *transversal hypergraph problem*, denoted by TRH, we mean a problem of checking, for given hypergraphs G and H, whether $G = H^d$. ◁

15.2.2. Characterization of Minimal Transversals of Hypergraphs. Obviously, T is a transversal of hypergraph $H = \langle V, E, M \rangle$ iff[1]

(135) $\quad \forall e \in E \exists v \in V[T(v) \wedge M(e, v)].$

---

[1] For the sake of clarity we use notation $\forall e \in E$, $\exists e \in E$ to indicate the domain of variable e.

It is a minimal transversal iff it is a transversal, i.e., (135) holds and additionally

(136)
$$\forall T' \Big\{ \big[\forall e \in E \exists v \in V[T'(v) \land M(e,v)] \land \forall w \in V[T'(w) \rightarrow T(w)] \big] \rightarrow$$
$$\forall u \in V[T(u) \rightarrow T'(u)] \Big\}.$$

Formula (136) is a universal second-order formula. Application of this formula to the verification whether a given transversal is minimal, is thus in CO-NPTIME. On the other hand, one can eliminate the second-order quantification by applying Lemma 6.1. To do this, we first negate (136):

(137)
$$\exists T' \Big\{ \big[\forall e \in E \exists v \in V[T'(v) \land M(e,v)] \land \forall w \in V[T'(w) \rightarrow T(w)] \big] \land$$
$$\exists u \in V[T(u) \land \neg T'(u)] \Big\}.$$

Formula (137) is equivalent to

(138)
$$\exists u \in V \exists T' \big[\forall w \in V[T'(w) \rightarrow T(w)] \land$$
$$\forall e \in E \exists v \in V[T'(v) \land M(e,v)] \land T(u) \land \neg T'(u) \big],$$

i.e., to

$$\exists u \in V \exists T' \big[\forall w \in V[T'(w) \rightarrow T(w)] \land$$
$$\forall e \in E \exists v \in V[T'(v) \land M(e,v)] \land T(u) \land$$
$$\forall w \in V[T'(w) \rightarrow w \not\approx u] \big],$$

and finally, to

$$\exists u \in V \exists T' \big[\forall w \in V[T'(w) \rightarrow (T(w) \land w \not\approx u)] \land$$
$$\forall e \in E \exists v \in V[T'(v) \land M(e,v)] \land T(u) \big].$$

After the application of Lemma 6.1 we obtain the following equivalent formula:

(139) $\exists u \in V \big[\forall e \in E \exists v \in V[T(v) \land v \not\approx u \land M(e,v)] \land T(u) \big].$

After negating formula (139) and rearranging the result, we obtain the following first-order formula equivalent to (136):

(140) $\forall u \in V \big[T(u) \rightarrow \exists e \in E \forall v \in V[(T(v) \land M(e,v)) \rightarrow v \approx u] \big].$

Let $H = \langle V, E, M \rangle$ be a hypergraph. In the sequel we use the notation $Min_H(T)$, defined by

(141)
$$Min_H(T) \stackrel{\text{def}}{\equiv}$$
$$\forall e \in E \exists v \in V[T(v) \land M(e,v)] \land$$
$$\forall u \in V \big[T(u) \rightarrow \exists e \in E \forall v \in V[(T(v) \land M(e,v)) \rightarrow v \approx u] \big].$$

We now have the following lemma.

LEMMA 15.4. For any hypergraph $H = \langle V, E, M \rangle$, T is a minimal transversal of H iff it satisfies formula $Min_H(T)$. In consequence, checking whether a given T is a minimal transversal of a hypergraph is in PTIME and LOGSPACE w.r.t. the size of the hypergraph.   ◁

15.2.3. Logical Specification of the TRH Problem.

15.2.3.1. *Specification of the* TRH *Problem in Second-Order Logic.* Let $G = \langle V, E_G, M_G \rangle$ and $H = \langle V, E_H, M_H \rangle$ be hypergraphs. In order to check whether $G = H^d$, we verify inclusions $G \subseteq H^d$ and $H^d \subseteq G$. The inclusions can be characterized in second-order logic as follows:

(142) $\forall e \in E_G \, \exists e' \in E_H^d \, \forall v \in V [M_G(e, v) \equiv M_H^d(e', v)]$

(143) $\forall e' \in E_H^d \, \exists e \in E_G \, \forall v \in V [M_G(e, v) \equiv M_H^d(e', v)].$

According to Lemma 15.4, formulas (142) and (143) can be expressed as

(144) $\forall e \in E_G \, \exists T [Min_H(T) \wedge \forall v \in V (M_G(e, v) \equiv T(v))]$

(145) $\forall T [Min_H(T) \rightarrow \exists e \in E_G \, \forall v \in V (M_G(e, v) \equiv T(v))].$

The above specification leads to algorithms which are intractable (unless PTIME = NPTIME). In the following sections we attempt to reduce the complexity by eliminating second-order quantifiers from formulas (144) and (145).

15.2.3.2. *The Case of Inclusion* $G \subseteq H^d$. Consider the second-order part of formula (144), i.e.,

(146) $\exists T \big[Min_H(T) \wedge \forall v \in V [M_G(e, v) \equiv T(v)] \big].$

Due to equivalence (141), Lemma 15.4 and Lemma 6.1,[2] formula (146) is equivalent to

(147)
$$\forall e' \in E_H \, \exists v \in V [M_G(e, v) \wedge M_H(e', v)] \wedge$$
$$\forall u \in V \big[M_G(e, u) \rightarrow$$
$$\exists e' \in E_H \, \forall v \in V [(M_G(e, v) \wedge M_H(e', v)) \rightarrow v \approx u] \big].$$

In consequence, formula (144) is equivalent to

(148)
$$\forall e \in E_G \, \forall e' \in E_H \, \exists v \in V [M_G(e, v) \wedge M_H(e', v)] \wedge$$
$$\forall e \in E_G \, \forall u \in V \big[M_G(e, u) \rightarrow$$
$$\exists e' \in E_H \, \forall v \in V [(M_G(e, v) \wedge M_H(e', v)) \rightarrow v \approx u] \big].$$

Thus the inclusion $G \subseteq H^d$ is first-order definable by formula (148). We then have the following corollary.

COROLLARY 15.5. For any hypergraphs

$$G = \langle V, E_G, M_G \rangle \text{ and } H = \langle V, E_H, M_H \rangle,$$

---

[2] Note that in the lemma of Ackermann the implication can be replaced by equivalence.

checking whether $G \subseteq H^d$, is in PTIME and LOGSPACE w.r.t. the maximum of sizes of hypergraphs G and H.   ◁

15.2.3.3. *The Case of Inclusion* $H^d \subseteq G$. Unfortunately, no known second-order quantifier elimination method is successful for the inclusion (145). We thus equivalently transform formula (145) to a form where Lemma 6.1 is applicable. The verification of the resulting formula in finite models is, in general, of exponential complexity. However, when some restrictions are assumed, the complexity reduces to deterministic polynomial or quasi-polynomial time, as shown below.

By (141), formula (145) is equivalent to

$$
(149) \quad \forall T \Big\{ \big[\forall e \in E_H \exists v \in V [T(v) \wedge M_H(e, v)] \wedge \\
\forall u \in V [T(u) \rightarrow \exists e \in E_H \forall v \in V [(T(v) \wedge M_H(e, v)) \rightarrow v \approx u]]] \\
\rightarrow \exists e \in E_G \forall v \in V [M_G(e, v) \equiv T(v)] \Big\}.
$$

Let us assume that the inclusion $G \subseteq H^d$ holds. If not, then the answer to the TRH problem for this particular instance is negative. Under this assumption, formula (149) is equivalent to[3]

$$
(150) \quad \forall T \Big\{ \big[\forall e \in E_H \exists v \in V (T(v) \wedge M_H(e, v)) \wedge \\
\forall u \in V [T(u) \rightarrow \exists e \in E_H \forall v \in V [(T(v) \wedge M_H(e, v)) \rightarrow v \approx u]]] \\
\rightarrow \exists e \in E_G \forall v \in V [M_G(e, v) \rightarrow T(v)] \Big\}.
$$

In order to apply Lemma 6.1 we first negate (150):

$$
(151) \quad \exists T \Big\{ \forall e \in E_H \exists v \in V [T(v) \wedge M_H(e, v)] \wedge \\
\forall u \in V [T(u) \rightarrow \exists e \in E_H \forall v \in V [(T(v) \wedge M_H(e, v)) \rightarrow v \approx u]] \wedge \\
\forall e \in E_G \exists v \in V [M_G(e, v) \wedge \neg T(v)] \Big\}.
$$

In order to simplify calculations, by $\Gamma(T)$ we denote the conjunction of formulas given in the last two lines of (151). Formula (151) is then expressed by

$$
(152) \quad \exists T \Big\{ \forall e \in E_H \exists v \in V [T(v) \wedge M_H(e, v)] \wedge \Gamma(T) \Big\}.
$$

Observe that $\Gamma(T)$ is negative w.r.t. T. Thus the main obstacle for applying Lemma 6.1 is created by the existential quantifier $\exists v \in V$ appearing within the scope of $\forall e \in E_H$.

Assume $E_H = \{e_1, \ldots, e_k\}$ and let $V_e \overset{\text{def}}{=} \{x \mid M_H(e, x) \text{ holds}\}$. Formula (152) can then be expressed by

$$
\exists T \Big\{ \exists v_1 \in V_{e_1} [T(v_1)] \wedge \ldots \wedge \exists v_k \in V_{e_k} [T(v_k)] \wedge \Gamma(T) \Big\},
$$

---

[3]By minimality of H^d and the assumption that $G \subseteq H^d$, the set inclusion expressed by $\forall v \in V [M_G(e, v) \rightarrow T(v)]$ is equivalent to set equality, expressed by $\forall v \in V [M_G(e, v) \equiv T(v)]$.

i.e., by

$$\exists v_1 \in V_{e_1} \ldots \exists v_k \in V_{e_k} \exists T \Big[T(v_1) \wedge \ldots \wedge T(v_k) \wedge \Gamma(T) \Big],$$

which is equivalent to

$$\exists v_1 \in V_{e_1} \ldots \exists v_k \in V_{e_k} \exists T \Big[$$
$$\forall v \in V[(v \approx v_1 \vee \ldots \vee v \approx v_k) \rightarrow T(v)] \wedge \Gamma(T) \Big].$$

The application of Lemma 6.1 results in the following first-order formula:

$$\exists v_1 \in V_{e_1} \ldots \exists v_k \in V_{e_k} \Big[\Gamma^{T(t)}_{(v \approx v_1 \vee \ldots \vee v \approx v_k)(v)} \Big].$$

In consequence, formula (150) is equivalent to

$$\forall v_1 \in V_{e_1} \ldots \forall v_k \in V_{e_k} \Big[(\neg \Gamma)^{T(t)}_{(v \approx v_1 \vee \ldots \vee v \approx v_k)(v)} \Big],$$

i.e., to

$$\forall v_1 \in V_{e_1} \ldots \forall v_k \in V_{e_k} \forall u \in V \Big\{ \Big[(u \approx v_1 \vee \ldots \vee u \approx v_k) \rightarrow$$

(153) $$\exists e \in E_H \forall v \in V[((v \approx v_1 \vee \ldots \vee v \approx v_k) \wedge M_H(e,v)) \rightarrow v \approx u] \Big]$$

$$\rightarrow \exists e \in E_G \forall v \in V[M_G(e,v) \rightarrow (v \approx v_1 \vee \ldots \vee v \approx v_k)] \Big\}.$$

The major complexity of checking whether given hypergraphs satisfy formula (153) is caused by the sequence of quantifiers $\forall v_1 \in V_{e_1} \ldots \forall v_k \in V_{e_k} \forall u$. We then have the following theorem.

THEOREM 15.6. For given hypergraphs G and H, such that $G \subseteq H^d$, the problem of checking whether $H^d \subseteq G$ is solvable in time $O(|V_1| * \ldots * |V_k| * p(n))$, where $p(n)$ is a polynomial,[4] n is the maximum of sizes of G and H, k is the number of edges in H, and for $e = 1, \ldots, k$, $|V_e|$ denotes the cardinality of set $\{x \mid M_H(e, x) \text{ holds}\}$. ◁

Accordingly we have the following corollary.

COROLLARY 15.7. Under the assumptions of Theorem 15.6, if all cardinalities $|V_1|, \ldots, |V_k|$ are bounded by a function $f(n)$, then the problem of determining whether $H^d \subseteq G$ is solvable in time $O(f(n)^k * p(n))$. ◁

In the view of the result given in [80], Corollary 15.7 can be useful if k is bounded by a (sub)logarithmic function, and $f(n)$ is (sub)linear w.r.t. n. For instance, if both k and $f(n)$ are bounded by $\log n$ then the corollary gives us an upper bound $O((\log n)^{\log n} * p(n))$ which is better than that offered by algorithm of [80]. Let us emphasize that in many cases $|V|$ and consequently $f(n)$ is bounded by $\log n$, since the dual hypergraph might be of size exponential w.r.t. $|V|$.

---

[4]Reflecting the complexity introduced by quantifiers inside formula (153).

The characterization provided by formula (153) is also related to bounded non-determinism. Namely, consider the complement of the TRH problem. The sequence of quantifiers $\forall v_1 \in V_{e_1} \ldots \forall v_k \in V_{e_k}$ appearing in formula (153) is transformed into $\exists v_1 \in V_{e_1} \ldots \exists v_k \in V_{e_k}$. In order to verify the negated formula it is then sufficient to guess k sequences of bits of size not greater than $\log \max_{c=1,\ldots,k} \{|V_e|\}$.

Thus, in the worst case, it suffices to guess $k * \log |V|$ bits. By the result of [69], mentioned in Section 15.2.1, $O(\log^2 n)$ guessed bits suffice to further solve the TRH problem in deterministic polynomial time. Thus the observation we just made is useful, e.g., when one considers the input graph H with the number of edges (sub)logarithmic w.r.t. n. Observe, however, that often n is exponentially larger than $|V|$.

15.3. Showing Decidability

In this section we show how second-order quantifier elimination can be used to prove decidability of particular problems.

Assume $Th(\bar{Q}, \approx)$ is a decidable finite[5] first-order (or fixpoint) theory over signature $\bar{Q}, \approx$ and let

$$A = \{\alpha_i(\bar{x}, \bar{Q}, \bar{R}, \approx) \mid i \in I\}$$

be a set of formulas over a signature $\bar{Q}, \bar{R}, \approx$. We shall consider the problem of checking whether $Th(\bar{Q}, \approx) \models \alpha$, for $\alpha \in A$. The method we consider depends on showing that for any $i \in I$,

$$Th(\bar{Q}, \approx) \models \forall \bar{R}[\alpha_i(\bar{x}, \bar{Q}, \bar{R}, \approx)] \equiv \beta_i(\bar{Q}, \approx),$$

where β is a first-order (or respectively, fixpoint) formula over signature $\bar{Q}, \approx$. In such a case the problem over $Th(\bar{Q}, \approx)$, expressed by $\alpha(\bar{Q}, \bar{R}, \approx)$, is decidable.

A particularly important case is when the signature of Th consists of $\approx$ only. As shown in [204] (see also Section 3.6.1, page 36), the fixpoint theory of equality is decidable.

EXAMPLE 15.8. Consider any finite classical first-order theory $Th(\bar{R}, \approx)$ positive w.r.t. relation symbols in $\bar{R}$. Let

$$A = \{\forall \bar{x}[\alpha(\bar{R}, \approx) \rightarrow P(\bar{x})] \mid P \in \bar{R} \text{ and}$$
$$\alpha \text{ is a classical first-order formula positive w.r.t. } \bar{R}\}.$$

Then the problem whether $Th(\bar{R}, \approx) \models \alpha$, for $\alpha \in A$, is decidable.

---

[5]Meaning that it can be axiomatized by a single formula being the conjunction of its finite number of axioms.

To show the decidability, it suffices to note that

$$Th(\bar{R}, \approx) \models \forall \bar{x}[\alpha(\bar{R}, \approx) \to P(\bar{x})] \text{ iff}$$
$$\models \forall \bar{R}[Th(\bar{R}, \approx) \to \forall \bar{x}[\alpha(\bar{R}, \approx) \to P(\bar{x})]] \text{ iff}$$
$$\models \neg \exists \bar{R}[Th(\bar{R}, \approx) \wedge \exists \bar{x}[\alpha(\bar{R}, \approx) \wedge \neg P(\bar{x})]].$$

All relation symbols in $\bar{R}$ except for P are positive in $Th(\bar{R}, \approx)$ as well as in $\exists \bar{x}[\alpha(\bar{R}, \approx) \wedge \neg P(\bar{x})]$. The elimination of quantifiers over $\bar{R}$ other than P is done by the DLS algorithm simply by removing those relation symbols from formulas. The remaining quantifier $\exists P$ can also be eliminated by a simple application of Ackermann's lemma (Lemma 6.1). The resulting formula, equivalent to $\neg \exists \bar{R}[Th(\bar{R}, \approx) \wedge \exists \bar{x}[\alpha(\bar{R}, \approx) \wedge \neg P(\bar{x})]]$, is a classical first-order formula containing $\approx$ as the only relation symbol. Verifying whether this formula is a tautology is known to be decidable (see also Section 3.6.1 for details). ◁

EXAMPLE 15.9. Consider any finite classical first-order theory $Th(\bar{R}, \approx)$ with axioms expressed by formulas of the form $\forall \bar{x}[\alpha(\bar{R}, \approx) \to P(\bar{x})]$, where $P \in \bar{R}$ and α is a classical first-order formula positive w.r.t. $\bar{R}$. Let A be the set of formulas positive w.r.t. $\bar{R}$. Then the problem whether $Th(\bar{R}, \approx) \models \alpha$, for $\alpha \in A$, is decidable.

To show the decidability, it suffices to note that

$$Th(\bar{R}, \approx) \models \forall \bar{x}[\alpha(\bar{R}, \approx) \to P(\bar{x})] \text{ iff}$$
$$\models \forall \bar{R}[Th(\bar{R}, \approx) \to \alpha(\bar{R}, \approx)] \text{ iff}$$
$$\models \neg \exists \bar{R}[Th(\bar{R}, \approx) \wedge \neg \alpha(\bar{R}, \approx)].$$

Since all occurrences of $\bar{R}$ in $\neg \alpha(\bar{R}, \approx)$ are negative, the DLS* algorithm succeeds to eliminate quantifiers $\exists \bar{R}$ and the resulting formula is a formula of the fixpoint theory of equality. Verifying whether it holds is then decidable (for details see Section 3.6.1). ◁

CHAPTER 16

Applications in Common-Sense Reasoning

In the last three decades, a great deal of attention has been devoted to logics of common-sense reasoning. Among the candidates proposed, circumscription, introduced by McCarthy [147] (for an overview, see also Lifschitz [139]), has been perceived as an elegant mathematical technique for modeling non-monotonic reasoning, but difficult to apply in practice. The major reason for this is the second-order nature of circumscription axioms and the involved complexity. There have been a number of proposals for dealing with the second problem ranging from compiling circumscriptive theories into logic programs [89], to developing specialized inference methods for such theories [94, 170].

An alternative solution to the complexity problems is to compile, where possible, second-order formulas into equivalent formulas of less complex logics, like the classical first-order or fixpoint logic. This approach has been advocated and represented in a number of publications including, e.g., [56, 128, 138, 171]. An overview of those approaches is provided by Doherty, Łukaszewicz and Szałas in [56], where it is shown that all known direct methods, except of the one based on a lemma given by Lifschitz in [139] (quoted as Lemma 16.2, page 212 below), are subsumed by the approach based on the DLS algorithm.

Applications of the DLS algorithm to reducing another form of circumscription, called domain circumscription, are provided in [57] and are discussed in Section 16.2.

16.1. Circumscription

Circumscription is basically a technique for minimizing chosen predicates, assuming that some other predicates are allowed to vary and all other predicates are fixed. Let us now formally define this concept.

DEFINITION 16.1. Let $\bar{P} = \langle P_1, \ldots, P_k \rangle, \bar{S} = \langle S_1, \ldots, S_m \rangle$ be disjoint tuples of relation symbols, and let $T(\bar{P}, \bar{S})$ be a first-order formula. The *second-order circumscription* of $\bar{P}$ in $T(\bar{P}, \bar{S})$ with variable $\bar{S}$, written $Circ(T; \bar{P}; \bar{S})$, is the second-order formula

$$T(\bar{P}, \bar{S}) \wedge$$

(154)
$$\forall \bar{X} \forall \bar{Y} \Big\{ \big[T(\bar{P}, \bar{S})_{\bar{X}, \bar{Y}}^{\bar{P}, \bar{S}} \wedge \bigwedge_{i=1}^{k} \forall \bar{x}_i [X_i(\bar{x}_i) \rightarrow P_i(\bar{x}_i)] \big] \rightarrow$$

$$\bigwedge_{i=1}^{k} \forall \bar{x}_i [P_i(\bar{x}_i) \rightarrow X_i(\bar{x}_i)] \Big\},$$

where $\bar{X}$ and $\bar{Y}$ are tuples of relational variables of the same arities as those in $\bar{P}$ and $\bar{S}$, respectively.   ◁

From the point of view of the elimination of second-order quantification, SCAN, DLS and DLS* consider only the second-order part of formula (154), i.e.,

$$\forall \bar{X} \forall \bar{Y} \Big\{ \big[T(\bar{P}, \bar{S})_{\bar{X}, \bar{Y}}^{\bar{P}, \bar{S}} \wedge \bigwedge_{i=1}^{k} \forall \bar{x}_i [X_i(\bar{x}_i) \rightarrow P_i(\bar{x}_i)] \big] \rightarrow$$

$$\bigwedge_{i=1}^{k} \forall \bar{x}_i [P_i(\bar{x}_i) \rightarrow X_i(\bar{x}_i)] \Big\}.$$

This approach works for a large class of formulas. However, in [**139**], Lifschitz formulated the following lemma, which works in many cases when DLS, DLS* and SCAN fail.[1]

LEMMA 16.2. If $T(P)$ is a first-order sentence of the form $\alpha(P) \wedge \beta(P)$, where $\alpha(P)$ is positive and $\beta(P)$ is negative w.r.t. P then $Circ(T(P); P; \emptyset)$ is equivalent to a first-order sentence.

PROOF. Consider $Circ(T(P); P; \emptyset)$ which, by (154), is

(155) $T(P) \wedge \forall X \Big\{ \big[T(P)_X^P \wedge \forall \bar{x}[X(\bar{x}) \rightarrow P(\bar{x})] \big] \rightarrow \forall \bar{x}[P(\bar{x}) \rightarrow X(\bar{x})] \Big\}.$

Since $T(P) \equiv \alpha(P) \wedge \beta(P)$, we have that (155) is

(156)
$$\alpha(P) \wedge \beta(P) \wedge$$
$$\forall X \Big\{ \big[\alpha(P)_X^P \wedge \beta(P)_X^P \wedge \forall \bar{x}[X(\bar{x}) \rightarrow P(\bar{x})] \big] \rightarrow$$
$$\forall \bar{x}[P(\bar{x}) \rightarrow X(\bar{x})] \Big\}.$$

Now observe that $\forall \bar{x}[X(\bar{x}) \rightarrow P(\bar{x})]$ is equivalent to $\forall \bar{x}[\neg P(\bar{x}) \rightarrow \neg X(\bar{x})]$. By assumption, $\beta(P)$ is negative w.r.t. P. We then have that $\beta(P)$ together with $\forall \bar{x}[X(\bar{x}) \rightarrow P(\bar{x})]$ imply $\beta(P)_X^P$ thus (156) can equivalently be simplified to

(157)
$$\alpha(P) \wedge \beta(P) \wedge$$
$$\forall X \Big\{ \big[\alpha(P)_X^P \wedge \forall \bar{x}[X(\bar{x}) \rightarrow P(\bar{x})] \big] \rightarrow \forall \bar{x}[P(\bar{x}) \rightarrow X(\bar{x})] \Big\}.$$

---

[1] And does not work in many cases when DLS, DLS* or SCAN work.

Consider now the second-order part of (157). It is equivalent to

$$(158) \qquad \neg \exists X \Big\{ \alpha(P)_X^P \wedge \forall \bar{x}[X(\bar{x}) \rightarrow P(\bar{x})] \wedge \exists \bar{x}[P(\bar{x}) \wedge \neg X(\bar{x})] \Big\}.$$

We now apply the DLS algorithm and obtain that (158) is equivalent to

$$\neg \exists \bar{x} \exists X \Big\{ \alpha(P)_X^P \wedge P(\bar{x}) \wedge \forall \bar{y}[X(\bar{y}) \rightarrow (\bar{y} \not\approx \bar{x} \wedge P(\bar{y}))] \Big\}.$$

By assumption, $\alpha(P)_X^P$ is positive w.r.t. X. Hence by applying Ackermann's lemma one obtains the following first-order formula which is equivalent to (158):

$$\neg \exists \bar{x} \Big\{ [\alpha(P)_X^P]_{\bar{y} \not\approx \bar{x} \wedge P(\bar{y})}^{X(\bar{y})} \wedge \forall \bar{z}[\bar{z} \not\approx \bar{x} \rightarrow P(\bar{z})] \wedge P(\bar{x})] \Big\};$$

thus (156) is also equivalent to a first-order formula, which proves the result.   ◁

16.1.1. Examples. Let us first consider two examples based on [56].

EXAMPLE 16.3. Let $T(Ab, On)$ be the theory

$$(159) \qquad \begin{array}{l} b1 \neq b2 \wedge B(b1) \wedge B(b2) \wedge \neg On(b1) \wedge \\ \forall x[(B(x) \wedge \neg Ab(x)) \rightarrow On(x)], \end{array}$$

where B and On are abbreviations for $Block$ and $Ontable$, respectively. We consider the circumscription of $T(Ab, On)$ with Ab minimized and On varied,

$$(160) \qquad \begin{array}{l} Circ(T(Ab, On); Ab; On) \equiv \\ T(Ab, On) \wedge \\ \forall X \forall Y \Big\{ \big[T(Ab, On)_{X, \ Y}^{Ab, On} \wedge \forall x[X(x) \rightarrow Ab(x)] \big] \rightarrow \\ \qquad\qquad\qquad\qquad\qquad \forall x[Ab(x) \rightarrow X(x)] \Big\}. \end{array}$$

In the following, we reduce

$$(161) \qquad \begin{array}{l} \forall X \forall Y \Big\{ \big[T(Ab, On)_{X, \ Y}^{Ab, On} \wedge \forall x[X(x) \rightarrow Ab(x)] \big] \rightarrow \\ \qquad\qquad\qquad\qquad\qquad \forall x[Ab(x) \rightarrow X(x)] \Big\}. \end{array}$$

Negating (161) and renaming a bound variable, we get

$$(162) \qquad \begin{array}{l} \neg \exists X \exists Y \Big\{ \big[T(Ab, On)_{X, \ Y}^{Ab, On} \wedge \forall x[X(x) \rightarrow Ab(x)] \big] \wedge \\ \qquad\qquad\qquad\qquad\qquad \exists y[Ab(y) \wedge \neg X(y)] \Big\}. \end{array}$$

Formula (162) is equivalent to

$$(163) \qquad \begin{array}{l} \neg \exists X \exists Y \Big\{ b1 \neq b2 \wedge B(b1) \wedge B(b2) \wedge \neg Y(b1) \wedge \\ \quad \forall x[(B(x) \wedge \neg X(x)) \rightarrow Y(x)] \wedge \\ \quad \forall x[X(x) \rightarrow Ab(x)] \big] \wedge \exists y[Ab(y) \wedge \neg X(y)] \Big\}. \end{array}$$

Using the background theory $T(Ab, On)$, we simplify (163):

(164)
$$\neg \exists X \exists Y \Big\{ \neg Y(b1) \wedge \forall x[(B(x) \wedge \neg X(x)) \rightarrow Y(x)] \wedge$$
$$\forall x[X(x) \rightarrow Ab(x)] \,] \wedge \exists y[Ab(y) \wedge \neg X(y)] \Big\}.$$

We first eliminate $\exists Y$ by an application of Ackermann's lemma to (164), obtaining

(165)
$$\neg \exists X \Big\{ \neg [B(b1) \wedge \neg X(b1)] \wedge$$
$$\forall x[X(x) \rightarrow Ab(x)] \wedge \exists y[Ab(y) \wedge \neg X(y)] \Big\},$$

which is equivalent to

$$\neg \exists y \exists X \Big\{ [\neg B(b1) \vee X(b1)] \wedge$$
$$\forall x[X(x) \rightarrow Ab(x)] \,] \wedge Ab(y) \wedge \neg X(y) \Big\},$$

i.e., to

(166) $\neg \exists y \exists X \big\{ X(b1) \wedge Ab(y) \wedge \forall x[X(x) \rightarrow (Ab(x) \wedge y \not\approx x)] \big\}.$

Applying Ackermann's lemma to (166) we eliminate $\exists X$:

(167) $\neg \exists y \big\{ Ab(b1) \wedge y \not\approx b1 \wedge Ab(y) \big\}.$

Formula (167) is equivalent to $\forall y \big\{ Ab(y) \rightarrow (y \approx b1 \vee \neg Ab(b1)) \big\}$, i.e., using theory $T(Ab, On)$, to $\forall y \big\{ Ab(y) \rightarrow y \approx b1) \big\}$, stating that there can be no abnormal objects other than $b1$.   ◁

EXAMPLE 16.4. Let $T(Ab, G)$ be the theory

(168)
$$\exists x \exists y[B(y) \wedge F(x, y) \wedge \neg G(x, y)] \wedge$$
$$\forall x \forall y[(B(y) \wedge F(x, y) \wedge \neg Ab(x, y)) \rightarrow G(x, y)],$$

where B, F and G are abbreviations for *Birthday*, *Friend* and *Gives-Gift*, respectively. Here $Ab(x, y)$ has the following intuitive interpretation: "x behaves abnormally w.r.t. y in the situation when y has a birthday and x is a friend of y". The circumscription of $T(Ab, G)$ with Ab minimized and G varied is

(169)
$$Circ(T(Ab, G); Ab; G) \equiv$$
$$T(Ab, G) \wedge$$
$$\forall X \forall Y \Big\{ [T(Ab, G)_{X,\,Y}^{Ab,G} \wedge \forall x \forall y[X(x, y) \rightarrow Ab(x, y)] \,] \rightarrow$$
$$\forall x \forall y[Ab(x, y) \rightarrow X(x, y)] \Big\}.$$

In the following, we reduce

(170)
$$\forall X \forall Y \Big\{ [T(Ab, G)_{X,\,Y}^{Ab,G} \wedge \forall x \forall y[X(x, y) \rightarrow Ab(x, y)] \,] \rightarrow$$
$$\forall x \forall y[Ab(x, y) \rightarrow X(x, y)] \Big\},$$

which is

$$(171) \quad \forall X \forall Y \Big\{ \big[\exists x \exists y [B(y) \land F(x,y) \land \neg Y(x,y)] \land \\ \forall x \forall y [(B(y) \land F(x,y) \land \neg X(x,y)) \to Y(x,y)] \land \\ \forall x \forall y [X(x,y) \to Ab(x,y)] \big] \to \forall x \forall y [Ab(x,y) \to X(x,y)] \Big\}.$$

Negating (171), we obtain

$$(172) \quad \neg \exists X \exists Y \Big\{ \exists x \exists y [B(y) \land F(x,y) \land \neg Y(x,y)] \land \\ \forall x \forall y [(B(y) \land F(x,y) \land \neg X(x,y)) \to Y(x,y)] \land \\ \forall x \forall y [X(x,y) \to Ab(x,y)] \land \exists x \exists y [Ab(x,y) \land \neg X(x,y)] \Big\}.$$

We remove $\exists Y$ first by an immediate application of Ackermann's lemma:

$$(173) \quad \neg \exists X \Big\{ \exists x \exists y [B(y) \land F(x,y) \land \neg (B(y) \land F(x,y) \land \neg X(x,y))] \land \\ \forall x \forall y [X(x,y) \to Ab(x,y)] \land \exists x \exists y [Ab(x,y) \land \neg X(x,y)] \Big\}.$$

We now remove $\exists X$ in (173). The most important DLS steps are the following:

$$(174) \quad \neg \exists u \exists z \exists X \Big\{ B(z) \land F(u,z) \land (\neg B(z) \lor \neg F(u,z) \lor X(u,z))] \land \\ \forall x \forall y [X(x,y) \to Ab(x,y)] \land \exists x \exists y [Ab(x,y) \land \neg X(x,y)] \Big\},$$

$$(175) \quad \neg \exists u \exists z \exists X \Big\{ B(z) \land F(u,z) \land \\ \forall x \forall y [(B(z) \land F(u,z) \land x \approx u \land y \approx z) \to X(x,y)] \land \\ \forall x \forall y [X(x,y) \to Ab(x,y)] \land \exists x \exists y [Ab(x,y) \land \neg X(x,y)] \Big\}.$$

An application of Ackermann's lemma now results in

$$(176) \quad \neg \exists u \exists z \Big\{ B(z) \land F(u,z) \land \\ \forall x \forall y [(B(z) \land F(u,z) \land x \approx u \land y \approx z) \to Ab(x,y)] \land \\ \exists x \exists y [Ab(x,y) \land \neg (B(z) \land F(u,z) \land x \approx u \land y \approx z)] \Big\},$$

which simplifies to

$$(177) \quad \neg \exists u \exists z \Big\{ B(z) \land F(u,z) \land Ab(u,z) \land \\ \exists x \exists y [Ab(x,y) \land \neg (B(z) \land F(u,z) \land x \approx u \land y \approx z)] \Big\},$$

i.e., to

$$(178) \quad \forall u \forall z \forall x \forall y \Big\{ \neg B(z) \lor \neg F(u,z) \lor \neg Ab(u,z) \lor \\ \neg Ab(x,y) \lor (B(z) \land F(u,z) \land x \approx u \land y \approx z)] \Big\},$$

and, finally, to

(179)
$$\forall u \forall z \forall x \forall y \Big\{ [B(z) \land F(u,z) \land Ab(u,z) \land Ab(x,y)] \rightarrow$$
$$(x \approx u \land y \approx z) \Big\},$$

which, states that there is at most one pair of individuals behaving abnormally in the considered situation. Together with the theory $T(Ab, G)$ one can conclude that there is actually exactly one such pair.   ◁

The following example illustrates the use of fixpoints in the context of circumscription.

EXAMPLE 16.5. Consider theory $T(R)$ consisting of the formula

(180) $\exists z[R(z)] \land \forall x \forall y[(R(x) \land P(x,y)) \rightarrow R(y)],$

where R and P stand for "rich" and "parent", respectively.

Consider $Circ(T(R); R; \emptyset)$,

(181)
$$Circ(T(R); R; \emptyset) \equiv T(R) \land$$
$$\forall X \Big\{ [T(R)_X^R \land \forall x[X(x) \rightarrow R(x)]] \rightarrow \forall x[R(x) \rightarrow X(x)] \Big\}.$$

In the following, we reduce

$$\forall X \Big\{ [T(R)_X^R \land \forall x[X(x) \rightarrow R(x)]] \rightarrow \forall x[R(x) \rightarrow X(x)] \Big\},$$

i.e.,

$$\forall X \Big\{ [\exists z X(z) \land \forall x \forall y[(X(x) \land P(x,y)) \rightarrow X(y)] \land$$
$$\forall x[X(x) \rightarrow R(x)]] \rightarrow \forall x[R(x) \rightarrow X(x)] \Big\},$$

which is equivalent to

$$\neg \exists z \exists X \Big\{ \forall y[(y \approx z) \lor \exists x[X(x) \land P(x,y)]) \rightarrow X(y)] \land$$
$$\forall x[X(x) \rightarrow R(x)] \land \exists x[R(x) \land \neg X(x)] \Big\}.$$

Now we apply Theorem 6.19 and obtain the following fixpoint formula

$$\neg \Big\{ \forall x[[\text{LFP } X(y).y \approx z \lor \exists x[X(x) \land P(x,y)]](x) \rightarrow R(x)]] \land$$
$$\exists x[R(x) \land \neg[\text{LFP } X(y).y \approx z \lor \exists x[X(x) \land P(x,y)]](x)] \Big\},$$

equivalent to (181).   ◁

16.2. Domain Circumscription

In many common-sense reasoning scenarios, we are given a theory specifying general laws and domain-specific facts about the phenomena under investigation. In addition, one provides a number of closure axioms circumscribing the domain of individuals and certain properties and relations among individuals.

Following Doherty, Łukaszewicz and Szałas [57], below we focus on a form of domain circumscription which subsumes other existing domain circumscription proposals in the literature, including [48, 72, 108, 142, 146].

DEFINITION 16.6. Let $\bar{P} = (P_1, \ldots, P_n)$ be a tuple of different relation symbols, $\bar{f} = (f_1, \ldots, f_k)$ be a tuple of different function symbols (including, perhaps, individual constants), $T(\bar{P}, \bar{f})$ be a theory and let R be a one-place predicate variable, and $\bar{X}$ and $\bar{Y}$ be tuples of relation and function variables of the same arities as those in $\bar{P}$ and $\bar{f}$, respectively. By $Ax(R, \bar{P}, \bar{f})$, sometimes abbreviated by $Ax(R)$, we shall mean the conjunction of:

- $R(a)$, for each individual constant a in T not occurring in $\bar{f}$;
- $R(Y_i)$, for each individual constant a in T such that a is f_i;
- $\forall x_1 \ldots x_n \{[R(x_1) \wedge \cdots \wedge R(x_n)] \to R(f(x_1, \ldots x_n))\}$, for each n-ary $(n > 0)$ function constant f in T not occurring in $\bar{f}$ and
- $\forall x_1 \ldots x_n \{[R(x_1) \wedge \cdots \wedge R(x_n)] \to R(Y_i(x_1, \ldots x_n))\}$, for each n-ary $(n > 0)$ function constant f in T such that f is f_i.

T^R stands for the result of rewriting $T(\bar{X}, \bar{Y})$, replacing each occurrence of $\forall x$ and $\exists x$ in $T(\bar{X}, \bar{Y})$ with "$\forall x[R(x) \to \ldots]$" and "$\exists x[R(x) \wedge \ldots$", respectively. ◁

DEFINITION 16.7. Let $\bar{P} = (P_1, \ldots, P_n)$, $\bar{f} = (f_1, \ldots, f_k)$ and $T(\bar{P}, \bar{f})$ be as in Definition 16.6. The *general domain circumscription for* $T(\bar{P}, \bar{f})$ *with variable* $\bar{P}$ *and* $\bar{f}$, written $Circ_D(T; \bar{P}; \bar{f})$, is the following sentence of second-order logic:

$$(182) \quad T(\bar{P}, \bar{f}) \wedge \forall Z \forall \bar{X} \forall \bar{Y} \{[\exists x[Z(x)] \wedge Ax(R, \bar{P}, \bar{f})_Z^R \wedge T^Z] \to \forall x[Z(x)]\}.$$

The second conjunct of the sentence (182) is called the *domain circumscription axiom*. ◁

It is not difficult to see that (182) asserts that the domain of discourse (represented by Z) is minimal with respect to T, where $\bar{P}$ and $\bar{f}$ are allowed to vary during the minimization.

If a is an individual constant, the variable corresponding to a is, in fact, an individual variable. Accordingly, we denote it by x_a, rather than by Y.

We shall write $Circ_D(T)$ as an abbreviation for $Circ_D(T; \emptyset; \emptyset)$, i.e., if neither relations nor functions are allowed to vary. This simplest form of domain minimization corresponds closely to McCarthy's original domain circumscription [146] with the augmentation described by Etherington and Mercer in [**72**].[2] We shall call it *fixed domain circumscription*.

We shall write $Circ_D(T; \bar{P})$ as an abbreviation for $Circ_D(T; \bar{P}; \emptyset)$, i.e., if some relations, but not functions, are allowed to vary. If $\bar{P}$ includes all predicate constant occurring in a theory T, then $Circ_D(T; \bar{P})$ is exactly *mini-consequence*, introduced by Hintikka [**108**] and improved by Lorenz [**142**]. Following [**142**], this form of minimization is referred to as *variable domain circumscription*.

16.3. Reducing General Domain Circumscription

In this section, following Doherty, Łukaszewicz and Szałas [**57**], we provide some reducibility results concerning various variants of general domain circumscription. In what follows, we assume that theories under consideration contain at least one individual constant symbol.

We shall frequently refer to the domain closure axiom, defined below.

DEFINITION 16.8. Let T be a theory without function symbols of positive arity and suppose that, for $n > 0$, $c_1, \ldots c_n$ are all the individual constants occurring in T. The *domain closure axiom for* T, written $DCA(T)$, is the sentence

$$\forall x[x \approx c_1 \vee \cdots \vee x \approx c_n].$$

Let $\bar{c}$ be a tuple of individual constants. By $DCA^{-\bar{c}}(T)$ we shall denote the sentence $\forall x \, x \approx c_1 \vee \ldots \vee x \approx c_n$, where $c_1, \ldots, c_n$ are all the individual constants of T excluding constants from $\bar{c}$. For $k \in \omega$, by $DCA^{+k}(T)$ we shall denote the sentence

$$\exists z_1 \cdots \exists z_k \forall x[x \approx z_1 \vee \cdots \vee x \approx z_k \vee x \approx c_1 \vee \ldots \vee x \approx c_n],$$

where $c_1, \ldots, c_n$ are all the individual constants of T. We also use notation $DCA^{-\bar{c}+k}(T)$ as a combination of the above.   ◁

REMARK 16.9. Assume that T is a theory. Then, for each formula A, $DCA(T)$ implies:

(183) $\begin{aligned} \exists x \, A(x) &\equiv [A(c1) \vee \cdots \vee A(c_n)] \\ \forall x \, A(x) &\equiv [A(c1) \wedge \cdots \wedge A(c_n)]. \end{aligned}$

This observation allows one to eliminate all second-order quantifiers whenever $DCA(T)$ holds since in this case all first-order quantifiers can be replaced by their equivalents given in (183) and DLS always works for open formulas.   ◁

---

[2]In fact, $Circ_D(T)$ is stronger in that it is based on a second-order axiom rather than on a first-order schema.

16.3.1. Fixed Domain Circumscription.

16.3.1.1. *Universal Theories.* It turns out that for universal theories without function symbols, domain circumscription allows the derivation of the domain closure axiom. Moreover, as a theorem of [57] (Theorem 16.10 below) shows, if T is a theory of that type, then domain circumscription for T is equivalent to $T \wedge DCA(T)$.

THEOREM 16.10. Let T be a universal theory without function symbols. Then $Circ_D(T)$ is always reducible into first-order logic with the DLS algorithm. Moreover, if A is the resulting formula, then A is equivalent to $T \wedge DCA(T)$.

PROOF. Let, for some $0 < k \in \omega$, $c_1, \cdots, c_k$ be all individual constants occurring in T. In this case $Circ_D(T)$ is equivalent to

$$(184) \qquad T \wedge \forall Z\big[(Z(c_1) \wedge \cdots \wedge Z(c_k)) \to \forall z[Z(z)]\big].$$

The second-order conjunct of (184) is equivalent to

$$(185) \qquad \neg \exists Z\big[Z(c_1) \wedge \cdots \wedge Z(c_k) \wedge \exists z[\neg Z(z)]\big].$$

The DLS algorithm transforms (185) into

$$(186) \qquad \neg \exists z \exists Z\big\{Z(c_1) \wedge \cdots \wedge Z(c_k) \wedge \forall u[Z(u) \to z \not\approx u]\big\}.$$

Applying Ackermann's lemma to (186), we get $\neg \exists z[z \not\approx c_1 \wedge \cdots \wedge z \not\approx c_k]$, which is equivalent to $\forall z[z \approx c_1 \vee \cdots \vee z \approx c_k]$.

Therefore $Circ_D(T) \equiv T \wedge \forall z[z \approx c_1 \vee \cdots \vee z \approx c_k]$.   ◁

Observe that according to our assumption, we consider only theories that contain at least one individual constant. This is only a technical assumption. If T has no individual constant symbols then

$$Circ_D(T) \equiv T \wedge \forall Z\big[\exists x[Z(x)] \to \forall z[Z(z)]\big].$$

The second conjunct of this formula is equivalent to $\neg \exists Z\big[\exists x[Z(x)] \wedge \exists z[\neg Z(z)]\big]$ which, according to the DLS algorithm, is equivalent to $\neg \exists x \exists z[z \not\approx x]$. Thus, in this case, $Circ_D(T) \equiv T \wedge \forall x \forall z[x \approx z]$.

16.3.1.2. *Semi-Universal Theories.* As regards semi-universal theories without function symbols we have the following theorem.

THEOREM 16.11. Let T be a semi-universal theory without function symbols. Then $Circ_D(T)$ is always reducible into first-order logic using the DLS algorithm. Moreover, if A is the resulted formula, then A implies $DCA^{+k}(T)$, where k is the number of existential quantifiers of T.

PROOF. Follows from Theorem 16.17 and the fact that the DCA axiom is unnecessary here. (See the proof of Theorem 16.17, page 222 and note that the DCA axiom is needed there to eliminate predicate variables corresponding to varying predicates only.)   ◁

The following example illustrates a reduction of domain circumscription of a semi-universal theory.

EXAMPLE 16.12. Let T be $\exists x[F(x)] \wedge B(Tweety)$, where B and F stand for $Bird$ and $Flies$, respectively. We shall reduce $Circ_D(T)$. The corresponding domain circumscription axiom is

$$(187) \qquad \forall Z\{[\exists x[Z(x)] \wedge Z(Tweety) \wedge \exists x[Z(x) \wedge F(x))]] \rightarrow \forall x[Z(x)]\}.$$

In the presence of $Z(Tweety)$, formula $\exists x[Z(x)]$ is redundant in (187). Thus (187) is equivalent to

$$(188) \qquad \neg \exists Z\{Z(Tweety) \wedge \exists x[Z(x) \wedge F(x)] \wedge \exists x \neg Z(x)\}.$$

To eliminate quantification over Z, DLS transforms (188) into the form

$$(189) \qquad \neg \exists x' \exists Z\{Z(Tweety) \wedge \exists x[Z(x) \wedge F(x)] \wedge \forall z[Z(z) \rightarrow z \not\approx x']\}.$$

Applying Ackermann's lemma, we get

$$(190) \qquad \neg \exists x'\{x' \not\approx Tweety \wedge \exists x[x' \not\approx x \wedge F(x)]\},$$

which is equivalent to $\forall x \forall x'[x' \approx Tweety \vee x' \approx x \vee \neg F(x)]$. Thus

$$(191) \qquad \begin{aligned} &Circ_D(T) \equiv \\ &\exists x F(x) \wedge B(Tweety) \wedge \\ &\forall x \forall x'[x' \approx Tweety \vee x' \approx x \vee \neg F(x)]. \end{aligned}$$

It can easily be verified that (191) implies $\exists z \forall x'[x' \approx Tweety \vee x' \approx z]$, i.e., $DCA^{+1}(T)$.   ◁

16.3.2. Variable Domain Circumscription.

16.3.2.1. *Universal Theories.* For universal theories we have the following counter-part of Theorems 16.10.

THEOREM 16.13. Let T be a universal theory without function symbols and suppose that $\bar{P}$ is a tuple of predicate symbols occurring in T. Then $Circ_D(T; \bar{P})$ implies $DCA(T)$. In consequence, $Circ_D(T; \bar{P})$ is always reducible to first-order logic.

PROOF. Observe that $Circ_D(T; (\bar{P}))$ implies $Circ_D(T)$ thus (by Theorem 16.10) implies $DCA(T)$. The reduction of $Circ_D(T; \bar{P})$ now easily follows from Remark 16.9.   ◁

EXAMPLE 16.14. Let theory T consist of $\forall x[R(x, a) \rightarrow R(a, x)]$ and consider $Circ_D(T; R)$. The second-order part of $Circ_D(T; R)$ is equivalent to:

$$(192) \qquad \forall X \forall Z\{[Z(a) \wedge \forall x[\neg Z(x) \vee (X(x, a) \rightarrow X(a, x))]] \rightarrow \forall z[Z(z)]\}.$$

In order to eliminate the quantifier over Z, DLS transforms it into a form required in Ackermann's lemma:

(193) $\quad \neg \exists X \exists Z \{ \forall x [x \approx a \rightarrow Z(x)] \wedge$
$$\forall x [\neg Z(x) \vee \neg X(x, a) \vee X(a, x)] \wedge \exists z [\neg Z(z)] \}.$$

An application of Ackermann's lemma, results in

(194) $\quad \neg \exists X \{ \forall x [x \not\approx a \vee \neg X(x, a) \vee X(a, x)] \wedge \exists z [z \not\approx a] \}.$

The elimination of X is now straightforward. The DLS algorithm finds out that the clause $\forall x [x \not\approx a \vee \neg X(x, a) \vee X(a, x)]$ can be removed, and thus results in $\neg \exists z [z \not\approx a]$ and we obtain that $\forall z [z \approx a]$ is a first-order equivalent of formula (192). ◁

The following example varies an individual constant.

EXAMPLE 16.15. Consider the theory T given by

(195) $\quad \begin{aligned} &S(c) \wedge S(d) \wedge \\ &\forall x [R(x, c) \equiv R(x, d)] \wedge \\ &\forall x [\neg R(x, c)] \wedge \forall y [\neg R(y, d)] \wedge \forall z [\neg R(z, z)]. \end{aligned}$

This theory was originally considered by Suchanek in [**197**]. Here $S(x)$, $R(x, y)$, c and d are to be read "the evidence says that x saw the victim alive", "the evidence says that x saw the victim alive after y saw her alive for the last time", "murderer" and "suspect", respectively. Suppose further that the police try to find all individuals who satisfy exactly those formulas that the (unknown) murderer does, comparing what is provable about the murderer with what is provable about a particular individual. To formalize this type of procedure, we should minimize the domain under consideration with all constant symbols, except of that referring to the murderer, allowed to vary. In our case, we minimize the domain of T with variable c. The intended conclusion is $d \approx c$.

The second-order part of $Circ_D(T, \emptyset, \{c\})$, after slight simplifications, is equivalent to

(196) $\quad \begin{aligned} &\forall x_c \forall Z \{ [Z(x_c) \wedge Z(d) \wedge S(x_c) \wedge \\ &\quad \forall x [Z(x) \rightarrow [(\neg R(x, x_c) \vee R(x, d)) \wedge (R(x, x_c) \vee \neg R(x, d))]] \wedge \\ &\quad \forall x [Z(x) \rightarrow \neg R(x, x_c)]] \rightarrow \forall s [Z(s)] \}. \end{aligned}$

Formula (196) is equivalent to

(197) $\quad \begin{aligned} &\neg \exists x_c \exists Z \{ Z(x_c) \wedge Z(d) \wedge S(x_c) \wedge \\ &\quad \forall x [Z(x) \rightarrow [(\neg R(x, x_c) \vee R(x, d)) \wedge (R(x, x_c) \vee \neg R(x, d))]] \wedge \\ &\quad \forall x [Z(x) \rightarrow \neg R(x, x_c)] \wedge \exists s [\neg Z(s)] \}, \end{aligned}$

which is transformed by the DLS algorithm to

(198) $\quad \begin{aligned} &\neg \exists x_c \exists Z \{ \forall x [(x \approx x_c \vee x \approx d) \rightarrow Z(x)] \wedge S(x_c) \wedge \\ &\quad \forall x [\neg Z(x) \vee \neg R(x, x_c)] \wedge \exists s [\neg Z(s)] \} \end{aligned}$

and then, after the application of Ackermann's lemma, to

(199)　　$\neg\exists x_c\{S(x_c) \wedge \forall x[\neg(x \approx x_c \vee x \approx d) \vee \neg R(x, x_c)] \wedge \\ \exists s[\neg(s \approx x_c \vee s \approx d)]\}.$

Therefore,

(200)　　$Circ_D(T, \emptyset, \{c\}) \equiv \\ T \wedge \forall x_c\{[S(x_c) \wedge \forall x[\neg(x \approx x_c \vee x \approx d) \vee \neg R(x, x_c)]] \rightarrow \\ \forall s[s \approx x_c \vee s \approx d]\}.$

It is easily seen, substituting d for x_c, that $Circ_D(T, \emptyset, \{c\}) \models d \approx c.$　　　　◁

16.3.2.2. *Semi-Universal Theories.* In the case of semi-universal theories we have the following corollary of Theorem 16.11.

COROLLARY 16.16. Let T be a semi-universal theory without function symbols and suppose that $\bar{P}$ is a tuple of predicate symbols occurring in T. Then $Circ_D(T; \bar{P})$ implies $DCA^k(T)$, where k is the number of existential quantifiers of T. In consequence, $Circ_D(T; \bar{P})$ is always reducible to classical first-order logic.　　　　◁

We also have the following theorem (see [57]).

THEOREM 16.17. Let T be a semi-universal theory without function symbols. Let $\bar{P}$ be a tuple of predicate symbols and $\bar{c}$ be a tuple of individual constants occurring in T. Then $Circ_D(T; \bar{P}; \bar{c})$ implies $DCA^{-\bar{c}+k}(T)$, where k is the number of existential quantifiers of T. In consequence, $Circ_D(T; \bar{P}; \bar{c})$ is always reducible to the classical first-order logic.

PROOF. Since T is semi-universal, it can be be written in the form

(201)　　$\bigwedge_i \exists x_{i1} \cdots \exists x_{is_i} \forall y_{i1} \cdots \forall y_{it_i} [T_i(\bar{X}, \bar{Y})]$

where each T is an open formula.

Let $c'_1, \cdots, c'_r$ be all individual constants occurring in T excluding those from $\bar{c}$. The second-order part of $Circ_D(T; \bar{P}; \bar{c})$ is then equivalent to

(202)　　$\forall \bar{Y} \forall \bar{X} \forall Z\{[Z(c'_1) \wedge \cdots \wedge Z(c'_r) \wedge \\ \bigwedge_i \exists x_{i1} \cdots \exists x_{is_i} \forall y_{i1} \cdots \forall y_{it_i} [Z(x_{i1}) \wedge \cdots \wedge Z(x_{is_i}) \wedge \\ (\neg Z(y_{i1}) \vee \cdots \vee \neg Z(y_{it_i}) \vee T_i(\bar{X}, \bar{Y})]] \rightarrow \forall z[Z(z)]\},$

i.e., to

(203)　　$\neg\exists \bar{Y} \exists \bar{X} \exists Z\{Z(c'_1) \wedge \cdots \wedge Z(c'_r) \wedge \\ \bigwedge_i \exists x_{i1} \cdots \exists x_{is_i} \forall y_{i1} \cdots \forall y_{it_i} [Z(x_{i1}) \wedge \cdots \wedge Z(x_{is_i}) \wedge \\ (\neg Z(y_{i1}) \vee \cdots \vee \neg Z(y_{it_i}) \vee T_i(\bar{X}, \bar{Y})] \wedge \exists z[\neg Z(z)]\}.$

Formula (203) is transformed by the DLS algorithm into

$$
\neg \exists\, x_{11} \cdots \exists x_{1s_1} \cdots \exists \bar{Y} \exists \bar{X} \exists Z \{
$$

(204)
$$
\forall u [(u \approx c_1' \vee \ldots \vee u \approx c_r' \vee
$$
$$
\bigvee_i (u \approx x_{i1} \vee \cdots \vee u \approx x_{is_i})) \to Z(u)] \wedge
$$
$$
\forall y_{i1} \cdots \forall y_{it_i} [\neg Z(y_{i1}) \vee \cdots \vee \neg Z(y_{it_i}) \vee T_i(\bar{X}, \bar{Y})] \wedge
$$
$$
\exists z\, \neg Z(z) \}.
$$

Let $B(u)$ denote the formula

$$
u \not\approx c_1' \wedge \cdots \wedge u \not\approx c_r' \wedge \bigwedge_i (u \not\approx x_{i1} \wedge \cdots \wedge u \not\approx x_{is_i}).
$$

Then the application of Ackermann's lemma to formula (204) results in:

(205)
$$
\neg \exists\, x_{11} \cdots \exists x_{1s_1} \cdots \exists \bar{Y} \exists \bar{X} \{
$$
$$
\bigwedge_i \forall y_{i1} \cdots \forall y_{it_i} [B(y_{i1}) \vee \cdots \vee B(y_{it_i}) \vee T_i(\bar{X}, \bar{Y})] \wedge \exists z [B(z)] \}.
$$

Thus formula (205) is equivalent to

(206)
$$
\forall x_{11} \cdots \forall x_{1s_1} \cdots \forall \bar{Y} \exists \bar{X} \{
$$
$$
\bigwedge_i \forall y_{i1} \cdots \forall y_{it_i} [B(y_{i1}) \vee \cdots \vee B(y_{it_i}) \vee T_i(\bar{X}, \bar{Y})] \to
$$
$$
\forall z [\neg B(z)] \}.
$$

By (201), the conjunction $T \wedge$ (206) implies

(207)
$$
\exists x_{11} \cdots \exists x_{1s_1} \cdots \forall z \neg B(z),
$$

where $\exists x_{11} \cdots \exists x_{1s_1} \cdots$ are all existential quantifiers of T. Replacing $B(z)$ in (207) by its definition, we get

(208)
$$
\exists x_{11} \cdots \exists x_{1s_1} \cdots \forall z [z \approx c_1' \vee \cdots \vee z \approx c_r' \vee \bigvee_i (z \approx x_{i1} \vee \cdots \vee z \approx x_{is_i})].
$$

It can now be easily observed that (208) is equivalent to $DCA^{-\bar{c}+k}(T)$, where k is the number of existential quantifiers of T. Given this, the elimination of predicate variables corresponding to varying predicate and individual constants follows from Remark 16.9.   ◁

16.3.2.3. *Arbitrary Theories.* For non-semi-universal theories without functions, neither the DLS algorithm nor its fixpoint generalization guarantee a reduction to classical first-order logic. However, the reduction can sometimes be obtained, as shown in the following example.

EXAMPLE 16.18. Let theory T be $\forall x \exists y S(x, y) \wedge \forall x \forall y [S(x, y) \to x \approx y]$. Then the second-order part of $Circ_D(T)$ is equivalent to:

(209)
$$
\forall Z \{ [\exists x Z(x) \wedge \forall x [Z(x) \to \exists y [Z(y) \wedge S(x, y)]]] \to \forall z [Z(z)] \}
$$

i.e., to

(210) $\neg \exists Z \{ \exists x Z(x) \wedge \forall x [Z(x) \rightarrow \exists y [Z(y) \wedge S(x,y)]] \wedge \exists z [\neg Z(z)] \}.$

We transform this formula to

$$\neg \exists z \exists x \exists Z \{ Z(x) \wedge \forall x [Z(x) \rightarrow [z \not\approx x \wedge \exists y [Z(y) \wedge S(x,y)]]] \}$$

and apply Theorem 6.19:

(211) $\neg \exists z \exists x [\text{GFP } Z(x).z \not\approx x \wedge \exists y [Z(y) \wedge S(x,y)]].$

Formula (211) is equivalent to

$$\forall z \forall x [\text{LFP } Z(x).z \approx x \vee \forall y [S(x,y) \rightarrow Z(y)]].$$

We now unfold the fixpoint formula

(212) $[\text{LFP } Z(x.z \approx x \vee \forall y [S(x,y) \rightarrow Z(y)]].$

Let $\Gamma(Z(x)) = (z \approx x \vee \forall y (S(x,y) \rightarrow Z(y))))$. Now:

$\Gamma^0(\text{FALSE}) \equiv \text{FALSE}$
$\Gamma^1(\text{FALSE}) \equiv z \approx x \vee \forall y (S(x,y) \rightarrow \text{FALSE}) \equiv z \approx x$ (by
   theory T)
$\Gamma^2(\text{FALSE}) \equiv z \approx x \vee \forall y (S(x,y) \rightarrow z \approx y).$

We show that $\Gamma^1(\text{FALSE}) \equiv \Gamma^2(\text{FALSE})$. It is easily observed that

$$\Gamma^1(\text{FALSE}) \rightarrow \Gamma^2(\text{FALSE}).$$

We thus have to show that $\Gamma^2(\text{FALSE}) \rightarrow \Gamma^1(\text{FALSE})$, i.e.,

$$z \approx x \vee \forall y [S(x,y) \rightarrow z \approx y] \rightarrow z \approx x.$$

Suppose that $z \not\approx x$ and $\forall y [S(x,y) \rightarrow z \approx y]$. Thus, replacing y by x we obtain that this formula implies $\neg S(x,x)$ which, using theory T, implies FALSE. Thus formula (212) reduces to $z \approx x$.

Formula (209) reduces now to $\forall z \forall x [z \approx x]$.   ◁

16.3.3. Variable Domain Circumscription with Functions.

For theories containing function symbols, the DLS algorithm always fails. However, it is sometimes possible to reduce domain circumscription for such theories using the fixpoint approach (see Examples 16.20 and 16.21). We also have the following theorem.

THEOREM 16.19. Let T be a semi-universal theory. Then $Circ_D(T)$ is always reducible to fixpoint logic.

PROOF. It can easily be observed that the negation of the second-order part of $Circ_D(T)$ consists of clauses containing at most one positive occurrence of Z. Thus it can be transformed into the form required in Theorem 6.19, i.e., $Circ_D(T)$ can be reduced to a fixpoint formula.   ◁

EXAMPLE 16.20. Let T consist of $\forall x[f(x) \approx a \lor f(x) \approx b]$. We reduce $Circ_D(T)$. The corresponding domain circumscription axiom is equivalent to

(213) $\forall Z\{[Z(a) \land Z(b) \land \forall x[Z(x) \to Z(f(x))]] \to \forall x[Z(x)]\}.$

Formula (214) is equivalent to

(214) $\neg \exists Z\{Z(a) \land Z(b) \land \forall x[Z(x) \to Z(f(x))] \land \exists x'[\neg Z(x')]\},$

which can further be transformed to

(215) $\neg \exists x' \exists Z\{Z(a) \land Z(b) \land \forall x[Z(x) \to (x \not\approx x' \land Z(f(x)))]\}.$

Now one can apply Theorem 6.19. Observe that in this case the fixpoint operator takes the form $[\text{GFP } Z(x).x \not\approx x' \land Z(f(x))]$ and so, after negating, the form

$\qquad [\text{LFP } Z(x).x \approx x' \lor Z(f(x))]$

which is equivalent to

(216)
$$x \approx x' \lor (x' \approx x \lor x' \approx f(x)) \lor$$
$$(x' \approx x \lor x' \approx f(x) \lor x' \approx f(f(x))) \lor$$
$$(x' \approx x \lor x' \approx f(x) \lor x' \approx f(f(x)) \lor x' \approx f(f(f(x)))) \lor \cdots$$

Observe that T implies that $f(f(f(x)))$ does not introduce new values (since for any x, $f(x) \approx a \lor f(x) \approx b$). Thus the third disjunct of (216) is equivalent to the second one, given T. Now we have

$\qquad [\text{LFP } Z(x).x \approx x' \lor Z(f(x))] \equiv (x' \approx x \lor x' \approx f(x) \lor x' \approx f(f(x))).$

Thus, after performing routine calculations, we conclude that $Circ_D(T)$ reduces to the conjunction of T and

(217) $\forall x'[x' \approx a \lor x' \approx f(a) \lor x' \approx f(f(a)) \lor x' \approx b \lor x' \approx f(b) \lor x' \approx f(f(b))].$

◁

EXAMPLE 16.21. Consider theory T from [197], consisting of $\forall x[x \approx f(f(x))] \land c \not\approx d$. Here $f(x)$ can be read "a spouse of x". We show a reduction of $Circ_D(T)$. The corresponding circumscription axiom, after some simplifications, is

(218) $\forall Z\{[Z(c) \land Z(d) \land \forall x[Z(x) \to Z(f(x))]] \to \forall x[Z(x)]\}.$

Formula (218) is equivalent to

(219) $\forall Z\{Z(c) \land Z(d) \land \forall x[Z(x) \to Z(f(x))] \land \exists s[\neg Z(s)]\},$

i.e., to

(220) $\neg \exists s \exists Z\{Z(c) \land Z(d) \land \forall x[Z(x) \to (Z(f(x)) \land x \not\approx s)]\}.$

Now, we apply Theorem 6.19. Note that in this case the fixpoint operator takes the form $[\text{GFP } Z(x).x \not\approx s \wedge Z(f(x))]$ and so, after negating, the form

$$[\text{LFP } Z(x).x \approx s \vee Z(f(x))],$$

equivalent to

$$(221) \quad x \approx s \vee (x \approx s \vee f(x) \approx s) \vee (x \approx s \vee (f(x) \approx s \vee f(f(x)) \approx s)) \vee \ldots$$

Observe that given T, the third disjunct of (221) is equivalent to the second one. Now, performing straightforward calculations, we obtain

$$Circ_D(T) \equiv T \wedge \forall s[c \approx s \vee f(c) \approx s \vee d \approx s \vee f(d) \approx s].$$

The above result states that the domain has to contain c and d, and all the results of applications of f. Since $f(f(x)) \approx x$, the second application of f does not give anything new. The minimal domain is then described by the resulting formula. ◁

CHAPTER 17

Applications in Databases

Second-order formalisms appear naturally in many contexts in database systems. Even the very basic problem of querying a database depends on finding a relation satisfying a given query. Here we ask whether there is a relation satisfying a query and look for the minimal such relation. Also non-monotonic reasoning database formalisms are basically second-order.

In the current chapter we show various applications of second-order quantifier elimination, in particular in querying databases, based on papers by Doherty, Kachniarz, Łukaszewicz and Szałas [**52, 58, 60**] and static verification of integrity constraints, based on the paper [**122**].

We shall focus on relational databases, as defined below.

DEFINITION 17.1. A *relational database DB*, is a relational structure

$$\langle U, r_1^{a_1}, \ldots, r_k^{a_k}, c_1, \ldots, c_l \rangle,$$

where U is a finite set, for $1 \leq i \leq k$, $r_i^{a_i}$ is an a_i-ary relation on U, and $c_1, \ldots, c_l$ are constants. By a *signature* of DB we shall mean the signature consisting of relation symbols $R_1^{a_1}, \ldots, R_k^{a_k}$ and constant symbols $C_1, \ldots, C_l$ together with equality $\approx$. ◁

Let $c_1, \ldots, c_n$ be all the constants from the alphabet under consideration. We write $\text{DCA}(M)$ to denote the *domain closure* axiom for a theory M,

$$\text{DCA}(M) \overset{\text{def}}{\equiv} \forall x \bigvee_{i=1}^{n} x \approx c_i.$$

We write $\text{UNA}(M)$ to denote the *unique name assumption* axiom for a theory M,

$$\text{UNA}(M) \overset{\text{def}}{\equiv} \bigwedge_{1 \leq i < j \leq n} c_i \not\approx c_j.$$

17.1. Local Closed World Assumption

Traditionally, an efficient means of representing negative information about the world in databases applies the *Closed World Assumption* (CWA). In this case, information about the world, absent in a database, is assumed to be false. In many realistic applications, CWA cannot safely be used. For example, from the lack of knowledge about obstacles a robot having incomplete information about the world should not deduce that actually there are no obstacles. New objects should be continually sensed or encountered. In applications such as this, an *Open World Assumption* (OWA), where information not known by the agent is assumed to be unknown, is the right choice to make, but complicates the use of negative information.

The CWA and the OWA represent two extremes. Quite often, a reasoning agent has information which permits the application of the CWA *locally*. For example, if a robot has a camera sensor, it can safely assume complete information about objects in the focus of attention of the camera.

An approach based on the second-order formalism to the local closed world assumption (LCW) has been proposed by Doherty, Łukaszewicz and Szałas in [60], where an earlier approach of Etzioni, Golden and Weld [73] has been substantially clarified and extended due to the use of second-order logic. The approach of [60] is based on the use of circumscription to minimize formulas in the context of theories. Using second-order quantifier elimination techniques, the original circumscribed theory is then reduced to a first-order or fixpoint formula. When the reduction is successful, one can viewing the reduced theory as a database query, the complexity of which is in PTIME.

Suppose that T is a finite first-order theory formalizing an agent's *knowledge*. Since T provides only incomplete information, not all facts about the world are known to the agent. In other words, only some of the information is locally closed relative to T, other information is unknown. We approximate an agent's knowledge by a pair $M, \mathcal{L}$, where M is a finite set of positive or negative ground literals and $\mathcal{L}$ is a set of first-order formulas, representing local closed-world assumptions. We write $M, \mathcal{L} \models \alpha$ to denote that a formula α follows from a pair $M, \mathcal{L}$. This notion is defined as follows.[1]

DEFINITION 17.2. Let $M, \mathcal{L}$ be a finite set of ground literals and a set of formulas representing closed-world information, respectively. Suppose that $\mathcal{L}$ consists of formulas $\beta_1, \ldots, \beta_n$. Let $\bar{R} = R_1, \ldots, R_n$ be a set of new predicates symbols of the arities equal to the number of free variables in $\beta_1, \ldots, \beta_n$, respectively. By an LCW-*based extension of* M, denoted by M', we shall understand the theory

---

[1]Recall that definitions of DCA and UNA are provided on page 227.

consisting of formulas of M, augmented by $\text{DCA}(M)$ and $\text{UNA}(M)$ as well as by the set of formulas $\forall \bar{x}[R_i(\bar{x}) \equiv \beta_i]$ $(i = 1, \dots n)$. ◁

The following definition provides us with the semantics of LCW.

DEFINITION 17.3. Assume $\bar{S}$ denotes the set of all predicate symbols occurring in $\beta_1, \dots, \beta_n$. Then $M, \mathcal{L} \models_{\text{LCW}} \alpha$ iff $CIRC(M'; \bar{R}; \bar{S}) \models \alpha$, where $\bar{R} = \langle R_1, \dots, R_n \rangle$. ◁

Note that Definition 17.3 provides the general case and semantics for reasoning under LCW. Now techniques similar to those discussed in Chapter 16 can be applied to eliminate second-order quantifiers and, in consequence, to reduce the complexity of reasoning to PTIME.

17.2. Query Languages

17.2.1. Semi-Horn Query Language. Much activity in the area of deductive databases has focused on the language DATALOG and its extensions which integrate recursion with negation. When adding negation to DATALOG one either ends up in languages of complexity in NPTIME or assumes a non-classical semantics for. There are many choices of such semantics and these choices influence not only the natural interpretation of the negation symbol in a query, but also the expressiveness of the language.

An important aspect of query language design is to achieve a good balance between the expressiveness of the language and the complexity of evaluating queries in the language. In Doherty, Łukaszewicz and Szałas [58] a purely declarative query language, SHQL, has been defined. Negation in SHQL is interpreted as classical negation, a class of mixed quantifiers is allowed in queries, and intentional and extensional predicates may occur anywhere in the query. What makes it efficient, is the possibility to eliminate second-order quantifiers appearing in queries.

SHQL is used as follows. Given the task of computing a definition of relation Q (or asking whether a tuple is an instance of Q) relative to a relational database B consisting of the relations $R_1, \dots, R_n$, we first provide an implicit definition of Q in terms of a SHQL theory, $T(Q)$. The goal is to compute an explicit definition of Q in deterministic polynomial time.

The computation process can be described in two stages. In the first stage, a PTIME compilation process is provided. It uses the DLS* algorithm. Given the SHQL query, $T(Q)$, we prefix it with an existential quantifier and input the formula $\exists Q[T(Q)]$ to DLS*. For SHQL queries the elimination of second-order quantifiers is guaranteed.

In the second stage, we use the explicit definition of Q output in the first stage to compute a suitable relation in the relational database that satisfies Q. Before computing the output relation, we first check to see that such a relation exists relative to the database. Suppose $T(Q)$ is the original query, B the relational database and $\Theta'(Q)$ the output of DLS* given the input $\exists Q[T(Q)]$. We say that the query $\Theta(Q)$ is a *coherent query relative to* B if $B \models \Theta'(Q)$. Assuming this is the case, we know that the output relation exists and can now compute the answer. Both checking that the query is coherent and computing the output relation can be done in deterministic polynomial time because these are fixpoint formulas (see Theorem 3.44, page 36).

DEFINITION 17.4. By a *semi-Horn formula w.r.t.* Q we understand any formula of the form

(222) $\forall \bar{x}[A(Q) \rightarrow Q(\bar{t})] \wedge B(Q),$

where $A(Q)$ is an arbitrary first-order formula positive w.r.t. Q and $B(Q)$ is an arbitrary first-order formula negative w.r.t. Q.   ◁

The dual forms are obtained by replacing Q by $\neg Q$ in (222), making C an arbitrary first-order formula positive w.r.t. Q.

Note that any conjunction of semi-Horn formulas w.r.t. Q can be transformed into a single semi-Horn formula by using the following equivalence:

$$\forall \bar{x}[A(\bar{x}, Q) \rightarrow Q(\bar{x})] \wedge B(Q) \wedge \forall \bar{x}[A'(\bar{x}, Q) \rightarrow Q(\bar{x})] \wedge B'(Q) \equiv$$
$$\forall \bar{x}[(A(\bar{x}, Q) \vee A'(\bar{x}, Q)) \rightarrow Q(\bar{x})] \wedge [B(Q) \wedge B'(Q)].$$

A similar equivalence applies for the dual forms.

Moreover, if we have many relations, we can easily encode these by a single predicate which has a vector of additional Boolean variables distinguishing between various relations. The resulting formulas are still semi-Horn formulas. Thus, we can safely assume that we always deal with a single predicate in our queries.

Semi-Horn formulas are strictly more expressive than Horn clauses. For instance, semi-Horn formulas express the complement of a relation which is not expressible by Horn clauses (see, e.g., Chandra [**34**]). Also existential quantifiers in the scope of universal quantifiers are not, in general, reducible to Horn clauses, but are allowed in semi-Horn formulas.

DEFINITION 17.5. By a SHQL *query* we mean any query expressed as a semi-Horn formula.   ◁

The semantics of the SHQL query $T(Q)$ is the minimal relation (maximal, in the case of the dual form of semi-Horn formulas) satisfying $T(Q)$, provided that such a relation exists (i.e., that the underlying database entails the coherence condition

$\exists Q T(Q)$). Observe that the definitions of minimal and maximal relations satisfying $T(Q)$ as well as the coherence condition are given by Corollaries 6.20 and 6.22 (see page 83).

The following theorem is due to [**58**].

THEOREM 17.6. Let B be a relational database.

- The minimal relation satisfying the SHQL query $T(Q)$ is computable in polynomial time in the size of the database.
- Any PTIME query can be expressed as a SHQL query provided that the domain of B is linearly ordered.

PROOF. The first part of the theorem can be proved by noticing that semi-Horn formulas reduce to fixpoint formulas and using the fact that fixpoint queries are computable in polynomial time.

To prove the second part of the theorem we use the following well known facts (see [**1**]):

- If the domain of the database is linearly ordered then fixpoint queries express all PTIME queries;
- Under the above assumption any fixpoint query can be expressed by taking fixpoint formula with a single least fixpoint with positive occurrences of the calculated predicate.

According to the above, it is sufficient to prove that a single fixpoint can be defined by an implicit query. Assume that the fixpoint to be defined is $[\text{LFP } P(\bar{x}).A(P)]$, where A is positive w.r.t. P. Then the SHQL query that defines this fixpoint is simply the formula $\forall \bar{x}[A(P) \rightarrow P(\bar{x})]$.   ◁

EXAMPLE 17.7. Assume we have a database B, containing information about whether persons are *realistic*, *smart*, or *experienced*, denoted by the unary extensional predicates, R, S, and E, respectively. Suppose we are interested in selecting all realistic persons and perhaps some others and we only want to consider those who are smart and experienced. Let Q denote the unary extensional predicate that describes the required relation. The first condition is then expressed by the formula

$$\forall x[R(x) \rightarrow Q(x)],$$

while the second condition is expressed by the formula

$$\forall x[Q(x) \rightarrow (S(x) \wedge E(x))].$$

The implicit query $T(Q)$ is then defined as the conjunction of the above formulas, where we are interested in obtaining the least relation Q satisfying

$$\forall x[R(x) \rightarrow Q(x)] \wedge \forall x[Q(x) \rightarrow (S(x) \wedge E(x))].$$

Thus the definition of minimal Q is given by $[\text{LFP} \, Q(x).R(x)]$ which is simply $R(x)$. The coherence condition is given by

$$\forall x[R(x) \rightarrow (S(x) \wedge E(x))].$$

Observe that our query forces this condition (by transitivity of implication), Thus, for instance, if a database contains an element e such that $R(e)$ and $\neg S(e)$, then the query is inconsistent with the database. $\lhd$

17.2.2. Meta-Queries. One of the particularly interesting domains of problems used to test the suitability of both representations and formalisms of database queries and reasoning is the domain of logical puzzles. Logical puzzles are quite often straightforward to state informally, yet prove to be quite difficult to represent and solve formally and often involve subtle issues in knowledge representation. Smullyan [**190**] has collected a number of puzzles to study problems related to topics such as self-reference and logical paradoxes. In particular, the solutions to a number of logical puzzles presented by Smullyan, such as some of the knights and knaves problems, are dependent on the generation of queries whose utterance contributes to the solution of the puzzles.

As an example, Smullyan [**190**], gives many puzzles, where the problem is to generate a single query that solves the problem (see also Example 17.8 below). Another example would depend on generating single queries or transactions to query rapidly changing databases.

The technique proposed by Doherty, Kachniarz and Szałas in [**52**] is based on the notion of a *meta-query* applied to a relational database. The idea is to first represent the problem to be solved by a first-order theory $T(Q)$ giving a (partial and implicit) definition of Q, where Q is the query we are looking for. Now we ask whether $\exists Q T(Q)$ and try to find an explicit definition of minimal or maximal Q satisfying $T(Q)$. The second-order formula $\exists Q T(Q)$ is called a *meta-query* because we do not actually ask the query but ask whether the query exists relative to the database contents.

It appears that the query language SHQL, discussed in Section 17.2.1, can serve as an efficient language to express meta-queries. The technology developed not only provides an answer as to whether a query exists (is consistent with the database of facts), but it also produces an explicit definition for the query which can be used to compute an answer. Polynomial time complexity of both answering whether a query exists and computing an answer to the query is guaranteed. In fact, all polynomial time meta-queries are provably expressible as SHQL queries.

The following examples, considered in [**52**], illustrate the idea.

EXAMPLE 17.8. As an example consider a puzzle given in Smullyan [**190**]:

"An island exists whose only inhabitants are knights and knaves. The knights on the island always tell the truth, while the knaves always lie. There are two roads. One of the roads leads to a castle and the other does not. An island visitor wants to ask an inhabitant of the island which road is the right road (leads to the castle), but the visitor does not know whether the person queried is a knight or a knave."

The solution to the puzzle is to find a query Q which indicates the right road no matter who the visitor queries, truthful inhabitants (knights), or lying inhabitants (knaves). In the following, assume that $R(x)$ means that an inhabitant x claims that a road chosen by the visitor is right (leads to the castle) and $K(x)$ means that x is a knight. Since the island is only inhabited by knights and knaves, $\neg K(x)$ asserts that x is a knave. We are interested in whether there is a query $Q(x)$, which when asked to an inhabitant x, allows us to distinguish between the right and wrong roads. If there is such a query then we should generate an explicit definition of the query. Based on the information supplied in the puzzle, query $Q(x)$ should satisfy the following conditions $T(Q)$:

(223) $\forall x[K(x) \rightarrow (Q(x) \equiv R(x))] \wedge \forall x[\neg K(x) \rightarrow (Q(x) \equiv \neg R(x))]$.

In consequence, asking whether a query satisfying (223) exists is expressed as the second-order formula

(224) $\exists Q\{\forall x[K(x) \rightarrow (Q(x) \equiv R(x))] \wedge \forall x[\neg K(x) \rightarrow (Q(x) \equiv \neg R(x))]\}$.

Formula (224) is equivalent to

$$\exists Q\{\forall x[Q(x) \vee (K(x) \equiv R(x))] \wedge \forall x[Q(x) \rightarrow (K(x) \equiv \neg R(x))]\}.$$

As a result we generate the following explicit definition of $Q(x)$:

(225) $Q(x) \equiv (K(x) \equiv R(x))$.

In addition, the coherence condition is always TRUE. This simply means that the query is always consistent and gives the right answer.

It is easy to see that this utterance stated by the visitor provides him with the necessary information about the castle road regardless of the status of who he makes the utterance to.   ◁

EXAMPLE 17.9. Let us consider a database storing, among others, patient demographic data (including parent–child relationships) as well as diagnosed disease cases. Let the relation $P(x, y)$ mean that x is a parent of y and $D(x)$ mean that patient x fell ill with a certain disease d. One may want to ask a query: "is there any data in the database confirming the hypothesis that the disease d is hereditary?". Here one wants to find a relation $A(x, y)$ containing all cases when both ancestor x and descendant y had the same illness d.

Assume that the query $A(x, y)$ has to satisfy

$$\forall x \forall y [A(x, y) \rightarrow (P(x, y) \vee \exists z (P(z, y) \wedge A(x, z)))] \wedge$$
$$\forall x [D(x) \rightarrow \exists z (A(z, x) \wedge D(z))].$$

The respective meta-query is expressed by the second-order formula

$$\exists A \forall x \forall y [A(x, y) \rightarrow (P(x, y) \vee \exists z (P(z, y) \wedge A(x, z)))] \wedge$$
$$\forall x [D(x) \rightarrow \exists z (A(z, x) \wedge D(z))].$$

According to Corollary 6.20, the explicit definition of the greatest $A(x, y)$ is given by:

$$A(x, y) \equiv [\text{GFP } A(x, y).P(x, y) \vee \exists z (P(z, y) \wedge A(x, z))]$$

and, by Corollary 6.22, the coherence condition, after simple transformations, has the form

$$\forall x [D(x) \rightarrow \exists z ([\text{GFP } A(x, y).P(x, y) \vee \exists z (P(z, y) \wedge A(x, z))]_{z,x}^{x,y}$$
$$\wedge D(z))]. \hspace{3cm} \triangleleft$$

17.3. Static Verification of Integrity Constraints

Integrity constraints are statements about database contents, expressed as classical first-order formulas (see, e.g., [1]) that are supposed to be satisfied by all possible instances of the database. In the existing implementations these conditions are checked dynamically during the database updates. In the case of software systems dealing with a rapidly changing environment and reacting in real time, checking integrity constraints after each update is usually unacceptable from the point of view of the required reaction time.

In a paper by Kachniarz and Szałas [122] a different approach, based on a static verification of integrity constraints, has been proposed. Assume that the database can be modified only by well-defined procedures (later called transactions), supplied by database designers. In such a case the task of verification of integrity constraints reduces to the following two steps:

(1) Verify that the initial contents of the database satisfies the defined constraints;
(2) Verify that all transactions preserve the constraints.

If both of the above conditions hold, a simple induction shows that all possible instances of the database preserve the integrity constraints. In such cases runtime verification of these constraints is no longer necessary.

Assume that $I(R_1, \ldots, R_n)$ is an integrity constraint involving relations (tables) $R_1, \ldots, R_n$ and is expressed as a classical first-order formula. In such a case the problem of checking the first of the above induction steps is in LOGSPACE and PTIME (see Theorem 3.27, page 29).

Consider a transaction which modifies relations $R_1, \ldots, R_n$ giving as a result relations $R'_1, \ldots, R'_n$. The second of the steps reduces to verification of whether the following second-order formula is a tautology:

(226) $\forall R_1, \ldots, R_n [I(R_1, \ldots, R_n) \rightarrow I(R'_1, \ldots, R'_n)]$.

In general this problem is totally undecidable. We shall show, however, that in numerous practical cases it can be reduced to decidable problems of acceptable complexity. The method is based on Lemma 6.1 and Theorem 6.19.[2]

DEFINITION 17.10. By an *integrity constraint* in a relational database DB we shall mean any classical first-order formula over the signature of DB.

By an *update* of a relational database DB we shall mean an expression of the form ADD $\bar{e}$ TO R or DELETE $\bar{e}$ FROM R, where R is an k-ary relation of DB and $\bar{e}$ is a tuple of k elements. By a *transaction* on a relational database DB we shall mean any finite sequence of *updates* on DB.   ◁

The meaning of ADD and DELETE updates is rather obvious. Namely, ADD e TO R denotes adding a new tuple e to the relation R, whereas DELETE e FROM R denotes deleting e from R:

- (ADD e TO R)(R) $\equiv R \cup \{e\}$
- (DELETE e FROM R)(R) $\equiv R - \{e\}$.

From the logical point of view, the above updates are formula transformers defined as follows, where $A(R)$ is a formula:

(227)   (ADD e TO R)($A(R(x))$) $\equiv A(R(x))^{R(x)}_{R(x) \vee x \approx e}$

(228)   (DELETE e FROM R)($A(R(x))$) $\equiv A(R(x))^{R(x)}_{R(x) \wedge x \not\approx e}$.

The result of applying transaction T to formula A is defined as the composition of updates appearing in T and is further denoted by $T(A)$.

The following definition is a basis for the presented approach.

DEFINITION 17.11. Transaction T is *correct with respect to integrity constraint* $I(R_1, \ldots, R_k)$ iff $\forall R_1 \ldots \forall R_k [I(R_1, \ldots, R_k) \rightarrow T(I(R_1, \ldots, R_k))]$ is a tautology.   ◁

In order to formulate the sufficient conditions that guarantee that the method works we have to define Ackermann's formulas[3] and universal Ackermann's formulas.

---

[2]The method based on Lemma 6.1 and using the well-known decidability of the classical theory of equality has been developed in [122]. Due to [204] it is extended to deal with recursive integrity constraints, too.

[3]We propose this term because of its correspondence to Ackermann's lemma.

DEFINITION 17.12. By an *Ackermann's formula w.r.t. relational symbols* $R_1, \ldots,$ R_k we shall mean:

(1) Any formula without symbols $R_1, \ldots, R_k$;
(2) Any formula negative w.r.t. $R_1, \ldots, R_k$;
(3) Any universally quantified disjunction of formulas of the form defined in the first item or literals, in which any symbol of $R_1, \ldots, R_k$ occurs at most once;
(4) Any conjunction of the above formulas.   ◁

DEFINITION 17.13. By a *universal Ackermann's formula w.r.t. relational symbols* $R_1, \ldots, R_k$ we shall mean any Ackermann's formula, where relational symbols $R_1, \ldots, R_k$ do not occur in the scope of existential quantifiers.   ◁

EXAMPLE 17.14. Formulas $\neg R(x) \vee \neg R(y) \vee \neg S(z)$ and $R(x) \vee x \not\approx y \vee G(y)$ are Ackermann's formulas w.r.t. relational symbols R and S, but $R(x) \vee R(y) \vee \neg S(z)$ and $R(x) \vee S(y)$ are not.   ◁

The method works also for dual forms of Ackermann's formulas, where all relational symbols $R_1, \ldots, R_k$ are replaced by their negations.

THEOREM 17.15. For any integrity constraint $I(R_1, \ldots, R_k)$ of database DB, expressed as a universal Ackermann's formula w.r.t. $R_1, \ldots, R_k$ and any transaction T modifying at most relations $R_1, \ldots, R_k$, it is possible to eliminate the second-order quantifiers from the formula:

(229) $\forall R_1 \ldots \forall R_k [I(R_1, \ldots, R_k) \rightarrow T(I(R_1, \ldots, R_k))]$

applying the DLS algorithm. Moreover, the resulting formula does not contain relation symbols $R_1, \ldots, R_k$ and its signature is included in the signature of DB.

PROOF.

Consider formula

$$\forall R_1 \ldots \forall R_k [I(R_1, \ldots, R_k) \rightarrow T(I(R_1, \ldots, R_k))],$$

where I is a universal Ackermann's formula and T is a transaction. This formula is equivalent to

(230) $\neg \exists R_1 \ldots \exists R_k [I(R_1, \ldots, R_k) \wedge \neg I'(R_1, \ldots, R_k)],$

where I' denotes the result of application of transaction T to I (i.e., the result of replacement of $R_i's$ by expressions of the form given in equations (227) or (228) corresponding to transaction updates). Since I' is obtained from a universal Ackermann's formula, relation symbols $R_1, \ldots, R_k$ do not appear in I' within the scope of existential quantifiers. In the next step move negation in formula (230) inside I'. Now relation symbols $R_1, \ldots, R_k$ do not appear in I' within the scope of universal quantifiers. Move all existential quantifiers binding variables occurring as arguments of $R_1, \ldots, R_k$ to the prefix of the formula. The resulting formula can now easily be transformed to the form required in Ackermann's lemma and the second-order quantifiers can be eliminated.

Observe also that the process of elimination of the second-order quantifiers based on Lemma 6.1 eliminates all occurrences of symbols $R_1, \ldots, R_k$ and does not introduce any new relation symbols (except $\approx$, which is assumed to be in the signature of database DB – see Definition 17.1). This proves the remaining part of the theorem.   ◁

THEOREM 17.16. Let $Th(Q_1, \ldots, Q_s, \approx)$ be a decidable first-order theory with a signature containing relational symbols $Q_1, \ldots, Q_s, \approx$. Let $I(R_1, \ldots, R_k)$ be a universal Ackermann's formula containing at most relation symbols $Q_1, \ldots, Q_s, \approx$ $, R_1, \ldots, R_k$ and let T be a transaction modifying at most relations $R_1, \ldots, R_k$. Then it is decidable to verify whether the formula equivalent to:

$$\forall R_1 \ldots \forall R_k [I(R_1, \ldots, R_k) \rightarrow T(I(R_1, \ldots, R_k))],$$

obtained as in Theorem 17.15, is a theorem of $Th(Q_1, \ldots, Q_s)$.

PROOF.

Observe that, according to Theorem 17.15, the signature of the formula resulting from the process of elimination of the second-order quantifiers contains at most symbols $Q_1, \ldots, Q_s, \approx$. By assumption, $Th(Q_1, \ldots, Q_s, \approx)$ is decidable. Thus it is decidable whether the resulting formula is a theorem of $Th(Q_1, \ldots, Q_s)$.   ◁

Since the classical equality theory is decidable, the following corollary holds.

COROLLARY 17.17. Let Th be a decidable first-order theory with signature containing only the symbol $\approx$. Let $I(R_1, \ldots, R_k)$ be a universal Ackermann's formula containing at most relational symbols $R_1, \ldots, R_k, \approx$ and let T be a transaction modifying relations $R_1, \ldots, R_k$. Then verification of whether the formula equivalent to:

$$\forall R_1 \ldots \forall R_k [I(R_1, \ldots, R_k) \rightarrow T(I(R_1, \ldots, R_k))],$$

obtained as in Theorem 17.15, is a tautology, is decidable.   ◁

The following example illustrates the considered method.

EXAMPLE 17.18. Consider a database containing mutually exclusive relations $M(x)$, meaning that x is a male, and $F(x)$, meaning that x is a female. No person can be both male and female, so the integrity constraint expressing this property can be defined as

$$I(M, F) \equiv \forall x [\neg M(x) \vee \neg F(x)],$$

which is a universal Ackermann's formula.

Consider transaction T moving a person a from F to M:

ADD a TO M; DELETE a FORM F.

Then $T(M(x)) \equiv M(x) \vee x \approx a$ and $T(F(x)) \equiv F(x) \wedge x \neq a$. According to the proposed method, the verification condition for integrity constraint I can be expressed as

(231) $\forall F \forall M \forall x [\neg F(x) \vee \neg M(x)] \rightarrow \forall z [\neg (F(z) \wedge z \not\approx a) \vee \neg (M(z) \vee z \approx a)].$

Formula (231) is equivalent to

$$\neg \exists F \exists M \forall x [M(x) \rightarrow \neg F(x)] \wedge \exists z [F(z) \wedge z \not\approx a \wedge (M(z) \vee z \approx a)].$$

An application of Lemma 6.1 to eliminate the second-order quantifier $\exists M$ results in

(232) $\neg \exists F \exists z [F(z) \wedge z \not\approx a \wedge (\neg F(z) \vee z \approx a)].$

Formula (232) is equivalent to

$$\neg \exists z \exists F \forall y [F(y) \vee y \not\approx z] \wedge z \not\approx a \wedge (\neg F(z) \vee z \approx a).$$

The next application of Lemma 6.1 results in $\neg \exists z [z \not\approx a \wedge (z \not\approx z \vee z \approx a)]$, i.e., $\forall z [z \approx a \vee (z \approx z \wedge z \not\approx a)]$, which is an obvious tautology.   ◁

Of course, the reduction to the classical first-order theory of equality is possible not only for integrity constraints expressed as universal Ackermann's formulas (see [**122**]). One can further extend the technique due to the decidability result of [**204**] (see also Section 3.6.2), as shown in the following example.

EXAMPLE 17.19. Let $R(x, y)$ stand for "x, y are relatives", j stand for "John" and m for "Mary". Consider the constraint

(233) $\forall x, y [R(x, y) \rightarrow R(y, x)]$

and the transaction ADD $\langle j, m \rangle$ TO R; ADD $\langle m, j \rangle$ TO R.

To prove correctness of the transaction we first consider the formula reflecting (226),

(234)
$$\forall R \Big\{ \forall x, y [R(x, y) \rightarrow R(y, x)] \rightarrow \\ \{ \forall x, y [R(x, y) \vee (x \approx j \wedge y \approx m) \vee (x \approx m \wedge y \approx j)] \rightarrow \\ [R(y, x) \vee (y \approx j \wedge x \approx m) \vee (y \approx m \wedge x \approx j)] \} \Big\}.$$

Formula (234) is equivalent to

(235)
$$\forall R \Big\{ \forall x, y [R(x, y) \rightarrow R(y, x)] \rightarrow \\ \{ \forall x, y [(x \approx j \wedge y \approx m) \vee (x \approx m \wedge y \approx j)] \rightarrow \\ [R(y, x) \vee (y \approx j \wedge x \approx m) \vee (y \approx m \wedge x \approx j)] \} \Big\}.$$

After negating (235), renaming variables and moving existential quantifiers into the prefix, we obtain

$$\exists x, y \exists R \Big\{ \forall x', y' [R(x', y') \rightarrow R(y', x')] \wedge$$
$$[(x \approx j \wedge y \approx m) \vee (x \approx m \wedge y \approx j)] \wedge$$
$$\neg R(y, x) \wedge (y \not\approx j \vee x \not\approx m) \wedge (y \not\approx m \vee x \not\approx j) \Big\}.$$

We eliminate $\exists R$ by applying Theorem 6.19:

(236)
$$\exists x, y \Big\{ [(x \approx j \wedge y \approx m) \vee (x \approx m \wedge y \approx j)] \wedge$$
$$\neg [\text{LFP } R(x', y').R(y', x')][y, x] \wedge$$
$$(y \not\approx j \vee x \not\approx m) \wedge (y \not\approx m \vee x \not\approx j) \Big\}.$$

Applying the decision procedure of Section 3.6.2 shows that formula (236) is equivalent to FALSE, which proves the correctness of the considered transaction.

The same can also be seen by noticing that

$$[\text{LFP } R(x', y').R(y', x')] \equiv \text{FALSE}$$

i.e., formula (236) is equivalent to

$$\exists x, y \Big\{ [(x \approx j \wedge y \approx m) \vee (x \approx m \wedge y \approx j)] \wedge$$
$$(y \not\approx j \vee x \not\approx m) \wedge (y \not\approx m \vee x \not\approx j) \Big\},$$

clearly equivalent to FALSE. ◁

CHAPTER 18

Applications in Approximate Reasoning

In many artificial intelligence applications one faces the problem of specifying vague concepts and relations and reasoning when such concepts are present. In fact, any model of a physical reality can only approximate this reality. In [148] McCarthy describes approximate concepts as those that cannot have complete if-and-only-if definitions. He observes that

> "The common sense informatic situation often involves concepts which cannot be made precise. This is a question of the information available and not about computation power. It is not a specifically human limitation and applies to computers of any possible power. This is not a claim about physics; it may be that a discoverable set of physical laws accounts for all phenomena. It is rather a question of the information actually available about particular situations by people or robots with limited opportunities to observe and compute."

Examples of approximate concepts/relations could be "the territory of Mount Everest", "fast speed", "to like very much", etc.

According to other literature (see, e.g., Williamson [218]), a concept is vague when it has borderline cases, i.e., some objects cannot be classified to the concept or to its complement with certainty. There are many approaches to deal with approximate theories. In this chapter, based on Doherty and Szałas [63] (see also Doherty, Łukaszewicz and Szałas [62]), vagueness is modeled by introducing similarity-based approximations of concepts. More specifically, the lower approximation of a concept consists of objects that are known to belong to the concept and the upper approximation of the concept consists of objects that might belong to the concept. This is a generalization of Pawlak's idea of approximations of his rough set theory [167] (see also, e.g., [55]).

There is a wide spectrum of choice as to what properties the similarity relation should have and how this affects the properties of approximate relations, e.g., stored in a database. This interaction is made precise due to a technique which permits specification of both approximation and similarity constraints and automatic translation between them, achieved by applying second-order quantifier elimination techniques.

18.1. Correspondences between Similarities and Approximations

There is a natural generalization of the notion of crisp relations where one uses intuitions from Pawlak's rough set theory [**167**], where relations are approximated by an upper and lower approximation. Rough sets can be generalized in such a way that one can consider a covering of the domain by similarity-based neighborhoods with lower and upper approximations of relations defined via the neighborhoods.

When taking this step and generalizing to approximate relations, there are many choices that can be made as regards the constraints one might want to place on the similarity relation used to define upper and lower approximations. For example, we would not want the relation to have the property of transitivity since similar things don't naturally chain in a transitive manner.

Whatever choices are made, one wants to ensure that these constraints are enforced while reasoning about approximate concepts. For example, for any relation, we would like to ensure that its lower approximation is a subset of its upper approximation. There are even constraints we might like to enforce that refer to the crisp relation of which we implicitly represent in terms of an upper and lower approximation. For example the lower approximation should be a subset of this crisp relation.

Following Doherty and Szałas [**63**], in this chapter we consider how correspondences between similarities and approximations can be computed using second-order quantifier elimination techniques. This method is analogous to techniques used in modal correspondence theory (see, e.g., Section 10.4, page 125 and Section 12.3, page 155).

18.1.1. Similarities, Neighborhoods and Approximations. Let us now introduce all the necessary concepts.

DEFINITION 18.1. By a *similarity structure* we understand any pair $\langle U, \sigma \rangle$, where U is a non-empty set and $\sigma \subseteq U \times U$. The relation σ is called a *similarity relation*.

By a *neighborhood function* we mean a function given by

$$n^{\sigma}(u) \stackrel{\text{def}}{=} \{u' \in U \mid \sigma(u, u') \text{ holds}\}.$$

By a *neighborhood* of u wrt σ we mean the value $n^{\sigma}(u)$.

Let $A \subseteq U$. The *lower and upper approximation of A wrt S*, denoted respectively by A_σ^+ and $A_\sigma^\oplus$, are defined by

$$A_\sigma^+ \overset{\text{def}}{=} \{u \in U \mid n^\sigma(u) \subseteq A\}$$
$$A_\sigma^\oplus \overset{\text{def}}{=} \{u \in U \mid n^\sigma(u) \cap A \neq \emptyset\}.$$

$\triangleleft$

An alternative characterization of approximations, formulated in the spirit of the Kripke semantics for modal logics, is provided by the following proposition.

PROPOSITION 18.2. Let $\langle U, \sigma \rangle$ be a similarity structure and $A \subseteq U$. Then

$$A_\sigma^+ = \{x \in A \mid \forall y \, [\sigma(x,y) \to y \in A]\}$$
$$A_\sigma^\oplus = \{x \in A \mid \exists y \, [\sigma(x,y) \land y \in A]\}.$$

$\triangleleft$

In order to specify constraints on approximate relations and similarity relations and to show correspondences between them, we introduce a language for approximation constraints.

DEFINITION 18.3. Let U be a set, $\bar{A}$ be a tuple of set symbols and $S = \langle U, \sigma \rangle$ be a similarity structure. *Set-theoretical terms over vocabulary* $\bar{A} \cup \{\sigma\}$ are defined as follows:

- For $A \in \bar{A}$, A is a set-theoretical term;
- If α is a set-theoretical term then $-\alpha, \alpha_\sigma^+, \alpha_\sigma^\oplus$ are set-theoretical terms;
- If α, β are set-theoretical terms then $\alpha \cup \beta$ is also a set-theoretical term.

If α and β are set-theoretical terms over $\bar{A} \cup \{\sigma\}$ then $\alpha \subseteq \beta$ is an *atomic set-theoretical formula over* $\bar{A} \cup \{\sigma\}$. The set of *set-theoretical formulas* is the least set which contains all atomic set-theoretical formulas and is closed under the classical propositional connectives.

$\triangleleft$

We also define $(\alpha \cap \beta) \overset{\text{def}}{=} -(-\alpha \cup -\beta)$ and $(\alpha = \beta) \overset{\text{def}}{=} (\alpha \subseteq \beta \land \beta \subseteq \alpha)$.

Given approximation constraints in the language above, we translate such constraints into formulas in a first-order language as follows.

DEFINITION 18.4. Let $U, \bar{A}, S$ be as in Definition 18.3. Let α be a set-theoretical term over $\bar{A} \cup \{\sigma\}$ and x be a variable over U. Then the *translation* $Tr(\alpha, x)$ *of set-theoretical terms* into first-order formulas is defined inductively as follows:

- $Tr(A, x) \overset{\text{def}}{=} A'(x)$, where $A \in \bar{A}$ and A' is a fresh unary relation symbol;
- $Tr(-\alpha, x) \overset{\text{def}}{=} \neg Tr(\alpha, x)$;
- $Tr(\alpha_\sigma^+, x) \overset{\text{def}}{=} \forall y \, [\sigma(x,y) \to Tr(\alpha, y)]$, where y is a fresh variable;
- $Tr(\alpha_\sigma^\oplus, x) \overset{\text{def}}{=} \exists y \, [\sigma(x,y) \land Tr(\alpha, y)]$, where y is a fresh variable;

- $Tr(\alpha \cup \beta, x) \overset{\text{def}}{=} Tr(\alpha, x) \vee Tr(\beta, x).$

The *translation* $Tr(\gamma, x)$ *of set-theoretical formulas* into first-order formulas is defined to satisfy $Tr(\alpha \subseteq \beta, x) \overset{\text{def}}{=} \forall x[Tr(\alpha, x) \rightarrow Tr(\beta, x)]$ and to preserve the classical propositional connectives.   ◁

EXAMPLE 18.5. Let a vocabulary consist of sets A, B, C and similarity relation σ. Then:

$$Tr((A \cup B)^+_\sigma \subseteq C^\oplus_\sigma, x) =$$
$$= \forall x \big[\forall y[\sigma(x,y) \rightarrow (A(y) \vee B(y))] \rightarrow \exists z[\sigma(x,z) \wedge C(z)]\big]. \qquad ◁$$

18.1.2. The Meaning of Inclusion $A^+_\sigma \subseteq A^\oplus_\sigma$. Consider now the very basic requirement in rough set theory that the lower approximation of a set should be contained in its upper approximation, i.e., for any set A we have $A^+_\sigma \subseteq A^\oplus_\sigma$. The translation of this approximation is given by

$$Tr(A^+_\sigma \subseteq A^\oplus_\sigma, x) = \forall x[Tr(A^+_\sigma, x) \rightarrow Tr(A^\oplus_\sigma, x)] =$$
$$\forall x \big[\forall y[\sigma(x,y) \rightarrow A(y)] \rightarrow \exists z[\sigma(x,z) \wedge A(z)]\big].$$

This gives rise to the following second-order formula:

$$\forall A \forall x \big[\forall y[\sigma(x,y) \rightarrow A(y)] \rightarrow \exists z[\sigma(x,z) \wedge A(z)]\big].$$

To apply Ackermann's lemma (Lemma 6.1), we first negate this formula and switch the order of initial existential quantifiers:

$$\neg \exists x \exists A \big[\forall y[\sigma(x,y) \rightarrow A(y)] \wedge \forall z[\neg \sigma(x,z) \vee \neg A(z)]\big].$$

Ackermann's lemma is then applied resulting in a logically equivalent first-order formula representing the following similarity constraint:

$$\neg \exists x [\forall z [\neg \sigma(x,z) \vee \neg \sigma(x,z)]].$$

After simplifying and negating again we find that the initial requirement is equivalent to $\forall x \exists z [\sigma(x,z)]$, i.e., to the seriality of σ, reflecting the axiom **D** of modal logics.

Seriality is a weaker requirement on σ than reflexivity, since reflexivity implies seriality. Assuming this is the only constraint placed on σ, what might this mean intuitively. In an epistemic context, one use of such a weak notion of similarity might be to represent a type of self-awareness, or lack of self-awareness in this case. Here is an example.

EXAMPLE 18.6. On a daily basis, humans often use many different relations of similarity concurrently. In common-sense reasoning these relations are generally kept apart, because this would lead to invalid conclusions. For example, assume we consider a similarity between parents and children in the sense that a child is similar to its parent. Suppose further that we do not want to mix this notion of similarity with other similarities, e.g., those of persons to themselves. More formally we can say that $\sigma(x, y)$ holds if x is a child of y. Since everybody has a parent, σ is serial. Obviously it is not reflexive, since no one is its own child. In this case it would not be symmetric or transitive.   ◁

18.1.3. The Meaning of Inclusion $A_\sigma^+ \subseteq A$. The properties we consider in this section and the next two sections are well-known topological properties if one considers the lower approximation to be the interior operation and the upper approximation to be the closure operation. From a modal logic perspective, the lower and upper approximations can be considered analogous to modal necessity and possibility, respectively.

We first translate the approximation constraint $Tr(A_\sigma^+ \subseteq A, x)$ into:

$$\forall x \big[\forall y[\sigma(x, y) \rightarrow A(y)] \rightarrow A(x)\big].$$

A straightforward calculation, as in Example 12.9, shows that the universal requirement

$$\forall A \forall x \big[\forall y[\sigma(x, y) \rightarrow A(y)] \rightarrow A(x)\big]$$

is equivalent to the similarity constraint $\forall x[\sigma(x, x)]$, i.e., to the reflexivity of σ.

18.1.4. The Meaning of Inclusion $A \subseteq (A_\sigma^\oplus)_\sigma^+$. We first translate the approximation constraint $Tr(A \subseteq (A_\sigma^\oplus)_\sigma^+, x)$ into a first-order formula:

$$\forall x \big[A(x) \rightarrow \forall y[\sigma(x, y) \rightarrow \exists z[\sigma(y, z) \wedge A(z)]]\big].$$

A straightforward calculation shows that the universal requirement

$$\forall A \forall x \big[\forall y[\sigma(x, y) \rightarrow A(y)] \rightarrow A(x)\big]$$

is equivalent to the similarity constraint $\forall x \forall y[\sigma(x, y) \rightarrow \sigma(y, x)]$, i.e., to the symmetry of σ.

18.1.5. The Meaning of Inclusion $A_\sigma^+ \subseteq (A_\sigma^+)_\sigma^+$. We first translate the approximation constraint $Tr(A_\sigma^+ \subseteq (A_\sigma^+)_\sigma^+, x)$ into:

$$\forall x \big[\forall y[\sigma(x, y) \rightarrow A(y)] \rightarrow \forall z[\sigma(x, z) \rightarrow \forall u[\sigma(z, u) \rightarrow A(u)]]\big].$$

Again, a straightforward calculation, as in Example 117, shows that the requirement

$$\forall A \forall x \big[\forall y[\sigma(x, y) \rightarrow A(y)] \rightarrow \forall z[\sigma(x, z) \rightarrow \forall u[\sigma(z, u) \rightarrow A(u)]]\big]$$

is equivalent to the similarity constraint $\forall x \forall z \forall u[(\sigma(x, z) \wedge \sigma(z, u)) \rightarrow \sigma(x, u)]$, i.e., to the transitivity of σ.

18.2. Weakest Sufficient and Strongest Necessary Conditions

18.2.1. Preliminaries. The notion of weakest sufficient and strongest necessary conditions, as discussed here, has been introduced by Lin in [**140**] and generalized by Doherty, Łukaszewicz and Szałas in [**59**] (see also [**55**]). Any sufficient condition can be considered as a lower approximation of a theory and any sufficient condition as its upper approximation, where approximations use a weaker language. Thus weakest sufficient and strongest necessary conditions are best approximations that one can obtain using a weaker language.[1]

DEFINITION 18.7. By *a necessary condition of a formula* α *on the set of relation symbols* P *under theory* T we shall understand any formula β containing only symbols in P such that $T \models \alpha \rightarrow \beta$. It is the *strongest necessary condition*, denoted by SNC $(\alpha; T; P)$ if, additionally, for any necessary condition ψ of α on P under T, we have that $T \models \beta \rightarrow \psi$.   ◁

DEFINITION 18.8. By *a sufficient condition of a formula* α *on the set of relation symbols* P *under theory* T we shall understand any formula β containing only symbols in P such that $T \models \beta \rightarrow \alpha$. It is the *weakest sufficient condition*, denoted by WSC $(\alpha; T; P)$ if, additionally, for any sufficient condition ψ of α on P under T, we have that $T \models \psi \rightarrow \beta$.   ◁

The set P in Definitions 18.7 and 18.8 is referred to as the *target language*.

The approach to compute strongest necessary and weakest sufficient conditions, developed in [**59**], is based on the use of second-order quantifier elimination techniques. According to [**59**], the weakest sufficient condition WSC $(\alpha; Th; P)$ and the strongest necessary condition SNC $(\alpha; Th; P)$ are characterized by the following lemma. It is assumed that theory Th is given by a finite number of axioms.

LEMMA 18.9. For any formula α, any set of relation symbols P and a closed finite theory Th,

$$\text{SNC}(\alpha; Th; P) \equiv \exists \bar{X}[Th \wedge \alpha],$$
$$\text{WSC}(\alpha; Th; P) \equiv \forall \bar{X}[Th \rightarrow \alpha],$$

where $\bar{X}$ consists of all relation symbols appearing in Th and α but not in P.

PROOF. By definition, any necessary condition β for α satisfies $Th \models \alpha \rightarrow \beta$, i.e., by the deduction theorem for first-order logic, also $\models Th \rightarrow (\alpha \rightarrow \beta)$, i.e., $\models (Th \wedge \alpha) \rightarrow \beta$. Thus also $\models \forall \bar{X}[(Th \wedge \alpha) \rightarrow \beta]$. Since β is required not to contain symbols from $\bar{X}$, we have

(237) $\models \exists \bar{X}[Th \wedge \alpha] \rightarrow \beta$.

---

[1]These approximations correspond to rough approximations, i.e., the underlying similarity appears to be an equivalence relation.

On the other hand, the minimal β, satisfying (237) and defining the required strongest necessary condition, is given by the equivalence $\exists \bar{X}[Th \wedge \alpha] \equiv \beta$.

By definition, any sufficient condition β for α satisfies $Th \models \beta \rightarrow \alpha$, i.e., by the deduction theorem for propositional calculus, also $\models Th \rightarrow (\beta \rightarrow \alpha)$, i.e., $\models (Th \wedge \beta) \rightarrow \alpha$. Thus also $\models \forall \bar{X}[(Th \wedge \beta) \rightarrow \alpha]$ which is equivalent to $\models \forall \bar{X}[(Th \wedge \neg \alpha) \rightarrow \neg \beta]$.

Since β is required not to contain symbols from $\bar{X}$, we have

(238) $\models \exists \bar{X}[Th \wedge \neg \alpha] \rightarrow \neg \beta$.

Maximizing β is the same as minimizing $\neg \beta$. On the other hand, the maximal β satisfying (238), defining the required weakest sufficient condition, is given by the equivalence $\exists \bar{X}[Th \wedge \neg \alpha] \equiv \neg \beta$, which is equivalent to $\neg \exists \bar{X}[Th \wedge \neg \alpha] \equiv \beta$, i.e., to $\forall \bar{X}[Th \rightarrow \alpha] \equiv \beta$.   ◁

EXAMPLE 18.10. Consider theory $T_1 = \{\forall x[Ab(x) \rightarrow (B(x) \wedge \neg F(x))]\}$, where B, F stand for "bird" and "flies", respectively. Consider SNC $(Ab(z); T_1; \{B, F\})$. According to Lemma 18.9, it is equivalent to

(239) $\exists Ab[\forall x[Ab(x) \rightarrow (B(x) \wedge \neg F(x))] \wedge Ab(z)]$.

By Lemma 6.1, formula (239) is equivalent to $B(z) \wedge \neg F(z)$.   ◁

EXAMPLE 18.11. Consider $T_2 = \{\forall x[\exists z[F(x, z) \vee M(x, z)] \rightarrow P(x)]\}$, where F, M, P stand for "father", "mother" and "parent", respectively. Consider the condition WSC $(P(y); T_2; \{M, F\})$. According to Lemma 18.9, it is equivalent to

(240) $\forall P[\forall x[\exists z[F(x, z) \vee M(x, z)] \rightarrow P(x)] \rightarrow P(y)]$.

Formula (240) is equivalent to

$$\neg \exists P[\forall x[\exists z[F(x, z) \vee M(x, z)] \rightarrow P(x)] \wedge \neg P(y)],$$

i.e., by an application of Lemma 6.1, to

$$\neg \neg \exists z[F(y, z) \vee M(y, z)]$$

which is equivalent to $\exists z[F(y, z) \vee M(y, z)]$.   ◁

18.2.2. Knowledge Compilation and Theory Approximation. The concept of approximating more complex theories by simpler theories has been studied, e.g., in [31, 59, 124, 140], mainly in the context of approximating arbitrary propositional theories by propositional Horn clauses. The concept of approximate theories is also discussed by McCarthy in [148]. It can easily be observed that strongest necessary and weakest sufficient conditions, as discussed in Section 18.2, provide us with best approximations of theories expressed in a richer language by theories expressed in a simpler language.

EXAMPLE 18.12. This example, in a propositional formulation, has been considered in [**124**] and then in [**59**]. Observe that a move from the propositional to first-order case is straightforward when we use weakest sufficient and strongest necessary conditions.

Consider the following theory T, where $C, Ph, Ps, Cog, RM, RD, RK$ respectively stand for "attends computer science", "attends philosophy", "attends psychology", "attends cognitive science", "reads McCarthy", "reads Dennett" and "reads Kosslyn":

(241) $\forall x[(C(x) \land Ph(x) \land Ps(x)) \to Cog(x)]$

(242) $\forall x[RM(x) \to (C(x) \lor Cog(x))]$

(243) $\forall x[RD(x) \to (Ph(x) \lor Cog(x))]$

(244) $\forall x[RK(x) \to (Ps(x) \lor Cog(x))]$.

Reasoning with this theory was shown to be quite complicated due to the large number of cases. On the other hand, one would like to check, for instance, whether a computer scientist who reads Dennett and Kosslyn is also a cognitive scientist. Reasoning by cases shows that this is true. One can, however, substantially reduce the theory and make the reasoning more efficient. In the first step one notices that Ph and Ps are not used in the query, thus they might appear redundant in the reasoning process. On the other hand, these notions appear in disjunctions in clauses (243) and (244). In this context we might consider

(245)   SNC $(\forall x[C(x) \land RD(x) \land RK(x)]; T; -\{Ph, Ps\})$

where $-\{Ph, Ps\}$ denotes all symbols in the language, other than Ph and Ps.

Formula (245) is equivalent to

$$\exists Ph \exists Ps\{(241) \land (242) \land (243) \land (244) \land$$
$$\forall x[C(x) \land RD(x) \land RK(x)]\}.$$

Performing simple calculations one obtains the following equivalent formula:

$$\forall x[C(x) \land RD(x) \land RK(x)],$$

which implies $\forall x[Cog(x)]$ and, hence, the formula also implies $\forall x[Cog(x)]$.

Assume that one wants to compute the weakest sufficient condition of being a computer scientist in terms of $\{RD, RK, RM, Cog\}$. We then consider

(246)   WSC $(C(x); T; \{RD, RK, RM, Cog\})$.

After eliminating quantifiers over Ph, Ps, C from the second-order formulation of the weakest sufficient condition, one obtains $RM(x) \land \neg Cog(x)$ as the formula equivalent to (246). Thus the weakest condition that, together with theory T, guarantees that a person is a computer scientist is that the person reads McCarthy and is not a cognitive scientist.   ◁

18.2.3. Abduction. As pointed out in [**140, 59**], the weakest abduction can be defined by a weakest sufficient condition.

The weakest sufficient condition corresponds to the weakest abduction.

EXAMPLE 18.13. Consider the theory:

$$T = \{\forall x[R(x) \rightarrow V(x)],$$
$$\forall x[B(x) \rightarrow R(x)]\},$$

where R, V, B stand for "red", "visible" and "ball", respectively.

Assume one wants to check whether an object is visible, the target language is $\{R\}$ and we consider WSC $(V(x); T; \{R\})$, which is equivalent to

$$\forall V \forall B[T \rightarrow V(x)].$$

After eliminating second-order quantifiers we obtain that

$$\text{WSC}\,(V(x); T; \{R\}) \equiv R(x).$$

If the target language is $\{B\}$, we consider WSC $(V(x); T; \{B\})$, which is equivalent to

$$\forall R \forall B[T \rightarrow V(x)].$$

After eliminating second-order quantifiers we obtain that

$$\text{WSC}\,(V(x); T; \{B\}) \equiv B(x).$$

When the target language is $\{R, B\}$, we consider WSC $(V(x); T; \{R, B\})$, which is equivalent to $\forall V[T \rightarrow V(x)]$. After eliminating second-order quantifiers we obtain that WSC $(V(x); T; \{R, B\}) \equiv \forall x[(B(x) \rightarrow R(x)) \rightarrow R(x)]$. ◁

18.2.4. Communication between Agents with Heterogeneous Ontologies. In the case of distributed architectures it is often necessary to exchange information between agents. In large-scale applications it is unavoidable that different agents use different vocabularies or even different ontologies.

Assume thus that agent M knows concepts (relations) $\bar{R}, \bar{S}$ and agent N knows concepts (relations) $\bar{S}, \bar{T}$, i.e., the common vocabulary of M and N consists of relations in $\bar{S}$. Suppose N asks query $A(S, T)$ to agent M, where $S \in \bar{S}$ and $T \in \bar{T}$. Of course, agent M does not know the concept T, but still has to provide a meaningful answer. One can consider at least the following policies for building the communication interface between M and N:

- M might approximate query $A(S, T)$ by "projecting out" the concept T it does not know and answer the query. In this case the resulting answer approximates the query in the sense that due to a more expressive language $A(S, T)$ can be more specific than $A'(S)$ which is obtained by removing T;

- M might ask N to approximate the query $A(S, T)$ by requiring that N "projects out" T and supplies the approximated query fully understood by M;

- M might ask N to approximate concept T and provide the approximation of T (which is a form of explanation provided by N). Based on the approximations of all concepts not understood by M and explained by N, M answers the query.

Of course, the dialogue might be much more advanced here. It is worth observing, however, that due to different knowledge possessed by both agents, in each case the answer might be more or less accurate.

It appears, as shown in **[61]** (for a more detailed discussion, see also **[55]**) that weakest sufficient and strongest necessary conditions can be applied in any of the policies listed above. The following example of **[61]** illustrates the technique.

EXAMPLE 18.14. Assume an agent Ag wants to select from a database all persons x such that $H(x) \vee Silny(x)$ holds. Assume further, that both agents know the terms H and S, standing for "high" and "sound", respectively. Suppose that the database agent does not know the term $Silny$.[2] Suppose, further that Ag lives in a world in which the condition $\forall y.[Silny(y) \to S(y)]$ holds. It is then natural for Ag to use

$$\text{WSC } (H(x) \vee Silny(x); \forall y[Silny(y) \to S(y)]; \{H, S\})$$
$$\text{SNC } (H(x) \vee Silny(x); \forall y[Silny(y) \to S(y)]; \{H, S\})$$

as an approximation to the original query, one that is understood by the database agent that processes the query. According to Lemma 18.9 these conditions are equivalent to

(247) $\forall Silny \{\forall y[Silny(y) \to S(y)] \to (H(x) \vee Silny(x))\}$

(248) $\exists Silny \{\forall y[Silny(y) \to S(y)] \wedge (H(x) \vee Silny(x))\}$.

By applications of Lemma 6.1, formula (247) is equivalent to $H(x)$, and (248) is equivalent to $H(x) \vee S(x)$. Thus, in the given target language and background theory, the set of tuples surely satisfying the original query are those satisfying $H(x)$ and those that might satisfy the original query are those satisfying the disjunction $H(x) \vee S(x)$. In other words, the lower approximation of the original query is $H(x)$ and its upper approximation is $H(x) \vee S(x)$.   ◁

---

[2]In Polish "Silny" means "Strong," but it is assumed that the database agent does not know the Polish language.

CHAPTER 19

Applications in the Semantical Analysis of Conditionals

A conditional is an expressions of the form "if then" (see, e.g., [**81, 194**]). There are various kinds of conditionals that fit into that pattern, such as counter-factual conditionals "if it were the case that α then it would be the case that β", causal conditionals "if α then causally β", etc. What is common to all these constructions is that the antecedent is connected to the consequent in such a way that the antecedent represents a condition or a context for the consequent. A counter-factual conditional is a conditional whose antecedent is false.

In the current chapter we shall discuss conditional reasoning and show applications of clausal second-order quantifier elimination techniques. We first start analyzing known systems and computing correspondences on the basis of Herzig [**106**].

In Section 19.2 we show how techniques can be applied to the approach of Gabbay [**81**]. These techniques are important, since here we deal with second-order quantifier elimination from formulas allowing relations of third order. Therefore we show how direct methods can be extended to cover such cases (see Lemma 7.8, which allows us to deal with relations of arbitrary order). The current chapter is based on the work of Gabbay and Szałas [**85**].

19.1. Language and Semantics

The language of conditionals assumes a basic logic, say $\mathcal{L}$, and extends its syntax by assuming that $\alpha > \beta$ is a formula, if α and β are. In what follows we shall assume that $\mathcal{L}$ is the classical first-order logic.

There are many possible choices as to the semantics. Beginning with the work of Stalnaker and Lewis [**193, 137**] several formal treatments of conditionals have been proposed. Most of them are based on the notion of similarity between possible worlds. Basically, a conditional $\alpha > \beta$ is TRUE in a world s if and only if β is true in every α-world most similar to s. Here we discuss the approach provided in Burgess [**30**], generalizing [**137**]. For the discussion of many other possible choices and results concerning such choices, see Herzig [**106**]. The *Burgess–Lewis* *semantics* is given by assuming a set W of worlds and a ternary relation on W such that for all $s \in W$, a binary relation $R_s(t, u)$ obtained from R by fixing s, is irreflexive and transitive. The intuitive meaning of $R(s, t, u)$ is that t is more similar to s than u. Assume that $\alpha(u)$ means that formula α is true in world u.

We shall consider the semantics with the *limit assumption*, expressed by the following second-order formula:

$$
(249) \quad \forall X \Big\{ \forall w \forall u \big[(X(u) \wedge \exists v R(w, u, v)) \rightarrow \\
\exists u'[X(u') \wedge (u' \approx u \vee R(w, u', u)) \wedge \\
\forall u''[X(u'') \rightarrow \neg R(w, u'', u')]]] \Big\}.
$$

Observe that the above formula can be expressed by means of a fixpoint formula by an application of Theorem 6.19. Namely, (249) is equivalent to

$$
(250) \quad \neg \exists X \Big\{ \exists w \exists u \big[(X(u) \wedge \exists v R(w, u, v)) \wedge \\
\forall u'[X(u') \rightarrow ((u' \not\approx u \wedge \neg R(w, u', u)) \vee \\
\exists u''[X(u'') \wedge R(w, u'', u')]]] \Big\},
$$

i.e., by applying Theorem 6.19, to

$$
(251) \quad \neg \Big\{ \exists w \exists u \exists v R(w, u, v) \wedge \\
[\text{GFP } X(u').(u' \not\approx u \wedge \neg R(w, u', u)) \vee \exists u''[X(u'') \wedge R(w, u'', u')]].
$$

Formula (251) is obviously equivalent to

$$
(252) \quad \forall w \forall u \forall v \Big\{ R(w, u, v) \rightarrow \\
[\text{LFP } X(u').(u' \approx u \vee R(w, u', u)) \wedge \forall u''[R(w, u'', u') \rightarrow X(u'')]] \Big\}.
$$

Let the limit assumption (249) (or, equivalently, (252)) hold. The semantics of $\alpha > \beta$ is then provided by

$$(\alpha > \beta)(w) \text{ is TRUE iff}$$

$$\forall u \Big\{ [\alpha(u) \wedge \exists v R(w, u, v) \wedge \forall s[A(s) \rightarrow \neg R(w, s, u)]] \rightarrow \beta(u) \Big\}.$$

Table 33 provides exemplary correspondences for axioms involving conditionals, obtained by applying SCAN, reported by Herzig in [**106**].

19.2. Another Approach

In [**81**] Gabbay has argued that conditionals often require an approach which differs from those quoted above. In this section we first recall the approach of [**81**] and then show second-order quantifier elimination over conditionals.

TABLE 33. Exemplary correspondences for axioms involving conditionals.

axiom	the corresponding property
$\alpha > \alpha$	TRUE
$\neg(\text{TRUE} > \text{FALSE})$	$\forall w \exists v[(\exists u R(w, u, v)) \rightarrow \exists s R(w, v, s)]$
$(\alpha > \beta) \rightarrow (\alpha \rightarrow \beta)$	$\forall w \forall u[\neg R(w, u, w)] \wedge \forall w \exists v R(w, w, v)$
$(\alpha \wedge \beta) \rightarrow (\alpha > \beta)$	$\forall w \forall u[(\exists v R(w, u, v)) \rightarrow (u \not\approx w \rightarrow R(w, w, u))]$

In the approach of [81] a conditional statement $\alpha > \beta$ asserts that β follows from α under "certain" conditions, which depend on the meaning of α and β and on the properties of the world in which $\alpha > \beta$ was uttered. For example, saying "if I were the president, I would have withdrawn from the East" one means that, the political situation being the same, β follows from α. So in order to falsify that statement, one has to present a possible world where both the general political situation is the same and I am president but where I do not withdraw from the East.

Generally, whenever a statement $\alpha > \beta$ is uttered in a world s, the speaker has in mind a certain set of statements $\Delta(\alpha, \beta, s)$ which is supposed to remain true and the speaker wants to express that in all worlds validating Δ, formula $\alpha \rightarrow \beta$ must hold. The set Δ depends both on α and β, for consider the statements:

(1) If New York were in Georgia, then New York would be in the South;
(2) If New York were in Georgia, then Georgia would be in the North.

Clearly, in the first sentence "Georgia is in the South" must retain its truth value and in the second "New York is in the North" must retain its truth value.

The truth value of $\alpha > \beta$, proposed in [81], is the following:

> $\alpha > \beta$ is TRUE at s iff in all possible worlds in which $\Delta(\alpha, \beta, s)$
> and α are TRUE, β is also TRUE.

If we take $\square$ to mean the modal necessity we get:

$$\alpha > \beta \text{ is TRUE at } s \text{ iff } \square\left(\bigwedge_{\delta \in \Delta(\alpha, \beta, s)} \delta \rightarrow (\alpha \rightarrow \beta) \right).$$

In order to avoid possibly infinite conjunctions, one can use a (third-order) relation $R(X, Y, x, y)$, where X, Y are sets of worlds and x, y are worlds,[1] and define

> $\alpha > \beta$ is TRUE at s iff $\alpha \rightarrow \beta$ is true in all worlds t
> where $R(\alpha(u), \beta(v), s, t)$ holds,

---

[1] The intuitive meaning of relation $R(X, Y, x, y)$ is that the world y is accessible from the world x relative to X and Y.

where u and v are fresh free variables. We understand $\alpha(u)$ and $\beta(v)$ as characteristic formulas for sets of worlds in which these formulas are true. For example, $\alpha(u)$ represents the set $\{u \mid \alpha(u)$ holds $\}$. In what follows we sometimes abuse notation and use set inclusion on formulas, identifying inclusion with the corresponding implication.

The semantics of conditionals can now be defined more precisely,

$$(253) \qquad \begin{aligned} s \models \alpha > \beta \text{ iff for all } t \text{ such that } R(\alpha(u), \beta(v), s, t), \\ \text{we have } t \models \alpha \to \beta. \end{aligned}$$

Since R is third-order, we can follow the direction indicated by Lemmas 7.1 and 7.4 (see pages 88 and 89, respectively). In fact, what we need is to allow relation symbols of third-order, too.

Based on (253) we shall consider a translation of formulas involving conditionals into the formulas of the classical first-order logic. This translation provides a precise semantics of conditionals, as understood further on.

DEFINITION 19.1. The *translation* $Tr(\alpha, x)$, where α is a formula and x is a world, is defined recursively:

$$\begin{aligned} Tr(\alpha, x) &\overset{\text{def}}{=} A(x), \text{ where } \alpha \in V_0 \text{ is a propositional variable and } A \\ &\qquad\qquad\qquad \text{is a unary relation symbol corresponding to } \alpha \\ Tr(\neg\alpha, x) &\overset{\text{def}}{=} \neg Tr(\alpha, x) \\ Tr(\alpha \circ \beta, x) &\overset{\text{def}}{=} Tr(\alpha, x) \circ Tr(\beta, x), \text{ where } \circ \in \{\neg, \vee, \wedge, \to, \equiv\} \\ Tr(\alpha > \beta, x) &\overset{\text{def}}{=} \forall y\big[R(A(u), B(v), x, y) \to \\ &\qquad\qquad\qquad (Tr(\alpha, y) \to Tr(\beta, y))\big], \\ &\qquad \text{where } u, v \text{ are fresh variables.} \qquad\qquad \triangleleft \end{aligned}$$

In order to find correspondences between axioms involving conditionals and properties of the considered accessibility relation we consider third-order formulas of the form $\forall \bar{A} \forall x \big[Tr(\alpha, x)\big]$, where α is the considered axiom and $\bar{A}$ is a sequence consisting of all relation symbols corresponding to propositions in A and introduced by the translation Tr.

In order to apply Lemma 7.8 and Theorem 7.9 we need to know the monotonicity properties of $R(X, Y, s, t)$, where R is the accessibility relation required in (253).

We can first observe that whenever A implies A' (in all worlds) then

$$(A' > B) \to (A > B)$$

should hold, too, meaning that

$$\begin{aligned} \forall y\big[R(A'(u), B(v), x, y) \to \big(A'(y) \to B(y)\big)\big] \to \\ \forall y\big[R(A(u), B(v), x, y) \to \big(A(y) \to B(y)\big)\big]. \end{aligned}$$

Therefore in order to make sure that $A(y) \to B(y)$ holds we would like to use the transitivity of implication and the facts that $A(y) \to A'(y)$ and $A'(y) \to B(y)$. But the latter fact is guaranteed for those y that are accessible from x via $R(A'(u), B(v), x, y)$. Thus $R(A(u), B(v), x, y) \subseteq R(A'(u), B(v), x, y)$ guarantees the desired property. We then assume that

(254) $A \subseteq A'$ implies $R(A(u), B(v), x, y) \subseteq R(A'(u), B(v), x, y)$,

which is up-monotonicity of R w.r.t. its first coordinate.

Also, whenever B implies B' (i.e., $B \subseteq B'$) then

$$(A > B) \to (A > B')$$

should also hold, which means that

$$\forall y \big[R(A(u), B(v), x, y) \to \big(A(y) \to B(y) \big) \big] \to$$
$$\forall y \big[R(A(u), B'(v), x, y) \to \big(A(y) \to B'(y) \big) \big].$$

Similarly to the previous case, we can notice that

$$R(A(u), B'(v), x, y) \subseteq R(A(u), B(v), x, y)$$

guarantees that this formula indeed holds. We then assume that

(255) $B \subseteq B'$ implies $R(A(u), B'(v), x, y) \subseteq R(A(u), B(v), x, y)$,

which is down-monotonicity of R w.r.t. its second coordinate.

Summarizing (254) and (255), we further on assume that R is up-monotone w.r.t. its first argument and down-monotone w.r.t. its second argument. In particular we make these assumptions in Examples 19.2–19.6 below.

19.2.1. Examples. In this section we show some examples of application of the considered technique, based on Gabbay and Szałas [**85**].

EXAMPLE 19.2. Consider the axiom

(256) $\alpha > \alpha$.

According to the semantics given by (253), axiom (256) is equivalent to

$$\forall A \forall x \big[\forall y [R(A(u), A(v), x, y) \to (A(y) \to A(y))] \big].$$

Since $A(y) \to A(y)$ is a tautology, the above formula and therefore also axiom (256), reduces to TRUE.   ◁

EXAMPLE 19.3. Consider the axiom

(257) $(\alpha \wedge \beta) \to (\alpha > \beta)$.

According to the semantics given by (253), axiom (257) is equivalent to

(258) $$\forall A \forall B \forall x \Big[\big(A(x) \wedge B(x) \big) \to \forall y [R(A(u), B(v), x, y) \to$$
$$(A(y) \to B(y))] \Big].$$

Formula (258) is equivalent to

$$\neg \exists A \exists B \exists x \Big[A(x) \wedge B(x) \wedge \exists y \big[R(A(u), B(v), x, y) \wedge A(y) \wedge \neg B(y) \big] \Big],$$

i.e., to

(259) $\neg \exists x \exists y \exists A \exists B \Big[A(x) \wedge B(x) \wedge R(A(u), B(v), x, y) \wedge A(y) \wedge \neg B(y) \Big].$

According to our assumption (254), relation $R(A(u), B(v), x, y)$ is up-monotone w.r.t. A, therefore A can be replaced by TRUE and we obtain the following formula equivalent to (259):

(260) $\neg \exists x \exists y \exists B \Big[R(\text{TRUE}, B(v), x, y) \wedge B(x) \wedge \neg B(y) \Big].$

Now observe that (260) is equivalent to

(261) $\neg \exists x \exists y \exists B \Big[\forall z \big[x \approx z \to B(z) \big] \wedge R(\text{TRUE}, B(v), x, y) \wedge \neg B(y) \Big].$

According to our assumption (255), formula

$$R(\text{TRUE}, B(v), x, y) \wedge \neg B(y)$$

is down-monotone w.r.t. B. Applying Lemma 7.8 we then obtain the following equivalent of (261):

$$\neg \exists x \exists y \Big[R(\text{TRUE}, x \approx v, x, y) \wedge y \not\approx x \Big],$$

which is equivalent to

$$\forall x \forall y \Big[R(\text{TRUE}, x \approx v, x, y) \to y \approx x \Big].$$

Slightly abusing our notation, the above formula is equivalent to

$$\forall x \forall y \Big[R\big(\text{TRUE}, \{x\}, x, y\big) \to y \approx x \Big].$$

Intuitively, our initial axiom (257) requires that the conjunction $A \wedge B$ implies the conditional $A > B$. This means that A should imply B in all worlds accessible from the current world via the relation $R(A(u), B(v), x, y)$, i.e., that

$$\forall y \big[R(A(u), B(v), x, y) \to (A(y) \to B(y)) \big].$$

To see the connection we consider two cases.

If $y \approx x$ then $A(y) \to B(y)$ holds since $A \wedge B$ holds in the current world x which is the same as y.

If $x \not\approx y$ then indeed $R\big(\text{TRUE}, \{x\}, x, y\big)$ should not hold for otherwise we could construct a model for $A \wedge B$ and $\neg(A > B)$, consisting of two worlds $\{x, y\}$ with x being the current world, and satisfying $A(x), A(y), B(x)$ and $\neg B(y)$. Now the set of worlds satisfying A would be $\{x, y\}$ and the set of worlds satisfying B would be $\{x\}$. Thus $R(A(u), B(v), x, y)$ is equivalent to $R(\{x, y\}, \{x\}, x, y)$.

If this was true then y would be accessible from x and $A(y) \to B(y)$ should be TRUE, which is not the case since $A(y)$ is TRUE and $B(y)$ is FALSE.   ◁

EXAMPLE 19.4. Consider the axiom

(262) $(\alpha > \text{TRUE}) \to \neg\alpha.$

According to the semantics given by (253), this formula is equivalent to

$$\forall A \forall x \big[\forall y[R(A(u), \text{TRUE}, x, y) \to (A(y) \to \text{TRUE})] \to \neg A(x)\big],$$

i.e., to $\forall A \forall x[\neg A(x)]$, which, even without eliminating $\forall A$, can be easily seen to be equivalent to FALSE. Therefore there is no frame satisfying axiom (262). On the other hand, (262) should be valid for counter-factuals. Therefore this example shows that, in some cases, counter-factuals cannot be adequately captured by the semantics we consider.

It would be interesting to check what formulas α would make the axiom (262) satisfiable in a frame. We are then interested in checking which formulas A satisfy in the current world x

(263) $\forall y\big[R(A(u), \text{TRUE}, x, y) \to (A(y) \to \text{TRUE})\big] \to \neg A(x),$

and these are exactly those which satisfy $\neg A(x)$, since formula (263) is equivalent to $\neg A(x)$, which is what should have been expected.   ◁

EXAMPLE 19.5. Consider the axiom

(264) $(\text{TRUE} > \alpha) \to \alpha.$

According to the semantics given by (253), this formula is equivalent to

$$\forall A \forall x \Big[\forall y\big[R(\text{TRUE}, A(v), x, y) \to A(y)\big] \to A(x)\Big],$$

i.e., to

$$\neg \exists x \exists A \Big[\forall y\big[\neg R(\text{TRUE}, A(v), x, y) \vee A(y)\big] \wedge \neg A(x)\Big],$$

and further to

(265) $\neg \exists x \exists A \Big[\forall y\big[\neg R(\text{TRUE}, A(v), x, y) \vee A(y)\big] \wedge \forall z[A(z) \to x \not\approx z]\Big].$

Observe that due to the assumption (255), formula $\neg R(\text{TRUE}, A(v), x, y) \vee A(y)$ is up-monotone w.r.t. A. Therefore we can apply Lemma 7.8 and obtain the following formula equivalent to (265):

(266) $\neg \exists x \forall y \big[\neg R(\text{TRUE}, x \not\approx v, x, y) \vee x \not\approx y\big].$

Formula (266) is itself equivalent to $\forall x \exists y \big[R(\text{TRUE}, x \not\approx v, x, y) \wedge x \approx y\big]$, i.e., to $\forall x \big[R(\text{TRUE}, x \not\approx v, x, x)\big]$, or to $\forall x[R(\text{TRUE}, \text{-}\{x\}, x, x)]$ (slightly abusing notation), which is a form of reflexivity $R(A, B, x, x)$ for all A and B such that $x \notin B$ (due to the down-monotonicity of R w.r.t. its arguments). Since TRUE >

TRUE is a tautology, combining this fact with our result we have that $R(A, B, x, x)$ validating axiom (264) holds for any formulas A and B and any world x. ◁

EXAMPLE 19.6. Consider the axiom

(267) $((\alpha > \neg\alpha) \to \neg\alpha) \to (\alpha > \text{FALSE})$.

According to the semantics given by (253), this formula is equivalent to

$$\forall A \forall x \Big[\big[\forall y \big[R(A(u), \neg A(v), x, y) \to (A(y) \to \neg A(y)) \big] \to \neg A(x) \big]$$
$$\to \forall z [R(A(w), \text{FALSE}, x, z) \to (A(z) \to \text{FALSE})] \Big],$$

i.e., to

$$\forall A \forall x \Big[\big[\forall y \big[R(A(u), \neg A(v), x, y) \to \neg A(y) \big] \to \neg A(x) \big] \to$$
$$\forall z [R(A(w), \text{FALSE}, x, z) \to \neg A(z)] \Big],$$

and further to

$$\neg \exists x \exists A \Big[\big[\forall y \big[R(A(u), \neg A(v), x, y) \to \neg A(y) \big] \to \neg A(x) \big] \wedge$$
$$\exists z [R(A(w), \text{FALSE}, x, z) \wedge A(z)] \Big],$$

and to

$$\neg \exists x \exists A \Big[\big[A(x) \to \exists y \big[R(A(u), \neg A(v), x, y) \wedge A(y) \big] \big] \wedge$$
$$\exists z [R(A(w), \text{FALSE}, x, z) \wedge A(z)] \Big],$$

and finally to

$$\neg \exists x \exists A \Big[\forall t \Big[A(t) \to \big(x \not\approx t \vee \exists y \big[R(A(u), \neg A(v), x, y) \wedge A(y) \big] \big) \Big] \wedge$$
$$\exists z [R(A(w), \text{FALSE}, x, z) \wedge A(z)] \Big].$$

By assumptions (254) and (254), $R(A(u), \neg A(v), x, y)$ is up-monotone w.r.t. A. Thus Theorem 7.9 is applicable and results in

$$\neg \exists x \exists z \Big[$$
$$R([\text{GFP } A(t).x \not\approx t \vee \exists y \big[R(A(u), \neg A(v), x, y) \wedge A(y) \big]](w), \text{FALSE}, x, z) \wedge$$
$$[\text{GFP } A(t).x \not\approx t \vee \exists y \big[R(A(u), \neg A(v), x, y) \wedge A(y) \big]](z) \Big],$$

equivalent to

$$\forall x \forall z \Big[$$
$$R([\text{GFP } A(t).x \not\approx t \vee \exists y \big[R(A(u), \neg A(v), x, y) \wedge A(y) \big]](w), \text{FALSE}, x, z) \to$$
$$\neg [\text{GFP } A(t).x \not\approx t \vee \exists y \big[R(A(u), \neg A(v), x, y) \wedge A(y) \big]](z) \Big],$$

being a condition on the class of frames validating the axiom (267). ◁

CHAPTER 20

Applications in Automatizing Duality

Duality theory, from the perspective of non-classical logic [**28**], studies the relationship between the semantics of a logic and its algebra, and the ways to obtain each from the other. Typically, the semantics is defined with reference to some relational structure, like a frame, the corresponding algebra is obtained by a power construction, and from the algebra the model structure can be recovered by imposing a relational structure on the set of ultrafilters. More generally, duality theory studies the relationship between algebras and relational structures without necessarily referring to any logic. The variety of relation algebras is a case in point. These algebras arose in response to the problem posed by Tarski [**205**] of finding equational axioms that would capture the calculus of binary relations, in the same way as the axioms for Boolean algebras capture the calculus of sets. Already Jónsson and Tarski in [**120, 121**] established that relation algebras stand in a duality relationship to generalized Brandt groupoids, and the relationship of algebras of relations to first-order logic was fully presented by Tarski and Givant in [**207**]. A different perspective on duality is that of Stone [**196**], who related Boolean algebras to topological spaces. It appears that the semantics of some logics are in full topological duality to their algebras.

The approach to duality theory presented here is based on Brink, Gabbay and Ohlbach [**26, 27**], where by the use of second-order quantifier elimination it is shown that the correspondence theory and the duality theory are very close to each other.

20.1. Power Structures and Duality

DEFINITION 20.1. Let F denote an operator on sets. F is a *normal* operator if whenever one of the arguments of the operator is the empty set then so is the outcome, i.e., $F(\ldots, \emptyset, \ldots) = \emptyset$. F is *completely additive* if when any of its arguments is an arbitrary union then so is the result, i.e., $F(\ldots, \bigcup_{i \in I} X_i, \ldots) = \bigcup_{i \in I} F(\ldots, X_i, \ldots)$. ◁

DEFINITION 20.2. Let R be an $(n+1)$-arity relation over a set U, i.e., $R \subseteq U^{n+1}$. Define the *power operation* $op(R)$ over R to be the function

$$op(R) : \mathcal{P}(U)^n \longrightarrow \mathcal{P}(U)$$

specified by:

$$y \in op(R)(X_0, \ldots, X_{n-1})$$
$$\text{iff} \quad \exists x_0 \in X_0 \ldots \exists x_{n-1} \in X_{n-1}[R(x_0, \ldots, x_{n-1}, y)].$$

Let $\mathcal{R} = \langle U, R_1, \ldots, R_m \rangle$ be a relational structure. The *power algebra* $\mathcal{B}(U)$ of $\mathcal{R}(U)$ is defined by

$$\mathcal{B}(U) = \langle \mathcal{P}(U), op(R_1), \ldots, op(R_m) \rangle. \qquad \triangleleft$$

THEOREM 20.3. (Jónsson and Tarski [**120, 121**]) Any Boolean algebra with operators is isomorphic to a subalgebra of the power algebra of some relational structure.

$\triangleleft$

This theorem tells us that Boolean algebras with operators arise from power algebras, extended with the Boolean set operations of intersection, union and complement, of relational structures, and gives a representation theorem.

DEFINITION 20.4. Let U be a set. For any n-ary operator $F : \mathcal{P}(U)^n \longrightarrow \mathcal{P}(U)$, the *base relation* $rel(F)$ underlying F is defined by

$$rel(F)(x_0, \ldots, x_{n-1}, y) \quad \text{iff} \quad y \in F(\{x_0\}, \ldots, \{x_{n-1}\}).$$

For any Boolean algebra $\mathcal{B}$ with operators $F_1, \ldots, F_m$, the underlying *relational structure* is defined by $\mathcal{R} = \langle U, rel(F_1), \ldots, rel(F_m) \rangle$. $\triangleleft$

THEOREM 20.5.

(1) Given any relation $R \subseteq U^{n+1}$, the base relation of the power operation of R is R, i.e., $rel(op(R)) = R$.
(2) If $F : \mathcal{P}(U)^n \longrightarrow \mathcal{P}(U)$ is a normal, completely additive operator then the power operation of the base relation of F is F, i.e., $op(rel(F)) = F$.

$\triangleleft$

20.2. Algebras Related to Modal Logic

How do the properties of power operators and their base relations translate to each other? The following result is a correspondence theorem for unary operators and binary relations.

THEOREM 20.6. (Brink [**25**])

(1) Suppose $F : \mathcal{P}(U) \longrightarrow \mathcal{P}(U)$ is any normal, completely additive operator. If R is the base relation of F, i.e., $R \subseteq U^2$ and $R = rel(F)$, then in each of the cases in Table 34, property (b) implies property (a).

TABLE 34. Correspondences between properties of unary operators and properties of binary relations.

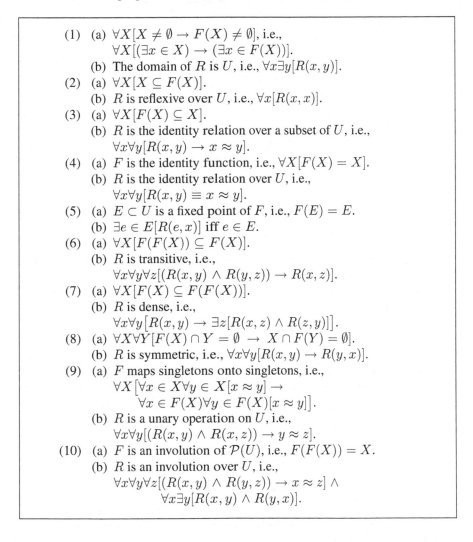

(1)   (a) $\forall X[X \neq \emptyset \rightarrow F(X) \neq \emptyset]$, i.e.,
            $\forall X[(\exists x \in X) \rightarrow (\exists x \in F(X))]$.
    (b) The domain of R is U, i.e., $\forall x \exists y[R(x, y)]$.

(2)   (a) $\forall X[X \subseteq F(X)]$.
    (b) R is reflexive over U, i.e., $\forall x[R(x, x)]$.

(3)   (a) $\forall X[F(X) \subseteq X]$.
    (b) R is the identity relation over a subset of U, i.e.,
            $\forall x \forall y[R(x, y) \rightarrow x \approx y]$.

(4)   (a) F is the identity function, i.e., $\forall X[F(X) = X]$.
    (b) R is the identity relation over U, i.e.,
            $\forall x \forall y[R(x, y) \equiv x \approx y]$.

(5)   (a) $E \subset U$ is a fixed point of F, i.e., $F(E) = E$.
    (b) $\exists e \in E[R(e, x)]$ iff $e \in E$.

(6)   (a) $\forall X[F(F(X)) \subseteq F(X)]$.
    (b) R is transitive, i.e.,
            $\forall x \forall y \forall z[(R(x, y) \wedge R(y, z)) \rightarrow R(x, z)]$.

(7)   (a) $\forall X[F(X) \subseteq F(F(X))]$.
    (b) R is dense, i.e.,
            $\forall x \forall y[R(x, y) \rightarrow \exists z[R(x, z) \wedge R(z, y)]]$.

(8)   (a) $\forall X \forall Y[F(X) \cap Y = \emptyset \rightarrow X \cap F(Y) = \emptyset]$.
    (b) R is symmetric, i.e., $\forall x \forall y[R(x, y) \rightarrow R(y, x)]$.

(9)   (a) F maps singletons onto singletons, i.e.,
            $\forall X[\forall x \in X \forall y \in X[x \approx y] \rightarrow$
                $\forall x \in F(X) \forall y \in F(X)[x \approx y]]$.
    (b) R is a unary operation on U, i.e.,
            $\forall x \forall y[(R(x, y) \wedge R(x, z)) \rightarrow y \approx z]$.

(10) (a) F is an involution of $\mathcal{P}(U)$, i.e., $F(F(X)) = X$.
    (b) R is an involution over U, i.e.,
            $\forall x \forall y \forall z[(R(x, y) \wedge R(y, z)) \rightarrow x \approx z] \wedge$
                $\forall x \exists y[R(x, y) \wedge R(y, x)]$.

(2) Conversely, let $R \subseteq U^2$ be any binary relation over U and let F be the power operation of R, i.e., $F : \mathcal{P}(U) \longrightarrow \mathcal{P}(U)$ and $F = op(R)$. Then F is normal and completely additive, and in each of the cases in Table 34, property (a) implies property (b).   ◁

TABLE 35. Modal axioms corresponding to properties in Table 34.

(1) $\Diamond$TRUE
(2) $X \rightarrow \Diamond X$.
(3) $\Diamond X \rightarrow X$.
(4) $\Diamond X \equiv X$.
(5) non-logical axiom: $\Diamond E \equiv E$.
(6) $\Diamond\Diamond X \rightarrow \Diamond X$.
(7) $\Diamond X \equiv \Diamond\Diamond X$.
(8) $\Diamond\neg\Diamond\neg X \rightarrow X$, i.e., $\Diamond\Box X \rightarrow X$.
(9) $\Diamond X \rightarrow \neg\Diamond\neg X$, i.e., $\Diamond X \rightarrow \Box X$.
(10) $\Diamond\Diamond X \equiv X$.

The definition of F in terms of R, as the power operation of R, is

$$y \in F(X) \quad \text{iff} \quad \exists x[R(x,y) \wedge x \in X].$$

Comparing this definition with the semantics of the $\Diamond$ operator of modal logic, an immediate connection is apparent. Recall, the definition of the semantics of the $\Diamond$ operator (Definition 10.3), here reformulated using the view of formulas as sets of worlds in which they are true:

$$x \models \Diamond X \quad \text{iff} \quad \exists y[R(x,y) \wedge y \in X].$$

It is clear that the function F is the algebraic version of the $\Diamond$ operator of modal logic modulo the arguments of the R relation being exchanged. In fact F corresponds to the $\Diamond^{\smile}$ operator of modal tense logic. F is the pre-image operator while the operator corresponding to the $\Diamond$ operator is the image operator. This difference is not crucial though. The dual operator of F corresponding to the modal $\Box^{\smile}$ operator is defined by:

$$y \in \overline{F(\overline{X})} \quad \text{iff} \quad \forall x[R(x,y) \rightarrow x \in X].$$

$\overline{X}$ denotes the complement of X, i.e., $\overline{X} = U \backslash X$.

The modal axioms corresponding to the algebraic properties in Table 34 are given in Table 35. In the table the X, Y denote universally quantified variables, while E in (5) denotes a constant.

Theorem 20.6 therefore tells us something out the duality between the algebras corresponding to modal logics and the induced relational structures. Consider for instance closure algebras [120] which are the algebras of the modal logic S4. The Kripke semantics of S4 is given by the theory of quasi-orders (a quasi-order is a binary relation which is reflexive and transitive). Analogously, Theorem 20.6 tells us that from any S4 relational structure, or frame, $\langle U, R \rangle$ with a set of worlds U

and a quasi-order R, one obtains the corresponding closure algebra

$$\mathcal{B}(U) = \langle \mathcal{P}(U), op(R) \rangle$$

with closure operator $op(R)$. Conversely, from any closure algebra $\mathcal{B}(U) = \langle \mathcal{P}(U), F \rangle$ over the powerset of U, one obtains a corresponding relational structure $\mathcal{R} = \langle U, rel(F) \rangle$ with quasi-order $rel(F)$, and axioms representing properties (a) of 2 and 6 translate to the respective properties (b) in Table 34.

20.3. Algebras Related to Relevance Logic

Boolean algebras with binary operators can be related to the relevance logic $\mathbf{R}^{\neg}$ (see Brink [25]). $\mathbf{R}^{\neg}$ is the extension of the relevance logic $\mathbf{R}$ of Anderson and Belnap [3] with a Boolean negation operation $\neg$. The semantics of $\mathbf{R}^{\neg}$ is given by relational Kripke structures and the algebraic version of the logic is the class of $\mathbf{R}^{\neg}$-algebras.

DEFINITION 20.7. [25] An $\mathbf{R}^{\neg}$-*Kripke structure* is a relational structure $\mathcal{U} = \langle U, R, {}^{*}, E \rangle$ where $R \subseteq U^3$, $E \subseteq U$ and $^{*} : U \longrightarrow U$ are such that the following hold.

(1) R is totally reflexive, i.e., $\forall x[R(x, x, x)]$.
(2) R is $(1, 2)$-symmetric, i.e., $\forall x \forall y \forall z[R(x, y, z) \rightarrow R(y, x, z)]$.
(3) R has identity elements in E, i.e., $\forall x \forall y \big[\exists e \in E[R(e, x, y)] \equiv x \approx y\big]$.
(4) R^2 is associative, i.e.,
$$\forall x \forall y \forall z \forall u \big[\exists v[R(x, y, v) \land R(v, z, u)] \equiv \\ \exists w[R(x, w, u) \land R(y, z, w)]\big].$$
(5) * is an involution, i.e., $\forall x[x^{**} \approx x]$.
(6) $\forall x \forall y \forall z[R(x, y, z) \rightarrow R(x, z^{*}, y^{*})]$.   ◁

DEFINITION 20.8. [25] An $\mathbf{R}^{\neg}$-*algebra* is an algebra $\mathcal{A} = \langle A, \lor, \neg, 1, \circ, {}^{*}, e \rangle$ such that the following hold for any $a, b \in A$.

(1) $\langle A, \lor, \neg, 1 \rangle$ is a Boolean algebra.
(2) * is an involution, i.e., $a^{**} \approx a$.
(3) * is additive, i.e., $(a \lor b)^{*} \approx a^{*} \lor b^{*}$.
(4) $\langle A, \circ, e \rangle$ is a commutative monoid (i.e., $\circ$ is an commutative, associative operation with identity e).
(5) $\circ$ is upper semi-idempotent, i.e., $a \leq a \circ a$ (where $\leq$ is the usual lattice ordering of the Boolean algebra).
(6) $a \circ b^{*} \leq \neg c$ iff $a \circ c^{*} \leq \neg b$.   ◁

An $\mathbf{R}^{\neg}$-algebra is a Boolean algebra with operators [25].

The constructions for the correspondence results and the representation theorem use power operations of relations but also power operations of operations [25].

DEFINITION 20.9. Let g be an n-ary operation over a set U, i.e., $g : U^n \longrightarrow U$. The *power operation* $op(g)$ over g is the function $op(g) : \mathcal{P}(U)^n \longrightarrow \mathcal{P}(U)$ given by:

$$op(g)(X_0, \ldots, X_{n-1}) = \{g(x_0, \ldots, x_{n-1}) \mid x_i \in X_i, 0 \leq i < n\}.$$

Let $\mathcal{U} = \langle U, g_1, \ldots, g_m \rangle$ be an algebra with a finite number of finitary operations. Then its *power algebra* is the algebra $\mathcal{P}(\mathcal{U})$ defined by

$$\mathcal{P}(\mathcal{U}) = \langle \mathcal{P}(U), \cup, -, U, op(g_1), \ldots, op(g_m) \rangle,$$

where $\cup, -$ denote set-theoretic union and complement.   ◁

We define $\circ$ as the power operation of the relation R by

$$X \circ Y = op(R)(X, Y) = \{z \mid \exists x \exists y [R(x, y, z) \wedge x \in X \wedge y \in Y]\}$$

and $\star$ as the power relation of the operation $*$ by

$$X^\star = op(\star)(X) = \{x^* \mid x \in X\}.$$

The next theorem correlates properties of R and $\circ$. We formulate the theorem more generally for any binary operator and any ternary relation. That is, the definition of F in terms of R, as the power operation of R, is

(268) $z \in F(X, Y)$ iff $\exists x \exists y [R(x, y, z) \wedge x \in X \wedge y \in Y].$

THEOREM 20.10. [25]

    (1) Let $F : \mathcal{P}(U)^2 \longrightarrow \mathcal{P}(U)$ be any normal, completely additive operator and let R be the base relation of F, i.e., $R \subseteq U^3$ and $R = rel(F)$. Then, in each of the cases in Table 36, property (b) implies property (a).

    (2) Conversely, let $R \subseteq U^3$ be any binary relation over U and let F be the power operation of R, i.e., $F : \mathcal{P}(U)^2 \longrightarrow \mathcal{P}(U)$ and $F = op(R)$. Then, F is normal and completely additive, and in each of the cases in Table 36, property (a) implies property (b).   ◁

Theorem 20.11 provides the correlation between properties of $*$ and properties of $\star$.

THEOREM 20.11. Let $G : \mathcal{P}(U) \longrightarrow \mathcal{P}(U)$ be the power operation of an operation $g : U \longrightarrow U$ defined by

(269) $G(X) = \{g(x) \mid x \in X\}$

and F the power operation of a binary relation R over U. Then, in each of the following cases, properties (a) and (b) are equivalent.

    (1) (a) $\forall X [X \subseteq G(G(X))].$
        (b) $\forall x [x \approx g(g(x))].$

TABLE 36. Correspondences between properties of binary operators and properties of ternary relations.

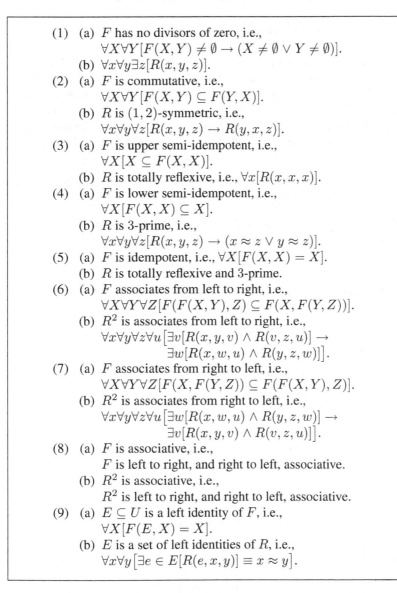

(1) (a) F has no divisors of zero, i.e.,
$$\forall X \forall Y [F(X,Y) \neq \emptyset \rightarrow (X \neq \emptyset \vee Y \neq \emptyset)].$$
(b) $\forall x \forall y \exists z [R(x,y,z)].$

(2) (a) F is commutative, i.e.,
$$\forall X \forall Y [F(X,Y) \subseteq F(Y,X)].$$
(b) R is $(1,2)$-symmetric, i.e.,
$$\forall x \forall y \forall z [R(x,y,z) \rightarrow R(y,x,z)].$$

(3) (a) F is upper semi-idempotent, i.e.,
$$\forall X [X \subseteq F(X,X)].$$
(b) R is totally reflexive, i.e., $\forall x [R(x,x,x)].$

(4) (a) F is lower semi-idempotent, i.e.,
$$\forall X [F(X,X) \subseteq X].$$
(b) R is 3-prime, i.e.,
$$\forall x \forall y \forall z [R(x,y,z) \rightarrow (x \approx z \vee y \approx z)].$$

(5) (a) F is idempotent, i.e., $\forall X [F(X,X) = X].$
(b) R is totally reflexive and 3-prime.

(6) (a) F associates from left to right, i.e.,
$$\forall X \forall Y \forall Z [F(F(X,Y),Z) \subseteq F(X,F(Y,Z))].$$
(b) R^2 is associates from left to right, i.e.,
$$\forall x \forall y \forall z \forall u \big[\exists v [R(x,y,v) \wedge R(v,z,u)] \rightarrow$$
$$\exists w [R(x,w,u) \wedge R(y,z,w)] \big].$$

(7) (a) F associates from right to left, i.e.,
$$\forall X \forall Y \forall Z [F(X,F(Y,Z)) \subseteq F(F(X,Y),Z)].$$
(b) R^2 is associates from right to left, i.e.,
$$\forall x \forall y \forall z \forall u \big[\exists w [R(x,w,u) \wedge R(y,z,w)] \rightarrow$$
$$\exists v [R(x,y,v) \wedge R(v,z,u)] \big].$$

(8) (a) F is associative, i.e.,
F is left to right, and right to left, associative.
(b) R^2 is associative, i.e.,
R^2 is left to right, and right to left, associative.

(9) (a) $E \subseteq U$ is a left identity of F, i.e.,
$$\forall X [F(E,X) = X].$$
(b) E is a set of left identities of R, i.e.,
$$\forall x \forall y \big[\exists e \in E [R(e,x,y)] \equiv x \approx y \big].$$

(2)   (a) $\forall X \forall Y \forall Z[F(X, G(Y)) \subseteq \overline{Z}$ iff $F(X, G(Z)) \subseteq \overline{Y}]$.
      (b) $\forall x \forall y \forall z[R(x, g(y), z) \rightarrow R(x, g(z), y)]$.   ◁

20.4. A Framework for Automating Duality

We are interested in the duality problem, i.e., determining the corresponding properties between an operation F and its underlying base relation R, or conversely between a relation and the corresponding power operation F. We now describe the framework of Brink, Gabbay and Ohlbach [27] within which the duality problem can be solved automatically. A case study which uses the framework for automatically computing the correspondences of Theorems 20.6 and 20.10 shows that the method works.

The duality problem comprises four subproblems. In the *top-down direction* (from (a) to (b) in Tables 34 and 20.10):

- Given a property (a) of F, find a suitable property (b) for R.
- Verify the equivalence of (a) and (b).

In the *bottom-up direction* (from (b) to (a) in Table 34 and 20.10):

- Given a property (b) of R, find a suitable property (a) for F.
- Verify the equivalence of (a) and (b).

The top-down direction is a problem of *second-order quantifier elimination*. This sequence of steps solves the problem.

- Define F in terms of R by:

  $Def(F, R)$:
  $\quad y \in F(X_0, \ldots, X_{n-1}) \quad$ iff
  $\quad\quad \exists x_0 \in X_0 \ldots \exists x_{n-1} \in X_{n-1}[R(x_0, \ldots, x_{n-1}, y)]$.

- Formulate the property (a) logically, as a formula $Fprop(F)$.
- Eliminate F from $Fprop(F)$, using the equivalence $Def(F, R)$ from left to right.
- Apply second-order quantifier elimination.

If the last step is successful the outcome is a property $Rprop(R)$ of R. The following then holds:

(270) $Def(F, R) \rightarrow (Fprop(F) \equiv Rprop(R))$.

Brink et al. [27] use the SCAN algorithm based on C-resolution for the last step, but the DLS algorithm or H-resolution can be used equally well.

The bottom-up direction of the duality problem is a problem of *second-order quantifier introduction*. The aim is to derive the property of the operation F from the property of the relation and the definition of F in terms of R. That is, we want to derive $Fprop(F)$ from $Rprop(R)$ and $Def(F, R)$ so that (270) holds. The bottom-direction therefore amounts to computing $Fprop(F)$ using *back-translation*. The framework of [27] uses two different methods.

The first method exploits that the property (270) is implied by this property

$$(271) \qquad \exists R[Def(F, R) \land Rprop(R)] \equiv Fprop(F),$$

for the particular R and $Fprop(F)$. A second-order quantifier elimination method can be used to eliminate the existentially quantified relation symbol R from

$$\exists R[Def(F, R) \land Rprop(R)],$$

the left-hand side of (271). If this succeeds then the formula returned has to be verified with the top-down method. If this succeeds then (270) is established.

Unfortunately, this method succeeds only in relatively few, simple cases. It does not succeed for example for the transitivity property [27].

The second method described in [27] uses first-order logic as a meta-framework and a first-order resolution theorem prover is used to generate the required property from a first-order encoding of $Def(F, R)$ and $Rprop(R)$. In particular, the encoding uses is a syntactic translation in which formulas are encoded as first-order terms and quantification of the set variables is encoded as first-order quantification of first-order variables. The problem specification consists of these parts:

- Semantic equivalences, determining the semantic encoding of all the classical connectives as functions.
- An equivalence encoding the definition of F, $Def(F, R)$, so that F is a function applied to terms.
- A suitable encoding of the relational property $Rprop(R)$.

Now answer resolution [37] is used to generate candidates for $Fprop(F)$. The problem specification defines the theory and answer resolution provides a method for automatically enumerating the theorems in the theory. Being an enumeration method, this approach produces a lot of theorems many of them are useless for answering the back-translation problem. Heuristic guidance of the theorem prover is therefore crucial to the success of this approach. In their case study Brink et al. [26, 27] show that standard theorem proving techniques and control mechanisms available in existing provers are sufficient to use this approach very successfully for actually generating the expected properties. Crucial to the success is that the scarch space of the prover is limited. This is done by limiting the number of connectives defined in the problem specification, limiting the size of terms representing formulas through assigning large weights to nested terms and using demodulation to completely prevent the nesting of certain functions. The OTTER theorem prover which supports these features was used in the case study. We direct the reader interested in details to [**26**].

Both of these back-translation approaches are different from the MSQIN approach described in Chapter 14. Using the MSQIN procedure, and a suitable generalization (which is possible), would present an alternative solution.

20.4.1. Examples. We conclude this chapter with examples illustrating the application of second-order quantifier elimination methods for the top-down direction of the framework, i.e., computing the correspondence properties of $\mathbf{R}^\neg$-Kripke structures.

EXAMPLE 20.12. We verify the equivalence (6) of Table 36. Using the Definition (268) of F in terms of R, the encoding in first-order logic of

$$F(F(X,Y),Z) \subseteq F(X,F(Y,Z))$$

is

$$\forall x \Big[\exists y \exists z [R(y,z,x) \wedge \exists u \exists v [R(u,v,y) \wedge X(u) \wedge Y(v)] \wedge Z(z)]$$
$$\to \exists y \exists z [R(y,z,x) \wedge X(y) \wedge$$
$$\exists u \exists v [R(u,v,z) \wedge Y(u) \wedge Z(v)]] \Big].$$

This is $Fprop(F)$ with F already eliminated. The predicates X, Y, Z are universally quantified and the aim now is to eliminate them. We use SCAN for this. Negating the formula we get

$$\exists x \Big[\exists y \exists z [R(y,z,x) \wedge \exists u \exists v [R(u,v,y) \wedge X(u) \wedge Y(v)] \wedge Z(z)]$$
$$\wedge \neg (\exists y \exists z [R(y,z,x) \wedge X(y) \wedge$$
$$\exists u \exists v [R(u,v,z) \wedge Y(u) \wedge Z(v)]]) \Big].$$

The input clauses to SCAN are therefore:

1. $R(b,c,a)$
2. $R(d,e,b)$
3. $X(d)$
4. $Y(e)$
5. $Z(c)$
6. $\neg R(y,z,a) \vee \neg X(y) \vee \neg R(u,v,z) \vee \neg Y(u) \vee \neg Z(v)$

Now use C-resolution, constraint elimination and purity deletion to eliminate X, Y and Z:

$$7.\ \neg R(y, z, a) \lor y \not\approx d \lor \neg R(u, v, z) \qquad\qquad 3.1, 6.2$$
$$\lor \neg Y(u) \lor \neg Z(v)$$

$$8.\ \neg R(d, z, a) \lor \neg R(u, v, z) \lor \neg Y(u) \lor \neg Z(v) \qquad 7, \text{c-elim.}$$

$$9.\ \neg R(d, z, a) \lor \neg R(e, v, z) \lor \neg Z(v) \qquad\qquad 4.1, 8.3, \text{c-elim.}$$

$$10.\ \neg R(d, z, a) \lor \neg R(e, c, z) \qquad\qquad\qquad 5.1, 9.3, \text{c-elim.}$$

SCAN returns the clauses 1, 2 and 10. Unskolemization is not difficult and gives:

$$\exists x \exists y \exists z \exists u \exists v \forall w [$$
$$R(y, z, x) \land R(u, v, y) \land (\neg R(u, w, x) \lor \neg R(v, z, w))],$$

equivalently

$$\exists x \exists y \exists z \left[R(y, z, x) \land \right.$$
$$\left. \exists u \exists v \left[R(u, v, y) \land \forall w [\neg R(u, w, x) \lor \neg R(v, z, w)] \right] \right].$$

Negating again we obtain

$$\forall x \forall y \forall z \left[\neg R(y, z, x) \lor \right.$$
$$\left. \forall u \forall v \left[\neg R(u, v, y) \lor \exists w [R(u, w, x) \land R(v, z, w)] \right] \right].$$

This can be equivalently rewritten to give us

$$\forall x \forall y \left[\exists v \left[R(x, y, v) \land \right. \right.$$
$$\left. \left. \forall z \forall u [R(v, z, u)] \to \exists w [R(x, w, u) \land R(y, z, w)] \right] \right],$$

which is what we wanted. $\triangleleft$

In the next two examples we use SCAN to verify the correlation between $\star$ and $*$ as stated in general terms in Theorem 20.11, as correlations between G and g. These show that second-order quantifier elimination methods can successfully be used to compute equivalent properties for power operations of relations as well as power operations of operators. These have not been considered in [26, 27].

EXAMPLE 20.13. Using the definition of G in terms of g given in (269), the encoding of $\forall X[X \subseteq G(G(X))]$ in first-order logic is:

$$\forall x \left[X(x) \to \exists u \exists v [X(v) \land u \approx g(v) \land x \approx g(u)] \right].$$

Negating and transforming into clausal form we get:

1. $X(a)$

2. $\neg X(y) \vee x \not\approx g(y) \vee a \not\approx g(x)$

One resolution step gives

3. $x \not\approx g(a) \vee a \not\approx g(x)$.

This simplifies to $a \not\approx g(g(a))$. Now restore the quantifier and negate. We get the required property $\forall x[x \approx g(g(x))]$. ◁

EXAMPLE 20.14. In this example we show (2) of Theorem 20.11. We prove that

$$\forall X \forall Y \forall Z \left[F(X, G(Y)) \subseteq \overline{Z} \text{ implies } F(X, G(Z)) \subseteq \overline{Y} \right]$$

equivalently reduces to $\forall x \forall y \forall z \left[R(x, g(y), z) \rightarrow R(x, g(z), y) \right]$. The equivalence of the conditions (6) of Definitions 20.7 and 20.8 now follows from the fact that g (i.e., $*$) is an involution.

Proceeding in the usual way we formulate the negation of the property (a) as a first-order formula, eliminate the operators F and G and apply a second-order quantifier elimination method. We get the clauses

1. $\neg R(y, z, x) \vee \neg X(y) \vee Y(u) \vee z \not\approx g(u) \vee \neg Z(x)$

2. $R(b, c, a)$

3. $X(b)$

4. $Z(d)$

5. $c \approx g(d)$

6. $Y(a)$

Applying SCAN reduces the problem (in several steps) to the set containing

7. $\neg R(b, z, d) \vee z \not\approx g(a)$

8. $R(b, c, a)$

9. $c \approx g(d)$

Clause 7. can be replaced by

10. $\neg R(b, g(a), d)$

Using 8. and 9. we derive

11. $R(b, g(d), a)$

What remains are clauses 10. and 11. Restoring quantifiers and applying negation gives us the required property. ◁

CHAPTER 21

Other Applications in Logic and Mathematics

In this chapter we show several applications of second-order quantifier elimination in classical logic and mathematics. The techniques are more general in that they can be applied in non-classical logics equipped with second-order semantics, provided that second-order quantifier elimination techniques are available for such logics. In particular we show applications to computing interpolants, structural transformation, give an analysis of specific second-order axioms and briefly mention further applications.

21.1. Computing Interpolants

21.1.1. Preliminaries. Given two languages L_1 and L_2 (with L the common language) and a consequence relation $\vdash$ on $L_1 \cup L_2$, we can formulate the interpolation property as follows:

- If $\alpha \vdash \beta$, with α a formula in L_1 and β in L_2, then there exists an H in L such that $\alpha \vdash H \vdash \beta$.

What we mean by common language L can vary.

(i) L may contain only constants, predicates and variables that are common to α and to β.
(ii) L may contain only connectives and quantifiers that are common to α and β.
(iii) L may contain refinements about the form of occurrence of the common items in α and β and how they appear in H (positive, negative, free, etc.).

It was Craig [46] who proposed and proved interpolation for classical first-order logic. Improvements along the lines of (iii) were put forward by Lyndon [143]. See Gabbay and Maksimova [83] for the most recent account.

The interpolation property was found important not only in formal developments of logic, but also in computer science applications. A summary of the rôle of the interpolation property in computer science and formal methods is given in [19].

Interpolation has important applications, including to the following areas:

- Automated theorem proving: in the case when a candidate for interpolant is found, the proof of the implication is often significantly simplified.
- Specification theory: interpolation is linked to modularization, information hiding, proof decomposition in the verification of complex software systems.
- Detection of information flow: in the case of interfacing highly secure software systems with less secure systems it is important to detect what information is revealed to the less secure systems. In such a case all interpolants occurring in reasoning about the interface should already be deducible by means of the less secure system.

One can easily observe that the interpolants can be expressed by means of second-order quantification. Namely, assume that $\alpha(\bar{P}, \bar{Q}) \rightarrow \beta(\bar{R}, \bar{Q})$ is a tautology of a given logic, where $\bar{Q}$ represents the common vocabulary. This means that $\forall \bar{P} \forall \bar{R}[\alpha(\bar{P}, \bar{Q}) \rightarrow \beta(\bar{R}, \bar{Q})]$ is a tautology of the second-order version of the considered logic. Thus

$$\exists \bar{P}[\alpha(\bar{P}, \bar{Q})] \rightarrow \beta(\bar{R}, \bar{Q}) \text{ as well as } \alpha(\bar{P}, \bar{Q}) \rightarrow \forall \bar{R}[\beta(\bar{R}, \bar{Q})]$$

are tautologies, too. Both $\exists \bar{P}[\alpha(\bar{P}, \bar{Q})]$ and $\forall \bar{R}[\beta(\bar{R}, \bar{Q})]$ are then interpolants. The question arises whether the interpolants can be expressed in the original language, i.e., whether the second-order quantification can be eliminated.

It is worth emphasizing here that the second-order characterization of interpolants is rather general and gives the possibility to compute interpolants for particular pairs of formulas even if the considered logic does not have the interpolation property. This follows from the fact that lack of an interpolation property means that there are pairs of formulas such that one implies the other but interpolants might still exist for many other pairs, even for the majority or all of the pairs of interest for a given application area.

It is worth emphasizing that the standard way of computing interpolants by extracting them from the proof of the implication in question, or using methods based on guessing models tend to be more complex than methods based on second-order quantifier elimination. Second-order quantifier elimination methods have the advantage that interpolants can be computed and returned directly.

There is another important point. Even if no interpolant exists for a pair of formulas in the native language or it exists but is hard to compute, it might still be useful to have it defined by means of fixpoints. Consider, for example, databases. Then, in a given logic, the interpolant one needs might not exist or be hard to compute, but second-order quantifier elimination might result in a fixpoint formula. On the other hand, from the point of view of querying a database, fixpoint formulas often have deterministic polynomial time complexity while second-order formulas end up at least in NPTIME.

21.1.2. Examples. The following examples illustrate the method.

EXAMPLE 21.1. Consider the following implication

$$\left.\begin{array}{l} \forall x[R(x) \to S(x)] \\ \land\ R(a) \\ \land\ \forall y[S(y) \to T(y)] \end{array}\right\} \to \exists y[S(y) \land T(y)].$$

It is a tautology of classical first-order logic. Therefore there exists an interpolant I such that formulas

$$\forall x[R(x) \to S(x)] \land R(a) \land \forall y[S(y) \to T(y)] \to I,$$
$$I \to \exists y[S(y) \land T(y)]$$

are both tautologies. In order to compute I we note that it can be expressed by the second-order formula

(272) $\exists R\{\forall x[R(x) \to S(x)] \land R(a) \land \forall y[S(y) \to T(y)]\}.$

Applying the lemma of Ackermann (Lemma 6.1) we obtain that

$$S(a) \land \forall y[S(y) \to T(y)],$$

which is equivalent to (272), and thus one possible interpolant. ◁

EXAMPLE 21.2. Consider the implication

$$\left.\begin{array}{l} \forall x \forall y\big[R(x) \to \big(S(x,y) \to (R(y) \land T(y))\big)\big] \\ \land\ R(a) \\ \land\ \forall x \exists y[S(x,y)] \end{array}\right\} \to \exists y[S(a,y) \land T(y)]$$

and the corresponding second-order formulation of an interpolant,

$$\exists R\{\forall x \forall y\big[R(x) \to \big(S(x,y) \to (R(y) \land T(y))\big)\big] \land R(a) \land \forall x \exists y[S(x,y)]\}.$$

In such a case neither DLS nor SCAN succeed to eliminate $\exists R$. However, DLS* applying Theorem 6.19, returns in this case

$$[\text{GFP }R(x).\forall y[S(x,y) \to (R(y) \land T(y))]](a) \land \forall x \exists y[S(x,y)]\}. \quad ◁$$

21.2. Structural Transformation

Conversion to conjunctive normal form (and therefore clausal form) may produce a formula whose size is exponential in the size of the original formula. The cause for the exponential blow-up is the rule based on distributivity of disjunction over conjunction. Standard, more efficient transformations into clausal form use structural transformation or formula renaming to avoid this blow-up [**24, 168, 208**]. We follow here the presentations found in, e.g., De Nivelle, Schmidt and Hustadt [**50**] as well as in Schmidt and Hustadt [**184**].

Let $\mathrm{Pos}(\alpha)$ be the set of positions of a first-order formula α. If λ is a position in α, then $\alpha|_\lambda$ denotes the subformula of α at position λ and $\alpha(\lambda/\beta)$ is the result of replacing $\alpha|_\lambda$ at position λ by β.

DEFINITION 21.3. *Structural transformation* associates with each element λ of $\Lambda \subseteq \mathrm{Pos}(\alpha)$ a relation symbol Q_λ and a literal $Q_\lambda(x_1,\ldots,x_n)$, where $x_1,\ldots,x_n$ are the free variables of $\alpha|_\lambda$, the symbol Q_λ does not occur in α and two symbols Q_λ and $Q_{\lambda'}$ are equal only if $\alpha|_\lambda$ and $\alpha|_{\lambda'}$ are equivalent formulas. Let

$$\mathrm{Def}_\lambda^+(\alpha) = \forall x_1 \ldots x_n\, [Q_\lambda(x_1,\ldots,x_n) \to \alpha|_\lambda] \quad \text{and}$$

$$\mathrm{Def}_\lambda^-(\alpha) = \forall x_1 \ldots x_n\, [\alpha|_\lambda \to Q_\lambda(x_1,\ldots,x_n)].$$

The *definition* of Q_λ is the formula

$$\mathrm{Def}_\lambda(\alpha) = \begin{cases} \mathrm{Def}_\lambda^+(\alpha) & \text{if } \alpha|_\lambda \text{ has positive polarity} \\ \mathrm{Def}_\lambda^-(\alpha) & \text{if } \alpha|_\lambda \text{ has negative polarity} \\ \mathrm{Def}_\lambda^+(\alpha) \wedge \mathrm{Def}_\lambda^-(\alpha) & \text{otherwise.} \end{cases}$$

Define $\mathrm{Def}_\Lambda(\alpha)$ inductively by: $\mathrm{Def}_\emptyset(\alpha) = \alpha$ and

$$\mathrm{Def}_{\Lambda \cup \{\lambda\}}(\alpha) = \mathrm{Def}_\Lambda\big(\alpha(\lambda/Q_\lambda(x_1,\ldots,x_n))\big) \wedge \mathrm{Def}_\Lambda(\alpha),$$

where λ is maximal in $\Lambda \cup \{\lambda\}$ with respect to the prefix ordering on positions. $\mathrm{Def}_\Lambda(\alpha)$ is a *structural transformation*, or *definitional form*, of α.   ◁

Λ is typically taken to be the set of all positions of subformulas which are non-atomic or non-literal.

THEOREM 21.4. Let α be a first-order formula. For any $\Lambda \subseteq \mathrm{Pos}(\alpha)$:

(1) $\alpha \equiv \exists \overline{Q}[\mathrm{Def}_\Lambda(\alpha)]$, where the relation symbols in $\overline{Q}$ are those introduced during structural transformation.
(2) $\mathrm{Def}_\Lambda(\alpha)$ can be computed in linear time.   ◁

PROOF. The first part is an easy consequence of Theorems 5.2 and 5.16 since either C- or H-resolution can be used to eliminate the introduced relation symbols again. More precisely, C- or H-resolution transform the clausal form of $\mathrm{Def}_\Lambda(\alpha)$ into a set of clauses equivalent to α. The result is also a consequence of Ackermann's lemma (Lemma 6.1).

The second part is not difficult to prove.   ◁

This shows that structural transformation amounts to the *introduction* of (existential) second-order quantifiers which can be successfully undone by second-order elimination methods.

In practice, one often wants to use the same symbols for variant subformulas, or subformulas which are obviously equivalent. In this case, Theorem 21.4 is also true, but the complexity of the reduction is bounded by a quadratic function.

21.2.1. Applications. Structural transformation has many uses in logic and automated theorem proving. In automated theorem proving it is used as an efficient method for producing clause sets. It can be used to define a linear (or quadratic) algorithm for transforming formulas into clausal form which causes merely a linear increase in size. It enables the preservation of the structure of the original formula in the first-order clausal form. This has various advantages, for example, first-order resolution proofs become more readable and can be more easily translated into tableau-style proofs as shown by Hustadt and Schmidt [115]. These ideas have been extended to an approach of simulating, and even developing, tableaux calculi and other calculi, cf. e.g. [50, 91, 113, 114, 115, 180, 186]. Structural transformation is also a vital part of decision procedures based on resolution which can be used to decide the majority of the familiar solvable classes of first-order logic and many extended modal and description logics, cf. e.g. [50, 86, 76, 112, 114, 183, 184, 185]. Practical experience, for example, with the first-order theorem prover SPASS [215], shows that structural transformation can significant improve the performance of a prover, cf. e.g. [156]. Structural transformation can also be seen to be the main idea underlying the second-order introduction rules used in the MSQIN procedure in Chapter 14 [182].

In logic, forms of structural transformation are known as *renaming* or *Scott reduction*. Our definition of structural transformation is more fine-grained (and efficient) than the form typically used in logic. Scott reduction is based on equivalences which ignore the polarities of the replaced formulas.

21.3. Analysis of Chosen Axioms

21.3.1. Characterizing Equality. Consider this simple second-order axiom:

(273) $\forall X[X(x) \rightarrow X(y)]$.

It is equivalent to $\neg\exists X[X(x) \wedge \neg X(y)]$, i.e., to

$$\neg\exists X\{\forall z[x \approx z \rightarrow X(z)] \wedge \neg X(y)\}.$$

An application of Ackermann's lemma results in $\neg[\neg x \approx y]$, i.e., $x \approx y$. This means that (273) is equivalent to $x \approx y$, i.e., implication within (273) suffices.[1]

---

[1]Usually equivalence rather than implication is considered in this context.

21.3.2. Well-Foundedness. Consider the following axiom:

(274)　　$\forall X\{\exists x X(x) \to \exists x[X(x) \wedge \forall y[R(y,x) \to \neg X(y)]]\}$.

It is equivalent to $\neg\exists X\{\exists x X(x) \wedge \forall x[X(x) \to \exists y[R(y,x) \wedge X(y)]]\}$. An application of Theorem 6.19 results in

(275)　　$\neg\exists x[\text{GFP}\,X(x).\exists y[R(y,x) \wedge X(y)]]$,

which is equivalent to

(276)　　$\forall x[\text{LFP}\,X(x).\forall y[\neg R(y,x) \vee X(y)]]$.

This is known to express the well-foundedness of R.

21.3.3. Critics Admiring Only One Another. The sentence "some critics admire only one another" cannot be formalized by classical first-order logic, but can be expressed by the following second-order formula (see [**141**]):

(277)　　$\exists X\{\exists x[X(x) \wedge \forall x \forall z[(X(x) \wedge A(x,z)) \to (x \not\approx z \wedge X(z))]]\}$,

where $A(y,z)$ stands for "y admires z" and the domain is, for simplicity, restricted to critics.

The formula (277) is equivalent to

(278)　　$\exists X\{\exists x[X(x) \wedge \forall x[X(x) \to \forall z[A(x,z) \to (x \not\approx z \wedge X(z))]]]\}$,

i.e., by an application of Theorem 6.19, to

$$\exists x[\text{GFP}\,X(x).\forall z[A(x,z) \to (x \not\approx z \wedge X(z))]].$$

21.3.4. Second-Order Induction. In this section we consider the second-order induction axiom. This particular analysis is from [**155**]. Assume $S(x,y)$ means that y is a successor of x. Then the second-order induction axiom can be formulated as:

(279)　　$\forall X[X(0) \wedge \forall x \forall y[(X(x) \wedge S(x,y)) \to X(y)]] \to \forall z[X(z)]$.

The formula (279) is obviously equivalent to

$$\neg\exists X[X(0) \wedge \forall x \forall y[(X(x) \wedge S(x,y)) \to X(y)]] \wedge \exists z[\neg X(z)],$$

i.e., to

(280)　　$\neg\exists X \forall y[(\exists x[X(x) \wedge S(x,y)] \vee y \approx 0) \to X(y)] \wedge \exists z[\neg X(z)]$.

An application of Theorem 6.19 to formula (280) results in:

$$\neg\exists z[\neg[\text{LFP}\,X(z).[z \approx 0 \vee \exists x[S(x,z) \wedge X(x)]]]],$$

i.e., in

(281)　　$\forall z[[\text{LFP}\,X(z).[z \approx 0 \vee \exists x[S(x,z) \wedge X(x)]]]]$.

The formula under the fixpoint operator in (281) is existential, therefore by Proposition 3.41 we have that the formula (281) is equivalent to the following infinite disjunction:

$$\forall z \left[\bigvee_{i \in \omega} [z \approx 0 \lor \exists x [S(x, z) \land X(x)]]^i (\text{FALSE}) \right].$$

Thus, by a simple calculation we obtain the well-known fact that the second-order induction (279) is equivalent to

$$\forall z \left[\bigvee_{i \in \omega} [S^i(0, z)], \right]$$

i.e., "every natural number is obtained from 0 by a finite number of applications of the successor relation".

21.4. More Applications

Second-order quantifier elimination methods have yet more applications than we have been able to cover in this book. The following gives a glimpse of some further applications.

21.4.1. Conservative Extensions of Theories.

Let T_1 and T_2 be theories. If for any formula α in the language of T_1 we have that $T_2 \models \alpha$ implies that $T_1 \models \alpha$, then T_2 is said to be a *conservative extension* of T_1. A particular instance of this problem of interest to ontology building is:

> The problem of determining whether the theory T_2 is a conservative extension of a theory T_1 included in it, i.e., $T_1 \subseteq T_2$ and for any formula α in the language of T_1, if $T_2 \models \alpha$ then $T_1 \models \alpha$.

View T_2 as the ontology obtained by adding specifications of new properties and definitions to the ontology T_1. If T_2 is a conservative extension of T_1 then T_2 does not contain any additional information of relevance to T_1 that does not already follow from T_1. For a knowledge engineer this is a useful test to be able to perform in order to check that adding new information to an ontology does not result in any unexpected interaction that would invalidate any properties of T_1 which may be essential for the domain of application.

Ghilardi et al. [92, 93] consider this problem for modal and description logics, but do not use second-order quantifier elimination methods.

If we assume the language of our theories is function free, the problem can viewed as an example of a second-order quantification problem which can be tackled with the techniques discussed in this book.

For simplicity assume that both theories are finite so their axioms can be expressed as their conjunction and can be viewed as a single formula. Then, slightly abusing notation, we can state that T_2 is a conservative extension of T_1 if

$$\models \forall X[(T_2 \to X) \to (T_1 \to X)],$$

which is equivalent to

(282) $\models \neg \exists X[(T_2 \to X) \wedge T_1 \wedge \neg X].$

Applying Lemma 6.1, we obtain that (282) is equivalent to $\models \neg(T_1 \wedge \neg T_2)$, i.e., to

(283) $\models T_1 \to T_2.$

Let $\bar{P}$ consist of all relation symbols in the language of T_2 but not in the language of T_1. Then (283) can be expressed as $\models \forall \bar{P}[T_1 \to T_2]$, i.e., as $\models T_1 \to \forall \bar{P}[T_2]$. Therefore we have the following lemma which can be used in showing conservativeness by first applying second-order quantifier elimination and then first-order theorem proving.

LEMMA 21.5. Let $T_1 \subseteq T_2$. Then $T_1 \models \forall \bar{P}[T_2]$ iff T_2 is a conservative extension of T_1, where $\bar{P}$ are the relation symbols of T_2 which do not occur in T_1.

21.4.2. Modular and Local Reasoning. The aim of hierarchical reasoning is to show that reasoning in extensions of base theories can be hierarchically reduced to reasoning in the base theory, and to provide complete methods for achieving this reduction and performing reasoning that exploits modularity and locality properties. There is no general solution of this problem, however complex classes of theories exist for which hierarchical reasoning is possible. Hierarchical methods have been developed and applied to various kinds of extensions of base theories by, e.g., [**15, 87, 174, 191**]. Sofronie-Stokkermans [**192**] gives an overview of results and applications which include modular reasoning, black-box combinations of provers, decision procedures for extensions and combinations of equational theories, interpolation-based verification, automatic complexity analysis, and recognizing locality.

21.4.3. Projection Computation. Wernhard [**216, 217**] studies and develops methods for projection computation, which can be seen to generalize second-order quantifier elimination. Given a scope S, which is a set of literals, the aim of *projection computation* is to reduce a given formula α to formula β that is logically equivalent to α but is expressed only in terms of the "patterns" in the scope S. Wernhard shows how the SCAN approach can be generalized and used for projection computation. Wernhard also introduces an abstract tableau-based framework for projection computation and knowledge compilation in propositional logic, which is shown to subsume and improve various existing approaches.

List of Tables

Bibliography

[1] ABITEBOUL, S., HULL, R., AND VIANU, V. *Foundations of Databases*. Addison-Wesley, 1996.

[2] ACKERMANN, W. Untersuchungen über das Eliminationsproblem der mathematischen Logik. *Mathematische Annalen 110* (1935), 390–413.

[3] ANDERSON, A. R., AND BELNAP, N. D. *Entailment: The Logic of Relevance and Necessity*, vol. 1. Princeton University Press, 1975.

[4] ARNOLD, A., AND NIWINSKI, D. *Rudiments of μ-calculus*, vol. 146 of *Studies in Logic and the Foundations of Mathematics*. Elsevier, 2001.

[5] AUFFRAY, Y., AND ENJALBERT, P. Modal theorem proving: An equational viewpoint. *Journal of Logic and Computation 2*, 3 (1992), 247–297.

[6] BAADER, F., CALVANESE, D., McGUINNESS, D. L., NARDI, D., AND PATEL-SCHNEIDER, P. F., Eds. *Description Logic Handbook*. Cambridge University Press, 2002.

[7] BAADER, F., AND HOLLUNDER, B. Embedding defaults into terminological knowledge representation formalisms. *Journal of Automated Reasoning 14*, 1 (1995), 149–180.

[8] BAADER, F., AND NUTT, W. Basic description logics. In Baader et al. [6], pp. 47–100.

[9] BACHMAIR, L., AND GANZINGER, H. Rewrite-based equational theorem proving with selection and simplification. *Journal of Logic and Computation 4*, 3 (1994), 217–247.

[10] BACHMAIR, L., AND GANZINGER, H. Equational reasoning in saturation-based theorem proving. In *Automated Deduction—A Basis for Applications*, W. Bibel and P. H. Schmitt, Eds., vol. I. Kluwer, 1998, ch. 11, pp. 353–397.

[11] BACHMAIR, L., AND GANZINGER, H. Resolution theorem proving. In *Handbook of Automated Reasoning*, A. Robinson and A. Voronkov, Eds., vol. I. Elsevier, 2001, ch. 2, pp. 19–99.

[12] BACHMAIR, L., GANZINGER, H., AND WALDMANN, U. Refutational theorem proving for hierarchic first-order theories. *Applicable Algebra in Engineering, Communication and Computing 5*, 3/4 (1994), 193–212.

[13] BALDONI, M. Normal multimodal logics with interaction axioms. In *Labelled Deduction*, D. Basin, M. D'Agostino, D. M. Gabbay, and L. Vigano, Eds. Kluwer, 2000, pp. 33–57.

[14] BARWISE, J. On Moschovakis closure ordinals. *Journal of Symbolic Logic 42* (1977), 292–296.

[15] BASIN, D. A., AND GANZINGER, H. Automated complexity analysis based on ordered resolution. *Journal of the ACM 48*, 1 (2001), 70–109.

[16] BASIN, D. A., MATTHEWS, S., AND VIGANÒ, L. Natural deduction for non-classical logics. *Studia Logica 60*, 1 (1998), 119–160.

[17] BERGE, C. *Hypergraphs*, vol. 45 of *North-Holland Mathematical Library*. Elsevier, 1989.

[18] BETH, E. W. On Padoa's method in the theory of definition. *Koninklijke Nederlandse Akademie van Wetenhappen A 56* (1953), 330–339.

[19] BICARREGUI, J., DIMITRAKOS, T., GABBAY, D. M., AND MAIBAUM, T. Interpolation in practical formal development. *Journal of the IGPL 9*, 2 (2001), 247–259.

[20] BLACKBURN, P., DE RIJKE, M., AND VENEMA, Y. *Modal Logic*. Cambridge University Press, 2001.

[21] BONATTI, B., LUTZ, C., AND WOLTER, F. Description logics with circumscription. In *Proceedings of the 10th International Conference on Principles of Knowledge Representation and Reasoning* (2006), P. Doherty, J. Mylopoulos, and C. Welty, Eds., pp. 400–410.

[22] BORGIDA, A., LENZERINI, M., AND ROSATI, R. Description logics for databases. In Baader et al. [6], pp. 472–494.

[23] BOROS, E., GUREVICH, V., KHACHIYAN, L., AND MAKINO, K. Generating partial and multiple transversals of a hypergraph. In *Automata, Languages and Programming* (2000), vol. 1853 of *Lecture Notes in Computer Science*, Springer, pp. 588–599.

[24] BOY DE LA TOUR, T. An optimality result for clause form translation. *Journal of Symbolic Computation 14* (1992), 283–301.

[25] BRINK, C. $R^\neg$-algebras and $R^\neg$-model structures as power constructs. *Studia Logica 48* (1989), 85–109.

[26] BRINK, C., GABBAY, D. M., AND OHLBACH, H. J. Towards automating duality. Technical Report MPI-I-93-220, Max-Planck-Institut für Informatik, Saarbrücken, Germany, 1993.

[27] BRINK, C., GABBAY, D. M., AND OHLBACH, H. J. Towards automating duality. *Computers and Mathematics with Applications 29*, 2 (1995), 73–90.

[28] BULL, R., AND SEGERBERG, K. Basic modal logic. In Gabbay and Guenthner [82], pp. 1–88.

[29] BULL, R. A. On modal logic with propositional quantifiers. *Journal of Symbolic Logic 34* (1969), 257–263.

[30] BURGESS, J. Quick completeness proofs for some logics of conditionals. *Notre Dame Journal of Formal Logic 22* (1981), 76–84.

[31] CADOLI, M. *Tractable Reasoning in Artificial Intelligence*, vol. 941 of *Lecture Notes in Artificial Intelligence*. Springer, 1995.

[32] CASTILHO, M. A., FARIÑAS DEL CERRO, L., GASQUET, O., AND HERZIG, A. Modal tableaux with propagation rules and structural rules. *Fundamenta Informaticae 3–4*, 32 (1997), 281–297.

[33] CHAGROV, A., AND CHAGROVA, L. The truth about algorithmic problems in correspondence theory. In *Advances in Modal Logic* (2006), G. Governatori, I. Hodkinson, and Y. Venema, Eds., College Publications, pp. 121–138.

[34] CHANDRA, A. K. Theory of database queries. In *Proceedings of the 7th ACM Symposium on Principles of Database Systems* (1988), pp. 1–9.

[35] CHANG, C. C. Some new results in definability. *Bulletin of American Mathematical Society 70* (1964), 808–813.

[36] CHANG, C. C., AND KEISLER, H. J. *Model Theory*. Elsevier, 1990.

[37] CHANG, C.-L., AND LEE, R. C.-T. *Symbolic Logic and Mechanical Theorem Proving*. Computer Science Classics Series. Academic Press, 1973.

[38] CHELLAS, B. *Modal Logic: An Introduction*. Cambridge University Press, 1980.

[39] CHURCH, A. A note on Entscheidungsproblem. *Journal of Symbolic Logic 1* (1936), 40–41.

[40] CONRADIE, W. On the strength and scope of DLS. *Journal of Applied Non-Classical Logics 16*, 3–4 (2006), 279–296.

[41] CONRADIE, W. *Algorithmic Correspondence and Completeness in Modal Logic*. PhD thesis, University of Witwatersrand, Johannesburg, South Africa, 2007.

[42] CONRADIE, W., GORANKO, V., AND VAKARELOV, D. Elementary canonical formulae: A survey on syntactic, algorithmic, and modeltheoretic aspects. In *Advances in Modal Logic, Volume 5*, R. A. Schmidt, I. Pratt-Hartmann, M. Reynolds, and H. Wansing, Eds. King's College Publications, 2005, pp. 1–26.

[43] CONRADIE, W., GORANKO, V., AND VAKARELOV, D. Algorithmic correspondence and completeness in modal logic: I. The core algorithm SQEMA. *Logical Methods in Computer Science 2*, 1:5 (2006), 1–26.

[44] CONRADIE, W., GORANKO, V., AND VAKARELOV, D. Algorithmic correspondence and completeness in modal logic: II. Polyadic and hybrid extensions of the algorithm SQEMA. *Journal of Logic and Computation 16* (2006), 579–612.

[45] COOK, S. A. The complexity of theorem proving procedures. In *Proceedings of the 3rd Annual ACM Symposium on the Theory of Computing* (1971), ACM, pp. 151–158.

[46] CRAIG, W. Linear reasoning: A new form of the Herbrand-Gentzen theorem. *Journal of Symbolic Logic 22* (1957), 250–268.

[47] D'AGOSTINO, G., MONTANARI, A., AND POLICRITI, A. A set-theoretic translation method for polymodal logics. *Journal of Automated Reasoning 3*, 15 (1995), 317–337.

[48] DAVIS, M. The mathematics of non-monotonic reasoning. *Artificial Intelligence 13* (1980), 73–80.

[49] DAWAR, A., AND GUREVICH, Y. Fixed point logics. *Bulletin of Symbolic Logic 8*, 1 (2002), 65–88.

[50] DE NIVELLE, H., SCHMIDT, R. A., AND HUSTADT, U. Resolution-based methods for modal logics. *Logic Journal of the IGPL 8*, 3 (2000), 265–292.

[51] DE RIJKE, M., AND VENEMA, Y. Sahlqvist's theorem for Boolean algebras with operators with an application to cylindric algebras. *Studia Logica 54* (1995), 61–78.

[52] DOHERTY, P., KACHNIARZ, J., AND SZAŁAS, A. Meta-queries on deductive databases. *Fundamenta Informaticae 40*, 1 (1999), 17–30.

[53] DOHERTY, P., KACHNIARZ, J., AND SZAŁAS, A. Using contextually closed queries for local closed-world reasoning in rough knowledge databases. In Pal et al. [**165**], pp. 219–250.

[54] DOHERTY, P., ŁUKASZEWICZ, W., SKOWRON, A., AND SZAŁAS, A. Approximation transducers and trees: A technique for combining rough and crisp knowledge. In Pal et al. [**165**], pp. 189–218.

[55] DOHERTY, P., ŁUKASZEWICZ, W., SKOWRON, A., AND SZAŁAS, A. *Knowledge representation techniques. A rough set approach*, vol. 202 of *Studies in Fuziness and Soft Computing*. Springer, 2006.

[56] DOHERTY, P., ŁUKASZEWICZ, W., AND SZAŁAS, A. Computing circumscription revisited. *Journal of Automated Reasoning 18*, 3 (1997), 297–336.

[57] DOHERTY, P., ŁUKASZEWICZ, W., AND SZAŁAS, A. General domain circumscription and its effective reductions. *Fundamenta Informaticae 36*, 1 (1998), 23–55.

[58] DOHERTY, P., ŁUKASZEWICZ, W., AND SZAŁAS, A. Declarative PTIME queries for relational databases using quantifier elimination. *Journal of Logic and Computation 9*, 5 (1999), 739–761.

[59] DOHERTY, P., ŁUKASZEWICZ, W., AND SZAŁAS, A. Computing strongest necessary and weakest sufficient conditions of first-order formulas. In *Proceedings of the International Joint Conference on Artificial Intelligence* (2000), pp. 145–151.

[60] DOHERTY, P., ŁUKASZEWICZ, W., AND SZAŁAS, A. Efficient reasoning using the local closed-world assumption. In *Artificial Intelligence: Methodology, Systems, and Applications, 9th International Conference, Proceedings* (2000), A. Cerri and D. Dochev, Eds., vol. 1904 of *Lecture Notes in Artificial Intelligence*, Springer, pp. 49–58.

[61] DOHERTY, P., ŁUKASZEWICZ, W., AND SZAŁAS, A. Approximative query techniques for agents with heterogeneous ontologies and perceptive capabilities. In *Proceedings of 9th International Conference on the Principles of Knowledge Representation and Reasoning* (2004), D. Dubois, C. Welty, and M.-A. Williams, Eds., AAAI Press, pp. 459–468.

[62] DOHERTY, P., ŁUKASZEWICZ, W., AND SZAŁAS, A. Similarity, approximations and vagueness. In *Rough Sets, Fuzzy Sets, Data Mining, and Granular Computing, 10th International Conference, Proceedings* (2005), D. Slezak, J. T. Yao, J. Peters, W. Ziarko, and X. Hu, Eds., vol. 3641 of *Lecture Notes in Artificial Intelligence*, Springer, pp. 541–550.

[63] DOHERTY, P., AND SZAŁAS, A. On the correspondence between approximations and similarity. In *Rough Sets and Current Trends in Computing, 4th International Conference, Proceedings*

(2004), S. Tsumoto, R. Slowinski, J. Komorowski, and J. W. Grzymala-Busse, Eds., vol. 3066 of *Lecture Notes in Artificial Intelligence*, Springer, pp. 143–152.

[64] EBBINGHAUS, H.-D., AND FLUM, J. *Finite Model Theory*. Springer, 1995.

[65] EBBINGHAUS, H.-D., FLUM, J., AND THOMAS, W. *Mathematical Logic*. Springer, 1994.

[66] EITER, T., AND GOTTLOB, G. Identifying the minimal transversals of a hypergraph and related problems. *SIAM Journal on Computing 24*, 6 (1995), 1278–1304.

[67] EITER, T., AND GOTTLOB, G. Hypergraph transversal computation and related problems in logic and AI. In *Proceedings of the 8th European Conference on Logics in Artificial Intelligence* (2002), M. Flesca, S. Greco, N. Leone, and G. Ianni, Eds., vol. 2424 of *Lecture Notes in Artificial Intelligence*, Springer, pp. 549–564.

[68] EITER, T., GOTTLOB, G., AND GUREVICH, Y. Normal forms for second-order logic over finite structures, and classification of NP optimization problems. *Annals of Pure and Applied Logic 78*, 1–3 (1989), 111–125.

[69] EITER, T., GOTTLOB, G., AND MAKINO, K. New results on monotone dualization and generating hypergraph transversals. In *Proceedings on 34th Annual ACM Symposium on Theory of Computing* (2002), pp. 14–22.

[70] ENGEL, T. *Quantifier Elimination in Second-Order Predicate Logic*. MSc thesis, Fachbereich Informatik, Universität des Saarlandes, Saarbrücken, Germany, 1996.

[71] ENGEL, T., AND OHLBACH, H. J. SCAN, 1994. http://www.mpi-inf.mpg.de/departments/d2/software/SCAN/.

[72] ETHERINGTON, D. W., AND MERCER, R. Domain circumscription: A revaluation. *Computational Intelligence 3* (1987), 94–99.

[73] ETZIONI, O., GOLDEN, K., AND WELD, D. S. Sound and efficient closed-world reasoning for planning. *Artificial Intelligence 89* (1997), 113–148.

[74] FAGIN, R. Generalized first-order spectra and polynomial-time recognizable sets. In *Proceedings of Complexity of Computation* (1974), R. Karp, Ed., North-Holland, pp. 43–73.

[75] FARIÑAS DEL CERRO, L., AND HERZIG, A. Modal deduction with applications in epistemic and temporal logics. In *Handbook of Logic in Artificial Intelligence and Logic Programming: Epistemic and Temporal Reasoning*, D. M. Gabbay, C. J. Hogger, and J. A. Robinson, Eds., vol. 4. Clarendon Press, 1995, pp. 499–594.

[76] FERMÜLLER, C., LEITSCH, A., HUSTADT, U., AND TAMMET, T. Resolution decision procedures. In *Handbook of Automated Reasoning*, A. Robinson and A. Voronkov, Eds., vol. II. Elsevier, 2001, ch. 25, pp. 1791–1849.

[77] FINE, K. Propositional quantifiers in modal logic. *Theoria 36* (1970), 336–346.

[78] FITTING, M. Interpolation for first order S5. *Journal of Symbolic Logic 67*, 2 (2002), 621–634.

[79] FRAYNE, T. E., MOREL, A. C., AND SCOTT, D. S. Reduced direct products. *Fundamenta Mathematicae 51* (1962), 195–228.

[80] FREDMAN, M. L., AND KHACHIYAN, L. On the complexity of dualization of monotone disjunctive normal forms. *Journal of Algorithms 21* (1996), 618–628.

[81] GABBAY, D. M. A general theory of the conditional in terms of a ternary operator. *Theoria 38* (1972), 97–104.

[82] GABBAY, D. M., AND GUENTHNER, F., Eds. *Handbook of Philosophical Logic*. D. Reidel, 1984.

[83] GABBAY, D. M., AND MAKSIMOVA, L. *Interpolation and Definability: Modal and Intuitionistic Logic*. Oxford University Press, 2005.

[84] GABBAY, D. M., AND OHLBACH, H. J. Quantifier elimination in second-order predicate logic. *South African Computer Journal 7* (1992), 35–43. Also published in *Proceedings of the 3rd International Conference on Principles of Knowledge Representation and Reasoning* (1992), B. Nebel, C. Rich, and W. R. Swartout, Eds, Morgan Kaufmann, pp. 425–436.

[85] GABBAY, D. M., AND SZAŁAS, A. Second-order quantifier elimination in higher-order contexts with applications to the semantical analysis of conditionals. *Studia Logics 87* (2007), 37–50.

[86] GANZINGER, H., AND DE NIVELLE, H. A superposition decision procedure for the guarded fragment with equality. In *Proceedings of the 14th Annual IEEE Symposium on Logic in Computer Science* (1999), IEEE Computer Society Press, pp. 295–303.

[87] GANZINGER, H., SOFRONIE-STOKKERMANS, V., AND WALDMANN, U. Modular proof systems for partial functions with Evans equality. *Information and Computation 204*, 10 (2006), 1453–1492.

[88] GARSON, J. W. Quantification in modal logic. In Gabbay and Guenthner [**82**], pp. 249–307.

[89] GELFOND, M., AND LIFSCHITZ, V. Compiling circumscriptive theories into logic programs. In *Proceedings of the 2nd International Workshop on Non-Monotonic Reasoning*, vol. 346 of *Lecture Notes in Artificial Intelligence*. Springer, 1989, pp. 74–99.

[90] GEORGIEV, D. *An implementation of the algorithm SQEMA for computing first-order correspondences of modal formulas*. Masters thesis, Sofia University, Bulgaria, 2006. http://www.fmi.uni-sofia.bg/fmi/logic/sqema/.

[91] GEORGIEVA, L., HUSTADT, U., AND SCHMIDT, R. A. Hyperresolution for guarded formulae. *Journal of Symbolic Computation 36*, 1–2 (2003), 163–192.

[92] GHILARDI, S., LUTZ, C., AND WOLTER, F. Did I damage my ontology? A case for conservative extensions in description logics. In *Proceedings, Tenth International Conference on Principles of Knowledge Representation and Reasoning* (2006), P. Doherty, J. Mylopoulos, and C. A. Welty, Eds., AAAI Press, pp. 187–197.

[93] GHILARDI, S., LUTZ, C., WOLTER, F., AND ZAKHARYASCHEV, M. Conservative extensions in modal logic. In *Advances in Modal Logic, Volume 6* (2006), G. Governatori, I. M. Hodkinson, and Y. Venema, Eds., College Publications, pp. 187–207.

[94] GINSBERG, M. L. A circumscriptive theorem prover. *Artificial Intelligence 39* (1989), 209–203.

[95] GÖDEL, K. Die Vollständigkeit der Axiome des logischen Funktionenkalküls. *Monatshefte für Math. und Phys. 37* (1930), 349–360. Also in [**212**].

[96] GOGIC, G., PAPADIMITRIOU, C. H., AND SIDERI, M. Incremental recompilation of knowledge. *Journal of Artificial Intelligence Research 8* (1998), 23–37.

[97] GOLDBLATT, R. *Logics of Time and Computation*, vol. 7 of *CSLI Lecture Notes*. Chicago University Press, 1987.

[98] GORANKO, V., HUSTADT, U., SCHMIDT, R. A., AND VAKARELOV, D. SCAN is complete for all Sahlqvist formulae. In *Relational and Kleene-Algebraic Methods in Computer Science* (2004), R. Berghammer, B. Möller, and G. Struth, Eds., vol. 3051 of *Lecture Notes in Computer Science*, Springer, pp. 149–162.

[99] GORANKO, V., AND VAKARELOV, D. Sahlqvist formulas unleashed in polyadic modal languages. In *Advances in Modal Logic, Volume 3*, F. Wolter, H. Wansing, M. De Rijke, and M. Zakharyaschev, Eds. World Scientific, 2002, pp. 221–240.

[100] GORANKO, V., AND VAKARELOV, D. Elementary canonical formulae: Extending Sahlqvist's theorem. *Annals of Pure and Applied Logic 141*, 1–2 (2006), 180–217.

[101] GORÉ, R. Tableau methods for modal and temporal logics. In *Handbook of Tableau Methods*, M. D'Agostino, D. Gabbay, R. Hähnle, and J. Posegga, Eds. Kluwer, 1999, pp. 297–396.

[102] GRAHAM, R. L., KNUTH, D. E., AND PATASHNIK, O. *Concrete Mathematics: A Foundation for Computer Science*. Addison-Wesley, 1994.

[103] GUSTAFSSON, J. An implementation and optimization of an algorithm for reducing formulas in second-order logic. Tech. Rep. LiTH-MAT-R-96-04, University of Linköping, Sweden, 1996. http://www.ida.liu.se/labs/kplab/projects/dls/.

[104] HENKIN, L. Some remarks on infinitely long formulas. In *Infinitistic Methods, Proceedings of Symposium on Foundations of Mathematics* (1961), pp. 167–183.

[105] HERZIG, A. *Raisonnement automatique en logique modale et algorithmes d'unification.* PhD thesis, University Paul-Sabatier, Toulouse, France, 1989.

[106] HERZIG, A. SCAN and systems of conditional logic. Research Report MPI-I-96-2-007, Max-Planck-Institut für Informatik, Saarbrücken, Germany, 1996.

[107] HINMAN, P. G. *Recursion-Theoretic Hierarchies.* Springer, 1978.

[108] HINTIKKA, J. Model minimization: An alternative to circumscription. *Journal of Automated Reasoning 4* (1988), 1–13.

[109] HORROCKS, I., HUSTADT, U., SATTLER, U., AND SCHMIDT, R. A. Computational modal logic. In *Handbook of Modal Logic*, P. Blackburn, J. van Benthem, and F. Wolter, Eds., vol. 3 of *Studies in Logic and Practical Reasoning.* Elsevier, 2007, pp. 181–245.

[110] HUGHES, G. E., AND CRESSWELL, M. J. *An Introduction to Modal Logic.* Routledge, 1968.

[111] HUGHES, G. E., AND CRESSWELL, M. J. *A New Introduction to Modal Logic.* Routledge, 1996.

[112] HUSTADT, U., AND SCHMIDT, R. A. Maslov's class K revisited. In *Automated Deduction—CADE-16* (1999), H. Ganzinger, Ed., vol. 1632 of *Lecture Notes in Artificial Intelligence*, Springer, pp. 172–186.

[113] HUSTADT, U., AND SCHMIDT, R. A. On the relation of resolution and tableaux proof systems for description logics. In *Proceedings of the 16th International Joint Conference on Artificial Intelligence* (1999), T. Dean, Ed., Morgan Kaufmann, pp. 110–115.

[114] HUSTADT, U., AND SCHMIDT, R. A. Issues of decidability for description logics in the framework of resolution. In *Automated Deduction in Classical and Non-Classical Logics* (2000), R. Caferra and G. Salzer, Eds., vol. 1761 of *Lecture Notes in Artificial Intelligence*, Springer, pp. 191–205.

[115] HUSTADT, U., AND SCHMIDT, R. A. Using resolution for testing modal satisfiability and building models. In *SAT 2000: Highlights of Satisfiability Research in the Year 2000*, I. P. Gent, H. van Maaren, and T. Walsh, Eds., vol. 63 of *Frontiers in Artificial Intelligence and Applications.* IOS Press, 2000, pp. 459–483. Also published as [**116**].

[116] HUSTADT, U., AND SCHMIDT, R. A. Using resolution for testing modal satisfiability and building models. *Journal of Automated Reasoning 28*, 2 (2002), 205–232.

[117] IMMERMAN, N. Upper and lower bounds for first-order expressibility. *Journal of Computer and System Sciences 25* (1982), 76–98.

[118] IMMERMAN, N. Relational queries computable in polynomial time. *Information and Control 68*, 1–3 (1986), 86–104.

[119] IMMERMAN, N. *Descriptive Complexity.* Springer, 1998.

[120] JÓNSSON, B., AND TARSKI, A. Boolean algebras with operators, part I. *American Journal of Mathematics 73* (1951), 891–939.

[121] JÓNSSON, B., AND TARSKI, A. Boolean algebras with operators, part II. *American Journal of Mathematics 74* (1952), 127–162.

[122] KACHNIARZ, J., AND SZAŁAS, A. On a static approach to verification of integrity constraints in relational databases. In *Relational Methods for Computer Science Applications* (2001), E. Orłowska and A. Szałas, Eds., Springer, pp. 97–109.

[123] KAPLAN, D. S5 with quantifiable propositional variables (abstract). *Journal of Symbolic Logic 35* (1970), 355.

[124] KAUTZ, H., AND SELMAN, B. Knowledge compilation and theory approximation. *Journal of the ACM 43*, 2 (1996), 193–224.

[125] KAVVADIAS, D. J., AND STAVROPOULOS, E. C. Evaluation of an algorithm for the transversal hypergraph problem. In *Algorithm Engineering, 3rd International Workshop* (1999), J. Scott Vitter and C. D. Zaroliagis, Eds., vol. 1668 of *Lecture Notes in Computer Science*, Springer, pp. 72–84.

[126] KNASTER, B. Un theoreme sur les fonctions d'ensembles. *Ann. Soc. Polon. Math. 6* (1928), 133–134.

[127] KOCHEN, S. B. Ultraproducts and the theory of models. *Annals of Mathematics 74* (1961), 231–261.

[128] KOLAITIS, P., AND PAPADIMITRIOU, C. Some computational aspects of circumscription. In *Proceedings of the 7th National Conference on Artificial Intelligence* (1988), vol. 346, pp. 465–469.

[129] KOLAITIS, P., AND VARDI, M. On the expressive power of variable-confined logics. In *Proceedings of the 11th Annual IEEE Symposium on Logic in Computer Science* (1996), pp. 348–359.

[130] KRACHT, M. How completeness and correspondence theory got married. In *Diamonds and Defaults* (1992), M. de Rijke, Ed., vol. 229 of *Synthese Library*, Kluwer, pp. 175–214.

[131] KRACHT, M. *Tools and Techniques in Modal Logic*. No. 142 in Studies in Logic and the Foundations of Mathematics. Elsevier, 1999.

[132] KRACHT, M., AND WOLTER, F. Normal monomodal logics can simulate all others. *Journal of Symbolic Logic 64* (1999), 99–138.

[133] KRIPKE, S. Semantic analysis of modal logic I. Normal propositional calculi. *Zeitschrift für mathematische Logik and Grundlagen der Mathematik 9* (1963), 67–96.

[134] KUEKER, D. W. Generalized interpolation and definability. *Annals of Mathematical Logic 1*, 4 (1970), 423–468.

[135] LEIVANT, D. Descriptive characterizations of computational complexity. *Journal of Computer and System Sciences 39* (1989), 51–83.

[136] LEMMON, E. J. *An Introduction to Modal Logic*. Blackwell, 1977.

[137] LEWIS, D. K. *Counterfactuals*. Blackwell, 1973.

[138] LIFSCHITZ, V. Computing circumscription. In *Proceedings of the International Joint Conference on Artificial Intelligence* (1985), Morgan Kaufmann, pp. 229–235.

[139] LIFSCHITZ, V. Circumscription. In *Handbook of Artificial Intelligence and Logic Programming* (1991), D. M. Gabbay, C. J. Hogger, and J. A. Robinson, Eds., vol. 3, Oxford University Press, pp. 297–352.

[140] LIN, F. On strongest necessary and weakest sufficient conditions. In *Proceedings of the 7th International Conference on Principles of Knowledge Representation and Reasoning* (2000), A. G. Cohn, F. Giunchiglia, and B. Selman, Eds., Morgan Kaufmann, pp. 167–175.

[141] LINNEBO, O. Plural quantification exposed. *Noûs 37* (2003), 71–92.

[142] LORENZ, S. A tableau prover for domain minimization. *Journal of Automated Reasoning 13* (1994), 375–390.

[143] LYNDON, R. An interpolation theorem in the predicate calculus. *Pacific Journal of Mathematics 9* (1959), 155–164.

[144] MAGNUSSON, M. DLS*, 2005. http://www.ida.liu.se/labs/kplab/projects/dlsstar/.

[145] MAKKAI, M. On a generalization of a theorem of E. W. Beth. *Acta Mathematica Acad. Sci. Hung. 15* (1964), 227–235.

[146] MCCARTHY, J. Epistemological problems of artificial intelligence. In *Proceedings of the 5th International Joint Conference on Artificial Intelligence* (1977), pp. 1038–1044.

[147] MCCARTHY, J. Circumscription: A form of non-monotonic reasoning. *Artificial Intelligence Journal 13* (1980), 27–39.

[148] MCCARTHY, J. Approximate objects and approximate theories. In *Proceedings of the 7th International Conference on Principles of Knowledge Representation and Reasoning* (2000), A. G. Cohn, F. Giunchiglia, and B. Selman, Eds., Morgan Kaufmann, pp. 519–526.

[149] MCCUNE, W. Un-Skolemizing clause sets. *Information Processing Letters 29* (1988), 257–263.

[150] NARDI, D., AND BRACHMAN., R. J. An introduction to description logics. In Baader et al. [6], pp. 5–44.

[151] NIEUWENHUIS, R., AND RUBIO, A. Paramodulation-based theorem proving. In *Handbook of Automated Reasoning*, A. Robinson and A. Voronkov, Eds., vol. I. Elsevier, 2001, ch. 7, pp. 371–443.

[152] NONNENGART, A. First-order modal logic theorem proving and functional simulation. In *Proceedings of the International Joint Conference on Artificial Intelligence* (1993), Morgan Kaufmann, pp. 80–85.

[153] NONNENGART, A. Strong Skolemization. Research Report MPI-I-96-2-010, Max-Planck-Institut für Informatik, Saarbrücken, Germany, 1996.

[154] NONNENGART, A., OHLBACH, H. J., AND SZAŁAS, A. Elimination of predicate quantifiers. In *Logic, Language and Reasoning. Essays in Honor of Dov Gabbay, Part I* (1999), H. J. Ohlbach and U. Reyle, Eds., Kluwer, pp. 159–181.

[155] NONNENGART, A., AND SZAŁAS, A. A fixpoint approach to second-order quantifier elimination with applications to correspondence theory. In *Logic at Work: Essays Dedicated to the Memory of Helena Rasiowa* (1998), E. Orłowska, Ed., vol. 24 of *Studies in Fuzziness and Soft Computing*, Springer, pp. 307–328.

[156] NONNENGART, A., AND WEIDENBACH, C. Computing small clause normal forms. In *Handbook of Automated Reasoning*, A. Robinson and A. Voronkov, Eds., vol. I. Elsevier Science, 2001, ch. 6, pp. 335–367.

[157] OHLBACH, H. J. *A Resolution Calculus for Modal Logics*. PhD thesis, University of Kaiserslautern, Germany, 1988.

[158] OHLBACH, H. J. Semantics based translation methods for modal logics. *Journal of Logic and Computation 1*, 5 (1991), 691–746.

[159] OHLBACH, H. J. Translation methods for non-classical logics: An overview. *Bulletin of the IGPL 1*, 1 (1993), 69–89.

[160] OHLBACH, H. J. SCAN—Elimination of predicate quantifiers: System description. In *Automated Deduction: CADE-13* (1996), M. A. McRobbie and J. K. Slaney, Eds., vol. 1104 of *Lecture Notes in Artificial Intelligence*, Springer, pp. 161–165.

[161] OHLBACH, H. J., NONNENGART, A., DE RIJKE, M., AND GABBAY, D. Encoding two-valued nonclassical logics in classical logic. In *Handbook of Automated Reasoning*, A. Robinson and A. Voronkov, Eds., vol. II. Elsevier Science, 2001, ch. 21, pp. 1403–1486.

[162] OHLBACH, H. J., AND SCHMIDT, R. A. Functional translation and second-order frame properties of modal logics. *Journal of Logic and Computation 7*, 5 (1997), 581–603.

[163] OMODEO, E., ORŁOWSKA, E., AND POLICRITI, A. Rasiowa-Sikorski style relational elementary set theory. In *Relational and Kleene-Algebraic Methods in Computer Science* (2004), R. Berghammer, B. Moeller, and G. Struth, Eds., vol. 3051 of *Lecture Notes in Computer Science*, Springer, pp. 213–224.

[164] ORŁOWSKA, E., AND SZAŁAS, A. Quantifier elimination in elementary set theory. In *Relational Methods in Computer Science* (2006), W. MacCaull, M. Winter, and I. Duentsch, Eds., no. 3929 in Lecture Notes in Computer Science, Springer, pp. 237–248.

[165] PAL, S. K., POLKOWSKI, L., AND SKOWRON, A., Eds. *Rough-Neuro Computing: Techniques for Computing with Words* (2003), Cognitive Technologies, Springer.

[166] PAPADIMITRIOU, C. H. *Computational Complexity*. Addison-Wesley, 1994.

[167] PAWLAK, Z. *Rough Sets. Theoretical Aspects of Reasoning about Data*. Kluwer, 1991.

[168] PLAISTED, D. A., AND GREENBAUM, S. A structure-preserving clause form translation. *Journal of Symbolic Computation 2* (1986), 293–304.

[169] POIZAT, B. Deux ou trois choses que je sais de L_n. *Journal of Symbolic Logic 47* (1982), 641–658.

[170] PRZYMUSINSKI, T. An algorithm to compute circumscription. *Artificial Intelligence 38* (1989), 49–73.

[171] RABINOV, A. A generalization of collapsible cases of circumscription. *Artificial Intelligence 38* (1989), 111–117.

[172] ROBINSON, J. A. A machine-oriented logic based on the resolution principle. *Journal of the ACM 12*, 1 (1965), 23–41.

[173] ROGERS, H. *Theory of Recursive Functions and Effective Computability*. McGraw-Hill, 1967.

[174] RYBALCHENKO, A., AND SOFRONIE-STOKKERMANS, V. Constraint solving for interpolation. In *Verification, Model Checking, and Abstract Interpretation, VMCAI 2007* (2007), B. Cook and A. Podelski, Eds., vol. 4349 of *Lecture Notes in Computer Science*, Springer, pp. 346–362.

[175] SAHLQVIST, H. Correspondence and completeness in the first- and second-order semantics for modal logic. In *Proceedings of the 3rd Scandinavial Logic Symposium* (1975), S. Kanger, Ed., North-Holland, pp. 110–143.

[176] SAVITCH, W. Relationships between nondeterministic and deterministic tape complexities. *Journal of Computer and System Sciences 4* (1970), 177–192.

[177] SCHAEFFER, T. The complexity of satisfiability problems. In *Proceedings of 10th ACM Symposium on Theory of Computation* (1978), ACM, pp. 216–226.

[178] SCHMIDT, R. A. *Optimised Modal Translation and Resolution*. PhD thesis, Universität des Saarlandes, Saarbrücken, Germany, 1997.

[179] SCHMIDT, R. A. Decidability by resolution for propositional modal logics. *Journal of Automated Reasoning 22*, 4 (1999), 379–396.

[180] SCHMIDT, R. A. Developing modal tableaux and resolution methods via first-order resolution. In *Advances in Modal Logic, Volume 6* (2006), G. Governatori, I. Hodkinson, and Y. Venema, Eds., College Publications, pp. 1–26.

[181] SCHMIDT, R. A. Efficient lazy second-order quantifier elimination in modal logic. Unpublished manuscript, 2006.

[182] SCHMIDT, R. A. Second-order quantifier introduction in modal logic. Unpublished manuscript, 2007.

[183] SCHMIDT, R. A., AND HUSTADT, U. A resolution decision procedure for fluted logic. In *Automated Deduction—CADE-17* (2000), D. McAllester, Ed., vol. 1831 of *Lecture Notes in Artificial Intelligence*, Springer, pp. 433–448.

[184] SCHMIDT, R. A., AND HUSTADT, U. Mechanised reasoning and model generation for extended modal logics. In *Theory and Applications of Relational Structures as Knowledge Instruments*, H. C. M. de Swart, E. Orlowska, G. Schmidt, and M. Roubens, Eds., vol. 2929 of *Lecture Notes in Computer Science*. Springer, 2003, pp. 38–67.

[185] SCHMIDT, R. A., AND HUSTADT, U. First-order resolution methods for modal logics. Manuscript. To appear in *Volume in memoriam of Harald Ganzinger, Lecture Notes in Computer Science*, Springer, 2006.

[186] SCHMIDT, R. A., AND HUSTADT, U. The axiomatic translation principle for modal logic. *ACM Transactions on Computational Logic 8*, 4 (2007), 1–55.

[187] SCHMIDT-SCHAUSS, M., AND SMOLKA, G. Attributive concept descriptions with complements. *Artificial Intelligence 48* (1991), 1–26.

[188] SIMMONS, H. The monotonous elimination of predicate variables. *Journal of Logic and Computation 4* (1994), 23–68.

[189] SKOLEM, T. Logisch-kombinatorische Untersuchungen über die Erfüllbarkeit und Beweisbarkeit mathematischen Sätze nebst einem Theorem über dichte Mengen. *Skrifter utgit av Videnskabsselskapet i Kristiania I*, 4 (1920), 1–36. Also in [212].

[190] SMULLYAN, R. *What is the Name of This Book?* Prentice Hall, 1978.

[191] SOFRONIE-STOKKERMANS, V. Hierarchic reasoning in local theory extensions. In *Automated Deduction—CADE-20* (2005), R. Nieuwenhuis, Ed., vol. 3632 of *Lecture Notes in Computer Science*, Springer, pp. 219–234.

[192] SOFRONIE-STOKKERMANS, V. Hierarchical and modular reasoning in complex theories: The case of local theory extensions. In *Frontiers of Combining Systems, 6th International Symposium, Proceedings* (2007), B. Konev and F. Wolter, Eds., vol. 4720 of *Lecture Notes in Computer Science*, Springer, pp. 47–71.

[193] STALNAKER, R. C. A theory of conditionals. In *IFS: Conditionals, Belief, Decision, Chance, and Time* (1981), W. L. Harper, R. C. Stalnaker, and G. Pearce, Eds., D. Reidel, pp. 41–55.

[194] STALNAKER, R. C., AND THOMASON, R. M. A semantic analysis of conditional logic. *Theoria 36*, 1–3 (1970), 23–42.

[195] STOCKMEYER, L. J. The polynomial-time hierarchy. *Theoretical Computer Science 3*, 1 (1976), 1–22.

[196] STONE, M. H. The theory of representations for Boolean algebras. *Notices of American Mathematical Society 6* (1937), 37–111.

[197] SUCHANEK, M. A. First-order syntactic characterizations of minimal entailment, domain-minimal entailment, and Herbrand entailment. *Journal of Automated Reasoning 10* (1993), 237–263.

[198] SVENONIUS, L. $\aleph_0$-categoricity in first-order predicate calculus. *Theoria 25* (1959), 82–94.

[199] SZAŁAS, A. On the correspondence between modal and classical logic: An automated approach. *Journal of Logic and Computation 3* (1993), 605–620.

[200] SZAŁAS, A. On an automated translation of modal proof rules into formulas of the classical logic. *Journal of Applied Non-Classical Logics 4* (1994), 119–127.

[201] SZAŁAS, A. Second-order quantifier elimination in modal contexts. In *Proceedings of the 8th European Conference on Logics in Artificial Intelligence* (2002), M. Flesca, S. Greco, N. Leone, and G. Ianni, Eds., vol. 2424 of *Lecture Notes in Artificial Intelligence*, Springer, pp. 223–232.

[202] SZAŁAS, A. On a logical approach to estimating computational complexity of potentially intractable problems. In *Proceedings of 14th International Symposium on Fundamentals of Computation Theory* (2003), A. Lingas and B. J. Nilsson, Eds., vol. 2751 of *Lecture Notes in Computer Science*, Springer, pp. 423–431.

[203] SZAŁAS, A. Second-order reasoning in description logics. *Journal of Applied Non-Classical Logics 16*, 3–4 (2006), 517–530.

[204] SZAŁAS, A., AND TYSZKIEWICZ, J. On the fixpoint theory of equality and its applications. In *Relations and Kleene Algebra in Computer Science* (2006), R. A. Schmidt, Ed., vol. 4136 of *Lecture Notes in Computer Science*, pp. 388–401.

[205] TARSKI, A. On the calculus of relations. *Journal of Symbolic Logic 6* (1941), 73–89.

[206] TARSKI, A. A lattice-theoretical fixpoint theorem and its applications. *Pacific Journal of Mathematics 5*, 2 (1965), 285–309.

[207] TARSKI, A., AND GIVANT, S. *A Formalization of Set Theory without Variables*, vol. 41. American Mathematical Society Colloquium Publications, 1987.

[208] TSEITIN, G. S. On the complexity of derivations in propositional calculus. In *Studies in Constructive Mathematics and Mathematical Logic, Part II*, A. O. Slisenko, Ed. Consultants Bureau, 1970, pp. 115–125. Reprint in *Automation of Reasoning: Classical Papers on Computational Logic* (1983), J. Siekmann and G. Wrightson, Eds, Springer, pp. 466–483.

[209] VAN BENTHEM, J. *Modal Logic and Classical Logic*. Bibliopolis, 1983.

[210] VAN BENTHEM, J. Correspondence theory. In Gabbay and Guenthner [**82**], pp. 167–247.

[211] VAN BENTHEM, J. Minimal predicates, fixed-points, and definability. *Journal of Symbolic Logic 70*, 3 (2005), 696–712.

[212] VAN HEIJENOORT, J., Ed. *From Frege to Gödel. A Source Book in Mathematical Logic, 1879–1931*. Harvard University Press, 1971.

[213] VARDI, M. Y. The complexity of relational query languages. In *Proceedings of the ACM SIGACT Symposium on the Theory of Computing* (1982), pp. 137–146.

[214] VIGANÒ, L. *Labelled Non-Classical Logics*. Kluwer, 2000.

[215] WEIDENBACH, C., SCHMIDT, R. A., HILLENBRAND, T., RUSEV, R., AND TOPIC, D. System description: SPASS version 3.0. In *Automated Deduction—CADE-21* (2007), F. Pfenning, Ed., vol. 4603 of *Lecture Notes in Artificial Intelligence*, Springer, pp. 514–520.

[216] WERNHARD, C. Semantic knowledge partitioning. In *Logics in Artificial Intelligence: 9th European Conference, Proceedings* (2004), J. J. Alferes and J. A. Leite, Eds., vol. 3229 of *Lecture Notes in Artificial Intelligence*, Springer, pp. 552–564.

[217] WERNHARD, C. *Automated Deduction for Projection Elimination*. PhD thesis, Universität Koblenz-Landau, Germany, 2008. To appear.

[218] WILLIAMSON, T. *Vagueness*. Routledge, 1994.

[219] ZOLIN, E. Modal logic applied to query answering and the case for variable modalities. In *Proceedings of the 20th International Workshop on Description Logics* (2007), D. Calvanese, E. Franconi, V. Haarslev, D. Lembo, B. Motik, S. Tessaris, and A. Y. Turhan, Eds., Bozen-Bolzano University Press, pp. 515–522.

Index of Notation

Subject Index